RECONSTRUCTION IN MISSISSIPPI

RECONSTRUCTION
IN
MISSISSIPPI

JAMES WILFORD GARNER, Ph.M.

LOUISIANA STATE UNIVERSITY PRESS
Baton Rouge

Printed in the United States of America by
The Colonial Press Inc.

To My Wife
Theresa Leggett-Garner

PREFACE

THE primary purpose of this work is to give a detailed study of reconstruction in Mississippi with reference to its political, military, economic, educational, and legal phases. A secondary purpose is to present a brief review of the Civil War so far as it affected directly the state of Mississippi or the people thereof, and, accordingly, special emphasis has been laid upon those results of the war that sustained more or less relation to the problems of reconstruction. Realizing the incompleteness of any history of reconstruction which concludes with the readmission of the state to the Union and the reëstablishment of civil government, the author has followed up the results of the congressional policy as they appeared in the period of " carpet bag " and negro domination, and has carried his narrative down to the final overthrow of the party that had been the especial beneficiaries of the congressional policy, — an event locally known as the " revolution of 1875."

The author is disposed to believe that a thorough study of the actual working out of reconstruction in its different relations and activities in any one of the Southern States will be of some value to the general student of American history, for, after all, the process and results in one state were essentially the same in all. So far as he knows no attempt has yet been made in this direction, and in undertaking to write such a history of Mississippi he has been possessed of a good many misgivings. More than one person to whom he applied for advice ventured the opinion that the smoke of battle had not sufficiently cleared away and with it the passions and animosities of the war to make it possible for any American to discover and set forth the facts of reconstruction without bias or prejudice. Although fully sen-

sible of the difficulties that beset the historian of this period,
the author does not sympathize with the view that the events
of that time cannot be narrated with reasonable fairness
and justice to all concerned. The time has come when the
history of reconstruction can be written, and it ought to be
written by a Southerner, for it is the Southerners who best
understand the problems which the reconstructionists undertook to solve and the conditions under which the solution
was worked out. This, of course, does not mean that the
history should be written from the Southern "point of view"
or from any other "point of view," unless it be that from
which the truth may be best discovered and presented.

The author of this book feels keenly his own prejudices,
but he has made an earnest effort to divest himself of every
influence arising from early environment or from later education that would tend to swerve him from a plain and
unprejudiced statement of the truth, and has endeavored to
set forth his findings without fear or favor, but with charity
for both reconstructionists and reconstructed. Most of the
events recorded in this book occurred before the writer was
born; not one of them is recent enough to come within reach
of his memory. He is not, therefore, handicapped by any
prejudices founded on personal observation or experience.

On the whole, the author concurs in the view of Lamar-
tine, that it is the province of the historian to *relate* and not
to *judge*. He has, therefore, except in a few instances where
opinions were clearly warranted by the facts, confined himself to a simple statement of the truth and left the reader to
form his own conclusions.

In concluding these preliminary remarks the author de-
sires to acknowledge his indebtedness to ex-Governor Adel-
bert Ames, ex-Governor R. C. Powers, Mrs. ex-Governor
J. L. Alcorn, ex-Senator H. R. Pease, Hon. C. E. Furlong,
Major Alvan C. Gillem, and Mrs. Betty Dent Smith for
placing at his disposal private papers of historical value; to
Hon. H. M. Street, Judge H. F. Simrall, and Hon. John R.
Lynch for information conveyed through private letters; to

Mr. R. H. Henry, editor of the Jackson (Miss.) *Clarion-Ledger*, for permission to examine his files; to General F. C. Ainsworth of the War Department for special courtesies; and to his wife for faithful and conscientious service in the preparation of the manuscript for the printer and in reading and correcting the proof.

The author desires to make special acknowledgments to his teacher, Professor W. A. Dunning of Columbia University, who in the midst of his academic duties found time to read the manuscript of this book and make many valuable suggestions.

JAMES WILFORD GARNER.

MORNINGSIDE HEIGHTS,
  NEW YORK,
    May 25, 1901.

CONTENTS

CHAPTER FIRST

SECESSION AND CIVIL WAR

CHAPTER SECOND

THE TRANSITION FROM CIVIL WAR TO RECONSTRUCTION

CHAPTER THIRD

PRESIDENTIAL RECONSTRUCTION

CHAPTER FOURTH

THE ECONOMIC ASPECTS OF RECONSTRUCTION

CHAPTER FIFTH

CONGRESSIONAL RECONSTRUCTION

CHAPTER SIXTH

CHAPTER SEVENTH

THE REËSTABLISHMENT OF CIVIL GOVERNMENT

CHAPTER EIGHTH

THE "CARPET-BAG" RÉGIME

CHAPTER NINTH

CHAPTER TENTH

CHAPTER ELEVENTH

THE REVOLUTION

INTRODUCTION

James W. Garner's *Reconstruction in Mississippi*, originally published in 1901, was the first and is generally considered the best of the books that members of the "Dunning school" wrote on Reconstruction in various Southern states. The head of this school, William A. Dunning, who had been born in New Jersey, taught history at Columbia University from the 1880's to the 1920's. Though Dunning produced only a few books of his own, these were quite influential, and so were his lectures and his conversations at Columbia. A remarkably effective teacher, he inspired his graduate students, many of them Southerners, to apply his approach to the Civil War and Reconstruction in a number of specialized studies. His students, in turn, influenced him through their research, and he acknowledged the writings of some of them in his general account *Reconstruction, Political and Economic, 1865–1877*, published in 1907.

Garner, born in Pike County, Mississippi, on November 22, 1871, had earned a B.S. degree from Mississippi Agricultural and Mechanical College and a Ph.M. from the University of Chicago before he entered Dunning's seminar at Columbia in 1900. He readily appreciated the qualities of Dunning, whom he was to remember as an excellent teacher, one who "not only knew his subject, but had the rare gift of presenting it in an attractive and forceful manner." Garner had already gained some teaching experience at Bradley Polytechnic Institute in Peoria, Illinois, and after receiving his Ph.D. he taught briefly at Columbia and at the University of Pennsylvania. Then, in 1904, he took a position as professor of political science at the University of Illinois, a position he was to hold until his death in 1938.

While at Illinois, Garner made for himself a distinguished career as a political scientist. He built up the university's political science department, of which he was at first both the head and the sole member, to one of the largest and most active in the country. He traveled abroad on a succession of honorific lectureships, in England, France, Switzerland, The Netherlands, India, and other parts of the world. He received honorary degrees from the University of Calcutta, the University of Lyons, Oberlin College, and Columbia University, and he was made a Chevalier of the French Legion of Honor. Meanwhile, his fellow political scientists recognized him as a leader of the profession when, in 1924 (two years after having recognized his mentor, Dunning, in the same way), they named him president of the American Political Science Association.

During these years Garner was a prolific writer, though in a field rather remote from that of his dissertation at Columbia. He contributed nearly three hundred articles to encyclopedias and professional journals, and he produced a dozen scholarly books. Almost all of these articles and books dealt with international relations or with general political science. In *Who's Who* he listed those of his works that he considered noteworthy. Among them were the following: *American Government* (1911), *Idées et Institutions Politiques Américaines* (1921), *Prize Law During the World War* (1927), *American Foreign Policies* (1927), and *Law of Treaties* (1935); but he included in this bibliography only one historical work, a four-volume history of the United States which he had written in collaboration with Henry Cabot Lodge (1906). Curiously, he made no mention of the book that will probably endure the longest—his first book, *Reconstruction in Mississippi*.[1]

From the outset, this work has received the sober, if qualified, approval of a wide variety of critics, and it continues to do so. A contemporary reviewer in *The Nation* thought that the "dismal story" had been "told impartially by Mr. Garner." Dunning himself commented on the "rigidly judicial spirit" his former student had shown. Years later, the outstanding Negro historian W. E. Burghardt DuBois characterized several of the Dunning-school studies as "thoroughly bad" but conceded that some, and especially Garner's, "though influenced by the same general attitude" of hostility to Radical Reconstruction, had a certain "scientific poise" and other redeeming qualities. Garner's *Reconstruction in Mississippi*, DuBois added, "conceives the Negro as an integral part of the scene and treats him as a human being." Howard K. Beale opined that a few of the Dunning students, "to a certain extent, and Garner, notably, escaped from the restricting frames of reference of the others." David Donald described the Garner book as "accurate, thor-

[1]Wendell Holmes Stephenson, *Southern History in the Making: Pioneer Historians of the South* (Baton Rouge, 1964), 149; *Who Was Who in America, 1897–1942* (Chicago, 1942), 441; Garner obituary in *American Political Science Review*, XXIII (1939), 90–91.

ough, and generally impartial." Vernon L. Wharton wrote: "Little that has been learned in the succeeding sixty years would serve greatly to alter or even to add to Garner's story. However, Garner did assume that Radical Reconstruction was wrong in principle and practice and that the restoration of native white rule was essential to the peace and progress of Mississippi. These assumptions resulted in some lack of consideration of the experiences, needs, and aspirations of the Negro majority, and in tendencies to discredit the character and testimony of those who took part in the Radical movement and to magnify the virtues of those who fought against it." [2]

In fact, Garner's book seems to have got a reasonably favorable reception in all quarters except one. Some of his fellow Mississippians were horrified to find him saying anything in exculpation of the Republican regime they had hated and had fought to overthrow. One of his severest critics was John S. McNeily, who prided himself on his ancestors' having settled in Mississippi in the time of Spanish rule. After serving in the Confederate army, McNeily became a professional journalist and an amateur historian. He edited a Democratic newspaper in Greenville and later in Vicksburg, and wrote a long and vigorous essay on "The Climax and Collapse of Reconstruction in Mississippi." In it he undertook to correct what he considered "grossly misleading deductions and errors" in Garner's work. McNeily was particularly offended by Garner's taking at face value a certain statement of a carpetbag official. The carpetbagger, McNeily said, "'could never have dreamed that his flimsy fiction would be accepted in a history of reconstruction, whose author is a native of Mississippi." [3]

In comparison with other natives of Mississippi who, before Garner, had written on Reconstruction in that state, he appears to be well balanced in his opinions and carefully

---

[2] *The Nation,* LXXIII (1901), 110; W. A. Dunning, *Reconstruction, Political and Economic, 1865–1877* (New York, 1907), 353; W. E. B. DuBois, *Black Reconstruction* (New York, 1935), 720; H. K. Beale, "On Rewriting Reconstruction History," *American Historical Review,* XLV (1940), 808–809; J. G. Randall and David Donald, *The Civil War and Reconstruction* (Boston, 1961), 780; V. L. Wharton, "Reconstruction," in Arthur S. Link and Rembert W. Patrick (eds.), *Writing Southern History: Essays in Historiography in Honor of Fletcher M. Green* (Baton Rouge, 1965), 300.

[3] J. S. McNeily, "Climax and Collapse of Reconstruction in Mississippi, 1874–1876," *Publications of the Mississippi Historical Society,* XII (1912), 312, 457, 459. For a biographical sketch of McNeily, see *ibid.,* VI (1902), 129 n.

restrained in his expression of them. One of the most important of the earlier writers was Ethelbert Barksdale, who had helped to lead the Democrats in overthrowing Republican rule and who afterward had served as a Democratic congressman from Mississippi. Barksdale contributed the Mississippi chapter to a collection of essays on the results of Reconstruction in the various states, a book that was put together and published as propaganda against a movement to secure congressional legislation for enforcing the Fifteenth Amendment in the South. This volume, *Why the Solid South?* (1890), probably did more than anything else to crystallize the Southern white, Democratic version of Reconstruction history. "In a word," Barksdale wrote of Mississippi (though he must have meant "in three words"), "mongrelism, ignorance and depravity were installed." Republicans "ruled and robbed," while "ignorance and knavery" prevailed over "intelligence and honesty." The Negro-and-carpetbagger government pretended to set up an educational system, but this was only "the convenient cover for all kinds of plundering schemes." Republican finances as a whole provided "a model of profligacy and extravagance." To all this, there could have been but one outcome. "The attempt of sectional agitators and philonegrists to reverse the abnormal [normal?] relation of the two races produced the inevitable consequence of strife and bloody conflict," Barksdale concluded. "It was worse than folly to suppose that the negro who had through all the ages shown his utter incapacity for self-government could be elevated from a state of slavery into the rulership of the race which history teaches . . . has never bent the suppliant knee to an inferior race." Similar language and similar themes can be found in the works of other Mississippi historians of the late nineteenth and early twentieth centuries. Much the same kind of interpretation can also be found in general histories by Northern historians of that time, historians such as James Ford Rhodes.[4]

That view of Mississippi Reconstruction, the Conservative view, may be summarized as follows: The Negroes, for racial reasons, were incapable of taking care of themselves, to say nothing of governing themselves. They needed to be guided

[4]H. A. Herbert (ed.), *Why the Solid South? Or, Reconstruction and Its Results* (Baltimore, 1890), 333–38. See also Dunbar Rowland, "The Rise and Fall of Negro Rule in Mississippi," *Publications of the Mississippi Historical Society,* II (1899), 188–99; Robert Bowman, "Reconstruction in Yazoo County," *ibid.,* VII (1903), 115–30; J. R. Lynch, "Some Historical Errors of James Ford Rhodes," *Journal of Negro History,* II (1917), 345–68.

and controlled; and the Black Code, which the legislature adopted in 1865, before the beginning of Radical Reconstruction, was a fair and appropriate means of providing the necessary control. Once enfranchised by the Reconstruction Acts of 1867, the Negroes sought to govern for their own benefit; they drew the color line against most of the whites. Those white men who aided and abetted Negro rule—the carpetbaggers and the scalawags—were contemptible, low-class, self-seeking, unprincipled types. The carpetbaggers were penniless adventurers who, as soon as the vote had been given to the Negroes, swarmed down from the North like a "Vandal horde" to exploit that vote, win office, and get rich. The "renegade scalawags, with white skin and black hearts," were Southern poor whites, the dregs of ante-bellum society, who seized the opportunity to better themselves at the expense of the more respectable folk. Together, these motley Republicans gave Mississippi for several years a regime of unbelievable extravagance and corruption. The constructive achievements of which they boasted, such as the establishment of public schools, were paltry in comparison with the ruinous taxes they imposed and the fantastic debt they ran up. The final overthrow of the Negroes and carpetbaggers, in the state election of 1875, was due to a virtuous though violent uprising of Mississippi whites. To some degree, the overthrow was facilitated by internecine quarrels within the Republican party and by the Democrats' positive appeal to Negro voters. The Democrats rallied practically all native white men, including those who formerly had cooperated with the Negroes and carpetbaggers, and even attracted many Negroes who were disgusted with the excesses of the dominant Republican faction.

Such, in brief, was the Conservative view, but there was also a Radical interpretation which traversed it at every major point. Just as the one version originated with Democratic politicians who had taken an active part in Reconstruction history, so the other originated with carpetbaggers and Negroes who had opposed them. Albert T. Morgan, who had come from Wisconsin to Mississippi and had become sheriff of Yazoo County, presented his case in his book *Yazoo* (1884). John R. Lynch, at one time a Negro congressman from Mississippi, disputed the Democratic charges in his book *The Facts of Reconstruction* (1913). Morgan praised the Mississippi Negroes as "the superiors of their former masters in physical strength, in manly courage, in political sagacity, and in love of country, and not inferior in any of the elements of good citizenship—general intelligence alone excepted." He condemned the mass of Mississippi white men as "a race once civilized but now reduced, by the inherent concupiscence of African slavery, to lecherous savages." Lynch described the Southern white Republicans, the so-called scalawags, as a group that numbered some of the "best and most substantial white men" of the state. Both writers defended the Republican program as a democratic attempt to provide for the general welfare of Mississippians, black and white. Both argued that the effort was largely frustrated, and the Republicans finally driven from power, by the terroristic tactics of their opponents.[5]

Besides the original Conservative and Radical versions of Mississippi Reconstruction, there is also a Revisionist interpretation, which has been developed by historians who were born too late to have taken part in the events of which they have written. The pioneer among the Revisionists, DuBois, though he did not devote himself specifically to Mississippi history, cast some light upon it in a brief article and a very long book. Donald took a new look at the Mississippi scalawags and the election of 1875, and Wharton left a significant volume whose scope was broader than its title, *The Negro in Mississippi, 1865–1890* (1947). In recent years the Revisionist trend in Reconstruction historiography has been greatly stimulated by the civil rights movement. The Revisionist interpretation, though more refined and better documented, is in spirit quite close to the Radical view—much closer to it than to the Conservative view. For instance, Donald confirmed and elaborated upon the Lynch thesis that a considerable number of respectable and well-to-do white Mississippians (possibly as many as 25 or 35 per cent of all the white voters in 1873) were temporarily Republicans. Most of these native whites, according to Donald, were former Whigs, and the Whigs had constituted "the wealthiest and best educated element in the state" before the war. Wharton, who was remarkedly free from racism, believed that Mississippi had been "extremely fortunate in the character of her most important Negro Republican leaders." [6]

There are, all together, four schools of Reconstruction

[5]A. T. Morgan, *Yazoo; Or, on the Picket Line of Freedom in the South* (Washington, 1884), 273, 357; J. R. Lynch, *The Facts of Reconstruction* (New York, 1913); Lynch, in *Journal of Negro History*, II, 352.

[6]W. E. B. DuBois, "Reconstruction and Its Benefits," *American Historical Review*, XV (1910), 781–99, and *Black Reconstruction;* David Donald, "The Scalawag in Mississippi Reconstruction," *Journal of Southern History*, X (1944), 447–60 (see especially pp. 448–49); V. L Wharton, *The Negro in Mississippi, 1865–1890* (Chapel Hill, 1947), 158.

historiography, whether considering Mississippi alone or the South as a whole (and there are, of course, differences regarding details among writers within each school). These are the Radical, the Revisionist, the Conservative, and the Dunningite, the last of which is, in the case of Mississippi, represented by Garner. The Revisionist view, as has been seen, is essentially a refinement and elaboration of the Radical view. The Dunning interpretation is, in the same way, closely related to the Conservative interpretation. Is Garner, whose book has won Revisionist praise and Conservative condemnation, to be classified as essentially a Revisionist?

As he indicated in the preface to his book, Garner had begun his study with a determination to do a thorough and impartial job. He not only looked into a large number of newspapers and state and federal documents; he also corresponded with former participants in Mississippi Reconstruction and sought letters from them. One of those to whom he wrote was Adelbert Ames, a native of Maine who had been the leading carpetbagger in Mississippi. He sent Ames a list of questions. What, for example, did Ames think were "some of the merits" of his administration as Mississippi governor? The elderly Ames replied to Garner, at that time a twenty-eight-year-old faculty member at Bradley Polytechnic Institute: "My dear Professor, when you appear before St. Peter at the gates of Heaven, what can you say in reply to his query as to 'the merits' of your earthly career?" Ames added: "To say that I acted conscientiously to the best of my ability does not seem to be sufficient." In this interchange, the old veteran comes off somewhat better than the eager but rather callow and bumptious scholar. Ames, feeling that he had nothing to hide, generously offered his personal papers to Garner. "My hope is," Ames wrote, "that as a young man, as I understand you to be, you will be free from the animosities and prejudices of those days." By the time Garner had completed his study, he was confident that, having felt "keenly his own prejudices" and having made, "an earnest effort to divest himself" of them, he had succeeded reasonably well in presenting an unbiased account.[7]

It is true that, having not yet reached his fourth birthday at the time of the 1875 election, Garner was too young to remember from his own experience the events about which he wrote. And there is no reason to doubt that he made a sincere attempt to recognize and counteract the Mississippi outlook with which he had been raised and educated. How

[7]Blanche Ames Ames, *Adelbert Ames, 1835–1933: General, Senator, Governor* (New York, 1964), 573; Garner, pp. vii–viii.

well he succeeded, and how close he came to the later Revisionist point of view, can be seen from a sampling of his and others' views on certain key issues of Mississippi Reconstruction.

"Even now," Garner said (1901), "the negro is not a model of industry, frugality, and foresight. He was much farther from it in 1866." This was but one of a number of deprecatory references that Garner made to Negroes in general. One group of them he called "poor deluded creatures." He took it for granted that Negroes were, by nature, inferior to whites and incapable of self-government. Indeed, he criticized Governor Ames on the grounds, among others, that Ames had "had an overconfidence in the mental and moral ability of the black race, so far as their ability to govern themselves was concerned," and that he had failed to realize "a superior race will not submit to the government of an inferior one." Even when Garner singled out an individual Negro, John R. Lynch, for commendation, he paid him the racist compliment that he was "distinctly Caucasian in his habits." In this assumption of Negro inferiority, Garner was much closer to the Conservative historians than to later Revisionists such as Wharton, who conceded that the whites had constituted the "dominant race" but assumed that they had been dominant because of "tradition, education, and superior economic and legal advantages," not because of an innate mental and moral superiority.[8]

Like the Conservative historians, Garner defended the Black Code, which had been designed to make dependent laborers of the former slaves, even depriving them of the right to buy or lease farms of their own. This and other features of the law, he admitted, were "unwise" because they gave Republicans in Congress a "pretext" for Radical Reconstruction; but such provisions were probably necessary. "The condition of things seemed to demand the immediate adoption of measures to check the demoralization of the freedmen, and compel them to labor." According to Wharton, however, the Black Code was an "entirely natural" but "almost entirely unnecessary product of its time and of the forces at work," and it "complicated rather than simplified the relations of the races." [9]

Garner implied that the Negroes, once in office, had discriminated against the whites. "In the first reconstruction legislature," he said, "the colored members consented to have a white man preside over their deliberations, but after-

[8]Garner, 296, 336, 353, 408; Wharton, *Negro in Mississippi*, 198.
[9]Garner, 116–18; Wharton, *Negro in Mississippi*, 93.

ward, as long as they were in power, with a temporary exception in 1873, a black skin was an indispensable qualification for the office of speaker, another illustration of their
greed for power." This charge of discrimination, as Wharton
was to point out, had originated with the Democrats, who
undertook to unite all native whites in opposition to the
blacks and justified this by contending that "the color line
had already been drawn by the Negro." Wharton commented
that the Democrats "ignored the fact that the Negroes had
from the beginning welcomed the leadership of almost any
white who would serve with them." Garner, too, ignored this
fact. His view of the Negroes was very different from that
of Wharton, who also pointed out: "Those in the legislature
sought no special advantage for their race, and in one of
their very first acts they petitioned Congress to remove all
political disabilities from the whites." [10]

In his treatment of carpetbaggers, Garner differed from
Conservative authors in taking a dispassionate and at times
even a somewhat sympathetic approach, yet he did not break
away completely from the Conservatives' stereotype. He accepted their definition of the carpetbagger as a Northerner
who had gone south to take advantage of the political opportunities that the Reconstruction Acts of 1867, by enfranchis-
ing the Negroes, had opened to him. Garner noted, however,
that most of the Northerners active in Mississippi politics after 1867 had arrived in the state before that year and
had come originally as planters and businessmen, not as
politicians. "It is incorrect, therefore, to call them 'carpet
baggers,'" he remarked. "They did not go South to get offices, for there were no offices for them to fill. The causes
which led them to settle there were purely economic, and not
political. The genuine 'carpet baggers' who came after the
adoption of the reconstruction policy were comparatively
few in number." Here Garner was on the verge of drastically
revising the carpetbagger concept, but he stopped short of
doing so. Forgetting his own admonition, he proceeded to
apply the term indiscriminately to all white Republicans
from the North, including the great majority whom he had
said the word did not fit. Albert T. Morgan, for example, had
arrived in Mississippi in 1865 and had invested (and lost)
some $50,000 in planting and lumbering enterprises before
going into politics. Yet Garner referred to him as "the well-
known 'carpet-bagger,' Colonel A. T. Morgan."

Garner tried to be fair to Morgan and others like him. He
wrote: "Morgan's correspondence shows that he is a man of

[10]Garner, 295; Wharton, *Negro in Mississippi*, 179.

education, and his political opponents testify that as an officer [sheriff] he was able and faithful." Nevertheless, when relating events in which Morgan had taken part, Garner followed the hostile reports of those political opponents much more closely than he did Morgan's own account. Similarly, he recounted Ames's Mississippi career in a basically antagonistic spirit even though he grudgingly praised Ames for his "personal integrity," "courteous demeanor," and "education and refinement." He said Ames failed as governor because of his prejudice against Southern whites as well as his overestimation of Southern Negroes and also because of "the circumstances surrounding his advent into Mississippi." But Garner admitted that Ames was innocent of peculation, as indeed were many other carpetbaggers. "The charge sometimes made that they were all thieves and plunderers has no foundation in fact." This relatively charitable judgment set Garner apart from his Conservative predecessors, and it was one of the main reasons for the complaints of his Conservative critics.[11]

Garner described and analyzed the carpetbaggers much more thoroughly than he did the scalawags. This word he used seldom, and only to refer to certain men as a group, not to individuals. Thus, with regard to the constitutional convention of 1868, he wrote: "There were twenty-nine native white Republicans, derisively called 'Scalawags.' Four of the Northern born Republicans had lived in the South before the war, and two of them had served in the Confederate army." These Northern-born Republicans he apparently excluded from the scalawag category, limiting it by implication to native white Republicans. In doing so, he made the term more restrictive than most people had done during Reconstruction and most historians have done since. By both popular and scholarly usage, it applies not only to native but also to Northern-born white Republicans in cases where these men had settled in the South before 1861 and had remained there during the war, giving active or merely passive support to the Confederacy. Garner's implied definition would leave out the man who, by common consent, was the greatest of Mississippi scalawags—James Lusk Alcorn. Born in Illinois and brought up in Kentucky, Alcorn had moved to Mississippi in 1844, when about thirty-three years old. During the war he served briefly and unenthusiastically as an officer of Confederate troops. Garner referred to him, er-

[11]Garner, 136, 309–10, 376 n, 408, 413–14; R. N. Current, "Carpetbaggers Reconsidered," in *A Festschrift for Frederick B. Artz* (Durham, 1964), 140–41.

roneously, as a "native Republican," but never as a scala-wag. Garner also refrained from using the term when men-tioning specific white Republicans, such as R. W. Flournoy and J. L. Wofford, who actually had been born in the South.

In dealing with men who are generally known as scala-wags, Garner was considerably more restrained but not much more sympathetic or understanding than were the writers of the Conservative school. He recognized Alcorn as a rich and respectable planter and a well-meaning politi-cian: "He seems to have been sincere in his professions." He dismissed Colonel Flournoy, however, as "the most extreme and obnoxious radical in the state," even though Flournoy was the wealthiest and most distinguished man of his own county, a man whom the county historian, a Democrat, after-wards described as "highly respected and beloved." Garner did not even approach a sophisticated conception of the scal-awags' identity, character, and role in Mississippi politics; it remained for the Radical Lynch and the Revisionists Wharton and Donald to throw some revealing light on these matters (and it remains for others to provide still more il-lumination).[12]

Garner accused the Republicans of levying burdensome and even confiscatory taxes. On this subject he agreed, in the main, with Conservative writers, yet he pointed out that, as of 1874, the local taxes in the thirty-nine counties with Democratic administrations seemed to be, on the whole, no higher than those in the thirty-four counties with Republi-can administrations. He did not entirely agree with Conser-vative writers on the question of governmental extrava-gance. Some of them charged that the Republicans had left a state debt of $20 million, and this figure came to be widely accepted. Garner concluded that Governor Ames, who had insisted that the debt amounted to no more than $500,-000, was substantially correct. And, though he too com-plained of excessive government spending, Garner revealed that annual state expenditures under the Republicans from 1870 to 1875 had averaged less than under the Democrats in 1865 and 1866. Wharton later concurred with Garner by say-ing there seemed to be "no correlation at all between the rate of taxation and the political or racial character of the counties," and he went beyond Garner by concluding that

[12]Garner, 187, 237, 243, 270, 279–81, 349; Wharton, *Negro in Mississippi*, 158; F. L. Riley, "James Lusk Alcorn," *Dictionary of American Biography*, I (New York, 1928), 137–39. See also A. W. Trelease, "Who Were the Scalawags?" *Journal of Southern His-tory*, XXIX (1963), 445–68.

the Republicans had given Mississippi "a government of greatly expanded functions at a cost that was low in comparison with that of almost any other state." [13]

On the issue of fraud and corruption, Garner broke completely with the Conservatives, who had written in emotional if rather vague language about "the most corrupt and colossal schemes of public robbery ever devised by a band of plunderers." Referring to the legislature that met in 1876, after the overthrow of the Republicans, Garner said the "majority of the Democratic members honestly believed that much official corruption" had existed, and the "most searching investigation was instituted in every department, with the confident expectation of unearthing numerous frauds." The Democrats found little, however, and Garner himself could verify only a few of the charges, and none involving more than comparatively trifling sums. "The only large case of embezzlement among the state officers during the postbellum period," he concluded, "was that of the Democratic state treasurer in 1866. The amount of the shortage was $61,962." Garner could have added, as both Lynch and Wharton later did, that the next important defaulter was also a Democratic state treasurer, the one who was elected in 1875. "His shortage," said Wharton, "was $315,612.19." Lynch maintained that, "when the insurrectionists [the Democrats] took charge of the government, every dollar of public money had been faithfully and honestly accounted for." [14]

Nevertheless, Garner's bitterest critic, the Conservative historian McNeily, repeated the theme of Republican corruption and accused Garner of falsifying the facts. McNeily indicated that Garner had confused the Democratic treasurer of 1866 with a much earlier state treasurer, Richard S. Graves, whose spectacular case was well known in Mississippi; he had been convicted of embezzlement and had escaped from jail by walking out in his wife's clothing after a visit from her. "The grossness of the perversion of history," McNeily protested, "in the misstatement of the time of the notorious Graves defalcation which occurred before the war, in 1843, can only be looked on as culpable carelessness." McNeily insisted that Garner was naive as well as careless. "As there were no public funds whose amounts would have made 'great embezzlements' possible," McNeily

[13]Garner, 312–13, 320–21; Wharton, *Negro in Mississippi*, 170, 180.

[14]Garner, 323, 412; Wharton, *Negro in Mississippi*, 179; J. R. Lynch, "A Letter on the Tragic Era," *Journal of Negro History*, XVI (1931), 114.

explained, "this implication of freedom from corrupt practice is exceedingly thin. The game of graft was not played that way. It consisted in a general practice of scrip speculation and warrant shaving, of falsified tax rolls, etc." McNeily's refutation itself was rather thin, and he presented no evidence to sustain it.[15]

Regarding public education, Garner credited the Republicans with a larger contribution than Conservatives did but with a smaller one than Revisionists were to do. "Did the Reconstruction regime give Mississippi her public schools?" one Conservative writer asked, and she came up with an essentially negative answer to the question. The Republican educational authorities had been so prejudiced and so corrupt, she argued, that "certainly Mississippians would have been justified in condemning the public school system." Instead of abandoning it upon the fall of the Negroes and carpetbaggers, however, the white Mississippians had taken it over and brought "success out of failure." Garner, too, felt that the system under the Republicans had serious faults, such as an administration that was "needlessly expensive" and that put the "entire management of the schools" in the control of the "non-tax-paying class." He minimized the white Mississippians' resistance to the establishment of schools; it did not appear, he said, that "there was any opposition by the more intelligent whites to an economical scheme of negro education." Yet he was fairly generous to the Republicans in his conclusion: "When the reconstructionists surrendered the government to the democracy, in 1876, the public school system which they had fathered had become firmly established, its efficiency increased, and its administration made somewhat less expensive than at first." Wharton was still more favorable to the Republicans. He gave them credit for setting up and maintaining a (biracial) school system which "was an amazing advance beyond anything the state had known before." He showed that the Democrats, in denouncing the schools, had raised the cry "that the new system involved an enormous expenditure, that the greater part of this was for the benefit of the Negroes, and that all of it came from the pockets of the whites." He blamed the Democratic leaders for the widespread burning of school buildings and of churches used as schools—a topic that Garner barely touched upon.[16]

[15]McNeily, in *Publications of the Mississippi Historical Society*, XII, 457–59.

[16]Elise Timberlane, "Did the Reconstruction Regime Give Mississippi Her Public Schools?" *ibid.*, 89; Garner, 356–57, 370; Wharton, *Negro in Mississippi*, 175, 245.

To what extent was the Democratic victory of 1875 due to intimidation and fraud? Such things went unmentioned in the Conservative kind of history that was taught to Mississippi school children. "In this contest," they were told, "thousands of the colored voters all over the State came boldly out on the side of the taxpayers, and with their assistance the Democratic Conservative ticket swept the State." Writing for adults, however, some of the Conservative historians frankly acknowledged the importance of violent and fraudulent techniques, justifying these on the ground that they had been absolutely necessary for redeeming the state from the "blighting curse of negro rule." The Conservative McNeily wrote: "A few negroes voted the Democratic ticket; a good many, from fear of bodily injury, or the policy declared in some counties of refusing employment to those who voted the radical ticket, remaining away from the polls. In some counties the ballot boxes were manipulated and the vote as polled changed. It was either that or a more violent recourse, for the decree had been registered that the carpetbagger must go." The carpetbagger Morgan agreed that murder and threats of it had formed the essence of the so-called Mississippi Plan of 1875. "Throughout that period the Republicans were as helpless as babes," Morgan said. "There was never any resistance at all by them to the violence of the enemy." He thought of the Democratic campaign as a renewal of the Rebellion. Similarly, the one-time Negro leader Lynch looked upon the Democratic party as a "reorganization of that part of the Confederate army" which resided in Mississippi, and he saw the Democratic campaign as an "insurrection" against the legitimate government of the state.

Garner took a different view. "In regard to the Republican charge of intimidation," he said, "it is undoubtedly true, as alleged, that intimidation was successfully practised by the whites, but, in most cases, it was resorted to before election day." All that, in any case, was a secondary factor. "A more important reason for the overthrow of the Republicans was the schism in their own ranks." Donald came to essentially the same conclusion in his 1944 article on Mississippi scalawags. "The triumph of the Democratic color-line policies, known as the Mississippi Plan of 1875, would seem to be due to the successful union of all southern whites into one party rather than to the intimidation of the Negro." But Wharton disagreed. In his account of the events of 1875, he made it clear that, in his opinion, the Democrats' use of "economic pressure" and, still more, their resort to "threats and actual violence" had played a decisive role. And Donald, in a later work, modified the judgment he had given in 1944.

He presented, in 1960, the following appraisal of the Mississippi Plan: "One part of the scheme had to do with arousing enthusiasm among the Democratic masses and with coercing the few remaining scalawags into leaving the Republican party. Its principal purpose, however, was to intimidate the Negroes." [17]

To sum up, Garner departed a long way from Conservative interpretations and anticipated Revisionist views on certain topics, but he remained in essential agreement with the Conservatives on others, though he eschewed the Conservatives' emotional and vituperative language. He showed the greatest originality and independence in his treatment of carpetbaggers and of Republican finances. In handling the scalawags, he was less successful, viewing them on the whole objectively but largely ignoring their background and significance. He gave the Republicans much more credit than the Conservatives had done, but somewhat less than Revisionists were to do, for the establishment of public schools. On the election of 1875, however, he differed more from the Radicals and Revisionists than from most of the Conservatives; certainly, he was with the Conservatives in spirit, hailing the 1875 campaign of the Democrats as a "most exciting" one that would "compare favorably with any political struggle that ever occurred on American soil." [18] Basically, he was no different from the Conservative writers—or from his fellow historians of the Dunning school—in his attitude toward Negroes. No one held more firmly than he to the conviction that Negroes were innately inferior, that they needed to be kept under strict control, that they abused the power which had been thrust upon them, and that they had to be turned out of office at almost any cost. He assumed that, throughout the Reconstruction conflicts in Mississippi, the Democrats and their allies were fundamentally right, and the Republicans fundamentally wrong.

All historians, whether they recognize them or not, hold basic assumptions of one kind or another. In the case of Garner, it is not strange that he reflected, to the extent that he did, the deep convictions with which he had been brought

[17]Robert Lowry and W. H. McCardle, *A History of Mississippi for Use in Schools* (New York and New Orleans, 1892), 232–33; Rowland, in *Publications of the Mississippi Historical Society*, II, 191; McNeily, *ibid.*, XII, 422; Morgan, *Yazoo*, 487; Lynch, in *Journal of Negro History*, XVI, 113; Garner, 396–97; Donald, in *Journal of Southern History*, X, 460; Wharton, *Negro in Mississippi*, 187, 190; Randall and Donald, *Civil War and Reconstruction*, 684–85.

[18]Garner, 372.

up. The remarkable thing is that he succeeded so well in breaking away from many of them. His book was, for 1901, an amazingly well-researched, accurate, and objective account of a portion of Mississippi history by a white Mississippian. No mere historiographical curiosity, this volume remains indispensable for the modern student of the subject. The student may take an antidote for some of its biases by reading, along with it, Vernon L. Wharton's book *The Negro in Mississippi, 1865–1900*, which treats much of the same material from a different point of view.[19] In the future, other scholars can be expected to come forth with new facts and new interpretations at various phases of the story. The next historian to produce a comprehensive study of Reconstruction in Mississippi will do extremely well if he proves himself as thorough in his research, as accurate in his statements of fact, and as nearly self-liberated from his prejudices as Garner was two generations ago.

RICHARD N. CURRENT

[19]Wharton's book was reprinted in a 1965 paperback edition as a "Harper Torchbook" by Harper & Row, New York. Lynch's *Facts of Reconstruction* is also valuable as a corrective supplement but is not widely available.

RECONSTRUCTION IN MISSISSIPPI

CHAPTER FIRST

SECESSION AND CIVIL WAR

I. THE RUPTURE WITH THE UNITED STATES

IT is necessary to a correct understanding of the history of the period which it is proposed to cover in this chapter to review briefly the steps leading up to the beginning of hostilities with the United States.

The perpetuation and extension of the system of negro slavery, the real cause of the Civil War, was declared by the Supreme Court of Mississippi in 1837 to be a part of the public policy of the state.[1] Three years before this decision was made, the people of the state repudiated unequivocally the doctrine of nullification and secession. On the 9th of June, 1834, the Democratic state convention, presided over by General Thomas Hinds, unanimously resolved that " a constitutional right of secession from the Union, on the part of a single state as asserted by the nullifying leaders of South Carolina, is utterly unsanctioned by the Constitution, which was framed to establish, not to destroy, the Union."[2] Secession in Mississippi was nothing more than an abstract question until the adoption by Congress of the policy of excluding slavery from the territories. What is believed to have been the first organized opposition to this policy was made by a state convention at Jackson in October, 1849. A number of resolutions was passed by this body, one of which declared that in certain contingencies their separate welfare might be consulted by the " formation

---

[1] Mitchell *vs.* Wells, 37 Miss. 254.
[2] Speech of J. A. Wilcox, Union Member of Congress from Mississippi, 1852, Globe, 32d Cong. 1st Ses. App. 284.

1

of a compact of union that would afford protection to their
rights and liberties." [1] Here was a formal declaration in
favor of secession as a "last resort." The convention in
all its deliberations followed the advice of Mr. Calhoun,
who in the previous July had sketched, in a letter to Colonel
Tarpley of the Supreme Court,[2] a plan of operations. Mississippi took a prominent part in the Nashville convention,
being represented by eight members, one of whom, Chief
Justice Sharkey, presided over the deliberations.

The enactment of the Compromise measures of 1850
gave additional impetus to the secession movement. These
measures were opposed by all the Mississippi delegation in
Congress, with the solitary exception of Senator Foote.
Jefferson Davis, his colleague, declared that every prominent
man in the state was opposed to the measures.[3] Southern
Rights Associations sprang up in nearly every community,
and the Compromise measures were universally denounced
from the stump. Foote says the press was well-nigh unanimous in favor of secession.[4] Upon the adjournment of Congress the delegation from Mississippi returned to the state
to give an account of their cause, and, with the exception
of Foote, to urge resistance to the action of Congress.
Albert Gallatin Brown said, in a speech at Jackson, "So
help me God I am for resistance ; and my advice to you is
that of Cromwell to his colleagues, "pray to God and keep
your powder dry.'"[5] Davis, McWillie, Featherston, and
Thompson spoke in a similar strain, while Foote bestirred
himself to vindicate his course before the people. The
legislature had already passed resolutions of censure against
him, declaring that the interests of the state were not safe
in his hands.[6] He then stumped the state, making in all
forty or fifty speeches, and urged the people to send delegates to a convention which he had presumed to call. Governor Quitman, the leader of the secession party, called the
legislature together in extraordinary session, and recommended measures, looking to the secession of the state in
case certain demands were not complied with.[7] The day
on which this message was read to the legislature, Foote's
convention assembled at Jackson. It adopted resolutions

---

[1] For the resolutions of the Convention, see speech of Senator R. B. Rhett,
Globe, 32d Cong. 1st Ses. App. 63.
[2] For the letter, see Globe, *Ibid.* p. 52.   [4] Casket of Reminiscences, p. 355.
[3] Memoirs of J. Davis, I. p. 465.   [5] Globe, *ibid.* p. 336.
[6] The resolutions are printed in the Globe, *ibid.* pp. 55, 56.
[7] Claiborne's Life of Quitman, II. p. 125.

indorsing his course, advocated acquiescence in the Compromise measures, warmly denounced the secession movement, and organized the Union party in Mississippi. The legislature, undisturbed by this "growl of whiggery" so near its doors, took up the governor's recommendation, and passed an act for a convention a year hence to "consider the state of Federal relations and the remedies to be applied."

The people of the state were now sharply divided into two political parties. One was the party of secession, organized in November, 1850, under the name of the Southern Rights Party, and which assumed the name of the Democratic State-rights Party in June, 1851. By some they were called "Resisters." It was composed of the bulk of the old Democratic party and a small element of State-rights Whigs. The Union party was organized on the day on which Foote's convention met; namely, the 18th of November, 1850. It was composed of old line Whigs and Union Democrats. The secession party had in its ranks a preponderance of the wealth and talent of the state, but lacked the concert of action and the audacity of the Union party. In the campaign that followed, the precise question involved, says Foote, was, "Will Mississippi join South Carolina in the act of secession from the Union?" The question was to be settled by the election of a governor and delegates to the state convention. Quitman, the most rabid of the "Resisters," was nominated by the Democrats for governor over Jefferson Davis, while Foote was chosen to be the standard bearer of the Union party. The election of delegates occurred a month earlier than the gubernatorial election. In the first election the Union party won by a majority of seven thousand votes. Quitman, mortified at this unequivocal condemnation of his policy, and almost certain that the convention which he had fathered would declare against him, retired from the race after issuing an address to the people.[1] This left the secession party without a leader, and the state election was but a month off. Jefferson Davis, who many felt should have received the nomination in the first instance, was persuaded to resign his seat in the Senate to lead their forlorn hope. Foote was elected governor, but the Union majority of seven thousand in September was reduced to less than one thousand in October.[2] The Union party elected a majority of the legislature, and three mem-

---

[1] Claiborne's Quitman, II. p. 146.
[2] Lalor, Cyclop. Pol. Sci., II. 860.

bers of Congress, and a Union Democrat was chosen to
succeed Foote in the United States Senate. The convention
met at Jackson November 10, 1851. It was composed of
ninety-three delegates and was, without question, the most
distinguished of the ante-bellum assemblages.[1] The purpose
of the convention, as stated by those who called it, was to
" demand a redress for past grievances, and a guarantee
against future assaults upon the rights of the people." No
such action as this, however, was taken; but instead the
convention resolved that the people would acquiesce in the
Compromise measures as a permanent adjustment of the sectional controversy. The convention furthermore resolved
that it held the Union second in importance only to the
rights and principles which it was designed to perpetuate,
and that the asserted right of secession was utterly unsanctioned by the Constitution.[2] Foote was sanguine enough to
believe that this put at rest forever the question of secession
in Mississippi, and he publicly declared in the Senate that no
man with secession sentiments could be elected to the most
insignificant office.[3] The secession movement really seemed
to be dead, but during the next ten years many events
occurred to reduce the numerical strength of the strong
Union party which Foote had built up in 1851. The infrac-
tions of the fugitive slave law, the Kansas struggle, the publication of " Uncle Tom's Cabin," the John Brown raid, and
the election of Lincoln intensified the feeling of hostility
toward the North. It was well illustrated in the John
Brown affair, on account of which the legislature, without
referring the bill to a committee, and almost without a dissenting vote, appropriated $150,000 to purchase arms. Reuben
Davis, a member of Congress from Mississippi, declared that
when the news of Lincoln's election reached Washington,
members from the South purchased long-range rifles to take
home with them, and some rejoiced that the end was near.[4]
Shortly after the election, the legislature was called together
in extraordinary session, and a state convention ordered to
meet on the 7th of January following to " consider the existing relations between the government of the United States
and the government of the people of Mississippi, and to adopt

[1] Some of the prominent members were William L. Sharkey, J. W. C.
Watson, Jason Niles, J. L. Alcorn, Wiley P. Harris, William Barksdale,
Charles Clark, and Amos R. Johnston.
[2] The resolutions are printed in Claiborne's Quitman, II. ch. xii.
[3] Globe, *op. cit.* p. 59.
[4] Recollections, p. 389.

such measures for vindicating the government of the state and the protection of its institutions as shall appear to be demanded." The governor was authorized to appoint commissioners to visit the other slave states, and inform them of the action of Mississippi, and to invite their coöperation in the adoption of efficient measures for their defence and safety. The commissioners at once bestirred themselves at the various Southern capitals, at all of which they were received in truly diplomatic style as ambassadors from foreign republics. Governors were formally notified of their arrival, audiences were granted, and their credentials submitted in the most formal manner. Committees of the legislature were appointed to wait upon them and extend the courtesies of the chambers, and their addresses were delivered before the joint session of the two houses. Complimentary resolutions were sometimes passed, and the proceedings in the reception of the commissioner enrolled on parchment, the great seal affixed, and the signatures of the officers of both houses attached. The instrument was then presented as the "response of a sister state to the friendly greeting of Mississippi." Their missions in most cases were successful.[1]

In the meantime the canvass for the election of delegates to the convention was proceeding. In a good many counties mass meetings were held, and resolutions adopted declaratory of the sense of the community on the all-absorbing question. Most of these, but by no means all, were in favor of secession. A very respectable minority were strongly opposed to secession. They bestirred themselves to secure the return of Union delegates, and were successful to the extent that about one-fourth of those chosen were Whigs, most of whom were opposed to secession, and some of whom had positive instructions to vote against an ordinance of secession. The secession contingent were divided among themselves as to the expediency of secession without the joint coöperation of a certain number of other slave states. They were designated as "coöperationists" and "immediate secessionists," the latter party constituting about two-thirds of the convention. The ultimate object of both was the same. As against the North, they were all united; they were all for resistance, the difference of opinion being only as to time and manner of procedure. The recognized leader of the "immediate secessionists" was Mr. L. Q. C. Lamar, who, on January 9,

---

[1] The addresses and reports of the Mississippi commissioners are printed in the Appendix to the Journal of the secession convention.

brought forward the ordinance of secession. Within an
hour's time it was adopted by a vote of 84 to 15.[1] An effort
to make the ordinance operative only upon the secession of
four other states was defeated by a vote of 75 to 25.   An
effort to have it submitted to the people for ratification or
rejection was defeated by a vote of 70 to 29.[2]   An amendment to secure further constitutional guarantees in the Union
was voted down by a majority of 78 to 21.

On the 12th of January Jefferson Davis delivered to
crowded galleries his farewell address, and then took formal
leave of the United States Senate.   He was followed on the
14th by his colleague, Senator A. G. Brown, who announced
his withdrawal in a few words without any attempt to be
dramatic or sensational.[3]   On the day of Davis's final leave-
taking, the Mississippi delegation in the lower house informed
the speaker, by a written communication, of their unqualified
approval of the action of the Mississippi convention, and
announced their withdrawal from the United States Congress.[4]
Mr. Gholson, the United States district judge, at once forwarded his resignation to the President.   The Mississippi
cadets at West Point withdrew, and the native Mississippians
in the regular army threw up their commissions and returned
home to enter the service of the Confederacy.[5]   The United
States marshals were requested by the convention to continue in the performance of their duties, so far as they
related to the completion of the census, and no further.
Postmasters and other officers and agents connected with the
mail service were "authorized" to continue in the discharge
of their duties until otherwise ordered by the convention.[6]

[1] Convention Journal, p. 16.
[2] One of the delegates, Mr. Flourney of Pontotoc County, remembered
chiefly for his radicalism after the war, says he voted for the ordinance upon
the promise of a number of the prominent secessionists that provision should
be made for submission to the people. Testimony before Kuklux Committee,
1871, p. 95.
[3] Globe, 36th Cong. 2d Ses. pt. i. p. 352.
[4] Ibid. p. 485.
[5] It appears from the report of the adjutant general that there were only
two cadets from Mississippi at West Point at the time of the passage of the
ordinance of secession. One resigned February 14 and the other December 23.
The convention instructed the senators and representatives in the Confederate
Congress to use their influence to have established in the South a military
school similar to that at West Point for the cadets of the seceding states.
Two hundred and forty-five officers of all grades resigned from the United
States army in 1861 to join the Confederacy. Of those credited to Mississippi
two became brigadier generals in the Confederate army. See G. W. Cullum's
Biog. Register of the Graduates of West Point.
[6] Journal, p. 19.

The United States land officers were authorized to continue in their offices and perform their duties according to the laws of the United States.[1] All citizens of the United States domiciled in Mississippi were declared to be citizens of the state, and the federal naturalization laws were re-enacted and applied to the state. At a second session of the convention, held in May, the Confederate Constitution was ratified by a vote of 78 to 7, after the rejection of several resolutions which had in view the taking of the sense of the people on the question. A number of ordinances was passed, the chief purpose of which was to place the state on a war footing.

Although the electorate was not directly consulted in the proceedings by which relations with the United States were broken off and a great war inaugurated, the work of the convention seems to have been thoroughly acceptable, if a judgment may be formed from the hearty response to the call of the governor for troops and from other popular manifestations of approval. On the night after the passage of the ordinance, the state Capital was brilliantly illuminated, and the " Bonnie Blue Flag " was sung for the first time in a local theatre by its author, who had witnessed the drama of secession. Reuben Davis relates that upon his return from Washington he found the rejoicing so great that he was rarely out of the sound of cannon from the time he entered the state until he reached his home at Aberdeen. The women of the state were almost unanimous for resistance, and the encouragement which they gave to the soldiers in the field and their sacrifices for the cause of the Confederacy were the subject of frequent acknowledgment by the legislature during the dark days of the war.

The responses to the governor's call were so ready, that, as early as the middle of May, he was compelled to announce that a sufficient number of troops to fill any probable requisition by the Confederate government had been tendered, and he was, therefore, under the " painful necessity " of informing those who were anxious to enlist, that no more companies would be received for the present.[2] " The call to arms," he said, " has been responded to in a manner unknown to modern times, and the call for means to support the volunteers is being answered in a way to gratify the heart of every patriot." The several railroads within the state tendered the free use of their cars for transporting troops and supplies, and prominent citizens in various portions of the state drew

[1] Journal, p. 134.   [2] Appleton's Ann. Cyclop. 1861, p. 475.

their personal checks for sums to be used in the purchase of arms. Senator Brown sent a draft for $500, while Jefferson Davis and Jacob Thompson guaranteed the payment in May of $24,000. A number of prominent citizens subscribed one hundred bales of cotton; one subscribed fifty hogsheads of sugar; another, one hundred kegs of powder. A gentleman of Vicksburg offered $1000 to aid in the equipment of every volunteer company raised in that city.[1] To what extent these demonstrations were made for the purpose of uniting the people, and possibly of frightening the North into an acceptance of the demands of the South, it is impossible to say. It is certain that as late as July the belief was widespread that there would be no war.[2]

II. WAGING WAR

Secession having been accomplished, the state proceeded to assert its sovereignty. On the 12th of January the Quitman battery hastened to Vicksburg, planted a number of cannon on the bluff, and a few days later, as the steamer *A. O. Tyler* from Cincinnati passed down the river, fired a shot athwart her bows and brought her to. This was done at the instance of the governor, who feared that a hostile expedition from the North was planning to seize the arsenal at Baton Rouge and certain forts in Louisiana. Upon receiving assurances that they were well garrisoned, the governor allowed the steamer to proceed, and steps were taken to make known to the people of the northwestern states that peaceful commerce on the Mississippi would not be interrupted. "This policy," said the governor, "will materially aid in preserving the peace between the southern and northwestern states." The convention adopted an ordinance recognizing the right of the riparian states to navigate the river for commercial purposes in time of peace, and declared its willingness to enter into "negotiations" with them for the enjoyment of that right. The hope was entertained that, by holding out commercial inducements to certain of

[1] See *Vicksburg Whig* of March 12, 1861, for names of these subscribers.

[2] Reuben Davis says Governor Pettus refused to purchase at a bargain certain improved ordnance machinery, for the alleged reason that there would be no war and that the military committees of the legislature were strongly in favor of disbanding certain of the troops after the battle of Bull Run, assigning as a reason that the last battle of the war had been fought. Recollections, pp. 404, 411.

the northwestern states, they might be detached from the Union. The hope, however, proved to be delusive.

So far as the possession of Federal property was concerned, Mississippi was less fortunate than some of her sister states. There was not a Federal arsenal in the state, and no fort except a small one at Ship Island, which had been neglected, and was, at the time of secession, unprepared for defence. There were some lighthouses, one or two marine hospitals, and possibly a small custom house on the coast. After the organization of the Confederate government, the title to this property, as well as that of waste and unappropriated land belonging to the United States, was vested by the state in that government. As soon as the governor was informed of the seizure of the arsenal at Baton Rouge, he sent a messenger to request the governor of Louisiana to divide the spoils. The latter responded by sending eight thousand muskets, one thousand rifles, six 24-pound guns, and a considerable amount of ammunition.[1] The post offices, with their funds and other property, were transferred to the service of the Confederacy. In some instances the funds were retained by the postmasters, but upon the establishment of the power of the United States in Mississippi, in 1865, they were compelled to account for all moneys appropriated to their own personal uses, or turned over to the Confederate government.[2]

The secession convention created the office of postmaster general, and provided for a postal system by reënacting all laws, contracts, and regulations of the United States for carrying the mail.[3] It does not appear, however, that a postmaster general for the state was ever appointed. The United States postal service was withdrawn on the 4th of February, it being impossible to continue it longer.

During the first year of the war Mississippi was free from the presence of the Union army, but with the beginning of 1862 the scene of the conflict shifted to the northern part of the state. From first to last forty-seven engagements were fought on Mississippi soil. The most noteworthy military operation was of course the siege of Vicksburg, which lasted for a period of forty-seven days. During these memorable days both citizens and soldiers were reduced to the most desperate straits for food. Mule meat was a delicacy, and was in great demand at a dollar per pound.[4]

[1] Message to the legislature, January 15, 1861.
[2] Report of Postmaster General, 1865–1866, p. 107.
[3] Convention Journal, p. 140.
[4] The *Vicksburg Citizen* of July 2, 1863, a tiny sheet printed on wall

There was scarcely a building that was not struck by shells, and many were completely demolished. To avoid death under such circumstances the inhabitants burrowed into the hillsides and lived in caves. Subjected to the burning sun, and to fogs and rains, thousands fell sick, so that one-third of Pemberton's army were in the hospitals at the time of the surrender. By the first of July the army was on the verge of mutiny for want of food,[1] and on the fourth Pemberton surrendered the city, and with it one of the largest armies of the war. There were at least thirty thousand men, over a hundred siege guns, and about four thousand small-arms lost to the Confederacy. The loss of higher officers was especially heavy, among the surrendered being one lieutenant general, three major generals, nine brigadier generals, and over a hundred colonels. Grant's first demand, that of unconditional and immediate surrender, was modified so that the men were allowed to march out with their side-arms and to retain their horses and other personal property. They were then released on parole and allowed to return to their homes. The importance of the surrender was not so much in the number of men or military supplies captured, but in the strategic value of the place. A few hours after the surrender, the river was lined with steamers along the levees. Less than a week later Port Hudson fell, and the Confederacy was cut in twain. On the 16th of July a St. Louis steamer reached New Orleans, and in the suggestive language of President Lincoln " the father of waters rolled unvexed to the sea."

The western boundary of the state having thus been secured, operations were pushed in every direction by the Union forces, so that by the end of the war there were few places that had not at one time or another been subject to military government and occupation. A year before Vicksburg fell, the towns in the northern part of the state, Corinth,

---

paper, said : " We are indebted to Major Gillespie for a steak of Confederate beef, alias meat. We have tried it and can assure our friends that they need have no scruples at eating the meat. It is sweet, savory, and tender, and so long as we have a mule left we are satisfied our soldiers will be content to subsist on it." Pemberton, in a report dated June 22, said in regard to the use of mule meat : " I am gratified to say it was found by both officers and men not only nutritious but very palatable and in every way preferable to poor beef." S. R. Reed, Vicksburg Campaign, p. 130.

[1] See Official Records, Series 38, Vol. 24, pt. i. p. 983, for an anonymous letter from one of the soldiers to Pemberton, warning him that the army was so near starvation that they were likely " to do anything." " I tell you plainly," he said, " you had better surrender us if you can't feed us. Men are not going to lie here and perish, if they do love their country."

Inka, Holly Springs, and Oxford, were occupied by the enemy in the first advance southward. At all these towns there was more or less destruction of property. At Holly Springs three blocks of buildings and the railroad depot were alleged to have been burned. The University buildings located at Oxford were for a while the headquarters of General Grant. From Oxford the army proceeded along the Mississippi Central railroad to Grenada, an important railroad center. The enemy reached here about the middle of December, 1862. Before evacuating the town the Confederate authorities burned fifteen or twenty locomotives and one hundred cars. Thousands of farmers abandoned their plantations and fled before the approaching army.

During the Vicksburg campaign most of the important towns in the southwestern portion of the state fell into the hands of the Federal authorities. The chief of these were Port Gibson, Grand Gulf, and Natchez. Natchez was a place of considerable wealth and culture, but, unlike Vicksburg, did not occupy a position of strategic value. It was never fortified by the Confederate authorities, inasmuch as it could be easily flanked above and below. There were never but two cannon in the place, and one of these was an old gun captured from Burgoyne at the battle of Saratoga, and kept in the town more as an article of curiosity than as a weapon of defence. It was finally melted and made into small-arms and bucklers for the Confederate service. When Farragut's fleet steamed up the river, the town surrendered without a struggle on July 13, 1863, and with it were captured ten thousand bales of cotton.

In May, 1863, Jackson, the capital of the state, fell into the hands of the Federal army. Early on the morning of the 14th of that month Grant telegraphed Halleck: "I will attack the state capital to-day."[1] On the following day he telegraphed: "This place fell into our hands yesterday, after a fight of about three hours. General Joe Johnston retreated north, evidently with the design of joining the Vicksburg force. I am concentrating my force at Bolton to cut them off if possible." On the 18th the Union generals had a banquet at the governor's mansion.[2] Shortly after the capture of Jackson, General Grant assembled the corps commanders at the state house and gave them orders. General Sherman was instructed to destroy the railroad tracks in and about Jack-

[1] Badeau's Grant, I. p. 243.
[2] Official Records, Series I. Vol. 24, Serial No. 38, p. 531.

son, and all property belonging to the enemy. How thoroughly he performed the task can be gathered from his report, made after the second raid upon Jackson. He says : " Indeed the city, with the destruction committed by ourselves in May last, and by the enemy during the siege, is one mass of charred ruins. . . . I then ordered all ordnance to be collected and destroyed, and put working parties to destroy the railroads. Besides the breaks at the north and south before recounted, twelve miles north and south of the town were absolutely destroyed ; every tie burned, and every rail warped so as to be utterly useless. About twenty platform cars, fifty box and passenger cars, were burned in the city and all the wheels broken. About four thousand bales of cotton used as parapets were burned. Two heavy rifled 6-inch guns with an immense pile of shot, shell, and fixed ammunition were destroyed and cast into Pearl River." General Steele with three brigades was sent to Brandon, where he destroyed three miles of track.

Among the buildings destroyed at Jackson were the Confederate Hotel, the railroad depots, the penitentiary, Greene's cotton factory,[1] the foundry, a hat factory, two bridges across Pearl River, the Catholic church, the office of the *Mississippian*, and the block of private buildings. The presses of the *Mississippian* were broken and the type scattered in the street. A number of books were stolen from the state library, some of which were returned in 1867 by General Ewing of Ohio.[2] The soldiers appear to have been turned loose on the town to work whatever destruction seemed to them desirable. A correspondent of the *Chicago Times* thus describes the work of plunder : " The first few hours were devoted by our soldiers to ransacking the town and appropriating whatever of value or otherwise pleased their fancy, or to the destruction of such articles as they were unable to appropriate or remove. Pianos and articles of furniture were demolished, libraries were torn to pieces and trampled in the dust, pictures thrust through with bayonets, windows broken and torn from their hinges. Finally after every other excess had been committed in the destruction of property, the torch was applied. The entire business portion of the city is in ruins except a few old

---

[1] Badeau says the owners of the cotton factory protested against its destruction on the ground that many women and poor families were employed in it, but Sherman decided that it must be burnt. Military Hist. of U. S. Grant, I. p. 250.

[2] See his letter in the *Hinds County Gazette* of April 13, 1866. See also Official Records, Series I. Vol. 24, pt. ii. p. 537.

frame buildings. One residence after another has been burned until none of the really fine ones remain, save those occupied by some of our general officers. Such complete ruin and devastation never followed the footsteps of an army before."[1] The correspondent of the *Chicago Tribune* gave another picture. He said: "Jackson, the formerly flourishing capital of the state, is in ashes, and all the region roundabout is laid waste, bridges destroyed, and everything which might be made useful to the rebels in making Jackson or Canton a base of supplies. There is not even substance for a band of guerrillas."[2] General Badeau says: "The importance of Jackson as a railroad centre and a depot of stores and military factories is annihilated and the principal object of its capture attained."[3]

But Jackson and the "country round about" was not the only community in Mississippi in which General Sherman's peculiar theory of war was applied. After the first occupation of Jackson he moved eastwardly along the line of the Alabama and Vicksburg railroad to Meridian, an important railroad centre in the eastern part of the state. He reached Meridian on February 15, 1864, and at once issued an order in which he said: "The destruction of the railroads intersecting Meridian is of great importance and should be done thoroughly. Every tie and rail for many miles in each direction should be absolutely destroyed or injured, and every bridge and culvert should be completely destroyed."[4] To accomplish this purpose the work of destruction north and east of the town was assigned to General McPherson, while that south and west was assigned to General Hurlbert. Three miles of track and three bridges were destroyed on the Vicksburg road, ten miles on the Selma road running east of Meridian, and thirty-five miles on the Mobile and Ohio road running north and south. Of course the town otherwise fared badly. Nearly every unoccupied building was destroyed, and a good many private residences as well, if we may believe the testimony of the inhabitants.[5] An Ohio volunteer says they had orders to burn all unoccupied houses, but the sol-

---

[1] Quoted by the *New York World* of Aug. 14, 1863.
[2] *Chicago Tribune* of Aug. 2, 1863. Relative to the charge that the town was pillaged Badeau says in his biography of Grant: "A hotel and a church were burned without orders, and there was some pillaging by the soldiers which their officers sought in every way to restrain." Mil. Hist. of U. S. Grant, I. p. 250.
[3] Mil. Hist. of U. S. Grant, I. 250.
[4] *New York Herald*, March 15, 1864.
[5] Letter from Meridian, *New York Times*, March 27, 1864.

diers were not very particular whether the houses were occupied or not.[1] "Houses were broken open and plundered, every horse, cow, and chicken in the place was seized, not a fence was left, the commissary stores were destroyed, and the slaves carried away with the army."[2] The railroad depot, two hotels (the Ragsdale and Burton houses), the Confederate machine shops, the hospital, twelve government sheds, the arsenal, a number of government warehouses, and the gunshops were among the public buildings destroyed.[3]

The other towns and villages in the path of his march suffered quite as much as Jackson and Meridian. Brandon, the first town of importance on the road east of Jackson, and the county seat of Rankin County, was one of these. An eyewitness thus describes the scene : "The work of destruction was most thoroughly done. The houses of prominent rebels were burned. Every horse and mule that could be found was seized upon, and the number became so great that a special detail was made to care for them. In fact, everything of an edible nature was levied upon and made an item in our commissariat. Thousands of blacks came into our lines. The railroad track was torn up, and every wagon, bridge, and depot was burned."[4] The editor of the *Hinds County Gazette* says the army destroyed his office and its equipments — the accumulations of twenty-five years.[5]

Seventy-six miles east of Jackson is the village of Decatur, the county seat of Newton County. It is reputed to have had thirty buildings burned. Lake Station near by lost two livery stables, the machine shops, three locomotives, a railroad water tank, a turntable, thirty-five cars, two saw-mills, and a quantity of lumber. At Enterprise, the chief place in Clarke County, the railroad depot, two flour-mills, fifteen thousand bushels of corn, two thousand bales of cotton, two hospitals, and other buildings were burned. At Marion, the county seat of Lauderdale, the railroad station and several other buildings were burned. Quitman, on the Mobile and

---

[1] Letter of Adjutant O. G. Phillips, 32d Ohio Volunteers, *New York Daily News*, March 21, 1864.

[2] *New York World*, March 14, 1864 ; *New York Herald*, March 15, 1864.

[3] A correspondent in the *New York Tribune* said : "Nearly every building in Meridian was destroyed save those occupied, and the smoking ruins with their blackened chimneys and walls standing as giant sentinels over the sorrowful scene sent a thrill of pity to the hearts of those whom stern war and military necessity compelled to apply the torch." Quoted by the *New York Express*, March 15, 1864.

[4] Correspondence of the *New York Tribune* dated March 21, 1864.

[5] *Hinds County Gazette*, April 13, 1866.

Ohio road about fifty miles below Meridian, had two flour-mills, a saw-mill, depot, and other buildings burned, while almost the entire length of the railroad between it and Meridian was destroyed. Other towns that met a similar fate were Lauderdale, Hillsboro, Bolton, and Canton. At the last mentioned place three locomotives, a number of cars, and the repair shops were burned.[1]

From Meridian the Sherman expedition returned to Vicksburg over substantially the same route which it had first travelled. He had been gone less than a month, had freed ten thousand slaves, captured seven thousand horses and mules, destroyed nearly three hundred miles of railroad, and several thousand bales of cotton.[2] General Sherman thus describes the character of his work: "We are absolutely stripping the country of corn, cattle, hogs, sheep, poultry, everything, and the new growing corn is being thrown open as pasture fields or hauled for the use of our animals. The wholesale destruction to which the county is now being subjected is terrible to contemplate."[3]

In summarizing his work, after the return from Meridian, General Sherman said: "We have destroyed three great arteries of travel in the state, which alone could enable the enemy to assemble troops and molest our passage of the Mississippi River; we have so exhausted the land that no army can exist during the season without hauling all his supplies in wagons. This seems to me to be a fitting supplement to the reconquest of the Mississippi River, and makes perfect that which would have been imperfect." His only complaint was the tendency of the troops to pillage and plunder.[4]

Although a vast amount of property was destroyed by the Sherman expedition, some of it wantonly no doubt, there is good reason to believe that the reports of the army officers, and especially the letters of the newspaper correspondents who followed the army, unduly exaggerated the importance of the expedition as a military operation. It was compared to a "frightful tornado sweeping everything in its course," while the country traversed was said to have been "a region which was as an Eden, but was now akin to a howling wilderness."[5] A local paper, on the other hand, described the

[1] *New York Tribune*, March 15, 1864.
[2] Correspondence of *New York Tribune*, March 21, 1864.
[3] Official Records, Series I. Vol. 24, pt. ii. p. 525.
[4] His official report is published in full in the *New York Times* of Sept. 20, 1863. He said: "There was and is too great a tendency to plunder and pillage that reflects discredit on us all."
[5] *New York Express*, March 15, 1864.

raid as an "abortion," and declared that the country ravaged
was a poor piney woods belt sparsely settled, while the property destroyed consisted chiefly of the villages, small cabins
along the road, and about fifty miles of railroad track.[1]

Sherman's theory of war was well described in a letter
which he addressed to a committee of Warre 1 County citizens
in 1864. "Our duty," he said, "is not to build up, but to
destroy the rebel army, and whatever of wealth and property
it possesses."[2]   But when, in the prosecution of war, as he
understood it, the non-combatants were reduced to starvation,
he was ready to extend them a helping hand.   In the latter
part of July, 1863, he informed Grant that he had desolated
the land for thirty miles around Jackson, and that there were
about eight hundred women and children who were likely to
perish of starvation unless they could receive some relief.
He asked for permission to give the mayor and a committee
of citizens two hundred barrels of flour and one hundred barrels of pork, if they would pledge themselves to devote it
to charitable purposes.[3]   The permission was granted and
the supplies issued.   At Clinton he left thirty days' rations
for five hundred people.   In each case written obligations
were taken that the provisions should be "held sacred for the
use of the impoverished inhabitants."   And thus he says,
"we shared with those whose homes had been burned by
war, freely of our stock of provisions on hand."[4]

The most notable Federal raid in Mississippi, aside from
Sherman's expedition, was that of Brigadier General B. H.
Grierson.   With seventeen hundred cavalry he started from
Lagrange, Tennessee, on the 17th of April, 1863, and moved
in a southwesterly direction across the state of Mississippi,
passing through or near the towns of Corinth, Ripley, New
Albany, Pontotoc, and Houston, in the northern part of the
state.   At the latter place he is alleged to have seized $10,000
from the county treasury, and to have destroyed the county
records.   He struck the Mobile and Ohio railroad near
Egypt, where the usual amount of destruction was wrought.
From here he continued his expedition, passing through the
towns of Starkville in Oktibbeha County, Louisville and
Philadelphia in Winston County, Decatur and Newton in
Newton County, at which latter place two railroad bridges,
four and one-half miles of railroad track, twenty cars loaded

---

[1] *Macon* (Miss.) *Confederate*, March 1, 1864.
[2] The letter is printed in full in the *New York Times* of Jan. 17, 1864.
[3] Official Records, Series I. Vol. 24, pt. ii. p. 530.
[4] *New York Times*, Sept. 20, 1863.

with supplies, and several miles of telegraph wire were destroyed. Crossing the Leaf River and burning the bridges behind him, he proceeded to Raleigh in Smith County, where it is alleged he seized $3000 from the county treasury. From thence he moved upon Westville in Simpson County, struck the New Orleans, Jackson, and Great Northern railroad at Hazlehurst, where he destroyed forty cars and a quantity of ammunition and stores. He then moved down the railroad to Brookhaven in Lincoln County, where he captured two hundred Confederate prisoners, a quantity of muskets, and five hundred tents. From Brookhaven he marched southward to Bogue Chitto, tearing up the railroad track and burning the bridges, trestles, and water tanks. At the latter place fifteen freight cars loaded with stores, together with the depot and other buildings, were burned. Ten miles below Bogue Chitto he swooped into the town of Summit, where he destroyed twenty-five freight cars and a quantity of government sugar. At this place he left the railroad, and taking a southwesterly course, proceeded to Liberty, in Amite County, in the meantime making feints on Osyka and Magnolia. From Liberty he marched to Greensburg, Louisiana, and finally to Baton Rouge, the terminus of his expedition. In seventeen days he had marched eight hundred miles, destroyed two hundred cars, a number of locomotives, bridges, depots, tanneries, between fifty and sixty miles of railroad, captured one thousand prisoners, twelve hundred horses, three thousand stand of arms, and a quantity of ammunition. Grierson estimates the value of property destroyed by him at $4,000,000.[1]

From Lagrange, his starting point, to Holly Springs, a newspaper correspondent in September, 1863, found only five plantations out of fifty occupied. In the majority of instances the buildings had been burned.[2] In August, 1863, General Winslow, with three cavalry regiments, made an expedition up the Mississippi Central railroad and destroyed a considerable amount of railroad property at Durant and vicinity. Panola and Coldwater were also visited.[3] In September, 1864, the university town of Oxford was "made free with" by a force under the command of General A. J. Smith.[4] In June, 1863, Colonel Mizner moved down the Mississippi and

---

[1] His official report of the expedition is printed in full in the *New York Times* of August 30, 1863. The *New York Herald* of May 18, 1863, contains an account from a newspaper correspondent. It agrees substantially with Grierson's report, except that in some cases the results are overstated.

[2] *New York Evening Express*, Sept. 21, 1863.

[3] *New York Herald*, Sept. 3, 1863.

[4] An eye-witness thus describes the work of destruction at Oxford: "In

Tennessee railroad, passing through five counties and playing havoc with the country, which he says was cleared of everything that an enemy could subsist upon.[1] In the following month Colonel Bussey made a raid upon Canton and destroyed a good deal of railroad property and six hundred bales of cotton.[2] In December, 1864, Colonel Osband moved up the Central road from Canton, destroying railroad property at Vaughan, Pickens, and Goodman. Twenty-six hundred bales of cotton, a quantity of government salt, and $160,000 worth of supplies were also destroyed.[3] About the same time General Davidson made an expedition across the southern part of the state, beginning at Baton Rouge and ending at Pascagoula. The people were thrown into considerable excitement, and the governor called out the reserves, but it appears that the amount of property destroyed was inconsiderable.[4]

These were the most noteworthy " Yankee raids " during the war. There were, of course, others of less importance. Generally, in the larger expeditions, detachments were sent out from the main line of operations to ravage the country. It should be observed also that in many cases these expeditions were either in pursuit of a Confederate force, or were pursued by one which likewise subsisted upon the country and destroyed property, especially when it was in danger of falling into the hands of the enemy. It is a mistake, therefore, to assume that the vast destruction of property was exclusively the work of the Union armies. Thousands, if not tens of thousands, of bales of cotton, many miles of railroad, quantities of stores, and some public buildings were destroyed by the Confederate forces.[5]

The part played by the people of Mississippi in the Civil

the meantime our advance had made free with Oxford, burning all the fine brick blocks fronting on the public square, and also the Court House, in one grand conflagration." " The houses of some prominent official rebels were also fired. The splendid mansion of Jacob Thompson, rebel Secretary of the Interior, with its gorgeous furniture, went up in crackling flames, a costly burnt offering to the ' Moloch of treason.' " Correspondence of the *Dubuque Times* in *New York Times* of Sept. 10, 1864.

[1] Official Records, Series I. Vol. 24, pp. 487 and 480.

[2] *Ibid.* pp. 551–554.

[3] *New York Times*, Dec. 17, 1864.

[4] *Memphis Argus*, Dec. 6, 1864.

[5] See Official Records, Series I. Vol. 42, pt. ii. p. 509, for a letter from the president of the Mississippi Central railroad to a Confederate general advising against the absolute destruction of the rolling stock and equipments, owing to the impossibility of replacing them. It was suggested that the same results might be accomplished by removing the rails and the parts of the engines most difficult of construction and placing them beyond the reach

War was an interesting one. Curiously enough the state furnished more troops to the Union army than it did to the Confederate army, the number being 545 whites [1] and 79,000 blacks.[2] By the census of 1860 there were 70,295 white males in the state, between the ages of eighteen and forty-five, while the total enlistments in the Confederate army during the war were 78,000. Down to November 1, 1863, forty-six regiments and a number of unattached battalions and cavalry companies had been organized and enlisted.[3] At the outbreak of hostilities the eagerness for military service, especially among the young men, was extraordinary. They clamored for assignment to duty, and exhibited an impatience at the dilatory methods of the mustering officers. The names of some of the companies tendered are significant. The following are selected at random: Abe's Rejecters, the Reuben Davis Rebels, the Tippah Tigers, the Blackland Gideonites, the Chunkey Heroes, the Benita Sharpshooters, the Rankin Rough and Readys, the Yankee Terrors, the Tullahoma Hardshells, the Oktibbeha Ploughboys, the Buena Vista Hornets, the Pontotoc Minutemen, etc. There were few great battles of the war, in which some of them did not take a more or less conspicuous part. Some idea of how they were sacrificed for the cause of the Confederacy may be gathered from the records of their commands. The Vicksburg cadets went out 123 strong, and but 6 returned; the "Sharpshooters" from the same place went to the front with an enlistment of 124, only 1 returned.[4] Of 125 men in the Quitman Guard from Pike County only about 25 lived to return. At the battle of Shiloh the Sixth Mississippi Regiment lost 300 men out of 425, the Sixteenth Mississippi at Sharpsburg lost over 63 per cent of those present, while the Twenty-ninth Mississippi lost at Chickamauga about 53 per cent of those present;[5] of the total enlistments it was estimated that about one-fourth were either killed in battle or died of wounds or of disease contracted in the service. With what persistence

---

of the enemy. Upon regaining possession of the road it would be possible to replace the missing material. Sherman charges that a block of buildings in Jackson was destroyed by Johnson upon his evacuation of that town in May, 1863.

[1] Official Records, Series III. Vol. 4, Serial No. 125, p. 1270.

[2] Report of Secretary of War.

[3] For the strength and organizations of these regiments see Official Records, Series IV. Vol. 2, pp. 929–936.

[4] *Vicksburg Journal*, Aug. 11, 1865.

[5] Gen. S. D. Lee, in Riley's History of Miss., p. 260.

the invasion of the Union army was contested may be inferred from the fact that more than 25,000 of the enemy lie buried to-day on Mississippi soil.[1]

Of the higher military officers of the Confederacy, Mississippi furnished a smaller proportion than some of the other states. Of the 8 full Confederate generals and 16 lieutenant generals, she furnished none. Of the 63 major generals, she furnished 5.[2] Of the 291 brigadier generals, she furnished 29.[3]

The martial spirit, so general at the outbreak of hostilities, to a considerable extent wore away as the war progressed, and voluntary enlistments became the exception. It was necessary, therefore, to bring the power of the state and Confederate governments to bear upon the indifferent individual who was capable of bearing arms, but who was not disposed to do so. Not until the territory of the state became the actual theatre of hostilities, however, was this power prominently called into requisition. On December 20, 1862, the governor recommended that the entire white male population between the ages of sixteen and sixty be enrolled in the state militia; that local officers be required to aid the military to enroll, and, if necessary, to arrest conscripts and send them to the proper camps. He recommended, furthermore, that every citizen convicted of evading or refusing to perform military service be disfranchised, required to leave the state, or be hired out, as such persons were "not fit to associate with brave and loyal men who return with honorable scars."[4] The legislature took up the recommendation, and enacted that all white males between the ages of eighteen and fifty were liable to militia service in the state, and that

[1] Report of Inspector of Nat. Cemeteries, Ex. Docs. No. 62, 41st Cong. 2d Ses. p. 57. They are buried at the following places: —

Natchez cemetery	.	.	.	2,994
Vicksburg cemetery	.	.	.	17,052
Corinth cemetery	.	.	.	5,671
Total	.	.	.	.	25,717

The names of 20,000 of these are unknown.

[2] They were S. G. French, W. T. Martin, Earl Van Dorn, E. C. Walthall, and W. H. C. Whiting. Martin is the only survivor.

[3] They were Wirt Adams, J. L. Alcorn, W. E. Baldwin, W. L. Brandon, S. Benton, W. F. Brantly, William Barksdale, Charles Clarke, D. H. Cooper, J. R. Chalmers, J. R. Davis, J. W. Frazer, S. J. Gholson, J. Z. George, S. W. Ferguson,* W. S. Featherston, B. G. Humphreys, Richard Griffeth, N. H. Harris, Robert Lowry,* M. P. Lowrey, Carnot Posey, C. W. Sears, P. B. Stark, J. A. Smith,* J. H. Sharp,* Evander McNair,* W. R. Miles,* and W. F. Tucker. Those indicated by a star are survivors. Barksdale, Griffith, Posey, and Whiting were killed in battle.

[4] Official Records, Series IV. Vol. 2, p. 250.

all such persons between the ages of eighteen and forty, or such other persons as might be called for by the Confederate government as conscripts then in the military service of Mississippi, be placed in camps of instruction. It was made the duty of all military officers to arrest deserters and deliver them to the nearest provost marshal.[1] This legislation was supplemented by a proclamation of the governor calling upon the people of the state to form companies for resisting the invasion. They were requested to meet, organize into companies of not less than twenty, and apply for a mustering officer who would be sent to muster them in. They were admonished, moreover, that it was a "burning disgrace" that while their sons and kindred were bravely fighting on other fields, the state was being successfully invaded, and the women subjected to insult and injury. "Let every man," the governor continued, "make it his business to lay all else aside and assist in organizing as many companies as possible in each county. By this course you will enable our arms in a short time to repel the invaders, secure the safety of your homes, and shed imperishable honor on your cause. Let no man forego the proud distinction of being one of his country's defenders, or he must hereafter wear the disgraceful badge of the dastardly traitor who refused to defend his home and country."[2] This proclamation was published two weeks before the capture of Jackson. On the 3d of November following, the governor sent in a message to the legislature reciting that cavalry raids were destroying the property of the country as well as the confidence of the people in the ultimate success of their cause — an element very essential, he said, to the successful termination of the contest. Again he recommended that every free white male between the ages of sixteen and sixty be included in the militia organization, and that such of these as were not called into actual service be organized for local defence against Federal raids or used for a police force.[3] Again the legislature came to his aid, and enacted that all persons between the ages of seventeen and fifty years, including those exempted or discharged from the Confederate service, as well as those who had substitutes, should be organized for the militia service as the governor might direct. The governor was empowered to offer a bounty of $50 for each enlisted person, and

[1] Act of Jan. 3, 1863 ; Laws, p. 67.
[2] The proclamation is printed in the *New York Herald* of May 22, 1863.
[3] Official Records, Series IV. Vol. 2, pp. 921–927.

to establish courts martial to try deserters.[1]   As another
inducement, the state undertook to guarantee to every soldier the value of his horse or gun when lost, if not due to
his own negligence.[2]   The legislature, furthermore, pledged
the faith of the state that so long as it had any means their
families should not be allowed to suffer during their absence
in the service.

In August of the following year the governor was authorized to call upon every able-bodied man in the state to assist
in repelling invasion at such place as he might direct.
About the same time General Forrest issued a spirited call
to all citizens between the ages of fifteen and sixty-five to
" rally to his support," the old men and the boys to take care
of the horses, while the soldiers did the fighting.   He was by
another act authorized to " order " into the militia service for
a period not exceeding thirty days all free white males between the ages of sixteen and fifty-five, including all persons
exempted from the Confederate service, with certain exceptions.   They were to be held for police duty, but in case of
invasion might be called into active service.[3]   In pursuance
of these acts the governor issued the usual proclamations.
In the first one he recited that the enemy in large numbers
were invading the state, and those capable of bearing arms
were requested to assemble at Grenada, Okalona, or Macon.
He appealed to them to come by companies, squads, or individuals.   He informed the Secretary of War that he would
probably be able to get four or five thousand men under this
call.[4]   The other proclamation reminded the people that all
previous exemptions and details were revoked, and that those
who failed to respond would be arrested, tried by court martial,
and forced into the military service for one year.   Of the latter act the *Jackson Clarion* said: " Those who have by artful
dodges and artifices kept out of the army cannot lay the flattering unction to their souls that they will escape this time.
They must respond now, or hide forever from the gaze of
brave men and enduring women, and, indeed, from the light
of day itself.   Numerous individuals who have hitherto kept
out of the service, as blacksmiths, etc., should be hunted up
and ferreted out, together with those who are hiding in the
woods."   An anonymous writer for the *New Orleans Times*,
in a communication from Pike County, declared that Governor Clarke had at last completely "subjugated" the state.

1 Laws, 1863, p. 105.   3 Act of Aug. 13, 1864.
2 *Ibid.* p. 123.   4 Official Records, Series IV. Vol. 3, p. 590.

"It is," the writer said, "a melancholy spectacle to see the old gray-haired men dragged out to the field, leaving a house full of little ones unprovided for."[1] It was certainly not a much less melancholy spectacle to see boys of sixteen dragged from their homes or the schools, and compelled to undergo the hardships of a service which was more than the average veteran could endure with comfort.

To enforce such laws it was necessary to maintain a small army of conscript officers. The law made it the duty of sheriffs to enroll conscripted persons, to arrest stragglers and deserters, to be "vigilant and active" in the detection, pursuit, and capture of such persons, to examine the leaves of absence and furloughs of all men absent from the army, and to see that they returned at the expiration of their furloughs. It was made the duty of all county and local officers to give the sheriff notice of stragglers and deserters. For every such person arrested and delivered up the sheriff was entitled to receive the sum of $5.[2] There were few complaints of desertions until the latter part of the year 1863. The occupation of a large part of the state by the Union armies induced many to lose faith in the ultimate success of the Confederate cause. Moreover, the great hardships and privations of military service increased after 1863 to such an extent that many who would otherwise have held out, abandoned the army and lay out in the woods or swamps.[3] Governor Clarke, in his inaugural address of November 16, 1863, paid his respects to the "no inconsiderable numbers who were evading military duty." To compel them to enlist he invoked the voice of an outraged public opinion. It is of course impossible to tell with any reasonable degree of accuracy how many were evading military service. It was said in January, 1864, that there were 92,016 white males in the state between the ages of sixteen and sixty, and only 66,982 on the muster rolls, leaving 36,034 who for some reason or other were not in the military service.[4] One of the conscript officials informed a Confederate Senator on December 29, 1864, that in his opinion there were not less than 7000 deserters in Mississippi. "I believe," he said, "that there are at this day in Mississippi alone a sufficient number of

[1] Quoted in *Richmond Examiner* of Nov. 14, 1864.
[2] Act of Jan. 3, 1863 ; Laws, p. 89.
[3] E. S. Dargan informed the Confederate Secretary of War, on March 4, 1864, that "public sentiment was much depressed" in Mississippi, and that many avoided service and even threatened to resist the authorities of the government. Official Records, Series I. Vol. 52, pt. ii. p. 635.
[4] Official Records, Series IV. Vol. 3, p. 103.

skulkers, deserters, idle officers, improper details, and useless exempts to give victory to any army." In his opinion the conscript department was a farce, and the officers ought to be in the field. During the previous five months he said only 235 men had been enlisted, and if the desertions from these enlistments were in proportion to those from the camps of instruction, not enough ever reached the army to form a company. He cited an instance in which 537 men were conscripted, and 302 of them deserted before leaving the state.[1] The reports of the Confederate Secretary of War show that from February, 1864, to February, 1865, 2031 deserters were returned to the army from Mississippi.[2] As a sort of last resort the governor, in November, 1864, issued a proclamation promising a general armnesty to all deserters and absentees who would forthwith report for duty. They were requested to report to the sheriff or other civil officer, and the people were advised to inform those interested.[3] The Confederate conscript officers seem to have had more success in apprehending deserters than did the state officers. Generals Forrest and Pillow made it exceedingly uncomfortable for such persons so long as they were in command in Mississippi. Of General Pillow's accomplishments a newspaper said: "General Pillow has during the months of September and October, 1863, returned from Alabama and Mississippi 26,000 infantry and cavalry. If the whole of the Confederacy could be placed under an administration of conscription distinguished by the vigilance, energy, and intelligence which seem to govern the district of Mississippi and Alabama, we should have no occasion to fear for the strength of our armies in the field or the success of our cause." [4] The legislature voted Forrest a sword and adopted a resolution of thanks, " hailing with delight " his avowed purpose, as expressed in a public address, of returning all stragglers and deserters to the army.

With the approach of the spring of 1865, the number of deserters became so large that Forrest was able to refer to

[1] Letter of H. W. Walter to J. W. C. Watson, Official Records, Series IV. Vol. 3, p. 976.
[2] Official Records, *ibid.* p. 1109.
[3] *Richmond Whig*, Nov. 14, 1864.
[4] *Richmond Sentinel*, Dec. 22, 1863. The desertions from the Confederate army do not seem to have been as great in proportion as those from the Union army. The United States Secretary of War in his report of Nov. 8, 1865, p. 81, says the number of deserters since his last report was 18,120. It appears also from the appendix to the same report, p. 29, that the number of deserters in Illinois from March, 1863, to March, 1866, was 5805. The large number of desertions was due to a considerable extent to the leniency of the government in punishing them.

them as "roving bands of deserters, stragglers, horse-thieves, and robbers, who consume the substance, and appropriate the property of the citizens."[1] In March, 1864, a conscript officer informed the Confederate Secretary of War, that there seemed to be more deserters in Choctaw County than anywhere else. He estimated the number at five hundred, one-half of whom were armed and in organized bands.[2] February 1, 1865, a prominent citizen of Holly Springs wrote that large numbers of deserters infested the country, robbing friend and foe alike, making the condition of its citizens truly pitiable.[3] About the same time, the governor proposed to General Taylor to call out the militia for thirty days to apprehend deserters,[4] whereupon Taylor urged him to call out also the old men and the boys for police purposes at home.[5] By an act of March 9 the governor was authorized to employ the militia for the purposes mentioned in his proposition to General Taylor.[6] Many of those who evaded military service took up their abode in the swamps of Pearl River, generally on Honey Island. This place became notorious as a nest of thieves and robbers.[7] It is alleged that public sentiment in Jones County, in the southeastern part of the state, was so opposed to the war that the county formally seceded from the Confederacy, and organized a government in opposition thereto. For a while the power of the Confederacy was expelled from the community, and Confederate wagon-trains are alleged to have been plundered by the adherents of the new power. A military force was despatched to the scene of the troubles, and the power of the Confederacy reëstablished.[8]

[1] Official Records, Series I. Vol. 49, Serial No. 103, p. 931.
[2] Ibid. Vol. 52, pt. ii. p. 791.
[3] Ibid. p. 950.
[4] Ibid. 939.
[5] Ibid. 941.
[6] Laws, 1865, p. 23.
[7] Honey Island is the scene of the events portrayed in Mr. Maurice Thompson's late novel, The King of Honey Island.
[8] For the alleged secession of Jones County from the Confederacy, see Magazine of American History, Vol. 16, p. 38. A recent writer in the publications of the Mississippi Historical Society asserts that there is no historical foundation for the story. There is unmistakable evidence of considerable opposition among the inhabitants to Confederate service, but on the other hand the story that an independent republic was established is a myth. In 1865 115 inhabitants of the county joined in a memorial to the legislature, praying that inasmuch as Jones County had become "notorious, if not infamous," in the annals of the Confederacy, its name might be changed and so "completely sunk out of sight that the hand of time might never resurrect it." Its name was accordingly changed to Davis, but the reconstructionists would have none of it, and restored its old name, by which it is known at the present time. See House Journal, 1865, p. 351.

In the enforcement of the conscript measures the state and Confederate governments sometimes came into conflict.   On the 4th of March, 1864, Governor Clarke wrote to Mr. Seddon, the Confederate Secretary of War, complaining that justices of the peace and other civil officers, exempt under his proclamation, were being forced into the Confederate service. He therefore " demanded " their discharge.[1]   On the 5th of April the legislature adopted a resolution protesting against the action of the Confederate government in thus conscripting the civil officers of the state.   Finally, the legislature adopted a resolution by which it was agreed that the state would waive her rights in the premises as to all officers, members, and agents not named in the constitution, and not necessary to the preservation of " our form of government."[2] A question involving the paramount authority of the Confederate government came before the courts in 1864.   A man who had been conscripted under state authority and by a state official for militia service in the state, was seized by a Confederate conscript officer and forced into the Confederate service.   Which government was supreme would have been a question for the Confederate Supreme Court, had there been such a tribunal.   He appealed to the Supreme Court of Mississippi.   Although its functions had practically been suspended during the war, it took cognizance of the case, and decided that the claims of the Confederate government should have the preference.[3]

It was a special complaint of Governor Clarke that the Confederate government would not indemnify state troops for the loss of their horses, bridles, and saddles.[4]   At another time he complained that the Confederate government impressed everything within its reach, and monopolized all the manufacturing establishments so that he could not even procure a blanket for the state troops.[5]

There is little doubt that in the enforcement of the almost merciless policy of conscription many persons not liable to military service were forced into the army.   On one occasion two hundred soldiers in Mississippi united in a petition to President Davis declaring that they were not liable as conscripts, and that unless they were allowed to return home their families would be reduced to starvation.[6]   In April,

[1] Official Records, Series IV. Vol. 3, p. 446.
[2] Resolution of Aug. 13, 1864.
[3] Simmons vs. Miller.
[4] Official Records, Series IV. Vol. 2, Serial No. 128, p. 300.
[5] Ibid. Series I. Vol. 52, pt. ii. p. 635.
[6] Ibid. p. 453.

1865, the legislature passed resolutions of censure against the Confederate Congress in conferring upon President Davis the power " to appoint military tribunals responsible only to him." The act was denounced as dangerous to the liberties of the citizen, and unconstitutional.[1] Its purpose was to increase the efficiency of the conscript service.

It remains to notice briefly the policy of the state toward the alien class domiciled within its limits, and toward the slave class. In a ·message to the legislature June 25, 1861, Governor Pettus suggested that as a " means of retaliation on a people who are raising armies to subjugate us," whether it would not be expedient and just to confiscate all the property of alien enemies within the state. It does not appear from the statutes, however, that the legislature ever took any action on the subject. But as the need for recruits increased, a sentiment developed in favor of pressing aliens into the service. Accordingly, in December, 1863, the legislature passed a law requiring all aliens between the ages of eighteen and forty-five to leave the state or volunteer in the Confederate service by the first of March following. The pretext for the act was that they were engaged in illegal trade with the enemy, and were guilty of extortion in dealing with the citizens.[2]

The policy of the Federal authorities in enlisting negroes of military age as they came into the lines, led President Davis to issue an order to his commanders in Mississippi to remove the slaves upon the approach of the enemy, to localities where they would not be in danger of being conscripted. Accordingly, the owners of slaves spirited them away to Texas or Alabama, where the Union armies had not yet penetrated. The result of the order was very different from what was expected. As soon as the Confederate commanders began to seize the negro men and transport them, they went over in great numbers to the lines of the Union army. In a message to the legislature November 21, 1863, the governor protested against Davis's order as " disastrous to the country " and calculated to " drive " the slaves into the hands of the enemy.[3] Upon his recommendation the legislature adopted a joint resolution requesting the governor to protect the people against the illegal impressment of slaves and other property by Confederate officers or pseudo officers, the effect of which was causing the slaves to go over to the enemy.[4]

---

[1] Resolution of April 5, 1864.
[2] Laws of 1863, p. 152.
[3] *New York Times*, Dec. 4, 1864.
[4] Resolutions of Nov. 20, 1863.

The successful employment of negro soldiers by the enemy aroused a sentiment in favor of the experiment in the Confederate army. Early in 1863 the governor was authorized by an act of the legislature to impress all male slaves between the ages of eighteen and fifty, together with tools, implements, wagons, teams, horses, timber, lumber, arms, ammunition, ordnance stores, etc., " for the purpose of repelling invasion and suppressing insurrection." The owners were to be allowed the same pay for each slave as the pay of an ordinary private soldier. The governor was authorized to furnish the Confederate commanders in the state with such number of slaves as might be necessary to give greater efficiency to the operations. The owner of thirty slaves impressed was allowed to send along an overseer to look after their health and general welfare. Provision was also made for indemnifying the owner of slaves killed while in the service.[1] With the approach of the year 1865 a sentiment developed in favor of actually enlisting the slaves as regular soldiers, and a few weeks before the collapse of the Confederacy, Congress authorized the President in his discretion, if he deemed it necessary to prosecute the war successfully, and maintain the sovereignty and independence of the Southern states, to call upon each state for its quota of three hundred thousand troops in addition to " those subject to military service under existing laws," to be raised from the whole population, irrespective of color. None were recruited under the act in Mississippi.

Occasional acts appear in the statutes of the time authorizing owners to emancipate certain slaves for faithful attendance upon their masters while in the army. The presence of free negroes seems to have been tolerated so long as their conduct was satisfactory to the Confederate authorities.[2]

---

[1] Laws of 1863, p. 84.

[2] The only record accessible to the author, relative to the policy of the state authorities toward free negroes in Mississippi, is an act of the legislature passed in 1861 authorizing the board of police in Pike County to issue licenses to such persons in their discretion to remain in the county. The act made it the duty of the sheriff to sell into slavery any free negro found, after the first of March following, without a license. Laws of 1861, p. 144.

III. PROBLEMS OF MILITARY OCCUPATION

Growing out of the occupation of the territory of the state by the military forces of the United States was the question of defining and establishing the relations that should exist between the conquerors and the conquered during the period of the occupation. Although the greater portion of the state was at one time or another occupied by the military forces of the enemy, a comparatively small portion of it was permanently held and governed. Thus the towns of Corinth and Holly Springs in the northern part, and Vicksburg and Natchez in the southwestern part, seem to have been almost the only places of importance where the administration of the local government was under the control of the military authorities for any length of time. It may be stated in general terms that wherever the army occupied and governed a district of territory the private law as it was found was not disturbed. Only the public law relations of the inhabitants were changed. The administration was sometimes modified by the removal of the civil officers, and the detail of military officials to perform their duties.

One of the knotty problems which the military commanders had to solve in the administration of the occupied territory, was the establishment of a code for the regulation of matters of trade and intercourse between the parts of territory under the control of the United States and those parts under the jurisdiction of the Confederacy. The difficulty arose from the necessity of procuring supplies for the use of the army and the destitute class, and at the same time of preventing supplies from falling into the hands of the enemy to be used for military purposes. There was a popular sentiment at the time that " trade follows the flag," and that the occupation of a given section of country ought to be accompanied by an immediate removal of all restrictions on trade and commerce. Grant saw the practical objection to the theory and protested against its application in the case of the territory under his control, but Secretary Chase and others fell in with the popular movement, and for a time the commander in Mississippi was considerably hampered in dealing with this difficult question.[1] It was the general's opinion that " any trade

---

[1] Badeau's Grant, I. p. 411 ; Shucker's Chase, p. 322.

whatever " with the Confederacy would reduce the military
strength of the United States at least 33 per cent.   " No
matter what restrictions," he said, "may be thrown around
trade, it will be made a means of supplying the enemy
with what they want.[1]   In 1862, while still in north Mississippi, he issued regulations for the government of persons
engaging in trade.   The purchase of cotton or other produce
at any military post was confined to those who had special
permission, and it was made an act of disloyalty to go beyond
the lines to make purchases.   The railroads were of course
controlled by the military authorities, and freight agents were
required to make daily reports of their shipments.   Licenses
were granted to loyal persons at all military posts to sell
articles of necessity, in small quantities, to those only who
were willing to take the oath of allegiance to the United
States.[2]   The purpose of this latter requirement was to aid
in building up the nucleus of a Union party in the state.
Grant's whole policy, in fact, was to encourage the inhabitants to return to their allegiance.   It is shown in his orders
and instructions to the division commanders and in his private
correspondence.   The policy was not entirely without results,
as will be seen later.

From time to time the regulations established for north
Mississippi were modified as experience or circumstances
dictated.   Thus, supply stores were authorized, the names
and addresses of purchasers were registered, together with
the date and amount of sale, and buyers were compelled
to make oath that the articles purchased were for their own
use.   The occupation of Vicksburg, together with the banks
of the Mississippi River above and below the city, made
more elaborate regulations necessary.   Thus, rules were
established for the government of express companies, requiring them to transmit packages in a certain manner, and
strictly according to military orders.[3]   Similarly, rules for
the regulation of the postal service, which was declared to
be established exclusively for the benefit of the military
authorities, were prescribed and enforced.   Mails were
required to be made up at military headquarters and sent
to the post office by army officers, and no letters were transmitted except those coming from designated military authorities.[4]   The great influx of speculators after the fall of

---

[1] Badeau's Grant, I. p. 411.
[2] Official Records, Series I. Vol. 52, pt. i. p. 303 ; see also *New York World*, Jan. 9, 1863.
[3] *New York Times*, Aug. 30, 1863.   [4] *Ibid.*

Vicksburg complicated matters, and for a while seriously embarrassed the military authorities in their efforts to permit only legitimate trade. The source of the trouble was the phenomenal rise in the price of cotton. This article could be stolen or bought for a nominal price and sold for fifty or seventy-five cents per pound. The effect was demoralizing, and officers of high rank in the army were known to neglect their duties to engage in the traffic. Quartermaster's teams were employed in hauling cotton to the river; soldiers were deprived of their rations, and hospitals of their supplies, because the wagons were being used for another purpose. Great scandals to the military service resulted from this practice, and finally the treasury department consented to leave the whole matter in the hands of Grant. He declared that many fortunes were made by men, all of whom were dishonest.[1] The surreptitious traffic thus carried on, from first to last was estimated to have aggregated at least $200,000,000.[2] A considerable number of these speculators seem to have been Jews from Cincinnati. Grant finally lost his patience and issued an order expelling *all* Jews in the department, and commanding them to depart within twenty-four hours. On account of its discriminating character the President rescinded the order. On the 22d of September, 1863, Grant laid down the law to the cotton speculators in "General Orders, No. 57." In plain terms they were informed that no person speculating in cotton would be permitted to remain in the department south of Helena. Actual residents, "well disposed to the government of the United States," were permitted to bring into any military post on the Mississippi River, cotton or other Southern produce of which they were the *bona fide* owners; and with special permission of the military authorities might ship the same to Memphis or New Orleans for sale. All cotton belonging to persons in arms against the United States was to be seized for the benefit of the government.[3] By another order, which does not seem to have been taken seriously, "permission" was granted to all persons to bring their cotton to the nearest military post, and voluntarily

[1] Quoted in Reed's Vicksburg Campaign, p. 148. Jan. 27, 1864, Sherman writes to a brigadier general at Vicksburg: "Encourage good laboring men, but give the cold shoulder to greedy speculators and drones. The moment they accumulate so as to trouble you, conscript them." Official Records, Series I. Vol. 32, Serial No. 58, p. 239.

[2] Shucker's Life of Chase, p. 323.

[3] *New York Times*, Oct. 4, 1863.

"abandon" it to the United States treasury agent, and in case they were able to prove to the satisfaction of the military authorities that they were, and ever had been, loyal to the government of the United States, they would be paid for it at the end of the war. A Memphis correspondent of the *New York World* wished to know if a single citizen of Mississippi had ever voluntarily surrendered a bale of cotton, or received a cent for it.[1] The probability is that no one ever did. The speculators that swarmed into Mississippi with the army by no means confined their transactions to dealings in cotton, but seem to have controlled to some extent the supply of the necessities of life. The evil became so flagrant that in August, 1864, an order was issued by General Dana fixing the maximum price of flour in the territory under his jurisdiction at $16 per barrel, pork at $57 per barrel, ham at forty-three cents per pound, bacon at thirty-three cents, soap at fifteen cents, and salt at $4 per bushel. The rule applied to all merchants and traders, as well as to the class known as speculators, and heavy penalties were imposed for its violation.[2]

Another problem which the exigencies of the war forced upon the military commanders related to the disposition of property which, as the result of successful invasion, had passed into their possession. While Grant was in north Mississippi he was directed by President Lincoln to seize and use any property which, in his opinion, would contribute to the success of the army, and to destroy such as appeared to be a military necessity, with the restriction that none should be destroyed in "wantonness or malice."[3] It was also made the duty of the military commanders to seize and apply to the support of the United States army, the property (*a*) of any officer in the army or navy of the Confederacy; (*b*) of any president, vice-president, member of congress, judicial or cabinet officer under the Confederate government; (*c*) of any insurrectionary state governor, member of the legislature or convention, or any judge of a state in secession; (*d*) of any officer in the Confederate service who had formerly held an office under the United States; (*e*) and of any person in a loyal state who had given aid, assistance, or comfort to those in arms against the United States.[4] The property comprehended under these five heads belonged to the class which

---

[1] *New York World*, Sept. 14, 1863.
[2] *New York Herald*, Sept. 2, 1864.
[3] Official Records, Series III. Vol. 3, Serial No. 124, p. 397.
[4] Act of July 17, 1862.

the government *confiscated* for its own use. Beside this class, was that included under the term *captured* property, such, for example, as Confederate cotton, stores, and military ordnance; and *abandoned* property, or that "deserted" by the owners who fled before the approach of the army, or who were voluntarily absent therefrom, and engaged either in arms or otherwise in aiding or encouraging the Confederate cause.[1] Most of the property included under the latter class was returned to the owners shortly after the termination of hostilities. Grant defined his policy with regard to the private property of non-combatants in an order issued from Vicksburg, August 1, 1863, in which he announced that such property would be "respected" unless it was found to be necessary for the use of the government, in which case it would be taken under direction of a corps commander, and be paid for at the end of the war upon satisfactory proof of loyalty. Sherman used less circumlocution in defining his policy toward the non-combatants. When a committee of the citizens of Warren County drew up a petition and presented it to him, reciting that their property had been unnecessarily destroyed or carried away by the soldiers, that their slaves had been enticed away from the plantations, and that the people were in a destitute condition and needed relief, he replied, cheerfully acknowledging the right of the citizens to meet and petition for redress, and the corresponding right of the military commander to protect them, but he said he knew of no nation that had attempted to feed and provide for the inhabitants of an insurgent district. "On account of firing on the steamboats," he said, "and the long and desperate resistance to the army, we are justified in treating all the inhabitants as combatants, and would be perfectly justified in transporting you all beyond the seas if the United States deemed it expedient." He told them that the people of Warren County had not assisted the government much, and were not, therefore, entitled to much protection, and his future policy would depend upon their conduct. In regard to the negro question his reply was anything but consoling. The United States, he said, had succeeded by right of war to the title hitherto held by the master, and in due season the slaves would be hired out, employed by the government, or removed to the camps where they could be conveniently fed, but in the meantime no one must molest them, or inter-

---

[1] Regulations Concerning Abandoned, Captured, and Confiscable Property, No. 3.

fere with the agents of the United States. In reply to the
request that he detail slaves from the freedmen's camps to act
as servants for those who had lost their servants, he said, " You
must do as we do — hire your own servants and pay them."
Relative to the future he said that everything was unsettled,
and that he would not advise any person to plant on an
extensive scale, for no one could see far enough into the
future to tell who might reap what they sowed. However,
he advised them to remain at home, put their houses and
grounds in order, and resume their former employments as far
as they were permitted to do so. Proceeding on the theory
that the government under which they lived was illegal, he
said : " You must establish a government before you can
have property. Of course we think our government (which
is still yours) is the best and easiest to put into operation
here." After advising them to take steps to establish a
loyal government and secure representation in Congress, he
added, " But General Grant, nor I, nor anybody else, can
give you any assurance or guarantees. The commander in
war is the judge, and he may take your house and your fields,
and turn you out helpless to starve. It may be wrong, but
that does not alter the matter. It is our duty to destroy,
not to build up; therefore do not look to us to help you.
Come out boldly and assert that the government of the
United States is the only power on earth that can insure to
the inhabitants protection to life, liberty, and property.
You will then have some reason to ask of us protection and
assistance, and not until then." [1]

Other inducements were held out to the inhabitants of
conquered districts to resume their allegiance. Thus after
the fall of Vicksburg it was ordered that inasmuch as all
Confederate soldiers had been driven out of that part of the
state west of the New Orleans, Jackson, and Great Northern
railroad which runs through the central part of the state
from north to south, and as it was "to the interest of the
citizens not to have armed bodies of men among them," the
most rigorous penalties would be inflicted upon all irregular
bodies of cavalry not mustered and paid by the Confederate
authorities. Moreover, all persons engaged in conscripting,
enforcing the conscription acts, or apprehending deserters,
whether regular or irregular, all citizens giving them encouragement, and all persons firing upon United States
transports, would be subjected to the same penalties. [2] The

[1] This letter is printed in the *New York Times* of Jan. 17, 1864.
[2] Gen. Orders, No. 50, *New York Times*, Aug. 30, 1863.

purpose of the order was to rid the country of the bands of deserters, stragglers, and guerillas who plundered the inhabitants, and at the same time leave the people free from Confederate influence, to develop a Union sentiment and return to their old allegiance, in case there was a desire to do so.

During the period of occupation it devolved upon the military authorities in some instances to assume the administration of the municipal governments within the territory occupied. To meet the necessary expenses it was customary to impose taxes on property and traffic. In Natchez the mayor was removed and the administration placed under the supervision of a provost marshal, who governed according to martial law. The city fund was turned over to the military authorities, wharf regulations were established by the general commanding, a commission for the trial of civil cases was instituted, permits were issued to citizens for a variety of purposes, and police duty was performed by the provost guard.[1] Loyal persons in Adams, Claiborne, and Jefferson counties were allowed to bring to the town for sale live stock, provisions, fuel, etc., for the use of the inhabitants, and to carry away small quantities of supplies, not exceeding the amount brought in. Persons engaging in the traffic were required to exhibit their oaths of allegiance at the lines.[2] The boundaries of the city, as a military administrative district, were extended so as to include the freedmen's camps and the plantations leased by the government. Beyond these lines no supplies could be sent except in accord with military regulations.[3]

One incident in the administration of the government by the military authorities may be cited as an illustration of its absolute character. This was a case of interference with the freedom of worship. After the occupation of Vicksburg by the military forces of the United States, the congregation of the Episcopal church practically ceased to attend service, on account of the action of the minister in offering prayer for the President of the United States. Upon the announcement that an old and highly respected minister would conduct the services on Christmas Day with the omission of the prayer for the President, a large congregation, among whom were a number of Union soldiers and officers, filled the church. Under fear of arrest by the military authorities, the timid

---

[1] Official Records, Series I. Vol. 48, Serial No. 101, p. 563.
[2] *Ibid.* Serial No. 102, p. 283.
[3] *Ibid.* Serial No. 101, p. 632.

pastor broke his promise and read the prayer according to the prescribed form of the Episcopal ritual, whereupon a young lady quietly arose and left the church. She was soon followed by three or four others. In the afternoon they were waited upon by the provost marshal and informed that they had incurred the displeasure of the commanding general, and must leave the city at once. Shortly thereafter copies of the following order were sent to the young ladies, and placarded at different places throughout the city: —

HEADQUARTERS 17TH ARMY CORPS, PROVOST MARSHAL'S OFFICE, VICKSBURG, MISS., Dec. 27, 1863.

The following named persons . . . having acted disrespectfully towards the President and government of the United States, and having insulted the officers, soldiers, and loyal citizens of the United States who had assembled in the Episcopal church on Christmas Day, by abruptly leaving the church at that point in the services where the minister prays for the welfare of the President and all others in authority, are hereby banished, and will leave the Federal lines within forty-eight hours, under penalty of imprisonment.

By order of

MAJOR GENERAL McPHERSON.[1]

This was followed shortly thereafter by the following special order: —

The parties ordered to proceed outside the Federal lines will report at the railroad depot to-morrow at 10 o'clock. They will be permitted to take their private baggage, and conveyance will be in readiness at Big Black Bridge with a flag of truce to take them to the Confederate lines, or so far as the flag may be permitted to proceed.

By order of

MAJOR GENERAL McPHERSON,
JAMES WILSON, LIEUT. COL., PROVOST MARSHAL.

The commanding general refused to extend the time to enable them to complete their preparations, but consented to allow the mother of one of the young ladies to accompany them. At the appointed time and place they "embarked in the presence of hundreds of Federal soldiers," and passed into the jurisdiction of the Confederacy.[2] The interference

[1] The order of banishment is printed in the *New York Evening Express* of Jan. 23, 1864.

[2] This order is printed in the *New York Daily News* of Feb. 2, 1864.

with the freedom of worship did not end with the banishment of the young ladies, for shortly thereafter the commanding general issued an order reciting that he had received notice that the pastors of "many" churches neglected to make any public recognition of allegiance to the government under which they lived, and to which they were indebted for protection, and omitted to offer prayer for the President. It was accordingly ordered that thereafter the ministers of such churches as had prescribed forms of prayer should read the same at each and every service, and other denominations, which had no such form of prayer, should on like occasions "pronounce a prayer appropriate to the times, and expressive of a proper spirit toward the chief magistrate of the United States." It was ordered that any minister who failed to do this should be immediately prohibited from exercising the functions of his office, and would render himself liable to be sent beyond the lines of the United States at the discretion of the general commanding. The provost marshal was charged with the execution of the order.[1] This order would have been regarded as rather a sacrilegious jest had not the commanding general proceeded to enforce it in the true Jacksonian spirit. The Right Reverend William Henry Elder, the bishop of Natchez, refused to read the prayer for the President, and on the 18th of June, 1864, was banished from the city and sent to the Confederate lines. After the expiration of about two months he was allowed to return and "pray for whom he pleased." At the same time the order making prayer for the President compulsory was "suspended until further orders." Henceforth all persons conducting divine worship were left "at liberty to manifest such measures of hostility as they may feel against the government and union of these states and their sympathy with the rebellion by omitting such supplications if they are so minded."[2] And henceforth, it may be added, the attempt to compel the adherents of one belligerent to pray for the success of the other was abandoned as an unprofitable if not an impossible task. Thereafter prayers for the President were given or withheld as the bishop directed. In July, 1865, he ordered that further prayers for the President be omitted until all troops should be removed from the state.[3]

There was no general interference with the press, although

---

[1] The order is printed in the *New York World* of July 12, 1864.
[2] The orders of banishment and recall are printed in the *New York Herald* of Sept. 6, 1864.
[3] See his letter to the clergy in the *New York Herald*, Aug. 3, 1865.

occasionally an editor was arrested for uttering "disloyal" sentiments.[1]

The degree of subjection under which the local civil governments were placed by the military power varied in different localities, and depended upon circumstances. It was very nearly absolute in Vicksburg and Natchez, while in northeast Mississippi, where there was more or less Union sentiment, the interference of the military authorities was nominal. Thus in Tishomingo County the local government remained intact throughout the period of Federal occupation, the inhabitants pledging themselves to do nothing in aid of the Confederate cause.[2] The running of regular trains through the county was permitted for the benefit of the citizens.[3]

Gradually the rigors of military rule were removed, and the municipalities left for the most part to govern themselves. Thus by February, 1864, the judicial district of Natchez had been reorganized and reëstablished. In April, 1865, the commander had placed the whole matter of civil government before the leading citizens of loyal persuasion, with the intention of permitting such a government, so far as it was not inconsistent with martial law.[4]

In August, 1865, General Slocum, commander of the Department of Mississippi issued an order reciting that no further reason existed for the practice of levying taxes upon property and trade of municipalities, and that henceforth the entire charge of municipal affairs should be left to the people, no taxes of any kind were to be imposed by the military authorities.[5]

IV. POLITICAL AND ECONOMIC ACTIVITY DURING THE WAR

Although state activity during the war was chiefly of a military nature, political functions were not entirely suspended. Both the state and local governments were maintained, the official organization being elaborated in some instances from military necessity, and restricted in others on

[1] The editor of the *Fayette Chronicle*, published in Jefferson County, was arrested in 1865 for indulging in severe criticism of the military rule to which he was subjected.

[2] Testimony of Robert A. Hill before reconstruction committee, p. 68.

[3] Official Records, Series I. Vol. 49, pt. i. p. 612.

[4] *Ibid.* Vol. 48, Serial No. 102, p. 175.

[5] *New York Herald*, Aug. 31, 1865.

account of the suspension to some extent of the business of civil government. Thus, in the prosecution of the war, it became necessary to create some new and unusual offices. For instance, there were, at one time or another, state salt commissioners, liquor dispensary agents, price commissioners, a superintendent of army records, etc. In the local governments there were indigent commissioners, salt commissioners, etc.

On the other hand, the suspension, to a considerable extent, of judicial business, made the judiciary, as it existed prior to the war, unnecessary, while the duties of certain other civil officers were so nearly nominal that the state was able to decrease its budget by a reduction of their compensation.[1] This was particularly true of the county probate judges. The regular appropriations for such institutions as the state library and the geological survey were discontinued. Although the state government continued intact from first to last, it was for a time, like the Continental Congress, a peripatetic institution with no permanent place of rest. Upon the approach of the Union army to Jackson in May, 1863, the state officials with the public archives fled to Meridian, in the eastern part of the state, but on account of poor accommodations there, the government soon moved to Enterprise, on the Mobile and Ohio railroad, some forty or fifty miles below Meridian. Upon the departure from Jackson, the governor being satisfied that the penitentiary would be burned, granted pardons to such of the convicts as were willing to enlist in the Confederate army, while those who were " unfriendly " to the Confederate cause, and likely to join the Union army, were sent to the penitentiary in Alabama.[2] In the autumn of 1863, the state government moved to Columbus, in the northeastern part of the state, where it remained until early in 1864. Upon the occupation of this part of the state, the seat of government was transferred to Macon in Noxubee County. The Supreme Court was authorized to meet anywhere in the state to prepare the cases pending for decision at the regular term, while the state printer was allowed to keep his office in any part of the state, and all publications required to be made at the seat of government were to be held valid, no matter where published. Upon the surrender of General Taylor, the officials with the

---

[1] The members of the legislature received only their actual expenses during the February session of 1865.

[2] Governor's message to the legislature, Nov. 3, 1863.   Official Records, Series IV. Vol. 2, pp. 921–927.

archives returned to Jackson, where shortly thereafter the
archives were seized by the military authorities of the United
States.   The legislature met regularly during the war, the
session of 1863 being held at Columbus, and those of 1864
and 1865 at Macon.   Its measures related almost solely to
the prosecution of the war and the relief of the destitute
women and children.

The functions of the Supreme Court were virtually suspended during the war, although its organization was maintained, and a few cases of special importance were heard and
determined.   At the April term of 1861 only three cases
were decided ; at the October term, twelve.   In 1862 there
were no meetings of the court.   At the April term of 1863
two cases were heard.   At the October term of 1864 two
cases were heard, and in 1865 none.   The functions of the
Confederate District Court appear to have been of even less
importance.   The United States district judges, who resigned their positions in 1861 to go with their states, were
reappointed by President Davis as Confederate district
judges in their respective districts, with the exception, it
seems, of Mr. Gholson, the United States district judge in
Mississippi.   In his place Judge Clayton was appointed, and
although he continued in office throughout the war, it does
not appear that he ever held a court.[1]   In August, 1864,
President Davis wrote to him complaining that the military
authorities were not receiving the proper assistance from the
civil power in Mississippi, and he ventured the suggestion
that if frequent sessions of the court were held near the lines
where trading with the enemy and other illegal practices
were common, great benefit would result therefrom.   Brandon, Jackson, and Canton were suggested as suitable places
for this purpose.[2]

The functions of the lower courts were to a considerable
extent suspended by an act of the legislature in 1861, which
practically closed them, so far as civil business was concerned.
All actions for debt or for the enforcement of contracts were
suspended until twelve months after the close of the war.
All sales under trust deeds, mortgages, and judgments were
likewise prohibited.[3]   Whatever may have been the opinion
of the bar as to the constitutionality of such legislation, none
of them ever had the temerity to bring the question to a test.

[1] J. A. Orr in Pubs. Southern Hist. Assoc., March, 1900, p. 98.   Ex-chief
Justice Campbell informs me that this statement is probably correct.
[2] Official Records, Series IV. Vol. 3, p. 598.
[3] Laws of 1861, p. 74.

Moreover, it was made unlawful to prosecute suit against any soldier in actual service.[1] These acts practically left the courts with criminal jurisdiction only, and as a no inconsiderable number of the criminal cases were settled by the military authorities, it is reasonable to suppose that the business of the courts was nominal.

The pressure upon the male population capable of bearing arms to go into the military service left the civil offices to be filled to a considerable extent by old men or soldiers disabled by wounds or disease. This was illustrated in the election of General Clarke to the governorship in 1863. Occasionally the qualifications for office or the practice of certain learned professions were made less rigorous, so as to enable those incapacitated for military service to fill them. Thus persons over sixty years of age were made liable to jury service,[2] and county clerks who were attorneys were permitted to practice before the courts.[3] Moreover, the number of civil officers and others exempted from military service was time and again reduced, so that in the end barely enough men were left to hold the offices. Thus all municipal officers under forty-five years of age were made liable to conscription. And so were all indigent commissioners, except one in each local district, all liquor dispensary agents under forty-five, all trustees of state institutions, all road overseers, all deputy sheriffs, except one in each county, all deputy circuit clerks, all school trustees, and all other officers appointed by any of the courts.[4] Only ordained pastors with regular charges, and teachers with two years' experience and with schools attended by at least twenty scholars, were exempt. An act of the Confederate Congress authorized the governor to exempt such persons from military service as were absolutely necessary to administer the civil government. This he did by public proclamation ; but the pressure upon the Confederate conscript officers for troops led them to seize in many instances those exempt under the governor's proclamation. The governor protested strongly against such proceedings, and recommended action by the legislature. The legislature also protested, but finally agreed to waive its rights as to all civil officers not named in the constitution and not necessary to the preservation of the American form of government.

The administration of local government was, more or less,

---

[1] Laws of 1864, p. 37.
[2] Laws of 1863, p. 120.
[3] Laws of 1864, p. 21.
[4] Resolution of Aug. 13, 1864.

interfered with by the movements of the Union army and
the destruction of the county records. It became necessary,
therefore, for the legislature to grant authority to the local
officials to take unusual action when circumstances demanded
it.   Thus they were empowered to remove the public records
to places of safety upon the approach of the enemy.[1] Even
then the records were frequently destroyed, and hence probate
courts were empowered to reinstate judgments, orders, and
proceedings from memory, and clerks were allowed to re-
register claims, the evidence of which had been destroyed.
They were also empowered to record anew deeds and wills
which had been burned, while the Supreme Court was
authorized to furnish the local authorities with transcripts
of records of cases removed to it.[2] Where appeals to the
Supreme Court were dismissed for want of prosecutors, or
because of the impossibility of filing a record, it was made
lawful for appellees at any time within two years to move
for a reinstatement of the case on the docket.[3] The absence
of attorneys and the difficulty of producing witnesses often
made it impossible to proceed with a trial.

In many counties it was impossible for tax assessors to
make their assessments on account of the presence of the
enemy.   In some instances boards of police were empowered
to extend the time for making the assessment, in other cases
assessments were directed to be made on the basis of the
old assessment, the rolls to be furnished by the auditor.
No assessment was attempted in 1865, and it was enacted
that the old assessment should continue in force until 1869.[4]

The same difficulty existed in the matter of collecting the
taxes.   In many cases the time had to be extended by act
of the legislature.   The property of absent soldiers was
exempt from distress and sale under execution.   Property
destroyed by the enemy or "run off," as in the case of live
stock and slaves, but still on the assessment rolls, was relieved of taxation, while the levee tax in the river counties
was suspended.

The effect of the presence of the Federal army on the
slave population made legislation necessary for the protection of owners.   In communities adjacent to the camps and
lines of the Federal army, owners were permitted to remove
their slaves from the state.   The same authority was granted
to executors, administrators, and guardians.   Powers of

[1] Laws of 1863, p. 90.
[2] Laws of 1864, p. 38.
[3] Laws of 1863, p. 220.
[4] Laws of 1864, p. 31.

commitment were given to justices of the peace, probate judges, and clerks, in the case of runaway slaves.

In attempting to meet the exigencies of the war the legislature did not always observe strictly the limits set to its action by the constitution, and in fact seems to have amended it by simple resolution, as occasion demanded. Thus the following enacting clause appears in a statute of April 5, 1864 : " Be it enacted that the constitution of Mississippi be and the same is hereby altered and amended," etc.[1] Again an act " amending " an ordinance of the secession convention occasionally appears.[2]

The chief task of the state and local governments during the war was to maintain the army and supply the wants of the destitute. Unfortunately the very year in which the war began there was a crop failure in parts of the state, which resulted in a widespread famine. One of the duties of the secession convention was to provide means for the relief of the famine-stricken inhabitants by sending an agent to the northwest to buy bread-stuffs.[3] For the purpose of meeting the increased demands upon the treasury the state tax was increased 50 per cent, a special tax of 3 per cent was levied upon all money loaned or employed in the purchase of securities, and provision was made for the issue of $1,000,000 of treasury notes.[4] This was soon followed by the famous " Cotton Money " scheme, under which treasury notes to the amount of $5,000,000 were issued and put into circulation. Any person who desired to accept these notes in payment for cotton, for which there was little demand on account of the blockade, could make application to the auditor, who issued notes equal to the value of the cotton at five cents per pound. The owner in turn promised to deliver the cotton at such time and place as the governor might direct by public proclamation.[5] By November, 1863, 8587 applications had been made for advances, and these notes eventually came to be the chief circulating medium of the state.

Before the end of the first year of the war an additional tax of 30 per cent on the state tax was imposed for the relief of the indigent. Shortly thereafter the state tax was again increased 25 per cent for the payment of interest on certain bonds issued to pay the Confederate taxes levied upon the citizens of the state.[6] In addition to flooding the country

---

[1] Laws of 1864, p. 36.
[2] Laws of 1861, p. 45, for example.
[3] *Vicksburg Whig*, March 30, 1861.
[4] Journal of Secession Convention, p. 128.
[5] Laws of 1861, p. 60.
[6] *Ibid.* p. 197.

with its own notes the state authorized the several railroads
to issue scrip. The Mobile and Ohio was empowered to
issue $300,000, the Mississippi Central $300,000, the Mississippi and Tennessee $125,000, the Southern $150,000, the
West Filiciana $50,000, the Grand Gulf and Port Gibson
$13,000, and the New Orleans, Jackson, and Great Northern
$300,000.[1]

Early in 1862 another issue of treasury notes to the amount
of $2,500,000 was made.[2] In 1864 another issue of $2,000,000
followed.[3] This was accompanied by an issue of $2,000,000
in bonds.[4] No official statement of the total expenditures
during the four years of the war is available to the writer.
According to one authority they were as follows : [5] —

1861	.	.	.	.	$ 1,824,161
1862	.	.	.	.	$ 6,819,894
1863	.	.	.	.	$ 2,210,794
1864	.	.	.	.	$ 5,446,732
		Total	.	.	$ 16,301,581

Most of this indebtedness was incurred in " aid of the rebellion," and was repudiated. The actual debt on October 25,
1865, was stated to be $4,979,324.[6] Of this $3,796,564 were
unredeemed cotton notes, which were declared to be unconstitutional in 1869. The real indebtedness, therefore, was
but little more than $1,000,000. A variety of expedients to
raise revenue were resorted to by the state government. In
the later years of the war, when specie was not to be had, a
tax in kind was levied. In 1865, it was 2 per cent on the
gross product of all corn, wheat, and bacon above a certain
amount. In addition, the counties were empowered to levy
a tax in kind of one-half of 1 per cent on the same products, for the benefit of the indigents.[7] The railroads were
allowed to pay their debts to the state, aggregating nearly
$1,000,000, in Confederate notes.[8] After the war, this act
was held to be unconstitutional, and the roads were required
to pay in sound money.[9] In 1864, provision was made for
the sale of 2,000,000 acres of public land (at a sacrifice, of
course), as a means of replenishing the treasury.[10]

The task of relieving the wants of the destitute class taxed

[1] Laws of 1861, p. 177.   [3] Laws of 1864, p. 22.
[2] Ibid. p. 286.   [4] Ibid. p. 23.
[5] Statement of Attorney General Harris Boutwell, Miss. Rept. 1875, p. 10.
[6] House Journal, pp. 82–83.   [8] Laws of 1863, p. 160.
[7] Laws of 1865, ch. i.   [9] Thomas v. Taylor, 42 Miss. 657.
          [10] Act of Aug. 13, 1864.

the energies of the state government quite as much as that of equipping and supporting the army. This did not become a serious problem until 1863, during which year the state was overrun by the enemy, and the country, to a considerable extent, desolated. Early in the year, provision was made by the legislature for the distribution of $500,000 in treasury notes among destitute families, and for the payment of which a tax equal to 50 per cent of the regular state levy was ordered.[1] In December following, a class of officers styled " Indigent Commissioners " was created to look after the needs of the destitute, and to distribute among them the funds appropriated by the state. There were five of these for each county. Another $500,000 of treasury notes was placed at their disposal. For the payment of these notes a tax equal to 150 per cent of the state levy was imposed. Payment of the tax was permitted to be made in kind at prices fixed by the state price commissioners. County boards were empowered to levy an additional tax equal to from 100 per cent to 300 per cent of the state levy. They were furthermore empowered to issue scrip to an amount not exceeding $20,000 per year, and to impress such supplies as were necessary.[2] Usually, where a county was fortunate enough to have a school fund, poor fund, or swamp land fund, the legislature cheerfully authorized its use for this purpose.[3] In 1864, $1,000,000 was appropriated for the relief of the indigent, and the commissioners were authorized to impress the surplus produce of all persons who had taken advantage of the Confederate exemption law as agriculturists. The commissioners were also empowered to impress the wagons and teams necessary to distribute the supplies. In any county where these provisions were inadequate to afford the necessary relief, the board of police was empowered to levy an additional tax, not exceeding 300 per cent of the state tax.[4] Similar provision was made in 1865, although the chief reliance was placed on the tax in kind, the amount of which was required to be delivered by the persons assessed to such destitute persons as the commissioners might direct.[5] As the end of the war drew near, the amount of destitution increased. The conditions were such in February, 1865, that the governor was prevailed upon to call an extraordinary session of the legislature, to afford relief to the sufferers. It was able to do

[1] Laws of 1863, p. 71.
[2] *Ibid.* pp. 111–122.
[3] *Ibid.* p. 196.
[4] Laws of 1864, p. 27.
[5] Laws of 1865, ch. i.

very little toward relieving their wants. What they needed above all else was peace. Fortunately, it was in sight.

One of the most perplexing problems of the civil government was how to procure salt and medicines, particularly quinine, morphine, and calomel, for the destitute of the state. The efforts put forth in this direction abundantly illustrate the commercial dependence of the South on the outside world. There were no salt works or mines in the state, the nearest mine being at New Iberia, Louisiana. By December, 1862, the want of salt had become the "most pressing necessity" of any in the state. The governor sent agents to Alabama, Virginia, and Louisiana to purchase a supply, but with the exception of the agent sent to Louisiana the missions were failures. The agent sent to Louisiana succeeded in reaching Vicksburg with forty thousand pounds, which was distributed among the poorer classes, and soon used up. The governor wrote to President Davis, October 17, 1862, that a relaxation of the commercial regulations was necessary to enable him to exchange cotton for salt. Many of the people, he declared, had none, and were compelled to eat their food without it.[1] Moreover, the pork and beef, more or less of which every family raised, could not be preserved or used without this all-important article. The governor asked the legislature to authorize him to impress a sufficient number of slaves to work the mine at New Iberia, and wagons and teams with which to haul the salt.[2] The permission was granted.[3] In the meantime, speculators were doing a thriving business, but the legislature came to the rescue of the people, and carefully regulated the price of the article, and imposed heavy penalties on those who exceeded the schedule prices in their charges.[4]

The next experiment of the governor was to send an agent with $20,000 and a steamboat to New Iberia. He secured a supply and started back, but was stopped by Lincoln's blockade in the Bayou Teche. The governor then entered into contracts with several foreigners who proposed to run the blockade. Fifty bales of cotton were placed at the disposal of a Frenchman, who deposited $10,000 in Confederate scrip as a security for the delivery of the salt. The salt was never delivered.[5] What became of the $20,000 paid the

---

[1] Official Records, Series IV. Vol. 2, p. 126.
[2] Message to the legislature, Dec. 20, 1862.
[3] Laws of 1863, p. 80.
[4] Laws of 1861, p. 144.
[5] Message of Governor Pettus, Nov. 3, 1863.

New Iberia agent and the fifty bales of cotton turned over to the Frenchman were subsequently the subjects of legislative investigation.[1] The governor also sent an agent to Virginia "to make contracts for salt water, intending to establish furnaces for the manufacture of salt on state account." This plan, like the others, was a failure. He then authorized a local firm domiciled in east Mississippi to manufacture salt on private account for the people of north and northeast Mississippi. Another agent was sent to Alabama to purchase salt, make contracts for its manufacture, or to establish furnaces and manufacture on state account. The agent entered into contracts for the delivery of a large amount, but like other contracts of this character they were never fulfilled.[2] The legislature now took action by appropriating $500,000 for procuring a supply, and authorized the governor to appoint a state salt agent charged with the general supervision of the salt administration. General West was appointed in April, 1863, to receive and distribute the supply, and to approve all contracts for the purchase or manufacture of salt on state account.

In December, 1863, a complete system for the manufacture of salt on state account was provided. Provision was made for a general agent to manage and direct its manufacture, and to distribute the same. He was empowered to appoint "one or two skilful manufacturers," each of whom, like himself, was required to give a bond of $60,000. They were authorized to erect the necessary buildings for the manufacture of salt, and establish a state depot as a centre for distribution among the counties. There was also to be a salt agent in each county.[3]

While the government was putting forth these efforts to manufacture salt, the inhabitants were digging up the dirt from the "smoke houses" and distilling it. In this way small quantities of a coarse article were obtained. Where salt water was obtainable, resort was had to the method of evaporation, by which process similar results were obtained.

Much of the legislation of the time was devoted to the encouragement of home manufactures and the growth of commodities necessary for the sustenance of life. To encourage the manufacture of leather, the taking and use of oak bark was permitted to any person,[4] and the governor was authorized to enter into arrangements with the govern-

[1] Resolution of Aug. 13, 1864.
[2] Message, *supra.*
[3] Laws of 1863, p. 163.
[4] Laws of 1861, p. 114.

ment for the purchase of the hides of all "Confederate" beeves slaughtered in the state. For the encouragement of cotton and wool manufactures a liberal bonus was offered for the manufacture of cards. The employees of tanneries, gun shops, cotton and woollen factories were exempt from military service.[1] To encourage the inhabitants to supply themselves with arms, all taxes were prohibited on bowie knives, sword canes, dirk knives, etc.[2] To encourage the growth of agricultural products necessary to feed the inhabitants, acts were passed to procure agricultural statistics,[3] and in order to turn the attention of the people from the growth of cotton, for which there was no demand, it was enacted that no person should be allowed to plant over three acres for each laborer employed, under a penalty of $500 per acre. Under an agricultural exemption law certain planters were relieved from military service. Another measure was passed to encourage the manufacture of wine from the native grape.[4]

The use of corn and other products in the distillation of spirituous liquors early became a matter of great complaint by the civil authorities. Besides withdrawing a large amount of agricultural products from the use of the army and the destitute, it supplied a temptation to the soldier to spend his earnings for drink. Early in 1863, the legislature made it unlawful to distil spirituous liquors from corn, rye, or other grain, sugar and molasses.[5] The law, however, does not appear to have been enforced, and in April the governor informed General Pemberton that the distillation ought to be stopped at once, that the civil remedies were too slow, and that if the general would make a requisition for corn, he would seize every bushel in the distilleries, and upon a requisition for copper he would even seize the stills themselves. The authority was given.[6] Even these measures did not prevent the evil, and finally the legislature in 1864 took heroic measures. It was made the duty of every person to destroy any distillery then existing as a public and common nuisance, and the failure of the sheriff to do his duty in the premises was to be punished by his removal from office. Moreover, all laws authorizing licenses for the sale of spirituous liquors were suspended for the remainder of the war, and the sale of the article was absolutely pro-

[1] Official Records, Series IV. Vol. 1, p. 1110.   [4] Laws of 1863, p. 146.
[2] Laws of 1861, p. 134.   [5] Ibid. p. 96.
[3] Ibid. p. 227.
[6] Official Records, Series IV. Vol. 2, pp. 511, 513.

hibited except for medicinal purposes. Provision was then made for two state distilleries for the manufacture of liquor. Dispensary agents were appointed in each county to supply those who had certificates from practising physicians. They were authorized also to sell to state and Confederate troops, and furnish destitute persons such quantities as were necessary, free of cost.[1] The difficulty of procuring the necessities of life was due not only to the scarcity but quite as much to the character of the currency and the exorbitant charges. Before the end of the first year of the war state and Confederate scrip had depreciated so that a soldier's pay for a month would barely buy him a coat. In December, 1862, flour was selling in North Mississippi for from $50 to $75 per barrel, salt meat was worth from 50 to 75 cents per pound ; the coarsest shoes sold for $5 a pair, while a pair that could have been easily bought in Chicago for $1.50 sold for $15 in Corinth and Holly Springs. Men's boots sold for $30 to $50 per pair, and calico brought $2 per yard.[2] At one time, while Johnson's army occupied Jackson, there were only three barrels of flour in the place. The regular price of the article was $200 per barrel.[3] In September, 1863, an ordinary horse in the country adjacent to Vicksburg was worth $1000, and a good mule brought $700. The price of shoes ranged from $75 to $100 a pair, and even watermelons brought from $10 to $25 apiece. At Enterprise, in the eastern part of the state, about the same time salt was selling at $45 per bushel, with an " upward tendency," flour at $50 a sack and $12 per pound. Cotton yarns were worth $30 per yard.[4]

An English traveller relates that while at Jackson, in the summer of 1863, he paid 35 cents good money for a square of " Confederate " soap about the size of a small billiard ball ; 50 cents for two small boxes of matches, of which the seller candidly told him not one in five would light ; and 5 cents for an envelope made out of a sort of slate-colored grocer's paper of Confederate production, with the words printed on it : —

> " Stand firmly by your cannon,
> Let ball and grape shot fly,
> Trust in God and Davis,
> And keep your powder dry ! "[5]

[1] Laws of 1864, Act of April 5.   [2] New York Times, Dec. 5, 1862.
[3] Memphis Correspondence in New York Evening Express, Sept. 21, 1863.
[4] Statement of the secretary of the Confederate Society, New York News, Oct. 27, 1863.
[5] Bentley, Two Months in the Confederacy, p. 101.

In October, 1863, flour was quoted at from $60 to $65 per barrel; in November, the price ranged from $90 to $100, while corn meal sold at $15 per bushel.[1] General Grierson says salt was in demand at $30 per bushel in that part of the state through which he passed in 1863.[2] President Goodman of the New Orleans, Jackson, and Great Northern railroad says there were locomotives in use on his line in July, 1863, that were worth $900,000 apiece (Confederate notes).[3]

In February, 1864, men's boots were selling for $200 per pair at Natchez, and coats were quoted at $350 each.[4] The adoption of the practice of the state government in impressing private property made it necessary to fix a schedule of prices to be paid for property thus taken. For this purpose two commissioners were appointed, and they divided the state into four "price" districts which corresponded roughly with east Mississippi, north Mississippi, central Mississippi, and south Mississippi; the western part of the state being largely in the possession of the enemy. The following was the schedule adopted in April, 1864, for the more important articles: bacon, $1.40 to $1.50 per pound; coffee, $5 per pound; corn, $1.75 to $3.10 per bushel; corn meal, $2.25 to $3 per bushel; flour, extra, $50 per barrel; horses, first class, $700; good jeans, $8 per yard; molasses, $7 per gallon; salt, $15 per bushel; army shoes, $10 per pair; soap, 75 cents per pound; woollen socks, $2 per pair; sugar, $2 per pound; green tea, $10 per pound; vinegar, $3 per gallon, and wool $5 per pound.[5] The prices were the same in all the districts, except in the case of bacon, corn, and corn meal, the price of which was considerably higher in the southern district. The price of cotton steadily increased during the war. At the time the blockade was proclaimed it was worth about 10 cents per pound. In December, 1862, it was worth 68 cents per pound; in December, 1863, the price had risen to 84 cents, and by December 1, 1865, it had reached $1.20.[6] The price of service and labor increased quite as much as the price of commodities. In 1864, a Jackson paper complained that the postage on a letter from Brandon to the trans-Mississippi department was 40 cents.[7]

[1] *Charleston Mercury*, Nov. 19, 1863.
[2] See his report, *supra*.
[3] Official Records, Series I. Vol. 52, pt. ii. p. 509.
[4] Cairo Correspondence, *New York Herald*, Feb. 15, 1864.
[5] Official Records, Series IV. Vol. 3, pp. 262–266. The price commissioners were Ex-Governor McRae and G. D. Moore, Esq.
[6] Shucker's Life of Chase, p. 322.
[7] The *Mississippian*, Aug. 13.

CHAPTER SECOND

The Transition from War to Reconstruction

I. THE PEACE SENTIMENT

DURING the first two years of the war there was no other feeling in the state than that of a determination to push the contest to a successful issue,[1] but with the fall of Vicksburg in July, 1863, and the virtual expulsion of the Confederates from the western part of the state, a peace sentiment began to develop in some localities. Many who had hitherto been hopeful of success, and who had given their earnest support to the cause of the Confederacy, now saw clearly that its failure was only a question of time. To continue in the support of a cause that was bringing misery and ruin to the people, and which was foredoomed to certain defeat, seemed the height of folly, especially to those who had in the beginning opposed the war. Prominent citizens of this class, for the most part old-line Whigs, like Judges Sharkey, Poindexter, and Yerger, took the lead in the movement for the conclusion of peace on the basis of a return to the Union. They petitioned General Grant to protect them against the raids of the Confederate cavalry which surged back and forth, stripping the country of horses, cattle, food, and forage.[2] The request was complied with, and it was ordered that the most rigorous penalties be inflicted on all irregular cavalry not in the regular Confederate service, and upon all conscription officers found west of the present Illinois Central railroad.[3]

[1] The *Jackson Mississippian*, in February, 1863, declared that the independence of the Confederacy would soon be acknowledged, and peace concluded. "Our opinion is," said the editor, "that the northern rump of a government has well-nigh spent its strength, and if it persists in urging the war upon the emancipation policy, it will find an enemy at home which will give it enough to do. We look upon our disenthrallment as one of the certainties of the future." Quoted by the *New York Times* of Feb. 3, 1863.
[2] *New York Times*, Sept. 26, 1863.   [3] *Ibid.* Aug. 30, 1863.

51

As early as the 27th of July, 1863, General Sherman reported that the leading citizens of Jackson and the surrounding country had "implored" him to take some action by which peace might be restored and the state readmitted to the Union. Both the army and the people, he declared, were dispirited and ready for peace.[1] A meeting had already been held at Jackson on the 21st of July to consider a plan of reorganization. Delegates from a number of towns were present, and the question of restoration was fully discussed. They asked for permission to reorganize the government in conformity with the Constitution and laws of the United States. Sherman at once informed his chief that he thought the movement should be received with favor, as it would constitute an "admirable wedge" which might be used to great advantage.[3] Subsequently he informed a committee that his government was still theirs, and it would be easy to put into operation in their county. "You are still citizens of the United States and of Mississippi," he said. "You have only to begin and form one precinct and then another. Soon your county will have such an organization as the military authorities will respect. One county will affect another, and the moment you can, by fair elections, send representatives to Congress, I doubt not that they will be received, and then Mississippi will be again as much a part of the United States as Kentucky or Indiana, and will soon have courts and law and all the other machinery of government."[4]

In the official report of his expedition to Jackson in September, 1863, he said : "I know that many of the best inhabitants of the state are now clamorous for peace on any terms perfectly acceptable to all who do not aim at the absolute destruction of this part of the United States."[5] There can be no doubt that Sherman's statement contained a large element of truth. Although, as he says, the peace party was made up of some of the most distinguished and best citizens of the state, it is impossible to form any intelligent idea of the numerical strength of the party. There were, doubtless, many who secretly favored peace, but who did not have the courage to announce their professions openly. To do this was in some communities not pleasant, in some, perhaps, not safe. It was a general belief in the

---

[1] *New York Express*, July 28, 1863.
[2] *New York World*, Aug. 7, 1863.
[3] Letter to General Grant, Official Records, Series I. Vol. 24, pt. ii. p. 530.
[4] *New York Times*, Jan. 17, 1864.
[5] *Ibid.* Sept. 30, 1863.

North that as the Federal armies penetrated the South those who had been "secretly" in favor of the Union would declare their allegiance to the United States. This did not happen, however, except in those parts of the territory that were permanently occupied by the military forces. In August, 1863, ex-Governor Brown, Judge Sharkey, and others took the oath of allegiance to the United States, the venerable ex-chief justice basing his justification on President Davis's prophecy that the fall of Vicksburg and Port Hudson would mean the inevitable destruction of the Confederacy. "Now," he said, "I take him at his word."[1] Similar action was taken by many citizens in the western part of the state, particularly in the vicinity of Vicksburg and Natchez. A newspaper correspondent in August, 1863, estimated that one-half of the inhabitants of Natchez, for the most part wealthy planters and slaveholders, were Union in sympathy.[2] The *Richmond Enquirer* said these men had had their "patriotism corrupted by love of cotton." Another correspondent thought nine-tenths of the inhabitants were anxious for peace and restoration to the Union.[3] The *Richmond Examiner* of August 1, 1863, announced that troops in "large numbers" were deserting Johnston's army at Jackson and going into the Union lines, whereupon the *Mobile Advertiser* declared that they were "whining for peace and reconstruction."

Notwithstanding this sentiment, the politicians flattered the people that they would yet win, and that a reconstructed Union must not be thought of. The outgoing governor in his message to the legislature in November, 1863, declared that independence or that which was worse than death were the only alternatives presented to the people, and the sooner the truth was fully realized and acted upon the better it would be for themselves and their children.[4] The incoming governor said in his inaugural that if there were any who deluded themselves with "visions of a reconstructed Union" and a "restored Constitution" let them awake from their dreaming. "Between the North and the South," he said, "there is a great gulf fixed. It can be passed only with dishonor, and in reconstruction we shall reach the climax of infamy."[5] To some extent the press concurred in these views. The *Meridian Clarion* favored prosecuting the war

---

[1] J. A. W. in *New York Times*, Sept. 26, 1863.
[2] *Ibid.* Aug. 16, 1863.   [3] *Ibid.* Aug. 2, 1863
[4] Official Records, Series I. Vol. 2, pp. 921–927.'
[5] *New York World*, Nov. 10, 1863.

as long as there was a man left to fight, and asserted that no step backward could be taken. "Our only course," it said, "is onward with vigor and energy. Let the people bear their burdens cheerfully. We have not yet learned to battle with adversity, like the Greeks and Dutch. When our territory is all overrun, our armies dispersed, and the people suffering from famine, we will learn what other nations have paid for their independence. If our people will remain firm, we shall never be reduced to that condition, but with strong arms and well-filled larders we shall achieve that grand triumph which will bring forth peans of praise from freemen in every part of the world."[1]

In the meantime the military authorities were bestirring themselves to encourage the development of a healthy sentiment in favor of reconstruction and the reëstablishment of civil government in conformity with the Constitution and laws of the United States. In April, 1864, Major General Dana, with this end in view, advised and gave countenance to the holding of a convention at Vicksburg in June. At the same time he said he had in contemplation the ordering of a civil government for both Natchez and Vicksburg, so far as it was consistent with the existence of martial law.[2] How these movements were disturbing the politicians may be gathered from a letter of Mr. Phelan, one of the Mississippi senators in the Confederate Congress. On October 2, 1864, he wrote President Davis : "The infernal hydra of reconstruction is again rearing its envenomed head in our state. If disasters intervene between this time and next autumn, you may anticipate a contest in Mississippi that will tax the powers and pain the souls of 'good men and true.' Only a Spartan band is left in the state, but the timid, the traitor, and the time-server are legion."[3]

The *Jackson Mississippian*, which, as we have seen, looked forward in February, 1863, to an early independence, went over to the peace party in November, 1864. In an editorial the editor pleaded for peace, and called upon both sides "to meet each other upon the halfway ground of mutual compromise, concession, and conciliation." "Beyond all doubt," he said, "the great body of the people desire peace, and the failure to conclude an honorable peace is due to moral cowardice."[4]

---

[1] Quoted in *New York Times* of Feb. 26, 1865.
[2] *New York Times*, May 9, 1865.
[3] Official Records, Series IV. Vol. 3, p. 709.
[4] Quoted in *New York Herald*, Nov. 28, 1864.

With the approach of the spring of 1865 the peace movement assumed greater proportions on account of the deplorable condition of the country. In some parts of the state
bands of deserters and stragglers infested the land, robbing
friend and foe alike ; dismounted cavalry took the horses of
the planters, while a victorious enemy seized their food and
clothing. The people were thoroughly tired of a conflict
which every day was further plunging them into ruin, and in
which there was no longer the slightest hope of success.
The efforts of the conscript officers and the flattering appeals
of the state and Confederate authorities could no longer be
depended upon to recruit the depleted ranks of the army. It
was patent to the most hopeful that the collapse of the Confederacy was very near, and that peace ought to be made
early enough in the year to enable the disbanded soldiers to
plant a crop, and thus drive away the starvation which
threatened their families. The Union sentiment was so
strong in Tishomingo County that as early as January, 1865,
the United States military authorities granted permission to
the inhabitants to hold regular sessions of the circuit, probate, and police courts upon certain conditions. At the
same time authority was granted to run trains on both railroads in the county for the private convenience of the
citizens.[1] Early in March a meeting was held in Newton
County, at which 229 persons were present ; resolutions were
adopted expressing their readiness to submit to the authority
of the United States, and invoking the protection of the Federal authorities against deserters, jayhawkers, and robbers.
About the same time similar action was taken by a meeting
"composed of respectable farmers " in Kemper County.[2]
An early movement looking to reconstruction also took
definite form in Jefferson County.[3] The *New York Tribune*
of March 25, 1865, published a long list of prominent persons
in Mississippi who " favored reconstruction on the basis of
the Union and the Constitution." The list includes the
names of the senators and representatives in the Confederate Congress.

It is not to be inferred, however, that these movements in
favor of peace represented the unanimous sentiment of the
people, even as late as March, 1865. There were counter
demonstrations here and there, which were usually harangued

[1] Official Records, Series I. Vol. 49, pt. i. p. 612.
[2] *Ibid.* p. 252.
[3] *Natchez Courier*, May 13, 1865.

by some politician who still professed to believe that their efforts would ultimately be crowned with success, and that peace concluded on any terms except recognition of independence was dishonorable, and not to be thought of for a moment. Such a meeting was held at Canton in Madison County on the first of March, 1865. One of the leading speakers was the chief justice, an "original secessionist," who declared that there could be no submission, no reconstruction, but only independence or death.[1] His speech was replied to by William Yerger, who represented the peace party. Yerger was a prominent Whig, and with possibly one exception was the leader of the Mississippi bar.

It is impossible to tell how formidable the peace party might have become, had the war continued a year longer. As Phelan suggests, it might have been sufficiently strong in numbers to produce a "contest" that would have pained the "good and true." However this may be, the time had now arrived when peace was in sight, and the politicians were powerless to prevent its further advent.

II. THE COLLAPSE OF THE CONFEDERACY

On the 9th of April General Lee surrendered, and on the 14th the news of the surrender was published for the first time in the Mississippi papers.[2] As most of the Mississippi troops were in General Richard Taylor's army, not yet surrendered, they were obliged to remain at the front until the planting season was well-nigh past. With the surrender of Johnston's army on the 26th of April, all the Confederate forces east of the Mississippi, except Taylor's, had laid down their arms. A week after the surrender of Johnston, Taylor sent General Dabney H. Maury to inform the troops that in all likelihood it would soon become his duty to surrender. General Maury was asked to explain to them that a surrender in such an event would not be the consequence of any defeat, but was simply yielding upon the best terms to the logic of events, and with a preservation of their military honor.[3] On the 6th of May, General Taylor surrendered to General Canby. From his headquarters at Meridian he issued a

---

[1] *New York Herald*, March 25, 1865.

[2] Official Records, Series I. Vol. 49, pt. i. p. 612.

[3] *Ibid.* p. 1272. General Maury was instructed by General Taylor to say to the soldiers that in being transported to their homes no Federal guard would be put over them, and that their private rights and property, and their

general order reciting the surrender of generals Lee and Johnston, events which, he said, practically ended the war.

In surrendering, the troops were accorded what are technically known as military honors. They were paroled by commissioners selected for that purpose, and were subjected to no humiliation or degradation. Both officers and men were allowed to retain their private horses. The bearing of General Canby was such as to evoke the highest praise from the Confederate general.[1] With the surrender of General Forrest two days afterward, all the Confederate soldiers east of the Mississippi River submitted to the authority of the United States. General Forrest, in his farewell address, appealed to the soldiers of his command to accept the situation in good faith, cheerfully submit to the authority of the United States, obey its laws, and aid in restoring peace.[2] Having given their paroles not to take up arms again against the United States, these ragged, hungry veterans of a lost cause returned to their homes to begin the work of restoration. The desolation which met their eyes was appalling. It was enough to fill the stoutest heart with despair.

Governor Clarke issued a proclamation from Meridian on the day of General Taylor's surrender, in which he informed the people of the state of the surrender of all the Confederate forces east of the Mississippi River, and announced that he had summoned the legislature to meet on the 18th of May to provide for calling a convention, and that the officers of the state government had been directed to return with the archives to Jackson. He enjoined all county officers to be vigilant in the preservation of order and the protection of

honor and feeling as soldiers and men would be zealously protected. He wished to assure them that he could say in perfect sincerity and with an unabated confidence in the justice of their cause, that there was but one course to take, and that was to manfully and honorably meet their responsibilities as citizens and soldiers. By pursuing such a course, they would secure the best conditions ever granted to an unfortunate side in an appeal to arms to settle national differences, and even their enemies would respect their manliness and consistency, and do justice to their motives.

[1] "This liberality and fairness," said General Taylor, "make it the duty of each and all of us to faithfully execute our part of the contract. The honor of all of us is involved in an honest adherence to its terms. The officer or man who fails to observe them is an enemy to the defenceless women and children of the South, and will deserve the severest penalties that can disgrace a soldier." The day before the surrender, General Maury issued an address to the soldiers of his command, largely Mississippians, at a place six miles east of Meridian.

[2] Official Records, Series I. Vol. 49, pt. i. p. 1289.

property, and asserted that sheriffs still had power to call out the *posse comitatus*, and that the militia would be kept under arms to maintain the peace. "The state laws," said he, "must be enforced as they now are until repealed. If the public property is protected, and peace preserved, the necessity of Federal troops in your counties will be avoided." Sheriffs were urged to continue to arrest all marauders and plunderers, and masters were informed that they would be held responsible, as heretofore, for the protection and conduct of their slaves. "Let all citizens," said he, "fearlessly adhere to the fortunes of the state, assist the returning soldiers to obtain civil employment, contemn all twelfth-hour vaporers, and meet facts with fortitude and common sense."[1] The governor evidently proceeded upon the belief that the business of reconstruction would be left to the existing state authorities.

But the North, flushed with victory, was in no mood to leave the work of restoration to the late Confederates, and a week after the publication of Governor Clarke's proclamation, a Federal brigadier general issued a proclamation from Natchez warning all good citizens of his district against any action, individually or collectively, armed or unarmed, under the authority of the "so-called Governor Clarke." "Martial law," he said, "still exists over the state of Mississippi, and steps are being rapidly taken by the proper authorities to protect life and property, and preserve order wherever needed."[2] He said the only body of persons that would be recognized was a convention authorized by the district commander to meet at Vicksburg, June 11. This meeting was the outcome of an appeal by Judge Burwell to the people of the state, in May, urging them to return to their allegiance, and inviting them to send delegates to a convention to take steps to pave the way for a restoration of Mississippi to her former place in the Union. This first movement in the

---

[1] Governor Clarke's proclamation is printed in the *Chicago Tribune* of May 24, 1865. Upon receiving an intimation from General Taylor of his intention to surrender, Governor Clarke made a hurried visit to Jackson and had a conference with a number of prominent gentlemen at the home of William Yerger, the purpose being to consult them as to the course they thought advisable for him to pursue after the armies had surrendered. He gave his own opinion that the proper course was to call the legislature together, send in a message exhorting the people to accept in good faith the results of the war, and recommend the sending of a commission to Washington to assure the President of their desire to be restored to the Union. His view of the case was unanimously approved by the conference. He returned to Meridian next morning, and was present at the surrender of Taylor's army. T. J. Wharton in *Memphis Commercial Appeal*, Dec. 29, 1895.

[2] *Chicago Tribune*, May 24, 1865.

direction of reconstruction was sanctioned and authorized by the department commander.[1]

The legislature which Governor Clarke had assumed authority to call, met at Jackson on the 18th of May. It was not prohibited by the military authorities from assembling, upon assurance that it met more as a committee of safety than as a legislative body, and that the meeting was informal, and would be of short duration. The governor sent in a message in which he adverted to his responsibility in calling the legislature together, spoke of the peculiar circumstances under which they met, and frankly admitted that the war had ended, and with it the power of the Confederacy. He expressed apprehension that the presence of the military power would render the reorganization of the states a delicate and difficult task, and to aid in its accomplishment, he advised the adoption of the speediest measures possible, consistent with the rights of the state and the liberties of the people. He spoke of the unanimity with which the convention had passed the ordinance of secession, insisted that there were causes which justified revolution and made secession a necessity, and declared that the people of Mississippi had taken up arms with no purpose of aggression, but for purposes of defence only. The people of the North, who had astonished the world by an exhibition of their power, could not now desire the abasement of a people whom they had found equal to themselves in all except numbers and resources. "The terrible contest," said he, "through which the country has just passed, has aroused in every section the fiercest passions of the human heart. Lawlessness seems to have culminated in the assassination of Mr. Lincoln. For that act of atrocity, so repugnant to the instincts of our hearts, you feel, I am sure, in common with the whole people, the profoundest sentiments of detestation." He recommended the calling of a convention to repeal the ordinance of secession and to enlarge the power of the legislature.[2]

The legislature remained in session about one hour. It was scarcely organized, and a brief message read, when the report came that General Osband had received orders to

[1] *Chicago Tribune*, May 12, 1865. A meeting of loyal persons from Mississippi, Tennessee, and Arkansas was held in Memphis on May 1, and resolutions were adopted declaring it to be their duty, as well as their desire, to return in good faith to their former allegiance. They pledged an " active coöperation " in any measures that had in view the restoration of civil law and the readmission of the state to the Union. The resolutions are printed in the *Chicago Tribune* of May 10, 1865.

[2] The message is printed in the *New York Times* of June 11, 1865.

arrest the members if they attempted to exercise general powers of legislation, whereupon they suspended the rules, passed their measures, and adjourned in great haste and confusion. The members, carrying their own baggage, hurried to the depot and took the first train that left Jackson.[1] During its brief session, the legislature made provision for a convention to meet July 3, for the appointment of three commissioners to proceed to Washington to confer with the President as to the course to be pursued by him, and adopted a resolution deploring the murder of President Lincoln. The military authorities, under instructions from the President, refused to recognize the organization of the existing state government, or the validity of any of its official acts, or the rightful authority of any party pretending to hold or exercise any office under such pretended government.

Two days after the meeting of the legislature the legal status was defined in a telegraphic despatch of General Canby to the commander of the Department of Mississippi. The commander was informed that by direction of the President he should recognize no officer of the Confederate or state government; and that he should prevent, by force, if necessary, the meeting of the legislature for purposes of legislation, and arrest and imprison any member who should attempt to exercise those functions. Civil officers of the state and Confederate governments were informed that they were not included in the "capitulation" of the military forces, and were advised to return to their posts, taking with them the archives and property in their custody, and await the action of the United States government. If this should be done in good faith, they might be allowed to remain at their homes without molestation, so long as they conducted themselves with propriety, and no attempt was made to evade the legal responsibilities which they had incurred. They were reminded of the importance of preserving the land, judicial, and other records in their possession.[2]

In pursuance of orders, Governor Clarke, while suffering from wounds, was arrested and imprisoned in Fort Pulaski, Savannah;[3] the other state officers were placed under guard,

[1] T. J. Wharton, *Memphis Commercial Appeal*, Dec. 19, 1895.

[2] Official Records, Series I. Vol. 48, Serial No. 102, p. 520.

[3] The arrest of Governor Clarke was witnessed by only a few persons. One of these has left a description of the incident. He says: "The old soldier, when informed of the purpose of the officer, straightened his mangled limbs as best he could, and with great difficulty mounted his crutches, and with a look of defiance said: 'General Osband, I denounce before high heaven and the civilized world this unparalleled act of tyranny and usurpation. I

and General Osband, on May 22, took forcible possession of
all the public property and archives of the state. The following day, General Canby telegraphed his approval of these
measures. The following is General Osband's report of his
action : —

COLONEL : — I have to report that the so-called legislature of
this state met here on the 20th inst. After receiving your despatch date 20th inst. I found them on the eve of adjournment.
To avoid any excitement, I did not interfere, as they expressly
stated to me that they did not meet as a legislature, but as a committee of public safety. They passed three acts, viz.: 1. To call
a convention. 2. To send three commissioners to Washington to
confer with the President and find what was necessary to bring
the state back to the Union. 3. To deplore the death of our late
President. The commissioners appointed are the oldest and most
ultra-Union men in the state. Upon the adjournment of the legislature, I immediately notified Governor Clarke that I could not
recognize the civil government of Mississippi, and having placed
the offices of the heads of the state departments under guard,
demanded the custody of public books, papers, and property, and
the executive mansion, appointing Monday 22d inst. for their delivery. At 9 A.M. Governor Clarke delivered to me all public
property of the state under protest, but without asking to have
force employed. I have designated an officer as commissioner to
receive from the heads of state departments with inventory, and
with certificates of completeness, the archives of the state, and to
seal the same to-day at noon.

E. D. OSBAND, *Brevet Brig. Gen.*

To LIEUT. COL. C. T. CHRISTIAN.
JACKSON, MISS., May 22, 1865.

Mississippi was now without a state government of any
kind. The governor was in prison charged with treason;
the legislature was forbidden to meet ; the archives and
public property were in the hands of the military ; the writ
of habeas corpus was still suspended, the President had not
yet officially announced the end of the war ; martial law was
supreme throughout the state. What would come next, no
one could foresee. This was a period of anxious uncertainty.
Many expected wholesale confiscation, proscription, and the
reign of the scaffold. People were thrown into more or less
terror. Some held their breath, indulging in the wildest

<hr>

am the duly and constitutionally elected governor of the state of Mississippi,
and would resist, if in my power, to the last extremity the enforcement of
your order. I only yield obedience, as I have no power to resist.' ''   T. J.
Wharton, *Memphis Commercial Appeal,* Dec. 29, 1895.

apprehension as to the character of the treatment they would receive from the United States. For days and weeks, frightened women lived in a state of fearful suspense, in hourly expectation of the beginning of all that their fruitful imaginations had pictured of Northern vandalism and rapacity. Old men, as well as some younger ones, shared largely in this belief. They desired some assurance from the Federal government as to what its policy would be. Hence the idea of a commission to Washington. During this period there would not have been much controversy about terms, but as the anticipated retribution was continually delayed, the worst apprehensions subsided, the equanimity of the people was restored, and the feeling of terror passed away with the issuance of the North Carolina proclamation of May 29.[1]

The commissioners selected by Governor Clarke to go to Washington and ascertain the wishes of the President were Ex-Chief Justice Sharkey and Hon. William Yerger. They were both old-line Whigs with strong Union proclivities, and, like the President, were natives of Tennessee. There were, to be sure, no safer men in the state to follow during this critical time than Sharkey and Yerger.[2] They proceeded at once to Washington, notified the President of their arrival and of the purpose of their mission, and solicited an interview. They were informed that they could not be received as commissioners of Mississippi, but only as private individuals. As such they were received with great cordiality and kindness, and were asked to suggest their proposed scheme of reconstruction. They represented to him the terrible condition of the country, the great destitution of the people, and the anarchy resulting from the subversion of civil law and the establishment of martial law. They asked that steps be taken to restore them to their original relations with the Federal union, and thereby insure peace and repose to the people. They proposed that the convention called by the legislature be allowed to meet and reorgan-

---

[1] As late as June 22, a Federal soldier stationed at Okolona (Lieutenant Colonel H. C. Forbes, Seventh Ill. Cavalry), in a letter to General Whipple, speaking of the great uncertainty upon the part of the people as to the probable policy of the government, said, "I am daily visited by hundreds of men asking information of vital interest without the ability to give more than a semi-intelligent guess toward the solution." Official Records, Series I. Vol. 49, Serial No. 104, p. 1024.

[2] Governor Sharkey says Jones Hamilton, Esq., went along as a sort of secretary to himself and Judge Yerger. "The fact is," said Sharkey, "we had no money to bear our expenses, and Colonel Hamilton, being a moneyed man, agreed to accompany us and pay the bills." Testimony before Reconstruction Committee. Report Committees, 1st Ses. 39th Cong. pt. iii. p. 137.

ize the state.   This the President rejected at once, as he said
he could not recognize for a moment any of the appointees
of rebel officers.   He then asked if they had read his North
Carolina proclamation, in which he had proposed a plan of
restoring civil government in that state, and if its terms
would be acceptable to them.   They replied that they had
read it, and next to the course proposed by their own legislature, they believed it would more nearly meet the approval
of the people.   They assured the President that the people
were anxious to be restored to their rights under the government, and that they intended to abide by and support the
Constitution and laws of the United States in good faith,
and in future conduct themselves as loyal citizens.   The
President told them that they must distinctly understand
one thing, and that was that the people of Mississippi must
recognize and abide by the order of things as brought about
by the war, including, of course, the abolition of slavery.
This, he said, was a *sine qua non* to the establishment of civil
government.   It was not his purpose to order or dictate anything ; but they must plainly understand that unless they
amended their constitution so as to conform to the facts of
the situation, so far as he was concerned he would never
consent to the reëstablishment of civil government in Mississippi.   With this understanding the commissioners withdrew and returned to the state, leaving the matter in the
hands of the President.[1]

III.   THE PRIVATE LAW STATUS DURING THE CIVIL
WAR

The collapse of the Confederacy and the consequent dissolution of the state government, organized in conformity
thereto, left the private law in a somewhat unsettled condition.   The chief judicial problem of reconstruction, therefore, was the adjudication of controversies growing out of
the Civil War.   In the determination of these questions it was
often necessary to define the public and private law status
of the state during the war.   As already pointed out in
another connection, the state and local governments were
maintained during the war, so far as the necessities for civil

---

[1] I have followed the account given by Judge Yerger in his speech before
the convention in June.   This speech is printed in the Convention Journal,
pp. 145–147, and also in the *Chicago Tribune* of Sept. 4, 1865.

government required. Officers were regularly chosen, and
were required to take an oath of allegiance to the Confederate government.   It was subsequently held by the High
Court of Errors and Appeals that the provision in the Constitution of the United States requiring members of the
state legislature to take an oath to support the national
Constitution was merely directory, and the failure to take
such an oath did not invalidate their legislation.[1] The state
legislature met regularly during the war, and enacted laws
which every inhabitant was bound to obey.   Transactions
involving millions of dollars were made in accordance with
formalities prescribed by the state government; contracts
were entered into; marriage relations were formed and
children born; estates of decedents were administered;
conveyances of property were made ; courts were held,
judgments rendered, and decrees executed in accordance
therewith; vested rights were acquired, and business relations
formed.   If the government under which these transactions
occurred was insurrectionary in its character, what, therefore, was their legal status upon the suppression of the
insurrection?   Clearly no sound principle of state policy, to
say nothing of reason, could be subserved by holding that
no government existed in the state from 1861 to 1865; that
the inhabitants were reduced to a state of anarchy; that all
executory contracts were voidable at the pleasure of either
party, and that all executed contracts were void; that all
rights acquired were unlawful; and that all relations formed
must, as far as possible, be undone.   To hold that all the
acts of the government during this period were illegal would
have led to consequences productive of incalculable mischief.[2]
These acts fall naturally into two classes : First, those the
primary purpose of which was to maintain peace and order,
and regulate the private relations of the inhabitants.   This
class of acts sustained no direct relation to the prosecution
of the war, but were measures which, in all probability, would
have been enacted had there been no war.   The second class
includes those done in "aid of the rebellion."   The Supreme
Court, after the war, uniformly held the acts of the first

[1] Hill *vs.* Boyland, 40 Miss. 618.
[2] The United States Supreme Court in the case of Thorrington *vs.* Smith
said obedience to the authorities of the Confederate government in civil
and local matters was a necessity and a duty upon the part of those domiciled
within its jurisdiction.   Without such obedience civil order was impossible.
The court, however, refused to recognize the Confederate government as *de
facto*, in the sense that its adherents in war against the *de jure* government
did not incur the penalties of treason.

class to be valid and binding as those done by a *de jure* government. On the other hand, it generally held the acts of the second class to be invalid.

Relative to the private law status during the war, the High Court said, in the case already cited, " The proposition that the citizens who owed at least temporary allegiance to the government which possessed their property and controlled by its power their persons during the period of such dominion were remanded to a state of nature as barbarians and outlaws in all their relations with one another, civil as well as criminal — as a judicial question, seems to us neither sanctioned by the principles of international law recognized by our highest judicial tribunals, nor by any code of morality known to civilized nations. Admitting," said the court, " that the ordinance of secession was a nullity, the state of Mississippi, neither in fact nor in legal contemplation, could be annihilated." This was the position taken by the United States Supreme Court in Texas *vs.* White the following year.[1] The attempt to secede only changed the relations toward the government of the United States, *i.e.* the public law relations, and not the relations between individuals composing the state, *i.e.* the private law relations. So far, therefore, as the private relations of the inhabitants were concerned, the government which existed in the state during the war was not only *de facto* but *de jure*.

The state convention of 1865, realizing the absolute necessity of recognizing the validity of certain of the governmental acts made during the previous four years, adopted an ordinance declaring all laws enacted since January 9, 1861, with two exceptions, so far as they were not in conflict with the laws and Constitution of the United States, nor in " aid of the rebellion," to be revived, ratified, and held valid and binding until altered or repealed by the proper authority.[2] All official acts of public officers ; all judgments, decrees, and orders of the courts, and all marriage relations properly contracted, were declared to be legalized, ratified, and confirmed. This ordinance was passed in August, 1865. But what was the status of the acts of the " insurrectionary " government during the period intervening between the surrender of the government, on May 22, and the adoption of the ordinance mentioned? A freedman in Noxubee County was indicted

---

[1] 7 Wall. 720.

[2] The two exceptions were the law in relation to crimes and misdemeanors, and an act of 1863 to enable railroads to pay moneys borrowed by them from the state before the war.

for stealing a gun on the 30th of May.   After conviction he
moved, in arrest of judgment, that at the time the offence
was committed, the constitution and laws of Mississippi were
suspended, or overthrown and destroyed, by the military
power of the United States, and that no such sovereignty as
the state of Mississippi existed.

The main question for decision was, therefore, whether
Mississippi had any legal or valid existence as a state on
the 30th of May, 1865, and if so, whether the laws of the
state for the punishment of crime, in force prior to January 9, 1861, continued in force after the overthrow of the
Confederacy.   The High Court of Errors and Appeals held
that the state of Mississippi on May 30, 1865, was the same
state as that which occupied her territorial limits before
January 9, 1861 ; that the constitution and laws were the
same, except in so far as they had been altered from time
to time by its own act ; that rights of property were to be
governed, contracts were to be construed, and crimes tried
and punished by the same laws that existed before the
adoption of the ordinance of secession.   It was declared
that the existence of the state as a sovereign state, *de jure*
and *de facto*, had never been interrupted or disturbed by
the ordinance of secession or by the progress or events of
the war, but, on the contrary, all the functions of government, executive, legislative, and judicial, continued in full
force and rightful operation.   Laws passed during the war
continued in force after the cessation of hostilities, and were
held to be valid and binding during the temporary suspension of functions consequent upon the occupation of the
territory by the military forces of the United States, and
after the restoration of those functions in October, 1865.
Consequently, offences against the criminal laws committed
during the war, or during the occupation of the state by
the armed forces of the United States, were indictable and
punishable as if those events had never occurred.[1]

In determining what acts were in " aid of the rebellion,"
the High Court usually took a liberal and just view.   One
of the most notable decisions involving this question was the
well-known " Cotton Money " case, decided at the October
term of 1869.   In May, 1866, a tender of one of these notes
was made to the sheriff of Hinds County, in payment of
taxes due the state.   The sheriff refused to receive it, alleging that the act under which this currency was issued was

---

[1] Harlan *vs.* The State, 41 Miss. 566.

illegal, having been passed by a revolutionary body calling itself the legislature of Mississippi. The High Court sustained the position of the sheriff, and held that the notes in question, having been issued at a time of great pecuniary want to supply a circulating medium, and to furnish the means by which an empty treasury might be replenished, were, in operation and in effect, in "aid of the rebellion," and therefore illegal and void.[1]

On the other hand, it was held that an act of the legislature in 1862, suspending the statute of limitations until two years after the close of the war, was valid,[2] and so was an act regulating the terms of the High Court.[3] Again, it was held that all deeds or other instruments of writing executed during the war, although not stamped as required by the laws of the United States, were valid if properly stamped at the close of the war.[4] A liquor law passed by the "insurrectionary" state government was upheld,[5] and so was an act authorizing trustees to invest funds in their keeping in Confederate securities,[6] and an act prohibiting suit against soldiers in active service.[7] Where application was made for a mandamus, to compel a county treasurer to pay a warrant of the board of police, issued in 1864 to a sheriff for taxes overpaid, it was held that the amount overpaid was undoubtedly in Confederate money, being taxes for the support of the rebellion, and should therefore be disallowed.[8]

In general, all acts necessary to the peace and good order of society, acts sanctioning and protecting marriage and domestic relations, acts governing descents, and regulating the conveyance and transmission of property, acts providing remedies for injuries to persons and property, and many other similar acts, which would be valid if emanating from a lawful government, were held to be valid, although proceeding from an unlawful government.

It was several times held that the state government reëstablished after the war was not bound by the acts and engagements of the "insurrectionary" government. Thus, it was said in the "Cotton Money" case that the government of the state of Mississippi as one of the United States, and the government of the state as a member of the Confederacy, were not identical, and the acts and obligations of the latter

---

[1] Thomas *vs.* Taylor, 42 Miss. 651.
[2] Buchanan *vs.* Smith & Barksdale, 43 Miss. 90.
[3] M. & O. R.R. *vs.* Math, 41 Miss. 692.   [6] Trotter *vs.* Trotter, 40 Miss. 704.
[4] Frazer *vs.* Daniels, 42 Miss. 121.   [7] Walker *vs.* Jeffreys, 45 Miss. 162.
[5] Licks *vs.* State, 42 Miss. 316.   [8] Files *vs.* McWilliams, 49 Miss. 578.

government were not *ipso facto* binding upon any government subsequently erected in the state ; that the laws enacted and obligations incurred during the war ceased upon the destruction of the government which enacted them, and were of no binding effect upon the government which succeeded. Thus it was held that the restored government was not bound to receive treasury notes issued by the " insurrectionary " government,[1] nor was it responsible for any claims for salaries of civil officers in the service of the latter government, its debts and obligations having perished with it.[2] Arrearages of taxes accruing during the war were not presumed to have been levied in " aid of the rebellion " ; but where the contrary was proven to be the case, they were held to be illegal, and could not be collected by the restored government.[3]

In regard to the status of state and Confederate money the court also took a liberal view. It took judicial notice of the fact that this currency was the chief circulating medium of the state during the war, and its use an absolute necessity. In a case involving this question the court said : " The use of such money became an absolute necessity of the condition of the people during the war, for without it they could neither have lived in the Confederacy nor have made their escape from it. There was no other means of securing food and clothing, and to hold that in giving, or receiving it, the people in their situation were guilty of an offence against the paramount law, would be a refinement of cruelty unworthy of a civilized nation or an enlightened age." [4] In accordance with this view it was held that where Confederate treasury notes, Mississippi cotton notes, and Mississippi treasury notes (military) were placed on deposit with a banker, an action of *indebitatus assumpsit* could be brought to recover their value from the banker who refused to deliver them to the depositor. Receiving this currency and giving his written promise to return it upon demand was not lending "aid to the rebellion." Again it was held that where a creditor in 1862 received under protest Confederate money in payment of a debt, he could not subsequently treat the payment as invalid and recover on his original demand by showing that at the time of the receipt of the money, military orders required its acceptance in payment of debts.[5] Where an administrator sold property for cash (Confederate money), and instead of

[1] Thomas *vs.* Taylor, 42 Miss. 651.   [4] Murrell *vs.* Jones, 40 Miss. 565.
[2] Buck *vs.* Vasser, 47 Miss. 531.   [5] Davis *vs.* M. & O. R.R., 46 Miss. 553.
[3] Dogan *vs.* Martin, 48 Miss. 11.

paying the decedent's creditors, as he might have done, kept the money until it was worthless, it was held that he was chargeable with the value of the money at the time of the sale.[1]   But it was held to be competent for an administrator in presenting his final account to show that the balance in his hands was Confederate money, and that he could not pay the debts of the estate with it or loan it to any person on any terms.[2] Similarly, where an administrator sold the personal estate of a decedent, receiving depreciated money therefor, and could show to the satisfaction of the court that he had been unable to use any or all of the same, he was chargeable only with the actual value of the amount on hand, and not used. Where an administrator sold property of an estate and took Confederate money in good faith and did not use it for his own purposes or mix it with his own funds, but kept it as a separate fund, and could not pay it out either to creditors or distributors, the administrator was not held responsible for the loss.   If, however, he used the money when he might have applied it to pay creditors, and did not do so, he was held to be charged with the value compared with the currency of the day.[3]   Where a note was given for Confederate money borrowed in 1862 payable in 1864 in such currency as would be generally received for debts at time of maturity, it was held to be an error to instruct the jury directing the value of the Confederate money to be ascertained at the maturity of the note.   The High Court declared the correct measure of recovery to be the value of Confederate money at the time of the loan.[4]

Where an action of mandamus was brought in 1873 to compel a county treasurer to pay a warrant issued by order of the board of police in 1864, for the sum of $75, it was held that payment in lawful money could be required only for the equivalent of the Confederate money at the date of the issue of the warrant.[5]

The status of contracts made during the war was the subject of a great deal of litigation during the reconstruction period.   The contracts about whose validity there was doubt were of three classes : first, those in which the consideration was a slave warranted for life, which slave was subsequently emancipated ; second, contracts for services or money

---

[1] Williams *vs.* Campbell, 46 Miss. 57.
[2] Still *vs.* Davidson, 51 Miss. 153.
[3] Moffatt *vs.* Loughbridge, 51 Miss. 211.
[4] Darcy & Wheeler *vs.* Shotwell, 49 Miss. 631.
[5] Clayton *vs.* McWilliams. 49 Miss. 313.

in " aid of the rebellion " ; and third, contracts based on Confederate money.

It was uniformly held by the Mississippi courts that a contract in which a slave was described as warranted for life, related only to the legal status of the property at the time of the warranty, and the contract was not affected by the subsequent emancipation of the slave by action of the government, and that such emancipation could not be set up in avoidance of payment of the purchase money of a slave so emancipated. It was held that the covenant was fulfilled if, at the time of the sale, the slave was by the then existing laws of the state in a condition which rendered him liable to servitude for the period of his life.[1] It was also held that a person sued on a note of this character could not allege as a defence that he was a citizen of a state in rebellion, was excluded from the benefit of the President's amnesty proclamation, and therefore not entitled to sue in the courts.[2]

In regard to the second class of contracts, the court invariably held that any agreement of whatsoever character that contemplated the giving of direct aid to the Confederacy was illegal and void. Thus it was held that a promissory note given in consideration that the payee serve as a substitute for the maker in the military forces of the state of Mississippi in the late war was a contract contrary to the public policy of the United States, directly in " aid of the rebellion," and therefore illegal and void.[3] An agreement to deliver cotton for the purpose of clothing and equipping military camps for the Confederate service was held to be illegal.[4]

Again, where the legislature during the war passed an act permitting the railroads of the state to pay in Confederate notes money which they had borrowed from the state before the war, it was held to be in "aid of the rebellion," and therefore void. The court said the purpose of the act was plainly to replenish an exhausted treasury, with a view of subverting the Constitution of the United States ; and that the money had been loaned by the legal government of the state, a member of the Federal union, and to that state alone was the obligation of the roads to repay it, and from that obligation they were not released by payment to any other government or authority. The court even refused to

[1] Williams vs. Williams, 43 Miss. 430.
[2] Wilkinson vs. Eliza Cook, 44 Miss. 367.
[3] Pickens vs. Eskredge, 42 Miss. 114.
[4] Cassell vs. Backrack, 42 Miss. 57.

admit the claim of credit for the value of the Confederate money at the time of payment.[1]   The same view was held by the court in 1876, when it had become democratic.[2]   Where, however, a man loaned money which he knew was wanted for the equipment of a company of Confederate cavalry, but without any stipulation to that effect in the contract, it was held to be a valid contract, and the money thus loaned might be recovered.[3]

In regard to the third class of contracts, the Mississippi courts uniformly held that where the parties were private individuals the contracts were valid and binding.[4]   Thus, where an agreement was made in 1864 to deliver on demand a certain amount of cotton, and the value of the cotton was paid to the owner in Confederate money, the latter could not recover the value of the cotton in lawful money of the United States.[5]   All contracts made between May 1, 1862, and May 1, 1865, for the payment of money were held to have presumed Confederate money, unless the contrary appeared on the face of the contract;[6] and where a contract was made to pay "dollars and cents," it was held to be competent to produce parol evidence to show that Confederate money was intended, and an administrator in settling his accounts was not precluded from showing that money described as "dollars and cents," and received by him, was in fact depreciated Confederate money.   This was not admissible, however, where he received other funds than the currency prescribed by the prevailing law.[7]   But where, during the war, a principal placed in the hands of his agent a number of notes and drafts by their terms payable in United

[1] M. & O. R.R. vs. State, 42 Miss. 115.
[2] N. O. St. L. & Chicago R.R. Co. vs. State, 52 Miss. 878.
[3] Walker vs. Jeffreys, 45 Miss. 162.
[4] Frazer vs. Robinson & Daniel, 42 Miss. 121 ; Murrell vs. Jones, 40 Miss. 566 ; Green vs. Sizer, 40 Miss. 530.   The Supreme Court of Louisiana as uniformly held that contracts founded on Confederate money as a consideration were illegal.   See Schmidt vs. Barker, 16 La. 261; the United States Supreme Court, in December, 1868, held that contracts for the payment of Confederate money, made during the war between private parties residing in the Confederacy, could be enforced in the courts of the United States after the return of peace.   Such currency, it said, must be considered as if it had been issued by a foreign government, temporarily occupying a part of the territory of the United States.   Such contracts have no necessary relation to the hostile government.   They are transactions in the ordinary course of civil society, and though they may indirectly and remotely promote the ends of unlawful government, are without blame, except where proved to have been entered into with actual intent to further insurrection.   Thorrington vs. Smith, 8 Wall. 1.
[5] Beauchamp vs. Comfort, 42 Miss. 94.
[6] Cowan vs. McCutcheon, 43 Miss. 207.
[7] Rogers vs. Tullos, 51 Miss. 153.

States currency, the agent having no instructions as to the kind of currency in which its collections were to be made, the action of the agent in accepting Confederate money was held to be wrongful, and he was liable to his principal for the full amount.[1]

The legality of business intercourse between citizens of Mississippi and citizens of that part of the country under the jurisdiction of the United States was another subject of litigation after the war. It was held that when at the beginning of the war a life assurance company of New York had an agent in Mississippi who remained during the war, the war did not *per se* revoke the agency, nor make it unlawful for the agent to receive premiums which were tendered, and a tender of the premiums saved the assured from being in default as to payment of premiums. The court furthermore held that unless it be necessary for their completion that some act be done calculated to aid and comfort the enemy, partly executed contracts, such as life assurance policies on which the premiums had, up to the war, been regularly paid, were not annulled by the war, but were suspended until its conclusion.[2] And where a citizen of Columbia, Tennessee, and the owner of a cotton plantation in Tunica County, Mississippi, entered into a contract with another citizen of Columbia during the occupation of that place by the Federal forces, the latter party agreeing to harvest the crop of cotton and transport it into the United States, with permission of the military authorities, it was held not to be a violation of the law, but an intention to comply with it.[3] But where a citizen of Jackson, Mississippi, entered into a contract with a citizen of St. Louis in 1863, it was held that in contemplation of law, they were enemies to each other, and were, therefore, prohibited from contracting or even holding intercourse.[4] Again, where a citizen of New Orleans in August, 1862, while that city was in possession of Federal troops, through his agent loaned Confederate money at Jackson, Mississippi, and took a mortgage on real estate to secure payment, it was held that the contract was illegal and void because intercourse between persons was forbidden by the law of nations, by the act of the United States Congress of July 13, 1861, and by the proclamation of the President.[5]

---

[1] McMath *vs.* Johnson, 41 Miss. 439; Bradford *vs.* Jenkins, 41 Miss. 328.
[2] Stratham *et al. vs.* New York Life Assurance Company *et al.* 45 Miss. 581.
[3] Shacklett *vs.* Polk, 55 Miss. 376.
[4] Shotwell *vs.* Ellis, 42 Miss. 439.
[5] Livingston Minns *vs.* John Armstrong, 42 Miss. 429.

Where the owner of land in Mississippi removed to Texas during the war, and left an agent to supervise and carry on his farm, such agency was not terminated by the Federal occupation of the territory in which the farm was situated, and a contract entered into between such agent and the Federal authorities to carry on the farm and work freedmen thereon did not terminate the agency or give the agent any power to defeat the interest of his principal, claiming the proceeds of the farm, but what he did on the farm, he did as agent, and the products belonged to the principal.[1] The farm in question was the Choctaw Bend plantation in Bolivar County. It was held that where a bill of exchange was drawn and endorsed by parties resident at Lexington, Mississippi, and accepted by parties residing in New Orleans after its occupation by the Federal forces in May, 1862, and transferred to parties in New York, the holders in New York were prohibited from transmitting to the agent at Lexington. After the capture of New Orleans, all intercourse between that city and Lexington, Mississippi, was forbidden by the force of public law and by the proclamation of the President.[2]

The effect of the President's Emancipation Proclamation and the exact date of the destruction of slavery in Mississippi was before the courts in a number of cases. Where on January 3, 1865, a man gave a note for $250 for the hire of a slave for one year, and in the course of the year the slave became free, and the maker of the note asked the court for an annulment on the ground of failure of consideration, the court refused to give the desired relief or to pass upon the question as to when the slave became free.[3] At the April term of 1869 the court was called upon to determine this question.

The case was an action of assumpsit upon a contract for hire of some negroes for the year 1863. It was alleged by the plaintiff that all slaves in Mississippi became free on the first of January, 1863, by virtue of the President's Emancipation Proclamation, and consequently, the plaintiffs were not liable for the fulfilment of a contract founded on a false consideration. The High Court held that the President's proclamation abolishing slavery was only operative and effective in that portion of the seceded states which the United States armies had occupied or might occupy after the proclamation should go into effect. The doctrine that one

[1] Shelby vs. Offutt, 51 Miss. 129.
[2] Darden vs. Smith, 44 Miss. 548.
[3] Herod vs. Thigpen, 43 Miss. 102.

belligerent may, by a mere proclamation or order, change
the status of a person residing in the interior of an enemy's
country, or their rights of property over which the belligerent
has no present power to enforce any order, the court pronounced to be unknown to the law of nations.   The rights
of property owners over slaves in Mississippi was not affected by the Emancipation Proclamation.   It was therefore
held that the abolition of slavery in Mississippi dated from
the adoption of the ordinance of the convention on that
subject in August, 1865, and not from the proclamation of
the President on January 1, 1863.[1]

[1] V. & M. R.R. Co. *vs.* Green, 42 Miss. 436.

CHAPTER THIRD

PRESIDENTIAL RECONSTRUCTION

I. THE INAUGURATION OF THE PRESIDENTIAL POLICY IN MISSISSIPPI

THE commissioners having assured the President that his North Carolina plan of reconstruction would be acceptable if no better could be had, he at once took steps to put it into operation in Mississippi by appointing Judge Sharkey provisional governor. It is doubtful if a better selection could have been made. Judge Sharkey was born of Irish parents on the river Holston in Tennessee, near the close of the eighteenth century. He was in General Jackson's army at the age of fifteen, and was present at the battle of New Orleans. He attended the common schools of Greenville, Tennessee, read law at Lebanon, emigrated to Mississippi, served in the legislature, and in 1833 went upon the bench as chief justice of the High Court of Errors and Appeals, where he presided with distinction for more than twenty years. Before the war, he was a Whig in politics and a Union man in his sympathies.[1] Being a non-combatant during the war, he escaped the legal penalties which attached to the action of most of his fellow-citizens, and was therefore eligible to office under the United States. His appointment was generally acceptable to the people of the North, although he was criticised by some for a decision which he had made years before concerning the status of a mulatto woman who had married a white man.[2]

Having no authority to appoint a state governor except as an exercise of the war power, the President appointed

---

[1] Judge Sharkey had been offered a place in President Taylor's Cabinet in 1848, but declined to accept political office, preferring to remain on the bench. No judge in the history of the state settled more legal questions or made more authoritative decisions than Sharkey, and his opinions in the Mississippi reports constitute a monument to his legal fame.

[2] *New York Herald*, July 9, 1865.

Judge Sharkey by public proclamation issued in his capacity as commander-in-chief of the army, and directed that he should be paid from the executive contingent fund.

The governor, however, said he did not regard himself as an official of the United States, nor even a constitutional governor,[1] and declined to accept compensation from the general government, saying that he was able to raise means at home for the support of his government. He did this by levying a special tax on stores, saloons, taverns, gaming tables, restaurants, pedlers, brokers, banking establishments, and ten dollars on every bale of cotton sent to market.[2]

The President's proclamation appointing Judge Sharkey governor declared it to be the duty of the United States to guarantee to each state a republican form of government, and in appointing a provisional executive to reorganize the government of the state, he was but carrying out the constitutional mandate. The proclamation made it the duty of the provisional governor to prescribe at the earliest possible moment such rules and regulations as might be necessary for calling a convention to be chosen by the "loyal" people for the purpose of altering or amending the constitution. No person was qualified to vote for a delegate or was eligible to membership in the convention unless he had taken and subscribed to the oath of amnesty prescribed in the President's proclamation of May 29, and he must in addition have been entitled to vote by the law of the state as it existed prior to January 9, 1861.[3]

The military commander of the department and all persons in the military or naval service of the United States were directed to aid and assist the governor in carrying out the purposes of the proclamation, and they were enjoined from hindering or discouraging the loyal people from organizing the government. The Secretary of State was authorized to put in force all the national laws, the administration of which

---

[1] Address before the legislature, Oct. 16, 1865.

[2] This tax schedule is printed in the *Chicago Tribune* of July 28, 1865. There was considerable objection among the merchants to the tax of $10 per bale on cotton, and many declined to pay it, whereupon the governor ordered that it should be doubled in every such instance, and the sheriff was directed to seize and sell at public auction a sufficient quantity to satisfy the tax. The receipts during Sharkey's administration were $152,218. The expenditures were $68,942. *New York Times*, Aug. 4, 1865.

[3] The substance of the oath was to faithfully support, protect, and defend the Constitution of the United States, and abide by and support all the laws and proclamations made during the war with reference to the emancipation of the slaves.

properly belonged to his department, and which were applicable to the state ; the Secretary of the Treasury was directed to nominate the necessary officers to put into execution the revenue laws, in each case the preference to be given to loyal persons residing within the district ; the Postmaster General was directed to reëstablish the postal service ; the district judge was instructed to proceed to hold courts according to law; and the district attorney was directed to libel and bring to judgment, confiscation, and sale such property as had become subject to confiscation ; the Secretaries of the Navy and of the Interior were likewise directed to enforce such laws as related to their respective departments.   On June 13, Secretary Seward notified Governor Sharkey of his appointment, transmitted therewith a copy of the President's proclamation, together with a copy of the official oath, and informed him that his salary would be $3000 per year.   Sharkey accepted the appointment reluctantly and with the understanding, he says, that he should not be interfered with by the military authorities in the administration of the civil government.[1]   On July 1, he issued a proclamation informing the people of the state of his appointment, and expressed a desire to carry out the President's wishes to restore civil government as speedily as possible.   To avoid the delay which would necessarily result from the separate organization of each county by special appointments, he reappointed by proclamation all officers who were holding at the time the government property and archives were surrendered to the military forces, that is, on May 22.   Inasmuch as it was necessary that the offices should be filled by incumbents who were loyal to the government of the United States, the governor expressly reserved the right to remove any one who might be an exception in that respect, and he earnestly invoked the loyal citizens of each county to give him timely and authentic information in regard to any officer who was obnoxious to this requirement.

The proclamation directed sheriffs to hold an election in each county on the 7th of August for delegates to a state convention to be held at Jackson, August 14.   The trustees of the state university were required to meet at Oxford, July 31, for the purpose of reopening the university.   The " unprecedented amount of lawlessness " in the state claimed the governor's especial attention.   " Crime," said he, " must be suppressed, and guilty persons must be punished."   He said

[1] H. Mis. Docs. December, 1868, No. 53, p. 37.

the commanding general had kindly offered to aid him in protecting the people and in apprehending offenders against the law, and he hoped that the people would give him timely information and render such other assistance as would enable him to carry out such a laudable object. He advised the people, when it should become necessary in consequence of their remoteness from a military post, to organize themselves into county patrols for the apprehension of offenders who, when caught, should be taken to Jackson for safe-keeping. He suggested that perhaps there were some who might have conscientious scruples about taking the amnesty oath, because of a belief that the Emancipation Proclamation was unconstitutional. This objection, he said, certainly could not be raised with propriety by those who denied that they were subject to the Constitution as the supreme law when the proclamation was issued. "Whether it be constitutional or not is a question which the people have no right to determine — that rests with the supreme judicial power of the United States, and until the Supreme Court has acted, the proclamation must be regarded as valid," he said. "The people of the South were in rebellion ; the President has the right to prescribe terms of amnesty — he has done so, and it is hoped the people will all cheerfully take the oath with a fixed purpose to observe it in good faith. Why should they now hesitate or doubt, since slavery has ceased to be a practical question ? It is the part of wisdom and of honor to submit without a murmur. The negroes are free — free by the fortunes of the war, free by the proclamation, free by common consent, free practically as well as theoretically, and it is too late to raise the technical question as to the means by which they became so." He assured his fellow-citizens that in accepting appointment from the United States he was actuated by no other motive than a desire to aid the people in reorganizing a civil government, and he ventured to suggest that their success in the late war would have proved to be the greatest calamity that could have befallen the country, and the greatest to the cause of civil liberty throughout the world. The proclamation was well received at the North, and met the approval of all the conservative men of the state.[1]

The governor's policy of reappointing all persons who were in office at the close of the war was the subject of

---

[1] The *New York Herald* of July 14 said it was excellent, and should be published throughout all the Southern states. The proclamation is printed in full in the *Herald* of the 13th, and in the *Times* of the 14th.

considerable complaint at the North.   The President telegraphed him August 22, complaining that reports calculated to do harm were circulating in "influential quarters,"
and urged upon him the importance of encouraging and
strengthening to the fullest extent the men of Mississippi
who had never faltered in their allegiance to the government.[1] The governor replied at once to this despatch declaring that he had endeavored both from inclination and duty
to avoid the appointment or recommendation of secessionists.
He assured the President that it had been an indispensable
requisite that applicants should be free from this objection.

He said he had required all officers before entering upon
their duties to take and subscribe to the oath of amnesty, a
copy of which in each case was transmitted to the governor's
office.   No one was eligible to office who was not included in
the President's amnesty proclamation, unless specially pardoned by him.   In counties where there were no persons who
could take the oath, special appointments were made.

There was no provision in Governor Sharkey's proclamation for the reorganization of the courts, and it was probably
his intention that those already in existence should not
again exercise their functions.   At this time the chief subjects of litigation were cotton, horses, and mules.   Owners
who had sold cotton during the war to be delivered at a
certain time, refused to deliver it upon the return of peace,
while cotton belonging to innocent persons was seized and
carried away by military authorities or treasury agents.   In
all such cases the military tribunals were the only resort.
Often without notice to the adverse party and on *ex parte*
showing, summary orders were made and enforced.   That
grievous wrongs sometimes resulted there can be little doubt.
When the provisional governor entered upon the discharge
of his duties he was besieged by aggrieved parties for relief.
To afford them a measure of relief, he revived by proclamation the replevin acts, and put them into operation.   They
provided a summary remedy before two justices of the peace
for recovery of property wrongfully taken or detained.   At

[1] Relative to his policy of reappointing those already in office, the governor testified in 1869: "I told the President precisely what I should do.   I
said : 'Mr. President, I cannot take this position and go there and fill every
office in the state.   I will have to do it by proclamation.   I will put those
men in office who held office before the war or during the war, reserving to
myself the power to remove them, and if I find them disloyal, I will remove
them.'   I appointed nobody to office knowingly who claimed to be a secessionist.   I was very careful in this respect."   H. Mis. Docs. 3d Ses. 40th
Cong. No. 53, p. 43.

first these were the only judicial tribunals provided for in the governor's scheme of jurisprudence. At a time when the rights of property were the chief subjects of litigation, such a system of judicature was notoriously insufficient.

Accordingly on the 12th of July the governor, by public proclamation, created a special court of equity to sit at Jackson with jurisdiction in all contracts for cotton or other personal property, and with power to proceed in a summary manner, on petition, to enforce specific performance, or annul contracts upon due notice to parties concerned. The court was further empowered to issue processes, punish for contempt, and appoint a clerk. The governor from time to time issued orders defining in detail the jurisdiction of the court, and modifying its procedure. The court seems to have been very unpopular, and its legality was attacked on the ground that the provisional governor had no power to establish such an extraordinary tribunal, and that it was unknown to the laws and constitution of the state, and its proceedings *coram non judice* and void.[1]

Another of Governor Sharkey's duties was to see that every individual who had served the Confederacy should be given an opportunity to take the amnesty oath prescribed by the President's proclamation of May 29, unless he was excluded from its benefits. During June and July, the military authorities were busy administering the oath, and those who were entitled to its benefits came up almost without exception, and took it, although to most of them it was gall and wormwood.[2] The oath was required to be subscribed to, and a copy transmitted to the government as a matter of record. The willingness of the applicant to take the oath was not regarded as conclusive evidence of his loyalty, and if the officer had good reason to believe that it was not being taken in good faith, he might withhold the privilege.[3]

---

[1] The Supreme Court at the April term of 1869 affirmed the validity of the Equity Court and held that the President of the United States, as commander-in-chief of the victorious army, had authority to appoint a provisional governor and invest him with power to establish such tribunals as in his judgment might be necessary.   Scott *vs.* Bilgerry, 40 Miss. 119.

[2] The *Jackson Mississippian* said that by the time the convention met there were comparatively few who had not taken the oath. It said : " We regard it as the solemn duty of every citizen in this trying hour to take the oath, and not by sullen indifference stand idly by while breakers surround the ship of state."

[3] The following incident is reported to have occurred at Hillsboro in Scott County while a provost marshal was administering the oath : *Prov. Marshal.* You wish to take the oath, do you ? — *Applicant.* Yes, sir. *P. M.* Have you been in the rebel army ? — *A.* Yes, sir. *P. M.* What was your rank ? — *A.*

It will be remembered that the President's proclamation excluded fourteen classes of persons from the benefit of the amnesty, but permitted them to make special application, and such clemency would be extended as might be consistent with the facts of the case, and the peace and dignity of the United States. In general, the excepted persons were those who left high official stations under the government of the United States to serve the Confederacy, those who acted as diplomatic agents of the Confederacy, or held military office above the rank of colonel ; those who left the army or navy of the United States to aid the Confederacy ; those who were educated at the military or naval academy, and afterward took up arms against the United States ; " rebel " governors ; and those who enlisted in the Confederate army, and whose taxable property exceeded $20,000 in value.[1] The majority of those in Mississippi, who were thus excluded from the amnesty, belonged to the latter class. The records of the Attorney General's office show that down to July 1, 1867, special pardons had been granted by the President to 949 residents of the state. Of these about 800 were persons worth over $20,000 ; about 90 had been postmasters ; 55, Federal tax collectors and assessors. The remainder had been United States commissioners, agents of various kinds, attorneys, receivers, mail carriers, contractors, etc. Pardons in every case were granted only upon the recommendation of some "loyal" person. Many of the recommendations from Mississippi were made by Governor Sharkey.[2]

Major. *P. M.* How much are you worth ? — *A.* I was rich once, but ain't worth a cent now. *P. M.* What has become of your property ? — *A.* It was destroyed first by one army and then the other, until it all went except the land, and there is not a fence or hedge on it. *P. M.* When did you enter the rebel army ? — *A.* In 1861. *P. M.* Voluntarily or involuntarily ? — *A.* I volunteered. *P. M.* What was your object ? — *A.* I was fighting for Southern rights. *P. M.* Have you changed your views since then ? — *A.* No, sir. *P. M.* Then how can you take the oath ? — *A.* Why, the fact is, I am subjugated. *P. M.* What good will taking this oath do you ? — *A.* I want to vote so as to keep down the niggerism suffrage party, and to save my neck. *P. M.* Do you feel any real loyalty to the government now ? — *A* (hesitatingly). I can't say that I do. *P. M.* If this country were to become engaged in a war with some European power, and that power should offer the South independence, what would you do ? — *A.* Well, I should act according to circumstances. *P. M.* But that is not loyalty. I insist on a direct answer. — *A.* Well, if I must speak out, I will. I should stand by my state, whichever way it went. *Chicago Tribune* of August 25.

[1] Richardson, Messages and Papers, VI. p. 312.

[2] See Sen. Ex. Docs. 1st Ses. 40th Cong. No. 32 for complete list of persons in Mississippi to whom special pardons were granted by the President, the date on which the pardon was issued, and the name of the person in each case who recommended the pardon, and the class to which the applicant belonged.

II. THE RECONSTRUCTION CONVENTION OF 1865

Meanwhile, the attention of the people was directed to
the convention which Governor Sharkey had ordered, and
the canvass for which was now in progress.   The chief issue
of the campaign was whether the convention should recognize fully the results of the war and declare the total and
final abolition of all property in slaves, including those owned
by widows, orphans, minors, and loyal persons ; or whether
some form of abolition should be adopted which would make
a distinction between the slave-holders on the one hand who
served the Confederate cause, and those on the other who had
opposed secession, had taken no part in the war, and had
given neither aid nor comfort to the enemies of the United
States.   To adopt the first course, would be to cut off all
right of judicial remedy by innocent slave-holders, should
such right of action ever be allowed by the United States in
its courts.   The candidates who favored the first course
insisted that it was for the interests of the state to yield to
military necessity and accept, unreservedly, the conditions
imposed by the Federal government.   The idea of compensation for slaves they believed to be delusive.   " If," said a
prominent candidate, " we obstinately hold on to the dead
body of slavery in any manner, we shall close and bar the
only door left open for readmission, and by so doing, enable
the radical party at the North — while we are chained down
as a conquered province under military rule — to consummate
the work in which they are now so earnestly engaged, of fas-
tening upon the South the odious principle of negro suffrage.
Everything with us depends upon decided enlightened action
by the great convention soon to assemble at Jackson." [1]   Many
candidates, on the contrary, favored taking no action upon
the question of abolition more than to recognize slavery as
abolished by the United States.   They did not purpose to

---

[1] This is the language of Judge Amos Johnston, one of the ablest of
the members of the convention.   *Chicago Tribune,* Aug. 2, 1865.   Judge
William Yerger, another candidate, strongly favored unconditional abolition.   He was sanguine enough to believe that it would insure the reëstablishment of civil government in the state, the speedy removal of the
troops, and the admission of their senators and representatives to Congress.   The *New York Daily News* of Aug. 7, 1865, contains the views of
Anderson, Johnston, Potter, Robb, and Yerger, on the leading issue of the
campaign.

have it appear as a matter of history that the abolition of slavery was an act of the state government.   As a prominent candidate of this persuasion put it : " My own opinion is that if this great act of oppression·is to be consummated, by which the Southern people are to be deprived of $4,000,-000,000 worth of property without compensation, it should be left to be recorded in history as the act of that government whose first and highest duty is, as far as its power extends, to protect and guard with equal care the interests and rights of the people of each and all of the states, and I should desire that the people of Mississippi should not by their action give sanction to this enormous public wrong." [1]   The press of the state was divided as between these two views. Of the two leading journals, the *Jackson News* and the *Clarion*, the latter favored an unequivocal recognition of the results of the war, while the *News* did not.   The *Clarion*, in an editorial, published the day before the meeting of the convention, declared that however reluctant they might be to yield their right to slaves as property, however much they might prefer gradual emancipation, no one could deny the fact that the freedom of the negro was already beyond cavil, and that no act of theirs could change his destiny. " We hear of candidates for the convention," said the editor, " who talk either of ignoring this question or protesting against emancipation and demanding compensation. Such a course, however proper it might be under other circumstances, at the present would inevitably result in the prolongation of military rule in the South, and would very probably lead to the reorganization of the states on the basis of negro suffrage.   It appears to us to be the duty of the convention to recognize the situation and at once change the Constitution to harmonize with this new order of things ; declare that slavery shall no longer exist in Mississippi, and let it be done in good faith, without protest or remonstrance."   The *Mississippian*, another Jackson paper said, " We think a decided majority of the convention will ignore quibbling and meet the issue of the hour like men of sense and candor." [2]

The Mississippi convention was the first of the Southern state conventions to assemble in pursuance of the President's

---

[1] Speech of Fulton Anderson, *Chicago Tribune*, Aug. 2.   Mr. Anderson said he did not think the taking of the amnesty oath created an obligation upon members of the convention to vote for the abolition of slavery, and as for himself, he intended to oppose it with all his power.

[2] Quoted in *New York World*, Aug. 22, 1865.

plan of reconstruction.   Its action was therefore watched
with keen interest by the people of all parts of the country.[1]
" If," said an influential New York paper, " Mississippi
moves into her place in the Union with a constitution that
will meet the approval of the government, we shall be able
to dismiss all further apprehension concerning the action of
any other Southern state."   The convention consisted of one
hundred delegates, all of whom, except two, were able to
qualify.   A majority of the members were old-line Whigs,
most of whom had opposed secession in 1861.[2]   It was
alleged that only one member, however, had actually opposed the power of the Confederacy.[3]   Seven members had
been delegates to the secession convention, all of whom
except one had voted against the ordinance.   Seven were
members of the reconstruction convention of 1868.   Governor Sharkey called the convention to order and administered the amnesty oath to each member.   He then laid
before them the following despatch from the President.   " I
am gratified to see that you have organized your convention
without difficulty.   I hope that without delay your convention will amend your state constitution abolishing slavery
and denying to all future legislatures the power to legislate
that there is property in man ; also that they will adopt the
amendment to the Constitution of the United States abolishing slavery.   If you could extend the elective franchise to
all persons of color who can read the Constitution of the
United States in English, and write their names, and to
all persons of color who own real estate valued at not less
than $250, and pay taxes thereon, you would completely
disarm the adversary and set an example the other states
will follow.   This you can do with perfect safety, and you
thus place the Southern states, in reference to free persons
of color, upon the same basis with the free states.   I hope
and trust your convention will do this, and, as a conse-

---

[1] The *New York Times* of Aug. 18 said the proceedings of the Mississippi convention commanded peculiar interest because Mississippi was the
state of Jeff Davis, because it was the second to secede, and because it produced more cotton than any other state and had nearly as many slaves as
any other.

[2] The secretary of the convention says the total number of Whigs was
seventy ; the *Vicksburg Herald* of Aug. 19 says the number was sixty.

[3] The *Chicago Tribune* of Aug. 29, 1865, said only one member of the
Mississippi convention had up to that time uttered anything that would pass
for union at the North.   That member was " Mr. Crawford from the state of
Jones, a county that had seceded from the Confederacy and maintained its
independence throughout the war."

quence, the radicals, who are wild upon negro franchise, will be completely foiled in their attempt to keep the Southern states from renewing their relations to the Union by not accepting their senators and representatives." A committee of fifteen was then appointed to inquire into and report to the convention such alterations and amendments of the constitution as were deemed to be necessary to secure the rehabilitation of the state government.[1] Another committee of fifteen was appointed to report to the convention such action as was deemed proper and expedient to be taken relative to the ordinance of secession, and what action should be taken with regard to such of the legislative and judicial acts of the state government passed since January 9, 1861, as were not in conflict with the Constitution of the United States. Foreseeing that the utterances of the members would be closely scrutinized by the people of the North, and knowing that the opinions expressed would be accepted as indicative of the spirit of the whole South, the convention determined that its debates should be reported in full and printed, so as to "vindicate the state from the aspersions constantly being cast upon her."[2]

A proposition to memorialize the President for the release and immediate pardon of Governor Clarke and Jefferson Davis was the subject of considerable debate. The more conservative members doubted the expediency of taking official action on a matter so delicate at that particular time. The convention had been called for a specific purpose, and to ask for the immediate pardon of the highest leaders of the Confederacy was not modesty, to say the least, and might defeat or embarrass their efforts at reorganization. The convention was composed largely of men whose political views were different from those of Davis, yet they had per-

---

[1] Convention Journal, p. 17.

[2] Ibid. p. 22. One of the members, an ex-major general in the Confederate army said : "It is important for us not only that the constitution which we shall adopt shall show the spirit of our people, but it is also important to show by the debates the spirit in which those propositions were discussed. It is necessary that we should show that it is a mistake to suppose that in surrendering we merely did it to gain time, and that there was still a disposition among the people to carry on the war against the Northern states. It is important in the present crisis that whatever can, should be done to assure the conservative people of the North that having first tried the logic of the schools, and failed in that, and having then resorted to the sterner logic of arms, and having failed in that also, we are now honestly disposed to return to our allegiance, and to make out of the disasters that have befallen us the best that we can." He thought there was no better way of showing the people of the North that they were earnest and sincere than by publishing the debates. *Ibid.* p. 27.

sonal sympathy for him, and were willing to take action in
his behalf as private individuals.[1] The resolution was finally
withdrawn.

The great question before the convention of 1865 was
that relating to the abolition of slavery. After all, it was
not a question of whether slavery should be abolished, but
how its extinction should be acknowledged. The convention
was unanimous in the opinion that slavery was a thing of the
past. The only question in their minds was whether they
should formally, by constitutional amendment, abolish the
institution as though there had been no war, or whether they
should adopt a resolution recognizing the extinction of
slavery as a result of the war, and saddle the responsibility
upon the government of the United States. In either case,
it would mean the loss of slavery. The latter course would
in a way satisfy their pride, but its expediency in the then
state of feeling at the North was very much questioned.
The committee of fifteen, to whom the matter had been
referred, brought in a report recommending the former
course. It submitted a constitutional amendment declaring
that slavery should no longer exist in the state of Mississippi.
No attempt was made to fix the responsibility upon the government of the United States. On the following day, a substitute was offered which was the same in substance as that
reported by the committee, but contained a preamble reciting
that slavery had been abolished by the action of the government of the United States.[2] Three or four members spoke
in favor of the substitute. They contended that slavery had
been destroyed by somebody, certainly not by the will of
the people of Mississippi. To declare slavery abolished by a
convention of the people would be an involuntary act, and
unnecessary. We acknowledge, they said, that it is abolished,
and we are willing to recognize the fact, but we think it due
to the state and ourselves that we should declare how slavery
has been abolished. We all took an oath to support the
Emancipation Proclamation — that proclamation dictates to
us that slavery was abolished by authority of the United
States. The world knows that the government of the
United States assumes responsibility and whatever honor
there may be for wiping away the stain of slavery. It was
due to posterity, they said, that in framing a constitutional
amendment on this point, the circumstances of abolition

---

[1] See speech of J. W. C. Watson, Convention Journal, p. 43.
[2] This substitute was offered by Hugh A. Barr, delegate from Lafayette
County. Convention Journal, p. 44.

should be distinctly set forth. For the sake of historical accuracy, they ought not to allow the naked fact of the abolition of slavery to go forth as the voluntary action of the people of Mississippi represented in convention, when everybody knew it was forced upon them by a conqueror.[1] The substitute was laid on the table.[2]

Several other substitutes were then offered, all of which sought to fix the responsibility for emancipation upon the United States. After the rejection of these, a series of resolutions offered by George L. Potter became the basis for all subsequent discussion on the subject. They arraigned the government of the United States for emancipating the slaves of innocent persons without compensation; and declared that the method by which slavery had been abolished was of doubtful validity, although the people of the state would recognize it as valid until annulled by the proper judicial tribunals or otherwise lawfully revoked.[3] Potter was one of the ablest members of the convention, and the leader of the non-conservatives. He defended his resolutions with some ability, and insisted that Mississippi was still in the Union precisely as before the war. He refused to recognize any power in the general government to dictate to the state changes in its constitution, and declared that the President had not exacted in plain terms the abolition of slavery.[4] He argued, moreover, that the ratification of the thirteenth amendment would not satisfy the radicals. Still greater concessions would be demanded until the whites and blacks were made equal. In view of this he was unwilling to cut off all hope of indemnity for the loss of their slaves. Small as the hope was, he was not willing to destroy it by an unconditional abolition of slavery, and by that act assume that the United States would never be just. True, the government could not pay them now, but it might exempt them from taxation.[5] The three ablest men in the convention, besides Potter, were Judges Watson, Johnston, and William Yerger, all of whom opposed the resolutions. Judge Watson declared that the circumstances under which they met to

---

[1] Convention Journal, p. 44.
[2] By a vote of 54 to 41.   [3] Convention Journal, p. 70.
[4] He had told the commissioners to Washington that the abolition of slavery was a *sine qua non* to the reëstablishment of civil government in Mississippi; he had told a South Carolina delegation that they had better see that "the friction of the Rebellion rub out slavery" if they desired readmission to the Union. See also his letter to Governor Sharkey, *supra*.
[5] Potter's speech was published in the *Chicago Tribune* and other Northern papers.

a great extent impaired their independence and freedom of action, that they were a conquered people, and the army of the enemy at that moment occupied their territory, and consequently they had no right to dictate to Congress terms of readmission to the Union. Judge Johnston pleaded with the convention to let the institution of slavery go, the question of compensation — everything, until they could relieve themselves and their posterity, and get some little guarantee, at least, that the children whom they were rearing would have a land to live in, and the privileges of free men. " Whatever," said he, " may have been our former glory, we are now vanquished and helpless, and in the power of the United States government. Gentlemen talk as if we had a choice, but we have no choice, and it is no humiliation to admit it. The only course we can pursue is that dictated to us by the powers at Washington." He assured gentlemen that none of them or any of their children would ever again see an African slave in this country. The sentiment of the entire civilized world taught them that they were alone in the support of slavery. He begged his fellow-members to act wisely, and they might hope for peace.[1]

By far the ablest speech in the convention was that of William Yerger, a man of conservative views, and one of the ablest lawyers that ever practised before the bar in Mississippi.[2] He told of his mission to Washington as one of the commissioners to see the President, of the numerous evidences he saw in the North of the determination of the people not to be " trifled " with, of the resolution of the President upon the slavery question, and of the peculiar circumstances under which they met and were there assembled. In regard to the views of the President, Mr. Yerger quoted him as saying : " In the proposed convention to alter and change the constitution, so as to restore your state to its

---

[1] This speech is printed in the *Chicago Tribune;* see also Convention Journal, p. 95 *et seq.*

[2] Like Governor Sharkey, Judge Yerger was a native of Tennessee, and a Whig in politics — a fact which practically excluded him from political life before the war. For a while, however, he occupied a seat on the Supreme bench with Judge Sharkey. In the celebrated case of Mississippi *vs.* Johnson, in which the court passed upon the validity of the Union bank bonds, Yerger, in the face of a popular feeling, violent and proscriptive, stood up fearlessly and nobly against repudiation, and declared that the state was legally as well as morally bound to pay the bonds. Although he knew it would cost him his ermine, he could not be deterred from following his convictions. His briefs in the Mississippi reports show that he was well versed in all branches of the law, and for a number of years he had the most lucrative practice of any attorney in the state.

relations with the Federal government, there ought to be incorporated an amendment, abolishing the institution of slavery." This was no order or dictation, only a distinct admonition, that unless it was done, so far as the executive was concerned, he would not give the support of the administration to the restoration of the state government, and they knew very well that without such support, they could not resist the overwhelming tide of fanaticism in the North, clamoring not only for abolition, but for universal suffrage and the social equality of the negro. Mr. Yerger said that everywhere on his journey to and from Washington, he made it his business to ascertain the public sentiment on that question, and he had found a fixed and universal sentiment that the abolition of slavery had been settled by the result of the war ; in the language of the President, "rubbed out by the friction of the war." There was no difference of opinion on that point. He did not hear a single utterance adverse to that view. He expressed surprise that there were members who seemed to overlook the fact of the war. Slavery was dead, and the state was under the absolute military control of the United States. It was folly to attempt to disguise the fact. It stared them in the face, wherever they went. It was palpable to the vision of every man. When they entered the gates of the capitol for the purpose of deliberating upon this question, they were compelled to pass armed and uniformed soldiers, pacing their daily march, and unless the President had been gracious enough to accord them the privilege of entering, they could not have done so. There were no civil courts in operation throughout the length and breadth of the state. The reign of civil law had given way to the reign of martial law. Trial by military commissions had taken the place of the ancient right of trial by jury. The writ of *habeas corpus* was no longer a privilege which they could claim. Almost daily, citizens were being taken out of the hands of the civil authorities, and tried before petty military tribunals, because the negro was excluded from giving testimony in cases in which he was interested. The question whether the Emancipation Proclamation made the negro free was an academic question and not a practical one. No master could institute action of replevin for recovery of his slave, or maintain a writ of *habeas corpus* for his recovery. Slaves went where they pleased, untrammelled and unfettered, and if molested by their former masters, they might appeal to the military tribunals of the United States for protection. He closed with an arraignment of the system of slave labor, and admonished his countrymen not to despair, but to look to the future. Although the destruction of the institution at this time, so suddenly and rudely, had worked great hardship upon many individuals, and had resulted in great pecuniary destitution, now that the loss had been sustained and could not be helped, they ought not to sit down and repine over the inevitable past, which they could not control, but look in hope to the future and to those things which might in some degree give compensation for what they had lost. "As men of sense, let us endeavor," he said, "to remedy what we cannot alter, and gather together whatever may tend to palliate our misfortunes. Of all the industrial systems, that of slavery was probably the most costly."[1]

Yerger's speech was listened to with the utmost attention, and after he had finished, Potter's resolutions were laid on the table by a large majority. This done, an ordinance was adopted by a vote of 87 to 11, declaring that the institution of slavery, having been destroyed in the state of Mississippi, neither slavery nor involuntary servitude, except in punishment for crime, whereof the party shall have been duly convicted, shall hereafter exist in the state.[2]

Thus perished slavery in Mississippi, killed in the house of its friends, and by those who loved the institution most. This was the great work of the convention. After all, it was but an involuntary acknowledgment of a fact already existing. This recognition might have been made on the first day of the convention ; but instead, a week was spent in trying to adopt a resolution which meant nothing. This act of abolition by the state of course destroyed all hope of a judicial remedy for the destruction of slave property. It applied to the widow, the orphan, and the loyal slave-holder, as well as to the most "guilty rebel." Yet there was a faint hope that in some good time, when the animosities and passions engendered by the war had passed away, the government of the United States would, in the spirit of justice, devise some scheme of compensation for the innocent at least. Few, however, allowed themselves to be seduced by such a hope, and even the most hopeful soon abandoned it.

The next important task of the convention related to the action to be taken with reference to the ordinances passed by the convention of 1861 — whether they should be declared

[1] Convention Journal, pp. 145-157. Yerger's speech is printed in the *Chicago Tribune* of Sept. 4, 1865.
[2] Convention Journal, p. 164.

"null and void" *ab initio*, or whether they should simply be "repealed" or "abrogated." To declare them "null and void," it was said, would be to impute to the convention that framed them incompetency, if not treason. It would discredit the secession convention, and cast a reflection upon the intelligence and patriotism of not only every member of that body, but upon every individual who obeyed them. Those who supported this view held that whether the ordinance of secession was lawful or unlawful, it was, nevertheless, an exercise of power by a sovereign state. It created a *de facto* if not a *de jure* government. The ordinance could no longer be maintained, and therefore the people of the state desired to see it "repealed," but not declared "null and void." They were ready to acquiesce in the result, they said, but they ought not to cast odium upon their predecessors. It was a common practice for legislative bodies to "repeal" acts whose constitutionality had been seriously questioned.[1] It was strenuously maintained by one of the members that if secession was not a reserved right, it was at least a right of revolution, and the ordinance was not, therefore, null and void, unless the right of revolution was null and void. The committee to whom the question had been referred, brought in a report declaring the ordinance of secession "null and void." The committee said that many of the delegates in the present convention did not recognize the right of secession, and had never recognized it, and to repeal the ordinance would be an admission upon their part that it had some original validity, and that the right existed and was recognized by the constitution. And besides, they said, to acknowledge the original validity of the ordinance by simply repealing it, would seriously prejudice their efforts to gain admission for their representatives in Congress.

Immediately after the reading of the report, an amendment was offered declaring the ordinance to be "of no force and effect." This was rejected. Another proposed that the ordinance be declared "null and of no binding force, since, in a war with the United States, the latter refused to recognize its legality or validity, and the state failed to maintain her asserted sovereignty."[2] Potter proposed to declare the ordinance "vacated and annulled." The report of the majority was finally adopted by a vote of 81 to 14.[3] After

---

[1] Convention Journal, p. 174.   [2] *Ibid.* p. 179.

[3] *Ibid.* p. 180. The *New York Times* of August 22 said that the form in which this declaration was made involved an absolute abandonment of the doctrine of secession, and committed the state to the true principle that there

declaring the ordinance of secession " null and void," the convention, oddly enough, " repealed " the other ordinances passed by the convention of 1861.

The ordinance of the convention of 1861 to raise funds for the defence of the state, the " Cotton Money " scheme, was left for the legislature to take such action upon as it might deem fit. In pursuance of this act, a large amount of money had been put in circulation, and for the convention to repeal it would have been equivalent to an act of repudiation. The sudden emancipation of the slaves had produced vast conditions which, it was thought, clearly called for some action by the convention. Offences such as larceny, assault, arson, and vagrancy were of almost daily occurrence. There was no state penitentiary in which offenders could be confined if convicted. The county jails were full to overflowing, and in nine cases out of ten they would not hold a desperate criminal twenty-four hours. The committee of fifteen brought in a report recommending the adoption of a resolution to punish grand larceny, robbery, rape, arson, and burglary with death by hanging.[1] The report was opposed, not on the ground of its severity, but because it was said to be clearly a matter which should be left to the legislature. The final action of the convention on this subject was the adoption of an amendment to the constitution, making it the duty of the legislature at its next session to provide by law for the protection and security of the person and property of the freedmen, and to guard them and the state against any evils that should arise from their sudden emancipation. The legislature was also empowered to provide by-laws for dispensing with a grand jury, and authorizing prosecution before justices of the peace in cases of petit larceny, assault and battery, affray, riot, unlawful assembly, drunkenness, vagrancy, and other misdemeanors of like character.

A memorial to the President of the United States in behalf of Governor Clarke and Jefferson Davis was adopted by the members in their individual capacity.[2] An ineffectual

---

is no such thing as a withdrawal from the Union, and that it was a full and final acknowledgment that the Federal Constitution is and of right supreme.

[1] Convention Journal, p. 258.

[2] The memorial was signed by 4633 women and by all the members of the convention except about ten, who were absent. The memorial declared that Governor Clarke was old, maimed in constitution, and wrecked in fortune ; that Davis was said to be deprived of the privilege of corresponding with his family and friends, and that he was suffering ill health and threatened with loss of eyesight. His family was reduced to poverty, resistance to the authority of the United States was at an end, there was an honest determi-

effort was made to have the constitution submitted to the people for ratification or rejection. The committee reported that it was inexpedient under existing circumstances. An attempt was then made to have the abolition amendment submitted. It was said that if the ordinance of secession had been submitted to the people, it would have been rejected. They did not want it to be said in the future that the abolition of slavery was forced upon the people of the state by the politicians. The report of the committee, however, was adopted.

Before adjourning, the convention, in a sort of unofficial way, nominated Judge Fisher of the Supreme Court for governor. He was an old-line Whig, and as a member of the court years before, had decided in favor of the validity of the Union bank bonds which were afterward repudiated. He took no part in the war, and upon the reëstablishment of Federal authority in the state, Governor Sharkey recommended him to the President for appointment as United States district judge, but for some reason or other he was not appointed. While on the eve of adjournment, the convention received a despatch from the President congratulating them on the progress they had made toward "paving the way for the readmission of the state to the Union." He told them that he would withdraw the troops and restore the writ of *habeas corpus* as soon as the state had resumed its "proper position in the Union." He expressed the confident hope that the example of Mississippi would be followed by the other Southern states.[1]

After a session of ten days, the convention adjourned with the understanding that it should be called together by the President if the "exigencies of the country" should require it. If no such necessity should arise within six months, it should be adjourned *sine die*. On the 28th of August, Governor Sharkey transmitted a copy of the constitution to the secretary of State, who at once replied that it would engage the early attention of the President.

On the whole, the work of the convention was satisfactory to the conservative people of the North. It abolished

nation of the people to return to their peaceful occupations and restore the prosperity that had once blessed the state. They declared that few of them "coincided" with Messrs. Davis and Clarke in their political opinions ; that most of them voted against secession, yet they did not doubt that Mr. Davis acted upon an honest and sincere conviction that his theory of the government was right.

[1] *New York Post*, Aug. 25, 1865.

slavery, and accorded to the negro certain civil rights, such
as the privilege of bringing suit in the courts and of acquir-
ing and holding real estate.   It was a disappointment to some,
that no step was taken to grant the negro political rights, even
in the most restricted form.   This afforded the radicals a
pretext for attacking the presidential policy of reconstruction.[1]

One of the measures of the convention was the ordering of
an election for the first Monday in October for state and
county officers and representatives in Congress.   The question of admitting negro testimony to the courts was the leading issue in the campaign, and candidates were required to
state their positions on this all-important subject.   The
Jackson News carried at its mast-head, " This is a white man's
country — President Johnson."   " The freedman and the
free negro," said the editor, " must stand on the same footing."   " Negroes as a class must be excluded from the witness
stand.   If the privilege is ever granted, it will lead to greater
demands, and at last end in the admission of the negro to the
jury box and ballot box."[2]   The *Clarion*, on the other hand,
was unequivocally in favor of negro testimony, declared that
the question whenever fairly presented had met popular approval, and that a revolution was taking place in the public
mind which would " astonish " those who were making such
violent opposition to it.[3]   The majority of the press concurred in the view taken by the *Clarion*, as did the leading
members of the bar.

The election took place October 2.   B. G. Humphreys,
a late brigadier general in the Confederate army, was elected
governor over Judge Fisher ;   and the party opposed to negro
evidence secured a majority of the members of the legislature,
which, it was said, insured the defeat of Governor Sharkey,
who was now a candidate for the United States Senate on the
negro testimony platform.   The party in favor of negro
testimony, however, secured the ablest leaders of the legislature.   At the same time, justices of the High Court of
Errors and Appeals and representatives in Congress were
chosen.   The new members of the court belonged to the
" original secessionist " party, while the congressmen elect
were all old-line Whigs except one, who was a Union Demo-

---

[1] Sumner, for example, declared that the Mississippi convention was little
more than a " rebel conspiracy to obtain political power." *New York
World*, Sept. 16, 1865.
[2] Quoted in the *New York Post* of Oct. 28, 1865.
[3] Issue of Nov. 19, 1865.

crat.[1] At the time of Humphreys' election he had not been pardoned by the President, and in fact had received no assurance that the pardon would be forthcoming in the event of his success at the polls.[2] He had never been regularly nominated as a candidate, but was brought forward in an informal way, and elected by his army comrades over the regular nominee, whose chief weakness had been his indifference to the success of the Confederacy. The result of the election was unfavorably regarded at the North, and was cited as an illustration of the popular preference for ex-Confederates as against Union men.[3] Humphreys had been a Whig before the war, and seems to have done what he could to prevent the adoption of an ordinance of secession, but when secession became a fact, he went with his state, according to the prevailing view of allegiance in the South. Although the President was disappointed at the defeat of Fisher, upon the recommendation of Governor Sharkey, he sent Humphreys a pardon in the first week of October. About the same time ex-Governor Clarke was released from confinement. The proclamation releasing him announced that the authority of the Federal government was sufficiently restored in Mississippi to admit of his "enlargement from custody," and directed that he be discharged on parole to appear at such time and place as the President might designate, to answer any charge preferred against him. Permission was given him to reside in Mississippi until further orders. He was informed that should the President see fit later on to grant him a full pardon, his parole would be discharged.[4] About the same time the President restored the privilege of the writ of *habeas corpus*, which had been suspended since December, 1863.

Governor Humphreys, having received his pardon, had himself inaugurated governor on the 16th of October, although for some time he was not recognized by the government of the United States as the real executive. Pardons

---

[1] Testimony of Governor Sharkey before reconstruction committee. The defeat of General Freemen in the Holly Springs district and Sylvanus Evans in the Vicksburg district was alleged to have been due to the fact that they favored the admission of negro testimony to the courts.

[2] When urged to become a candidate, Humphreys said : "I am yet an unpardoned rebel. I have taken the amnesty oath and forwarded an application for a special pardon, and am desirous of renewing my allegiance to the United States, although the President may not be equally as desirous of restoring me to the rights of citizenship." *New York World*, Sept. 9, 1865.

[3] *New York Tribune* of Oct. 9, 1865.

[4] The proclamation is printed in Savage's Life of Johnson, p. 95.

continued to be sent to Governor Sharkey for distribution, and he remained, as before, the medium through which the official correspondence between the United States and the state of Mississippi was carried on.   The day after the inauguration, Sharkey telegraphed Seward that his successor had been duly elected and installed as governor, that the other state officers had qualified, that the legislature was in session, and the civil government of the state was in fact complete.[1] The Secretary of State promptly replied that it was the expectation of the President that he should continue his functions as provisional governor until further notice from the department.

On November 17, the President telegraphed confirming Seward's despatch, and informed Governor Sharkey that his services as provisional governor were not yet dispensed with, and that he should continue to perform any and all the functions of that office, and report from time to time what progress was being made by the legislature.   The governor was furthermore requested to make such suggestions from time to time as he might deem proper.   The President admonished him before retiring to have the Thirteenth Amendment ratified by the legislature, and such laws enacted for the protection of freedmen in person and property as justice demanded.   He was urged to use his influence with the legislature to secure the admission of negro testimony in the courts.   " I do hope," the President wrote, " that the Southern people will see the position they now occupy, and will avail themselves of the favorable opportunity of once more restoring civil government."   Governor Sharkey was requested to show the despatch to Governor-elect Humphreys, whom the President now seems to have recognized as a sort of quasi governor.

III. CONFLICTS BETWEEN THE CIVIL AND MILITARY AUTHORITIES

Governor Sharkey's powers were somewhat vaguely defined.   His functions were partly civil and partly military. In some respects he was a United States officer, in others a state officer.[2]   The state was still held and occupied as con-

---

[1] Correspondence of Provisional Governor Sharkey, *op. cit.* p. 78.

[2] The Supreme Court of the state subsequently held that Governor Sharkey was a United States officer.   Scott *vs.* Bilgerry, 40 Miss. 119.   He was regularly commissioned by the President, and official communications were trans-

quered territory. The military commander of the Department of Mississippi had been instructed to coöperate with and aid Governor Sharkey in the performance of his duties, but in no instance to interfere with him. The existence of martial law, the suspension of the writ of *habeas corpus*, and what was practically a dual executive—one civil, the other military,— necessarily led to confusion and conflicts. From the time of the surrender of the civil government on May 22 until June 13, when Governor Sharkey took charge, the administration of civil affairs was entirely under the supervision of the military authorities. At the time of the surrender of the archives, Major General Peter J. Osterhaus was commander of the Department of Mississippi. On the day Governor Sharkey assumed control, General Osterhaus divided the military district of Mississippi into five sub-districts, each being put in charge of a sub-commander.[1] On June 23, General Osterhaus was superseded in command of the Department of Mississippi by Major General W. H. Slocum, United States volunteers, with headquarters at Vicksburg.[2] General Slocum continued in command during the remainder of Governor Sharkey's administration, and was superseded by General Thomas J. Wood on November 14, 1865.[3]

During the first weeks of Governor Sharkey's administration, the military and civil authorities came into conflict. The conflict arose from the action of General Osterhaus in forcibly taking a man from the custody of a civil magistrate, while the former was undergoing trial for shooting a negro taken in the act of robbery.

General Slocum proceeded to try the offender by a military commission, and when a circuit judge attempted to release him on a writ of *habeas corpus*, Slocum not only disregarded the writ, but had the judge arrested in true Jacksonian style.[4] Governor Sharkey complained to Secretary Seward that the judge in question was an appointee of the provisional governor, and was competent to try the slayer

mitted to him through the Department of State. The majority report of the reconstruction committee says the duties of the provisional governor were ancillary to the withdrawal of the military forces.

[1] Official Records, *op. cit.* p. 990. The sub-districts were as follows: I. Southwest Mississippi, headquarters Vicksburg; II. Northwest Mississippi, headquarters Grenada; III. Northeast Mississippi, headquarters Okolona; IV. East Mississippi, headquarters Meridian; V. Southeast Mississippi, ——.
[2] *Ibid.* p. 1039.
[3] Report of Secretary of War, 1866–1867, p. 50.
[4] The judge who was arrested for issuing the writ denounced the act as not only a violent and strong-handed injustice to him as an officer acting above personal and political considerations, but a blow by the mailed hand

of the negro; that the law under which he acted made no
distinction between the killing of a negro and a white man;
and that if the military authorities had jurisdiction in such
cases, they might try all offences, and consequently there
would be no necessity for civil government. He furthermore
denied that martial law existed in the state, and declared
that if it had ever existed, the President's proclamation appointing him provisional governor, and his declaration that
the military should aid, and not interfere with, the civil
authorities, in effect abolished it. Slocum justified his course
upon the practice of the civil authorities in prohibiting negro
testimony in the courts, and declared that so long as he remained in command of Mississippi, and until the laws of the
state admitted their testimony to the courts, negroes should
be placed under the protection of the United States, and
such cases as the one in question should be referred for
settlement to the military tribunals.[1] Slocum's position
was approved by the President, who informed Governor
Sharkey that he saw no reason for interfering, and that the
government of the state would be provisional only, until the
civil authorities should be restored with the approval of Congress. Four days later Seward wrote, saying, " Upon due
consideration the President is of the opinion that it is inexpedient to rescind the suspension of the writ of *habeas corpus*. Anarchy must in any case be prevented, as the process
of reorganization, though seemingly begun very well, nevertheless is yet only begun." [2]

There were other cases of conflict between the military and
civil authorities like the one described. In every instance,
the offence alleged was committed by a white man against
a negro. The whites claimed the right to be tried according to the laws of the state, and not by military commissions.[3] On July 25 an order came from the War Department

of military power against civil authority in the exercise of its most valued
and hitherto most respected function. The following was Stanton's order :

" WASHINGTON, Aug. 13, 1865.

" MAJOR GENERAL SLOCUM : Colonel Samuel Thomas, assistant commissioner of the Freedman's Bureau, has been directed to turn over to you a man
who had been arrested by his order for shooting a negro. You will receive
the man into your custody, cause him to be tried before a commission, and
carry its sentence into effect. If any efforts be made to release him by *habeas
corpus*, you are directed to disobey the writ and arrest the person issuing it
or attempting to execute it, and report for further orders. By order of the
President.   (Signed)   E. M. STANTON, *Secretary of War*."
—-From *Chicago Tribune*, Sept. 28, 1865.
   [1] Ex-Docs. No. 26, 1st Ses. 39th Cong. p. 55.   [2] *Ibid.* p. 60.
   [3] The *Jackson Daily News*, in a fiery editorial, demanded to know who

directed to General Slocum, who had in the meantime succeeded to the command of the Department of Mississippi,
instructing him to proceed at once with the trials, by
military commissions, of all persons charged with "capital
and other gross assaults" upon colored soldiers of the army,
and to prosecute, promptly and vigorously, all similar cases
of crime in the department. The Secretary of War declared
that because the President had accorded a provisional government to Mississippi, the fact should not be allowed to
abridge or injuriously affect the jurisdiction heretofore properly assumed by military courts in that region during the
war. Especially was the continued exercise of that jurisdiction called for in cases of wrong or injury done by citizens to
soldiers, and in cases of assault upon, or abuse of, colored citizens generally. "Where, indeed," ran the order, "the local
tribunals are either incapable or unwilling to do full justice or
properly punish offenders, Mississippi is still, to a very considerable extent, under the control of the military authorities.
The rebellion, though physically crushed, has not been officially announced or treated either directly or indirectly as a
thing of the past, the suspension of the writ of *habeas corpus*
has not been terminated, nor has military law ceased to be enforced in proper cases, through the agency of military courts
and military commanders in all parts of the country." Here
was a distinct definition of the status in Mississippi.

A more notable instance of disagreement between the civil
and military authorities arose from the attempt of Governor
Sharkey to organize the state militia. On August 17, he
issued a proclamation calling upon the people of the state
to organize under the militia laws a force for the apprehension of criminals and the suppression of crime. He declared
that parties of bad men had banded themselves together
in different parts of the state for the purpose of robbing
and plundering, that outrages of various kinds were being
perpetrated, and that the military force of the United States
within the state was insufficient to protect life and property.
He especially urged those who were liable to military service,
and who were familiar with military discipline, to organize in
each county, if practicable, at least one company of cavalry,
and one of infantry, as speedily as possible. He most ear-

was the governor of Mississippi — Sharkey, Slocum, or Osterhaus. It protested against the "repeated and outrageous assumption of Osterhaus," and
called upon Governor Sharkey to resign if he were not sustained. The people were indignant, said the editor, that he should be made the puppet of
United States military authorities. Quoted by the *Chicago Tribune* of Sept.
4, 1865.

nestly appealed to the young men of the state who had so distinguished themselves for gallantry in the late war, to respond promptly to a call in behalf of a suffering people.[1]

On the next day, there appeared in the Jackson papers a call to the young men of Hinds and Madison counties to meet at certain designated places on the 22d and 24th of August, to organize companies and elect officers. General Osterhaus, commander of the sub-district in which these counties were situated, informed Governor Sharkey that he was in duty bound to prohibit all military organizations not recognized as a portion of the United States army unless formed under special authority of the War Department or of Major General Slocum. He declared that the number of troops in Hinds and Madison counties was amply sufficient to give the civil authorities all the assistance they might need to suppress crime, if the civil authorities would only coöperate sincerely with the military authorities by furnishing them information promptly and voluntarily.[2] Governor Sharkey, replying to the letter of General Osterhaus on the 22d, expressed great regret that he should have felt compelled to take that view of the case, and begged to remind him that for twelve or thirteen consecutive nights, passengers travelling between Jackson and Vicksburg in the stagecoach had been robbed at places within a few miles of his headquarters. In addition to these robberies, the governor declared that information reached him daily of outrages committed in various parts of the state where there was no military force. He declared that the people were constantly calling upon him for protection which he could not give, and it was the purpose of his proclamation to afford them a means of relief. "If further justification," said he, "were needed, I may say that in the last interview I had with the President, in speaking of anticipated troubles, he stated distinctly to me, that I could organize the militia if it should become necessary." He thought the necessity was now manifest, claimed the authority of the President for his action, and until his instructions were changed, he said he should feel it his duty to carry out the line of policy adopted.[3]

[1] His proclamation is printed in Appleton's Ann. Cyclop. for 1865, p. 582.
[2] Report of Carl Schurz, Sen. Docs. 1st Ses. 39th Cong. No. 2, p. 104.
[3] The Chicago Tribune said that Sharkey's plan virtually proposed to reorganize the rebellion army after the loyal army had been disarmed and disbanded, and would enable them to drive every Northern man out of the state, make the condition of the freedmen intolerable, and revive a reign of terror. Issue of Sept. 13, 1865.

Carl Schurz, who was visiting the state at the time as a special commissioner of the President, telegraphed to Washington, protesting against the organization of the militia as proposed by Governor Sharkey. A military force, he insisted, made up of the young men who had fought in the ranks of the Confederacy, organized independently of the United States forces, would be superior in strength to the latter, and would be certain to bring about collisions between the white militia and the colored troops, and thereby increase in a tenfold degree the difficulties that beset the people. The President, too, seems to have doubted the expediency of this policy, although he had given Governor Sharkey to understand that he might organize the militia in certain contingencies. On the 21st of August, the President telegraphed Governor Sharkey to call upon General Slocum whenever he needed military authority to preserve order and suppress crime. He was advised not to organize the militia until further advances were made in the restoration of state authority. The President promised the governor that the military should be withdrawn, and the right of *habeas corpus* should be restored at the earliest possible moment it was deemed safe to do so.[1] To this, the governor replied on the 25th, that the failure to organize the military would leave them in a helpless condition, that General Slocum had no cavalry, and not force enough to protect the people, and that his negro troops did more harm than good when scattered through the country.[2] On the 24th, General Slocum cut the Gordian knot by issuing the somewhat notorious General Order "No. 22" in which he described the "herculean efforts" of Mississippi for four years to overthrow the government of the United States; declared that she had been compelled through sheer exhaustion to submit to the national authority; that the duty of preserving order and executing the laws and orders of the War Department devolved upon the military authorities; that Governor Sharkey had not thought proper to consult with the War Department relative to his course; and that the proposed organization of the young men would be certain to increase rather than lessen the difficulties that beset the people. It was therefore ordered that district commanders give notice at once to all persons within their respective districts that no military organizations except those under control of the United

---

[1] Correspondence of Governor Sharkey, Sen. Docs. 1st Ses. 39th Cong. No. 26, p. 229. [2] *Ibid.* p. 230.

States would be permitted within their respective commands, and all attempts to organize the militia would be arrested. The order declared that most of the crimes had been committed against Northern men, government couriers, and negroes, and that henceforth, when an outrage of this kind was reported, a military force would be sent to the locality, and every citizen within ten miles of the place where the crime occurred would be disarmed by the officer in command. Any citizen who possessed information that would lead to the capture of the criminal, and who refused to divulge it, should be arrested and held for trial.[1]

In the meantime, the President had telegraphed General Schurz, saying that he presumed General Slocum would cause no order to be issued interfering with Governor Sharkey's efforts to restore the functions of the state government without first consulting the United States government, and giving his reasons for the proposed interference. He expressed the belief that there could be organized in each county a force of citizens to suppress treason, preserve order, enforce the civil authority of the United States, and enable Congress to reduce the army, and thereby diminish the enormous expenses of the government. "If there is any danger," said he, "from such organization for the purpose indicated, the military are there to detect and suppress on first appearance any movement insurrectionary in its character." He declared that one of the great objects to be sought in the work of restoration was to induce the people to come forward in the defence of the state and the Federal government. The people must be trusted with their government, and if trusted, he believed they would act in good faith and restore their former constitutional relations with the Union. The proclamation authorizing the restoration of the state government of Mississippi required the military to aid the provisional governor in the performance of his duties. It in no way authorized the military to interfere or throw impediments in the way of consummating the object of his appoint-

---

[1] This order is printed in Appleton's Ann. Cyclop. for 1865, p. 582. The substance of it appears in Schurz's report and Sharkey's correspondence cited above. This emphatic stand of the general made him popular at the North, and he was immediately brought forward by the New York Democrats as a candidate for Secretary of State. The *Chicago Tribune* commenting upon the proposal to nominate him, said : "His overriding of Governor Sharkey would make him a strong candidate. General Orders, No. 22, entitles him to membership in full standing in the Union party simply on the score of its eminent fitness and unquestionable propriety." Issue Sept. 11, 1866.

ment without advising the government of the intended interference.[1]

Governor Sharkey now telegraphed the President official notice of General Slocum's action, and called his attention to their last interview. General Slocum, he said, had thought fit to issue an order to prevent such organization, and to arrest those who attempted it. "There is a condition," said the governor, "that must be settled, and it rests with you to do it. I wish to be able to vindicate myself when trouble comes, as we apprehend it will." [2] By way of reply the President, on August 30, telegraphed Governor Sharkey a copy of the despatch previously sent to Carl Schurz. The governor asked for permission to publish the despatch, which was readily granted, although the President said it was not originally intended for publication.[3] On the same day an order was sent from the War Department directing General Slocum to revoke his proclamation interfering with the organization of the militia.[4] On September 4, General Orders No. 23, published from the headquarters of the Department of Mississippi, countermanded the order previously issued to prohibit the organization of the militia. This ended the controversy so far as Sharkey and Slocum were concerned. The citizens of the state were naturally jubilant over Sharkey's triumph and Slocum's discomfiture.[5] Slocum was equally humiliated and threatened to resign — a course which he was strongly urged to pursue by many in the North, who thought his further continuance would be dishonorable to his profession. The organization of the militia accordingly proceeded, and was not interfered with until 1867, when it was disbanded in pursuance of the reconstruction acts which abolished all militia organizations in the Southern states.

[1] The telegram to Schurz is printed in the *Chicago Tribune* of Aug. 13, 1865.

[2] Sharkey's correspondence, p. 231.

[3] *Chicago Tribune*, September 12.

[4] The order is printed in the *Chicago Tribune* of Sept. 12, 1865. It is as follows : —

"WAR DEPARTMENT, WASHINGTON, Sept. 2.

"MAJOR GENERAL SLOCUM: Upon the 19th of August Governor Sharkey issued a proclamation calling for the formation of militia companies in each county to detect criminals, punish them, and preserve good order in places where the military forces of the United States were insufficient. If you have issued any order countermanding this proclamation or interfering with its execution, you will at once revoke the same. Acknowledge the receipt of this order, and telegraph your action.

"By order of the President of the United States.

"T. T. ECKERT, *Secretary of War.*"

[5] *Chicago Tribune*, Sept. 12, 1865.

The charge that the militia in its efforts to suppress crime did not always proceed according to due process of law seems not to have been entirely without foundation. By a proclamation of November 3, 1865, Governor Humphreys warned militia commanders that it was their duty to aid the civil authorities in the suppression of crime, and not to take the law into their own hands and act as judge and jury. Oppression, he said, toward any class of the people was contrary to law and to good policy.[1]

A constant source of friction between the civil and military power was the presence of negro troops in the state.[2] Many and earnest were the appeals to the President to order their removal and the substitution of white troops. There was a natural feeling of humiliation on the part of the whites in being ordered about by negro troops, and it was alleged, moreover, that poor discipline was maintained among them, and that they sometimes even plundered and robbed the citizens.[3] A noisy, boisterous squad of colored troops on the public square of a village never failed to arouse the angry passions of the whites, and often led to altercations.

On the 25th of August the President telegraphed Governor

---

[1] The proclamation is printed in the *New York Times* of Nov. 19, 1865. The *Holmesville* (Miss.) *Independent* of Dec. 3, 1865, contains a proclamation by a militia commander complaining that certain persons not belonging to any regularly organized militia company were shooting negroes on "private account." The order was widely circulated by the opponents of the militia, who said it was a virtual admission that shooting negroes was an exclusive prerogative of the militia.

[2] The mustering out of the Sixteenth Corps at Vicksburg on August 1 left only a few white troops in the state, The President, on Jan. 5, 1866, informed the House of Representatives that there were 39 white commissioned officers in the volunteer service in Mississippi and 338 negro officers, and that the total number of enlisted men was 1071 whites and 8784 blacks, making a total of 10,193. There were no regular troops in the state. Ex. Docs. 1865–1866, No. 71, p. 3.

[3] This allegation seems to have been partly sustained by the testimony of District Commander General Wood. In his report he says : " The diffusion of troops at many posts under inexperienced and negligent commanders, more especially if the posts occupied are surrounded by a large population of citizens, is one of the greatest enemies to efficiency and discipline. Looseness of discipline leads to many and useless conflicts with the citizens, and many complaints from the latter of outrages and lawlessness on the part of the troops are the necessary consequence." Report Sec. War, 1866–1867, p. 51.

An example of their treatment of the whites was the action of a company at Raymond in suspending a United States flag over the sidewalk and compelling the school children to pass under it on their way to and from school. *Hinds County Gazette*, Oct. 28, 1865.

A negro officer while on a public mission in Summit, Pike County, had the brass buttons and shoulder straps cut from his coat in broad daylight by two white men who gave him an hour to leave the town. Report of J. H. Mathews, Sub. Com. 1st Ses. 39th Cong. p. 146.

Sharkey in regard to negro troops " which seem to be producing so much dissatisfaction," that the government did not
intend to irritate or humiliate the people of the South, but
would be magnanimous and remove the cause of their
complaint at the earliest period practicable.[1]

Sharkey's successor seems to have regarded the removal
of negro troops as the chief end of his administration. He
represented to the President that the negro garrisons " did
infinite mischief by misrepresenting the purposes and intentions of the state government, and by circulating reports
among the freedmen that the lands would be divided among
them, and by advising them not to work for their late
masters."[2] He said, " I have yet to learn that United
States troops are needed in Mississippi to restore order.
On the other hand, I have found them a disturbing element,
a nuisance, and a blighting curse to the quiet and happiness
of both races."

The governor finally sent a special commission to Washington " to lay before the President the condition of affairs
as regards negro troops and the danger of insurrection"
among them, to secure if possible their removal, and to procure arms for the state militia.[3] In reply to a memorial of
the legislature, the President wrote on November 14 to the
governor-elect that the troops would be withdrawn from
Mississippi when, in the opinion of the government, peace,
order, and the civil authority could be maintained without
them. " Every step," said he, " will be taken while they are
there to enforce strict discipline and subordination to the
civil authority, and there can be no greater assurance than
has really been given."[4]

The conduct of the white officers who generally commanded the negro troops was not always above reproach, and
they were, to some extent, responsible for the conduct of the
private soldiers. General Wood reported that one of the
chief sources of complaint from the white citizens was the conduct of the white officers in neglecting their duties to " dab-
ble " in cotton alleged to have belonged to the Confederacy.

---

[1] Correspondence of Provisional Governor Sharkey, p. 60.

[2] In reply to a remonstrance from the provisional governor of South Carolina, Seward wrote on the 26th of August informing him that the colored soldiers were soldiers in the United States army, and that no discrimination
founded on color was intended or could be made by the government in the
assignment to service. Cor. Prov. Gov. Sharkey, 116.

[3] House Journal, 1865, p. 376.

[4] Savage's Life of Johnson, Appendix, p. 107.

The abuse became so great that he was compelled to issue an order forbidding the officers from engaging in the traffic.[1] It was also a general complaint that white officers inflamed the minds of the negroes by making "incendiary" speeches to them. They advised the negroes not to work for their old masters unless assured of good wages, and to resist by force every infringement of their rights and liberties. The commander of a colored regiment at Jackson is alleged to have told an audience of negroes that they must defend their rights even to the "click of the pistol, and at the point of the bayonet."[2] The President was deluged with representations of this nature from private citizens, from the governor, and from the legislature. On November 17 he wrote in reply to an appeal for the removal of negro troops : "The people of Mississippi may feel well assured that there is no disposition on the part of the government to dictate arbitrarily what action should be had ; but, on the contrary, to supply and kindly advise a policy that it is believed will result in restoring all the relations which should exist between the states comprising the Federal union."

"It is hoped that they will appreciate and feel the suggestions herein made, for they are offered in that spirit which should pervade the bosom of all those who desire peace and harmony, and a thorough restoration of the Union. There must be confidence between the government and the states, and while the government confides in the people, the people must have faith in the government. This must be mutual and reciprocal, or all that has been done will be thrown away."[3]

Early in January, General Wood was asked by the commanding general if, in his opinion, the number of troops in Mississippi could be reduced consistent with a due regard to the enforcement of the laws, the preservation of order, and the protection of life, liberty, and property. General Wood, in reply, recommended the withdrawal of seven of the negro regiments.[4] The authority to muster them out was imme-

---

[1] Report of Secretary of War, 1866–1867, p. 51.

[2] New York Herald, Nov. 13, 1865. The Jackson News, commenting on this address, declared it to be of such a character as would have secured a coat of tar and feathers, if nothing more, in times past. "We are entitled," it said, "to peace, and we demand the removal of the negro troops from our midst. We hope this matter will be fully investigated, and if the United States cannot and will not protect us from such outrages, we must protect ourselves." Quoted in Chicago Tribune of Nov. 17, 1865.

[3] New York Herald, Nov. 26, 1865.

[4] Report of General Wood in Report of Secretary of War, 1866–1867, p. 52.

diately granted, but before they could be collected at the points at which the mustering out was to take place, an order was received from the War Department suspending the former order, and directing that they be retained in the service to work on the levees of the Mississippi. Under this arrangement, the colored regiments remained in the service until February, but were never called for by the officer in charge of the work. About the middle of March they were mustered out, greatly to the satisfaction of the white inhabitants. In the month of April, an order came directing General Wood to muster out the remaining negro regiments, and by the 20th of May, 1866, all negro troops in Mississippi had been removed. This left but one small battalion of regular infantry.

The governor took great pleasure in congratulating the legislature in October on the removal of the negro troops, and the transfer of the Freedmen's Bureau to the control of officers of the regular army. The whites were now, he said, relieved from the "insults, irritations, and spoliations to which they were so often subjected," and the negroes from the "demoralization which was fast sinking them into habits of pauperism, idleness, and crime."

In February, through the influence of General Wood, the district organization of the state was abolished, and post commanders were required to report direct to the department commander, the records of the district being at the same time transferred to Vicksburg. General Wood was anxious to simplify the somewhat complex military organization then existing, for he believed that he could thereby maintain better discipline. He had the Department of Mississippi abolished in August, 1866, and the state erected into a command called the district of Mississippi, with five companies of troops at Vicksburg, one at Natchez, one at Jackson, and one at Grenada. To enforce rigid discipline and to prevent outrages on the citizens and unnecessary conflicts with them, he ordered troops to remain in their camps and cantonments when not absent on duty, and to receive tactical instruction twice a day of not less than one hour at each lesson. These, and other regulations of General Wood, brought about an improvement in discipline and a reduction in the number of complaints of outrages. His administration in Mississippi was the subject of favorable comment by the press of the state.[1] He advised the freed-

[1] The *Clarion* of Feb. 11, 1866, said: "It is gratifying to record the pleasant fact that we have for a department commander one who is so universally

men in counties not permanently under martial law to resort to the civil courts for a redress of their grievances. At the same time the civil authorities were informed, respectfully but firmly, that state laws making discriminations between citizens on account of color and race could not be enforced, and that all prosecutions or suits growing out of events connected with the late war were strictly prohibited. The higher executive and judicial officers of the state, as a rule, admitted the justice of his order, and as a consequence, no serious conflicts between the civil and military occurred.[1]

In December, 1866, Governor Humphreys applied to General Wood for permission to disarm the freedmen of the state in conformity with the state law prohibiting them from carrying arms without special licenses. It was currently believed that there was to be a negro insurrection about Christmas time. The freedmen had conceived the notion that the government intended to divide the lands of their late masters among them as a sort of Christmas present. Governor Humphreys believed that when the negroes discovered their mistake, they would rise against the whites and inaugurate a general massacre. General Wood, believing that there was no ground for this apprehension, and regarding the state law prohibiting freedmen from bearing arms as unjust and unconstitutional, declined to give his

kind to our people and considerate of their rights. We are convinced that the principles that animate him are of the purest character, and that he has at heart the honor and welfare of the whole nation." The *Vicksburg Herald* said that he had proved himself to be a high-toned and fair-minded gentleman in his dealings with the citizens, while he had never been remiss in the duties he owed to the government.

[1] Correspondence of Governor Sharkey, p. 54. General Wood in his report said: " Most of the suits or prosecutions prohibited by military orders or laws of the United States and of cases arising under the laws of the state making discriminations on account of race or color, have been adjusted either by equitable decisions in the state courts, or by transfer, under the act of Congress approved May 11, 1866, to the courts of the United States, and I think it is not going too far to say that substantial justice is now administered throughout the state by the local judicial tribunals to all classes of persons, irrespective of race or color, or antecedent political opinions. It is unfortunately too true that many outrages and crimes have been committed by the vicious and criminal upon the weak, and that these crimes have in many cases gone unpunished. But when it is remembered what a terrible social, political, and military convulsion the nation has passed through in the war of the Rebellion, when it is borne in mind what a vast population of slaves was suddenly emancipated by the violence of war, and that the late slaves now occupy as freed people the very same soil, in the closest juxtaposition to the formerly dominant class, on which the two races lived in the relation of master and slave, it should not, perhaps, be a matter of surprise that so many outrages and crimes occur and go unpunished, but rather a matter of marvel that so few occur."

assent to the proposed disarmament.   He informed the governor, however, that his request should be submitted to the President for such action as he might choose to take. General Wood's position was sustained by the President. Governor Humphreys then issued an order directing the state militia not to attempt to enforce that statute.[1]

IV. THE STATUS OF THE FREEDMEN

The suggestion of President Johnson that, if the Mississippi convention could extend the elective franchise to persons of color who were able to read the Constitution of the United States, and to those who owned real estate of a certain amount, it would " completely disarm the adversary," does not appear from the published debates to have received any attention whatever from that body.   It is highly probable that the unanimous sentiment of the convention was against the idea of political rights for the negro in any form.   But his freedom being accomplished, it was necessary to confer upon him the civil rights incident to such freedom, one of which was the right to testify before the courts.   It will be remembered that at this time negro testimony was not allowed in the civil courts, not even in cases in which the negro was a party litigant, although it was a common law right.[2]   On account of this it was alleged to be difficult to convict white men of maltreating negroes, and consequently the military authorities of the United States had adopted the practice of removing all cases in which negroes were involved, from the civil courts to military tribunals under the management of the Freedmen's Bureau.   This was a source of great irritation to the whites.   The bureau officials were charged with abusing this power, and in some cases they, no doubt, screened black criminals from just punishment.[3]

[1] Correspondence of Governor Sharkey, p. 54.   General Wood took occasion to say that during his administration of military affairs in Mississippi the civil governor heartily coöperated with him in every effort to secure the restoration of law, order, and prosperity among the people, and for the enforcement of strict and impartial justice to all classes.

[2] It appears that the first official to admit negro testimony in his court was the mayor of Vicksburg.   His action was the subject of a great outcry upon the part of those opposed to negro evidence, and the *Jackson News* demanded that Governor Sharkey remove him from office.

[3] General Slocum had to issue an order to correct alleged abuses of this kind.   Sen. Docs. 1st Ses. 39th Cong. p. 19.

On September 20, Colonel Samuel Thomas, assistant commissioner of the Freedmen's Bureau, proposed to Governor Sharkey to transfer to the civil authorities the right to try all cases in which the rights of freedmen were involved, upon condition that the judicial officers and magistrates of the provisional government would take for their mode of procedure the laws then in force, except in so far as they made a distinction on account of color, and allow negroes the same rights and privileges as were accorded to white men before the courts.   This meant that they were to have the rights of bringing suit and of giving testimony.[1] Governor Sharkey informed Colonel Thomas that in his opinion the negro could already sue and be sued in any court of the state as a result of the action of the convention in abolishing slavery, one incident to their right of person and property guaranteed by the Constitution of the United States being their competency to testify before any court of justice.[2]

On September 25, Governor Sharkey issued a proclamation reciting Colonel Thomas's proposition, and expressed a belief that the abolition of slavery carried with it the abolition of all laws which constituted a part of the system and established principles of slavery, a fact which entitled the negro to sue and be sued, and to testify in the courts.   In order, therefore, to secure to the people of the state the right of trial before their own officers and under their own laws, rather than by military tribunals and by military law, he ordered that in all civil and criminal trials in which the rights of freedmen were involved, either for injuries done their person or property, or in matters of contract, their testimony should be received, subject to the rules of evidence as regarded competency and credibility in the case of white witnesses.   He announced his acceptance of Colonel Thomas's proposition, and requested that no freedman's court should thereafter be organized, and that those already in existence be closed, and instructed to transfer the cases pending before them to the civil authorities.[3]

---

[1] *Chicago Tribune*, Oct. 12, 1865.

[2] Sharkey's letter to Thomas is published in the *Chicago Tribune* of Oct. 10, 1865.

[3] *Chicago Tribune*, October 12.   The *Tribune* of October 6 announced that the mayor of Vicksburg, a "secessionist," was allowing negro testimony in his courts, and had agreed to impose the same penalties on the whites as on the negroes, whereupon the bureau officials were instructed to interfere in no case with the city officials in the discharge of their duties, but to turn over to them all cases in which the rights of negroes were involved.

Sharkey's arrangement with Colonel Thomas was not very popular with the whites, who, as much as they disliked to be tried before military courts in their controversies with freedmen, disliked still more the admission of negro testimony to the civil courts, which it was believed would practically destroy their usefulness. There was, however, a comforting thought among the opponents of negro testimony, namely, that the "bargain" between Sharkey and Thomas had only temporary force, and the legislature soon to be elected might set it aside. As already pointed out in another connection, this was the principal issue in the campaign for the election of state and local officers. It was also pointed out that those opposed to negro testimony secured a majority of the seats in the legislature. It remained now to see what policy the legislature would pursue. It met October 16, and on the same day Humphreys was inaugurated. With regard to the status of the freedmen he said in his inaugural: "The highest degree of elevation in the scale of civilization to which they are capable morally and intellectually must be secured to them by education and religious training; but they cannot be admitted to political or social equality with the white race. It is due to ourselves and to the white immigrants invited to our shores, and it should never be forgotten to maintain the fact, that ours is and it shall ever be, a government of white men." He urged that the state deal justly with them, but that they should be required to choose some employment that would insure the maintenance of themselves and families, and that they should be compelled to fulfil their labor contracts.[1] On the 20th, he sent in a message in which he declared that the people of Mississippi, under the pressure of Federal bayonets, and urged on by the misdirected sympathies of the world in behalf of the African, had abolished slavery, and had solemnly enjoined upon the state legislature through their state constitution the duty of providing for the protection and security of the person and property of the freedman, and of guarding him and the state against any evils that might arise from his sudden emancipation. The negro, he said, was free, whether the people liked it or not, but freedom did not make him a citizen or entitle him to political or social equality with white men. The Constitution and justice, however, did entitle him to protection in his person and property, for which there could be no sure guarantee

---

[1] The inaugural address is printed in Appleton's Cyclop. for 1865, and in the *New York Herald* of October 29.

without an independent and enlightened judiciary. "The courts, therefore," he continued, "should be opened to the negro, and he be permitted to testify and introduce such testimony as he or his attorney may deem essential to establish the truth of his case. It is an injustice to our courts and juries to say that they will not protect innocent white or black men from false testimony and the perjury of black witnesses." [1]

The President's views in regard to the status of the freedmen were well known to the governor and the legislature. It is clear from the President's correspondence with Sharkey that the grant of political as well as civil rights in a limited form to the negro was a part of his policy of reconstruction. As early as the 21st of August he had urged Sharkey to have the convention ratify the Thirteenth Amendment, or recommend it to the legislature for ratification. He advised "promptness and circumspection" on this point, and declared that the proceedings in Mississippi would exert a powerful influence on the other states which were to act afterward. [2] But notwithstanding the well-known wishes of the President, the governor failed to say anything concerning the ratification of the Thirteenth Amendment, which no doubt would have gone very far toward securing favorable action upon it, and consequently the success of the presidential policy of reconstruction.

After listening to the governor's message, the legislature received the report of the special committee appointed by the convention to prepare such laws and amendments as might seem expedient in view of the abolition of slavery. The committee reported that its labors had been made difficult by the incorporation among them of a large class of freedmen afflicted with " poverty of mind, poverty of thought,

[1] Relative to Humphreys' message on negro testimony the *New York Times* of December 3 said : " The recommendations are sensible and practicable, but were made with a wry face and with bad grace. He accepts the abolition of slavery fully and without reserve, but could not avoid saying it was done under pressure of Federal bayonets." The message is printed in full in the *Chicago Tribune* of Nov. 30, 1865, and in the *New York Times* of Dec. 3, 1865.

[2] Again, on the first of November, the President telegraphed Governor Sharkey that " The action of the Mississippi legislature is looked forward to with great interest at this time, and a failure to act will create the belief that the act of your convention abolishing slavery will hereafter be revoked. The argument is, If the convention abolished slavery in good faith, why then should the legislature hesitate to make it a part of the Constitution of the United States ? " He told the governor that he trusted in God that the legislature would adopt it and make the way clear for the admission of senators and representatives to their seats.

poverty of means, poverty of self-government, poverty of energy, and rich in idleness with all their miseries."

The committee declared that it had "labored earnestly to secure justice, employment, labor, income, reward, home, comfort, security, health, sobriety, good morals, and protection to person and property." The report recommended a series of measures by means of which it was hoped to meet "the alarming condition brought about by the emancipation of the colored race." "While some of the legislation," the report declared, "might seem rigid and stringent to the sickly modern humanitarians, it could never disturb or retard the good and true of either race." [1]

The legislature at once took up the recommendations of the governor and the committee, and pursuant to the spirit of both, passed a number of acts concerning the freedmen which have come down to us under the name of the "Black Code" of 1865. It is for the enactment of these measures that the legislature of 1865 is best known. One of these was an act to regulate the relation of master and apprentice as it related to freedmen, free negroes, and mulattoes. This act made it the duty of the civil officers to report to the probate courts of their respective counties, semi-annually, all negroes under eighteen years of age who were orphans, or who were without means of support, and the court was required to apprentice them, their former owners being given the preference when in the opinion of the court they were suitable or competent persons. Males were to be bound until they were twenty-one years of age, females, until eighteen. Masters were empowered to inflict moderate chastisement for misbehavior. They were entitled to judicial remedy for recovery of runaway apprentices, and it was made a penal offence to entice or persuade apprentices to run away. [2]

An act to prevent vagrancy provided that all freedmen, free negroes, and mulattoes in the state over the age of eighteen years, found on the second Monday of January, 1866, or thereafter, with no lawful employment or business, or found unlawfully assembling themselves together either in the day or night time, together with all white persons so assembling with them on terms of equality, or living in adultery or fornication with negro women, should be deemed vagrants,

---

[1] The report was written by the chairman, Mr. Hudson of Yazoo. It is printed in full in the *Chicago Tribune* of Oct. 26, 1865.
[2] Pamphlet Acts of 1865, p. 86.

and upon conviction should be fined, in case of a negro, not exceeding $50, and in case of a white man, not exceeding $200, and in addition, be imprisoned at the discretion of the court, not exceeding ten days for the negro, and six months for the white man.   Jurisdiction was conferred on all justices of the peace, mayors, and aldermen to try offenders against this law without a jury.   Upon the failure of the convicted party, if a negro, to pay within five days the fine imposed upon him, the sheriff was to hire him out for a sum equal to the amount of the fine.   If the offender could not be hired out, he was to be treated as a pauper.   It was also made the duty of the Board of Police in every county to levy a poll-tax not exceeding $1 on each negro between the age of eighteen and sixty, the sum to constitute a freedmen's pauper fund to be expended exclusively for the colored poor.   Failure to pay the tax was to be deemed *prima facie* evidence of vagrancy, and it was made the duty of the sheriff to arrest the offender and hire him out for the amount of the tax plus the costs.[1]

An act to confer civil rights on freedmen gave them the right to sue and be sued, to implead and be impleaded in all the courts of law and equity of the state, to acquire and hold personal property and dispose of it as white persons, but it was expressly provided that they could not rent or lease land except in incorporated towns or cities where the corporate authorities were empowered to control the privilege.   They were given the right to marry in the same manner, and under the same regulations as white persons, provided that the clerk should keep a separate record of their marriages. All negroes who had cohabited together, as husband and wife, were to be held as legally married, and their issue as legitimate.   Intermarriage between whites and negroes was punishable by life imprisonment in the penitentiary.[2]   The right to testify in the courts was granted freedmen, but only in cases in which they were a party, either as plaintiff or defendant, and in all cases their testimony was to be made subject to the rules and tests of the common law, as to competency and credibility.   By another provision, they were

---

[1] Pamphlet Acts of 1865, p. 90.

[2] The first instance of intermarriage between the races in Mississippi occurred at Jackson in June, 1866. It was the case of a negro man and a white woman. They were tried in the circuit court, found guilty, and sentenced to imprisonment in the county jail for six months, and to pay a fine of $500 each. The military officers looked on with interest while the judge commented upon the depravity of the woman, but they did not interfere. *Hinds County Gazette*, June 22, 1866.

required to have a lawful home or employment, and written evidence thereof, by the second Monday in January, following, and annually thereafter. If living in an incorporated town, freedmen were required to obtain a license from the mayor, if in the country, from a member of the Board of Police, authorizing them to do irregular job work, which license might be revoked at any time for good cause. All contracts with freedmen, for labor for a longer period of time than one month, were required to be made in writing, and in duplicate to be read to the freedman before an officer, or two disinterested white persons of the county, and if he should quit the service of his employer before expiration of his contract, without good cause, his wages for the time he had served were to be forfeited. Civil officers were required to arrest freedmen who should run away from their contracts, and carry them back to the place of employment. For making the arrest, the officer was to be entitled to $5.10 per mile for each mile intervening between the place of arrest and the place from which the offender escaped, the sum to be paid by the employer and held as a set-off for so much against the wages of the deserter. Attempts to persuade freedmen to quit the service of their employers were punishable by a heavy fine. Other stringent provisions were adopted to compel colored laborers to fulfil their contracts.[1] Another act prohibited them from carrying firearms, dirks, or knives. For disturbing the peace by engaging in riots, practising cruelty to animals, making seditious speeches, using insulting language or gestures, or for exercising the functions of a minister without a license from a regularly organized church, a fine of not less than ten or more than a hundred dollars was imposed, and the offender was liable to imprisonment not exceeding thirty days.[2]

The legislation in regard to freedmen was completed by the reënactment of all the penal and criminal laws applying to slaves, except so far as the mode and manner of trial and punishment had been altered by law. This legislation created a storm of opposition in the North. The various acts were printed entire in many newspapers, and severely commented upon by editors.[3] It was said that their enforcement

[1] Pamphlet Acts of 1865, p. 82.   [2] *Ibid.* p. 165.
[3] The *Chicago Tribune* of Dec. 1, 1865, said, relative to this legislation : " We tell the white men of Mississippi that the men of the North will convert the state of Mississippi into a frog pond before they will allow any such laws to disgrace one foot of soil in which the bones of our soldiers sleep and over which the flag of freedom waves."

would mean a reëstablishment of slavery in another form. The reënactment of the old slave code, they said, was a return to slavery pure and simple. The vagrant act applied only to negroes. Only the negro was required to have a home within a certain time. It deprived him of the ancient right of trial by jury. Offences that had no relation to idleness, as the non-payment of taxes, for example, were denominated vagrancy, and punished as such.

Such was the Northern view of the legislation of 1865. The unpopularity of this legislation was not confined to the North. The sentiment in favor of it was by no means unanimous in Mississippi. The *Clarion*, the most influential journal perhaps in the state, regarded the action of the legislature as in many respects " unfortunate," and expressed the hope that the legislature possessed patriotism and wisdom enough to correct the mistake.[1] The *Vicksburg Herald* said the legislature had failed to do its duty, and the convention should be reassembled.[2] Petitions with this end in view came to the president of the convention from many parts of the state. The *Columbus Sentinel* characterized those responsible for these measures as a " shallow-headed majority more anxious to make capital at home than to propitiate the powers at Washington." " They are," said the editor, " as complete a set of political Goths as were ever turned loose to work destruction upon a state. The fortunes of the whole South have been injured by their folly." [3] Judge Campbell expressed the opinion that some of their acts were " foolish," [4] and Judge Watson declared that they went "entirely too far " in the matter.[5]

Prohibiting the freedmen from renting land outside of towns and cities was clearly unwise. Moreover, the movement of negroes to the towns and cities was one of the special complaints of the whites at this time, and yet, strangely enough, their legislation, instead of encouraging the freedmen to rent land in the country, tended to drive them to the towns, where they must suffer from idleness, vice, and disease. It would clearly have been the part of expediency to allow them not only to rent land, but to acquire homes and own real estate in the country. The constitution of 1865 invested the freedmen with the right to acquire and hold property without any qualification or limit as to kind or character, and in some instances the local courts refused

---

[1] Issue of Jan. 7, 1866.   [2] Issue of Dec. 4, 1865.
[3] Quoted by the *Hinds County Gazette* of Dec. 23, 1865.
[4] Boutwell Report, 1876, p. 933.   [5] *Ibid.* p. 1000.

to be bound by the acts of the legislature. Allowing them
to testify only in cases in which they were parties seems to
have been unwise. If they were competent witnesses either
for the prosecution or defence in cases in which either
plaintiff or defendant was a white man and the other party
a negro, there was no good reason why they should not have
been permitted to testify when both parties were white.
This was not only illogical, but worked positive inconvenience and injury to white litigants. In cases in which both
parties were white, negro testimony was not allowable,
although it might have been the only evidence available.[1]
Manifestly such legislation at this time was folly. Those
who were responsible for it assuredly did not understand the
temper of the North.[2] It was such legislation as this, begun
in Mississippi and adopted in other Southern states, that led
the radicals, when Congress met in December, to set aside
President Johnson's reconstruction measures. It gave them
a pretext to subvert the partially reconstructed state governments and remand the South to despotic military rule.
They cited this action as proof sufficient that the South had
not accepted the abolition of slavery in good faith, and it
doubtless led some conservative Republicans to adopt the
view that immediate negro suffrage was a political necessity.

[1] Chief Justice Campbell, as good a lawyer as ever wrote a brief in Mississippi, while on the circuit bench, was one of the first judges to admit negro
testimony in his court. In October, 1865, a white man was convicted of murder in his court by a white jury upon negro testimony. The judge in pro-
nouncing sentence delivered an opinion that completely demolished the
arguments of those who criticised his action. He said : " The idea that it is
dangerous to admit negro testimony against whites, and that combinations
among freedmen to fabricate false testimony will result in unjust convictions,
will be dissipated in the mind of every sensible man who calmly reflects on
the fact that it is usually difficult to convict of crime even on the testimony
of whites, and that a jury of white men with all their knowledge of negro
character, jealousy of caste, and prejudice against this innovation in the law
of evidence, and a white judge with a court house crowded with white spec-
tators, with white men as attorneys on both sides, will not be likely to be
deceived and duped into improper convictions." His full opinion in this case
is printed in the *New York Times* of Oct. 11, 1865. Sharkey and Alcorn,
the two senators-elect, upon invitation delivered addresses before the legislature, and admonished the members that it was a matter of policy and justice
that the negro should be allowed to testify, and warned the legislature that
if they refused him the right, the United States government would extend it
to him. *New York Herald*, Nov. 6, 1865.

[2] S. S. Cox, one of the conservative Democratic leaders in Congress during
reconstruction times, said : " It is surprising that the intelligent men of Mississippi could have persuaded themselves, after the terrible experience through
which they had passed, that the triumphant North, now thoroughly imbued
with the anti-slavery sentiment, would for a moment tolerate this new slave
code." *Three Decades*, p. 395.

However, something should be said in explanation of these measures. The sudden emancipation of the slave population, and the too generous course of the government in furnishing them with the means of subsistence during their idleness, not only deranged the labor system of the South, but demoralized the colored laborers to such a degree that to the planters of the state in 1865 the outlook was disheartening. The freedman was made to believe that liberty meant license, that as he had been freed from slavery by a powerful government, he would also be clothed and fed by it whether he chose to labor or not. He was told by unscrupulous Freedmen's Bureau agents and negro soldiers that he ought not to work for his former master for any promise of compensation, that his freedom was not secure so long as he remained on the old plantation, and that the government in due time expected to confiscate the land of the late masters and divide it up among the slaves. As a result, the freedmen left the plantations and moved to the towns or military camps, refusing to make contracts or to fulfil them when made. The amount of robbery and larceny was alarming. The farmer's swine were stolen for pork, his cows were penned in the woods and milked, and his barns and cotton houses were broken open.[1]

If he was fortunate enough to procure laborers to plant his fields, he had no assurance that they would remain with him until the crop was harvested. In fact, it was almost certain that they would not. The legislature was made up for the most part of small planters, none of the able members of the convention having been chosen to seats in it. There was, however, a respectable minority of able men who made unanswerable arguments against such legislation. One of these was Judge Simrall, subsequently a justice of the Supreme Court. The time was unpropitious for calm and deliberate action. The condition of things seemed to demand the immediate adoption of measures to check the demoralization of the freedmen, and compel them to labor. Laws were passed, most of which, when impartially enforced, as they generally were, did not work injustice to the negro. Their purpose was to force him to cease his roving and become a producer. The law against vagrants was not more severe than those of

---

[1] Cotton stealing was so prevalent that the legislature passed an act at this session making it unlawful in some counties to send cotton to market except in bales, or to buy cotton after dark. If brought in bags it was *prima facie* evidence of being stolen cotton. Other measures were provided for checking the crime. See act of November 25, Laws of 1865, p. 168.

many Northern states.[1] The refusal of the legislature to accord the negro civil and political rights was, of course, due to prejudices and traditions which constituted a part of the very fabric of Southern society, and the sudden banishment of which was not an easy task.

On the 30th of November, General Howard telegraphed the assistant commissioner of the Freedman's Bureau that as long as the bureau remained in Mississippi it would continue to protect the freedmen in the right to lease lands, and that the act of the legislature denying them the right was not recognized at Washington as valid. He directed, furthermore, that an investigation be made in all cases where freedmen were arrested for violation of the above law, and the facts be reported to Washington, in order that prompt redress might be afforded. Thereupon the governor sent Judges Yerger and Acker to Washington, to lay before the President the measures of this legislature relating to freedmen, and to request him to indicate such as the military authorities would be allowed to disregard. He informed the legislature, October 1, 1866, that the President had assured him that none of the acts should be nullified except by the courts of law.

[1] At the time this legislation was enacted the statutes of Wisconsin denominated as "vagrants" all idle persons who had no visible means of support, and all persons wandering abroad and not giving a good account of themselves, or who begged bread from door to door. Vagrancy was punishable by imprisonment not exceeding ninety days. Revised Statutes of 1878, p. 465.

The New York statutes denominated such persons as "tramps," and upon conviction they were to be imprisoned at hard labor in the nearest penitentiary for a period not exceeding six months. Revised Statutes of 1881, Vol. III. p. 1898.

In Maine all persons who refused to work, or who had no ordinary calling or lawful business, were required to be sent to the workhouse. All vagabonds or idle persons going about begging in town or country, or neglecting their calling or employment, or misspending what they earned and not providing support for themselves and families, were imprisoned not exceeding six months. Revised Statutes of 1871, p. 260.

In Massachusetts the laws against vagrancy were almost identically the same as in Wisconsin. If any difference, they were more severe. Supp. to Gen. Stats. Vol. I. 1860–1872, ch. 235, p. 510.

In Indiana any person, male or female, over fourteen years of age, who had made no reasonable effort to procure employment, or who had refused to labor and was found begging from door to door, was subject to a fine of $50. Going about begging and asking subsistence was vagrancy. Revised Statutes of 1881.

In Connecticut all idle persons who had no means of supporting themselves, all beggars who wandered abroad from place to place without lawful business, and all who misspent what they earned, were subject to imprisonment at hard labor not exceeding sixty days. Revision of 1866, ch. 4, p. 642.

The legislature not only declined to confer upon the freedmen such civil and political rights as the President had
advised, but refused to accept the requirements of the congressional policy. On December 4, the joint standing-com-
mittee on state and Federal relations, to which had been
referred the documents and resolutions relative to the proposed Thirteenth Amendment, brought in a report in which
it was declared that the first and main article of the amendment had already been adopted by the state of Mississippi,
in so far as her own territory was concerned, and was a
part of her constitution in almost the same language as the
proposed amendment ; that it was not possible for the state
by any act or in any manner to change the status of the
slave as fixed by the convention ; that slavery had been
abolished in good faith ; the state would abide by it, and
consequently the adoption of the proposed amendment could
have no practical effect in Mississippi. The chief objection
was the second section, which empowered Congress to enact
the appropriate legislation to carry the first section into
effect. Slavery having been totally abolished, they said they
could see no necessity for this second provision. Slavery
existed legally nowhere in the United States except in
Kentucky and Delaware, and the Thirteenth Amendment was
not necessary to coerce the people of those states to abolish
it. Moreover, they said, the second section contained a
dangerous grant of power by the states at a time most
unpropitious for enlarging the powers of the Federal government. Besides, it was unwise and inexpedient to reopen a
subject which would afford a theme for radicals and demagogues to use against the best interests of the country, and
Mississippi was unwilling to give her deliberate consent to
leave any question open from which further agitation could
arise. The question of slavery being settled in all the states
except two, the public mind should be withdrawn from a
subject "so irritating in the past, and the door as effectively
closed against all future agitation as it was possible for
human wisdom to do." Such was the argument against the
ratification of the Thirteenth Amendment.

The report concluded : " Connected as the provisions are,
a ratification of the first and a rejection of the second would
be inoperative and of no effect, therefore the rejection of
both is recommended." The report was adopted.[1] This

[1] The *Vicksburg Herald* of November 9 asked : "Shall Mississippi ratify
the Thirteenth Amendment? We answer, *No !* ten thousand times, no !"
The editor was willing that the section abolishing slavery should be ratified,

was the second step in the defeat of President Johnson's plan of reconstruction. The proposed Fourteenth Amendment met the same fate the following year. The governor in transmitting it to the legislature said it had been proposed by a Congress of less than three-fourths of the states, in "palpable violation" of the rights of more than one-fourth of the states ; that it was an "insulting outrage," and a denial of the equal rights of so many worthy citizens who had shed glory and lustre upon their race and section, both in the forum and in the field ; that it was such a gross usurpation of their rights that a mere reading of it would cause the legislature to reject it. He recommended its rejection, and the legislature unanimously adopted the recommendation.[1]

Governor Sharkey, who had asked to be relieved from the duties of provisional governor at the time of Humphreys' inauguration on October 16, was informed by Seward on the 14th of December that the time had come when, in the judgment of the President, the care and conduct of affairs in Mississippi might be remitted to the properly constituted authorities, chosen by the people thereof, without danger to the peace and safety of the United States.

He was instructed to transfer the papers and property of the state, then in his custody, to Governor Humphreys. The President acknowledged the fidelity, loyalty, and discretion which had marked the governor's administration. On the same day, the President sent a despatch to Governor Humphreys tendering him the coöperation of the United States government, whenever it might be found necessary in effecting the early restoration and the permanent prosperity and welfare of the state of Mississippi. This completed the reconstruction of the state according to the presidential policy.

but not the section empowering Congress to enact the legislation necessary to carry into effect the first.

[1] Senator-elect Sharkey, in a letter to Humphreys, dated Washington, Sept. 17, 1866, advised against the ratification of the Fourteenth Amendment on the ground that it had not been proposed by two-thirds of the Congress of the United States. *New York Herald*, Oct. 6, 1866.

CHAPTER FOURTH

The Economic Aspects of Reconstruction

I. ECONOMIC PROBLEMS

As a result of the events described in some of the preceding chapters, one would naturally not expect the economic outlook to have been very encouraging at the beginning of reconstruction. The people were generally impoverished; the farms had gone to waste, the fences having been destroyed by the armies or having decayed from neglect; the fields were covered with weeds and bushes; farm implements and tools were gone; live stock had disappeared so that there were barely enough farm animals to meet the demands of agriculture; business was at a standstill; banks and commercial agencies had either suspended or closed on account of insolvency; the currency was in a wretched condition; the disbanded Confederate soldiers returned to their homes to find desolation and starvation staring them in the face; there was no railway or postal system worth speaking of; only here and there was a newspaper still running; the labor system in vogue since the establishment of the colonies was completely overturned, and the laborers were wandering aimlessly about the country refusing to perform their accustomed toil. Worse than all this, was the fact that about one-third of the white breadwinners of the state had either been sacrificed in the contest or were disabled for life, so that they could no longer be considered as factors in the work of economic reorganization.[1] Another class of dependents were the widows and orphans, the support of whom claimed a no inconsiderable share of the state's bounty during the reconstruction period. The number of dependent orphans alone was estimated to be ten thousand.[2] Many of the women

---

[1] According to one authority, of the 78,000 troops furnished by Mississippi to the Confederate army, 12,000 were killed or died of wounds received, and 16,000 died of disease contracted while in the service. *Hinds County Gazette*, Feb. 2, 1866.

[2] Appeal of Rev. C. K. Marshall in *New York Times* of Feb. 27, 1866.

had never been accustomed to perform domestic service, and consequently found themselves at a great disadvantage in the struggle which now ensued.[1] There was hardly a home in the state in which there was not mourning for some member of the family who had been killed in the war. A Northern newspaper correspondent said it looked as if one-half the adult males of the state had disappeared. A family that had not lost a member was an anomaly, and, for the most part, those who had fallen were the young and vigorous, who were so much needed in the work of economic reorganization. A traveller, who was present at a meeting of three hundred people in the town of Aberdeen in 1865, declared that at least one-third of them had lost either a leg or an arm, while one-half of the remainder bore unmistakable evidences of severe campaigning. To supply this class of persons with artificial limbs, one-fifth of the state revenues were appropriated in 1866. Another traveller found only five hundred of the original inhabitants in the town of Corinth, these being chiefly women and children and old men. Instead of shops, stores, and warehouses, he saw only fortifications and piles of débris. Still another tells a pathetic story of an incident which came under his observation in July, 1865, while visiting the home of an old citizen in Monroe County. Ten years before, the traveller had known the man in question as the possessor of a happy home of five sons and two daughters. Upon inquiry as to the whereabouts of the eldest son, he was informed that the son had been killed at Shiloh. The second son had died of smallpox in the army, and all the others had either been killed in battle or had died of disease contracted while in the service. The two daughters whom he had known in 1855 as charming girls of thirteen and seventeen respectively were both dressed in mourning, each having lost a husband in the war. The mother, heartbroken with grief, had died a raving maniac. A more pathetic sight than this aged survivor, who wept bitterly as he spoke of his bereavements, would be difficult to imagine, yet the desolation of this household had its counterpart in thousands of others in the state. Our traveller records that as he continued his journey through a part of the state which he had known years before, he found here and there an old man occupying the former mansion ; but

---

[1] A Northern gentleman relates that while travelling in Smith County in 1865 he found a woman and four daughters who had never cooked a meal in their lives. They had flour but could not make bread, and cows which they could not milk.

in the place of the feast there was famine, and in the place
of enjoyment there was sadness.[1]

The state census of 1866 furnishes some interesting facts
concerning the effect of the war upon the population of the
state. It appears that between 1860 and 1866 there was a
decrease in population of 66,585, and what seems strange, the
proportional decrease among the blacks was more than four
times that of the whites, the decrease among the whites being less than 3 per cent, while that of the blacks was about
13 per cent. The following exhibit tabulated from the
United States census of 1860 and the state census of 1866
is given in illustration: —

White population, 1860	353,899
" " 1866	343,400
Decrease	10,499
Black population, 1860	437,404
" " 1866	381,258
Decrease	56,146

The census returns showed that Hinds County alone had
4000 fewer negroes than at the beginning of the war.
What became of the 56,146 negroes puzzled those of the
North who reflected upon the question. The Southerners
said they had died from disease and starvation resulting from
their sudden emancipation, and the explanation was not entirely without foundation. Governor Humphreys relates
that he had 59 juvenile blacks at the close of the war, and
only about 20 survived the "hardships" of emancipation.
Governor Sharkey told the reconstruction committee in
1866 that one-half the negroes of the state had perished since
the close of the war, and he was positive that the race was
doomed to an early extinction. Ludicrous as Sharkey's
prophecy may seem now, it is certain that the condition of
the blacks in 1865 did not present a very hopeful prospect
for their future.

When it comes to reckoning up the economic loss apart
from the population, the student encounters great difficulty
in reaching any intelligible results. Besides the destruction
of the railroads with their rolling stock, the levees, fences,
bridges, public and private buildings, growing crops, saw
and grist mills, factories, machine shops, and live stock, there
was the emancipation of the slaves, which is generally counted

[1] Letter in *Chicago Tribune* of Aug. 25, 1865.

as one of the items in the loss account. The assessed value of personalty (including slaves) in 1860 was $351,636,175 ; in 1870 it was $59,000,430.[1] During the same time the value of realty decreased from $157,836,737 to $118,278,460. The figures for 1866 are not available. A local authority estimates the actual loss in one county (Hinds) as follows:[2] —

22,353 slaves emancipated	$11,176,000
200 buildings burned	600,000
Growing crops destroyed	500,000
10,000 bales of cotton burned	3,000,000
Vehicles, furniture, etc., destroyed . . .	200,000
Stores, barns, etc.	250,000
Live stock carried away	2,000,000
Depreciation in value of lands	10,000,000
Total	$25,926,000

The estimate is based upon no actual records of property destroyed, and is no doubt largely in excess of the real amount. However this may be, Hinds County suffered much from the ravages of the armies, and the actual loss did probably reach several million dollars, independently of the emancipation of the slaves. The following exhibit from the United States census and the estimates of the Department of Agriculture, imperfect as it may be, furnishes some idea of the economic situation in 1866:[3] —

	1860.	1866.
Number of horses	117,570	69,355
" mules	110,723	71,316
" oxen and other cattle . .	522,263	401,110
" sheep	352,632	253,895
" swine	1,532,768	717,884
Value of live stock	$41,891,692	$23,530,710

The statistics relative to the production of cotton in 1866 are not available, but it is significant that the cotton crop, which in 1860 amounted to 1,202,507 bales, as late as 1870 had reached only 565,559 bales.

The condition in which the war left the levees along the banks of the Mississippi River may be cited as another illus-

---

[1] In 1860 the number of slaves was 436,631, valued at $218,000,000.
[2] *Hinds County Gazette*, Feb. 2, 1866.
[3] Report Dept. of Agr. 1860, p. 105 ; *ibid.* 1866–1867, pp. 57, 68 ; Compendium Ninth Census, p. 752.

tration of its economic effects. At the outbreak of hostilities,
310 miles of continuous levees stretched from the base of the
hills near the Tennessee line to Brunswick Landing in Warren County, protecting from overflows the Yazoo basin comprising 4,000,000 acres of as fertile land as there is on
the globe, and constituting the heart of the cotton zone of
the United States. Although sparsely settled, this region
in 1860 produced 220,000 bales of cotton and 2,500,000
bushels of corn.[1] During the progress of hostilities the
levees which protected it were cut in many places by one or
the other of the contending armies. The floods of 1867 completed the destruction, so that by 1870 many of the hitherto
well-kept farms were covered with weeds and bushes, while
the steamboats lay idle at the wharves along the Yazoo and
Tallahatchie rivers. With the reëstablishment of civil government in 1870, the country was divided into levee districts,
placed under the jurisdiction of levee boards which were
empowered to assess taxes on cotton and land, and employ
engineers to superintend the reconstruction of the levees.
This was one of the chief problems of economic reconstruction.

The war played quite as much havoc with the printing-
presses as with the railroads and levees. Upon the approach
of the Union army, the newspaper establishments were usually removed to less exposed districts, where publication was
sometimes continued, but more often suspended. It often
happened, however, that owing to the suddenness with
which a detachment of Federal cavalry would swoop into a
village, the unsuspecting editor was prevented from removing his type to a place of safety. In some instances the
presses were destroyed, and the type thrown into a neighboring well or river, or, as in the case of the *Jackson Mississippian*, scattered about the streets and tramped into the mud.
Sometimes presses were taken possession of, and the paper
continued to the end of the war as a Union sheet by some
of the soldiers. This was the case with the *Vicksburg
Citizen*, the *Natchez Courier*, and a Corinth paper. In one
case a press captured at Jackson by the Sixteenth Infantry
was carried away and kept for the use of the army. It
is still in possession of that regiment, and at present is
doing duty in the Philippine Islands.[2] A local authority
says the "events of the war" reduced the number of papers
in the state from fifty to about one dozen, most of which

---

[1] Memorial to Congress, H. Mis. Docs. 1867–1868, No. 14.
[2] *New York Times*, Feb. 11, 1901.

were "half sheets," and that in November, 1865, only four-teen were running.[1] However, with the return of peace a perfect mania for the establishment of newspapers took possession of the people, and by April, 1866, fifty were in operation, ten of them being dailies.

One of the largest items in the loss account was the cap-ture or destruction of cotton. The records of the United States Claims Commission furnish an imperfect idea of the amount seized by the Union forces. No records of the amount destroyed by the Confederate forces are available to the writer. The Confederate government, at one time or another, owned 127,341 bales in Mississippi valued at $7,947,455.[2] It was held as security for loans, and was generally stored on the plantations waiting for the removal of the blockade so that it could be exported. Much of this, as well as cotton not belonging to the Confederacy, was captured by the military forces of the United States. The amount of Confederate cotton thus seized in Mississippi was estimated at 60,000 bales, or nearly one-half the amount owned by the Confederacy in the state.[3] Of the remainder, some was removed to Texas, or burned to prevent capture, some was concealed in the woods or swamps where the bag-ging decayed from dampness, while a no inconsiderable part was sold by the slaves, at a nominal sum, to speculators who swarmed about the country. Private cotton seized was of three kinds: first, that abandoned by the owners upon the approach of the enemy; second, that captured in the course of military operations; and third, that confiscated on account of the use to which it was being put in aid of the Confederate cause. In the case of abandoned cotton, the owner was en-titled to recover its value if, upon the conclusion of peace, he could furnish satisfactory proof of loyalty throughout the war. The same was true of cotton improperly captured. Of course, nothing could be recovered for confiscated cotton.

It is difficult to ascertain with any degree of accuracy the amount of cotton seized by the government under each of these heads. The report of the Secretary of the Treasury shows that *after* June 1, 1865, 36,898 bales were collected in Mississippi by the cotton agents. Most of it seems to have belonged to the class known as "captured" cotton, and was collected in the months of July, August, and September, 1865. About two-thirds of the amount was gathered in the

---

[1] *Hinds County Gazette*, Nov. 4, 1865.
[2] Ex. Docs. 39th Cong. 2d Ses. No. 97.
[3] H. Mis. Docs. No. 190, 44th Cong. 1st Ses. pp. 40–42.

counties of Noxubee, Lowndes, Oktibbeha, and Monroe.[1] These seizures were doubtless a small portion of the total amount which at one time or another passed into the possession of the United States. Between 1872 and 1878 claims were filed for $6,285,240 on this account.[2] Up to June 30, 1868, the Court of Claims had awarded to residents of Mississippi $890,227 for captured and abandoned property, the claimants in each case being able to satisfy the government of their loyalty or to adduce satisfactory proof that the property had been improperly seized. The bulk of it was captured in Coahoma, Claiborne, Jefferson, Noxubee, Newton, Hinds, Washington, Warren, and Yazoo counties.[3] During this period, a few claims from Mississippi amounting to less than one thousand bales were also adjudicated by the Secretary of the Treasury. In 1871, a commission was created by Congress to hear and determine all claims for cotton alleged to have been improperly seized by the United States authorities in the South. Claimants were compelled to establish positive proof of loyalty in order to secure an award. Residing in the Confederate lines as a matter of choice, voting for secession candidates, holding civil or military office under the Confederacy, furnishing it supplies, arming or equipping any person for its service, subscribing to its loans, selling cotton or any other produce to the Confederate authorities, or doing anything whatsoever to aid the Confederate cause, were, by the rulings of the commission, acts of disloyalty. The following exhibit shows the number of claims from Mississippi adjudicated by the commission, the amounts claimed, and the amounts allowed during each year of its existence: —

Year.	Amount claimed.	Amount allowed.
1872	$490,977	$108,975
1873	710,883	83,188
1874	1,097,617	147,251
1875	559,018	57,996
1876	711,760	54,833
1877	1,078,820	53,051
1878	391,262	26,210
1879	1,134,727	34,201

[1] Ex. Docs. No. 23, 43d Cong. 2d Ses. p. 58. The amount collected in Noxubee was 11,665 bales, in Lowndes 10,592 bales, in Monroe 6185 bales, in Oktibbeha 2168 bales.

[2] Tabulated from the seven annual reports of the United States Cotton Claims Commission.

[3] See Ex. Docs. 44th Cong. 1st Ses. No. 189. The total awards for all the Southern states was $9,545,293.

The court was aided in its labors by special claims commissioners in each state, whose duties were to administer oaths and to take testimony and forward it to Washington.[1] Four hundred and sixty-three claims for the value of 32,444 bales of cotton were filed before the commission by residents of Mississippi.[2] By an act of June 15, 1878, it was provided that all claims not reported should be forever barred thereafter. Five thousand seven hundred and two cases in all were left unadjudicated.

The total amount of the awards was, of course, a very small proportion of the value of the property destroyed. All claimants were regarded as *prima facie* disloyal during the war, and the burden of proof rested upon them to show the contrary. The history of a single one of these claims is herewith presented as an illustration of the difficulties which claimants had to confront.

On the 5th of October, 1864, Colonel Osband, the commander of a negro regiment, took possession of the house of Mr. Edward McGehee, a wealthy planter in Wilkinson County. McGehee says the negroes ransacked his house, became intoxicated from wine found in the cellar, insulted his family, struck him about the head and cursed him, demanded his money and valuables, and finally ordered him to remove his furniture, as they intended to burn his house. As he removed the furniture, they either stole it or chopped it to pieces with axes, so that nothing but a piano was saved. They then burned the dwelling-house, stables, and gin house, together with 350 bales of cotton, and evidences of debt amounting to $30,000. After the close of the war he filed a claim for $134,962. He testified that he was originally a Whig, and in all sectional or state-rights contests he was a Union man, that he had " earnestly and warmly opposed secession," but when secession became a fact he " acquiesced." The committee to whom his claim was referred reported that it did not appear from his testimony whether his sentiments and prayers were for the Union or for the Confederacy, and that he did not make out a case entitling him to relief. They asked to be discharged from further consideration of his claim.[3] A majority of these claims met a similar fate.

---

[1] The commissioners for Mississippi were E. P. Jacobson, I. V. Blackman, and J. T. Moseley.

[2] For the name of each claimant and the number of bales claimed, see Ex. Docs. 43d Cong. 2d Ses. No. 23, p. 58 *et seq.*

[3] Sen. Reports, 41st Cong. 2d Ses. No. 83.

As already intimated, the character of the currency was such as to materially hinder the work of speedy economic reconstruction. The circulating medium consisted chiefly of about four million dollars of "cotton notes" issued at the beginning of the war, and the notes issued by several of the railroads by permission of the legislature. After the surrender of Lee, the millions of state and Confederate treasury notes were of course worth nothing. There was also great uncertainty as to the status of the so-called "cotton money." It will be remembered that these notes were advanced in consideration of pledges for the delivery of an equivalent of cotton upon the demand of the governor, who was authorized to issue his proclamation for delivery as soon as the Federal blockade was raised. On the 8th of January, 1866, Governor Humphreys called upon all those to whom advances had been made to fulfil their promises and deliver the cotton at certain specified points. It was, of course, a great hardship, inasmuch as the cotton notes had fallen in value to fifteen or twenty cents on the dollar.[1] This proclamation had the effect, however, of causing a rise in the value of cotton money to seventy-five cents on the dollar, and speculators were soon doing a good business. There was still much uncertainty as to whether the act under which this money was issued was in aid of the Confederate cause or not. If the former was the case, the act would be declared unconstitutional, and the money would be worthless. Public opinion was divided on this question. The *Jackson News* advised the people not to be "humbugged" by purchasing or dealing in cotton money, said it was veritable trash, and not a dollar would ever be redeemed. The *Hinds County Gazette*, however, said the people did not believe in repudiation and dishonor, and that no court in Mississippi would hold the cotton notes void.[2] The editor congratulated an "old and valued friend" who had succeeded in buying $2500 worth in Jackson for thirty cents on the dollar. He declared that many persons were purchasing it to pay debts with, as they should do, and that one bale of cotton would buy enough to lift a debt of $2000.[3] The *News* was right. The Supreme Court held the cotton money act to be null and void, as being in "aid of the rebellion."[4] For ten years after the close of the war, the government of the state was conducted on a credit basis by means of "warrants," which ranged

---

[1] *Hinds County Gazette.*
[3] Issue of Feb. 2, 1866.
[2] Issue of Feb. 23, 1866.
[4] Thomas *vs.* Taylor, 42 Miss. 651.

in value from about forty cents on the dollar to ninety-nine cents in 1876.

Superadded to the difficulty of a deranged currency was the burden of paying two Federal taxes. The first of these was Mississippi's quota of the twenty million direct tax levied by Congress in 1861. The President had been authorized to collect the amount with accrued interest at 6 per cent at the close of the war. On July 1, 1862, in pursuance of an act of Congress, he imposed a penalty equal to 50 per cent of the quota on all states " in rebellion," the same to be a lien on the land thus taxed until paid.[1] By a subsequent act, the privilege of redemption was denied to any person who could not present a clean record for loyalty. The amount of Mississippi's quota, together with the penalty, was $413,000. The landowners complained that the mode of assessment would work a great hardship upon them, inasmuch as the tax was levied on property, the value of which was several times as great in 1862 as in 1865. Moreover, they said, $200,000,000 worth of slaves had been emancipated in the state since the imposition of the tax, and the vast amount of property destroyed by the authority of the United States in Mississippi, such as courthouses, penitentiaries, asylums, and other public buildings, should be made a partial offset to the tax. It was levied, they said, at a time when the state did not have a representative in Congress, the people were not able to pay, and it would consequently mean the confiscation of their lands. In view of these facts, Congress was asked to relieve the state from the payment of the tax, or at least from the penalty of 50 per cent ; or make a reasonable deduction for public property destroyed by the United States; or make a change in the mode of assessment and valuation ; or give a reasonable extension of the time for its payment and for the privilege of redeeming lands sold for non-payment of the tax.[2] By an act of July 2, 1866, the Secretary of the Treasury was directed to suspend the collection of the direct tax in the late seceded states until January 1, 1868. At the time of this act, $69,947 had been collected in Mississippi.[3] No lands in Mississippi were sold for non-payment of the tax.

The tax on cotton was levied in 1863, when, of course, none of the cotton-producing states had representatives in the

[1] Official Records, Series III. Vol. 3, Serial No. 124, p. 185.
[2] Laws of 1866, p. 267.
[3] Report Secretary of the Treasury, 1867–1868, p. 286.

Congress of the United States. A small amount was collected in 1863 and 1864, but what proportion of this came
from Mississippi does not appear from the reports of the
Commissioner of Internal Revenue. The following exhibit
shows the rate of the tax and the amount collected in
Mississippi for each year after the war so long as the law was
in operation : [1] —

Year.	Rate.	Amount.
1866	3 cents per lb.	$756,289
1867	2½ " "	4,640,664
1868	2¼ " "	3,521,702
		Total $8,918,655

The weight of this burden is only appreciated when it is remembered that the cotton crops of 1866 and 1867 were almost
failures. The amount contributed by Mississippi in 1867
and 1868 was six or eight times the expenditures of the state
government, and was estimated to be about one-fourth of the
value of the crops.[2] Moreover, there was a general feeling
that inasmuch as it was practically a tax on exports, the burden was in violation of the Constitution. The Secretary of
the Treasury recommended the repeal of the tax as a means
of restoring the productive power of the Southern states as
rapidly as possible. " Even in their deplorable condition,"
he said, " more than two-thirds of our exports last year consisted of their products, and it is the crop of the present
year (1867), small though it is, that is to save us from the
ruinous indebtedness to Europe." [3] For a time this view
was not acceptable to Congress, and, in fact, an attempt was

[1] Report Secretary of the Treasury, 1867–1868, p. 260.   The total amount
contributed by the Southern states in the form of a tax on cotton while they
were unrepresented in Congress was as follows : —

1863	.	.	.	.	$ 351,311
1864	.	.	.	.	1,268,412
1865	.	.	.	.	1,772,983
1866	.	.	.	.	18,409,654
1867	.	.	.	.	22,500,947
1868	.	.	.	.	23,769,078
	Total		.	.	$68,072,385

[2] Memorial H. Mis. Docs. 40th Cong. 2d Ses. No. 66.
[3] Report Secretary of the Treasury, 1867–1868, p. xxix.

made to increase the tax to five cents per pound. The New York Chamber of Commerce memorialized Congress against such a measure, declared that taxation without representation was tyranny, that the cotton tax was in spirit at least a violation of the Constitution, that the proposed increase " lacked an impartiality which was calculated to provoke hostility at the South," and instead of such measures Congress ought by just and generous legislation to seek "to lift up those cast down, and inspire them with hope of better days."[1] The tax was repealed in 1868. For a long time cotton planters carefully preserved their tax receipts in the belief that the amount collected from them would be returned.[2]

The deranged economic conditions, together with the general impoverishment, led to a demand on the legislature to stay for a time the collection of all debts. The legislature yielded to the pressure in 1866, and passed a law suspending all laws for the collection of debts until January 1, 1868. It was vetoed by the governor, passed over his veto, and subsequently declared unconstitutional by the Supreme Court. The *Hinds County Gazette* denounced the law as a ruinous measure, and declared that nineteen of every twenty men were opposed to it.

One of the chief economic problems of reconstruction was the readjustment of the labor system in conformity with the new conditions growing out of emancipation. Not one planter in ten believed that free negro labor could be made profitable. Carl Schurz relates that while on his tour of inspection through the South in 1865 every planter with whom he talked, without a solitary exception, declared emphatically that negroes would not work without compulsion. At the time these views were expressed, the negroes were taking a sort of protracted holiday. It was but a temporary impulse, and they soon returned to the plantations and begged for employment, although it will be admitted that their labor was of a very unreliable character. They refused to contract for the whole year, but insisted upon employment by the month, according to the rule established by the Freedmen's Bureau. This was of course a very inconvenient method for the cultivation of the cotton plant. On account of the moral certainty that the negro would make a change

[1] Sen. Mis. Docs. 39th Cong. 1st Ses. No. 109.
[2] The Supreme Court of the United States was divided in opinion as to the constitutionality of this tax, and no decision was ever reached. The opinion in the recent case of Coe *vs.* Errol, 116 U.S. 517, however, sustains a tax of this kind.

of employers at the end of the month, it was almost useless
to attempt a crop on such a plan.   For a while, in the
autumn of 1865, they refused to make contracts under any
circumstances, in the belief that the lands were to be divided
among them about Christmas time.   The *Jackson Clarion* of
December 2 declared that the question of labor for the coming year was getting to be "interesting," and, to be sure,
it looked very much as if the lands would lie idle if negro
labor was to be the only dependence of the planters.   In
this situation, the planters began to turn their attention to
the importation of white immigrants from the North or from
Europe.   The *Hinds County Gazette* advised the people to
form associations and send agents abroad for this purpose.
The advice was followed, and "immigrant clubs" were
formed in many communities.   A prominent planter of
Lowndes County said Columbus was "fairly alive" on the
subject, and that unless white laborers could be had, one-
third of the lands in the county would lie idle, and the
remainder would be poorly cultivated.   It was his opinion
that it would be cheaper to pay a German $25 per month
than a negro $12.50.[1]   A correspondent of the *Cincinnati
Commercial* said he had never seen such anxiety among the
Southern people for the introduction of white immigrants.
These movements met with very little success.   Of the
162,918 immigrants who arrived at New York between January 1 and October 3, 1865, but 21 found their way to Mississippi.   The outlook was so discouraging that quite a few of
the inhabitants prepared to emigrate to some of the Spanish-
American countries.   Some of the late Confederate generals
were the leaders of the emigration movement.[2]   General
Sterling Price wrote from Cordova, Mexico, in December
1865 :   "I pray to God that my fears for the future of the
South may never be realized, but when the right is given to
the negro to bring suit, testify before the courts, and vote in
elections, you all had better be in Mexico."[3]   General Jubal
A. Early, another Confederate soldier who had emigrated to
Mexico, gave, however, a discouraging view of the situation, and advised emigrants not to take their families.[4]
The Choctaw *Herald* of December 1, 1866, announced that
several families had left that county for Brazil, and that
they were "merely pioneers of a large colony" which was

---

[1] *De Bow's Review*, June, 1867, p. 585.
[2] The *Mexican Times* of Nov. 11, 1865, is quoted as containing a list of
fifty-one prominent Confederate soldiers who had taken up their abode in
Mexico.   [3] *De Bow's Review*.   [4] *Ibid.* 1866, p. 666.

preparing to move there. General Wood, formerly of Natchez, went to Brazil shortly after the close of the war, to make arrangements for transplanting a colony of Mississippians to that country. Upon his return to the United States, he published the result of his mission, relative to which the *Hinds County Gazette* said : " Sensible and practical men should not permit themselves to be led astray by such visionary men. Better submit and endure wrongs than be exiles in a foreign land."[1] The *Jackson Clarion* of July 25, 1867, published a letter from a returned emigrant who declared that the emigration movement was a " delusion gotten up for the benefit of speculators." As soon as it became evident that free negro labor could be made profitable, and that the admission of the negro to the witness stand and the jury box would not be accompanied by the terrible results predicted, the emigration movement died out entirely.

Although few immigrants came from Europe, there were causes at work which led to the immigration of that class of persons from the North which came later to bear the name of " carpet baggers." These causes were the cheapness of the lands and the high price of cotton. Many of these immigrants were soldiers in the Union army, who during their stay in Mississippi had been attracted by the prospects of great profit in cotton growing. At the close of hostilities, cotton was worth a dollar per pound, and land could be bought at a song. Newspapers contained whole columns of advertisements of plantations for sale at a " sacrifice." One pamphlet advertised a list of one hundred " fine plantations " at greatly reduced prices. One of these consisted of 2690 acres, of which 1100 were in cultivation, and a house which in 1859 cost $22,500 at the rate of $10 per acre.[2] A plantation three miles from Corinth was sold for 35 cents per acre. Commenting upon these facts, a local paper declared that a finer opening for legitimate speculation was never presented.[3] A correspondent of a Northern journal informed its readers that the cheapness of the lands " amazed " those who knew something of their value in former years; and to him the productiveness of the half-cultivated fields was even more amazing. The Union soldiers who settled in the state after being mustered out, made frequent appeals through private letters and through the press to their Northern friends to join them in the South. A colony of Ohioans in Noxubee and Lowndes coun-

---

[1] Issue of March 9, 1866.
[2] See list in *De Bow's Review*, December, 1866, p. 667.
[3] *Hinds County Gazette*, June 1, 1866.

ties addressed a communication to the *Cleveland Republican*, saying, "We should like to see more of our Buckeye friends turn their attention in this direction. The inducements offered far surpass anything in the West. Fine improved plantations, varying in size from 200 to 300 acres, convenient to the railroad, are offered at from $10 to $25 per acre ; improved and well-timbered tracts at from $3 to $8 per acre. Our treatment by the citizens has been uniformly kind, their conduct toward us has been open and generous, and we have many times been under obligation to them for kind services." The result of such representations was a considerable influx of Northern immigrants. The majority of them rented plantations, although in some instances they came as purchasers, and in others as common laborers. The belief was general among the Northern settlers that they could by the introduction of scientific methods revolutionize cotton planting. The impression also existed that in view of their relations to the negro race, free negro labor could be made to yield greater returns than where Southern whites were the employers. This, however, did not prove to be true. The remorseless energy and thrift of the Northern planter, and the exacting nature of the service which he demanded, did not appeal to the slow-going freedman, who was accustomed to the patience and forbearance of the Southerner. None of the planters were so quick to declaim upon the unreliability of negro labor as those who had helped to emancipate the negro.

So far as revolutionizing the methods of cotton culture was concerned, it is not too much to say that a majority of the Northern planters were unsuccessful, and with the inauguration of the reconstruction policy in 1867, they virtually abandoned the business and became office holders.[1] It is incorrect, therefore, to call them "carpet baggers." They did not go South to get offices, for there were no offices for them to fill. The causes which led them to settle there were purely economic, and not political. The genuine "carpet baggers" who came after the adoption of the reconstruction policy were comparatively few in number.

The virtual failure of the attempt to procure a supply of

---

[1] This opinion is based upon an examination of the "personal testimony" given by a large number of these men before the various reconstruction committees that investigated affairs in Mississippi. One of the Northerners who had an experience of this kind was Governor Andrews of Massachusetts. He is reputed to have "sunk" $30,000 on a plantation in Issaquena County. He attributed the failure to negro labor.

white laborers by immigration made it necessary, therefore, to fall back upon the negro. The chief problem was how to devise a plan that would secure a reasonable return to the planter, and a corresponding reward for the toil of the laborer. There were certain economic elements that facilitated the solution of the problem. Thus, the white man owned the land, the stock, and the farming implements ; the freedman furnished the labor. But the relative values of each was a question to be determined by experiment. Some of the planters adopted the plan of renting land to freedmen for a stipulated sum of money, but the difficulty of collecting rent in this form led to its early abandonment. A better plan was to rent for a stipulated portion of the crop, say one-third. The most common method adopted, however, was the "share" system. Few freedmen possessed farm animals or implements or sufficient standing with the mercantile class to secure credit for the necessary supplies while the crop was growing. The planter, therefore, agreed to furnish the land, the seed, the farm implements and animals, and furnish the merchant with security for any supplies which the freedman might need. On the other hand, the freedman was to plant, cultivate, and gather the crop for a certain portion of it. This was usually one-half. In some instances, the farmer furnished the rations in addition, and received two-thirds of the crop. In Amite County, the value of labor and board was reckoned as being equivalent to the use of the land and animals ; in Washington County, one-fourth of the crop was paid for the labor, and one-third where the laborer furnished his own supplies. In Winston County, three-tenths of the crop was given for the labor. On the Yazoo, one-fourth of the gross product was paid for labor when the laborer furnished his own rations. In Tippah, the use of the farm, tools, and stock was regarded as an equivalent for the labor, rations, and feed for the stock. The scheme, however, by which the planter furnished the tools and animals and the freedman the labor, each receiving one-half of the crop, was in the end adopted everywhere.

The "share" system was disastrous to the planters of Mississippi in 1866 and 1867. On account of overflows, droughts, and insects, the yield was not sufficient to pay for the food and clothing of laborers. The failure, however, was not due solely to unfavorable seasons, but in a great measure to the unreliable character of negro labor. Even now, the negro is not a model of industry, frugality, and foresight. He was much farther from it in 1866. His undertakings

nearly always resulted in failure.   He was peculiarly unfitted
for the cultivation of the cotton crop, which requires careful
attention the greater part of the entire year.   Free to go
where he pleased, and to own fire-arms, he hunted and fished,
attended " frolics " and protracted meetings, while the grass
choked his cotton to death.   The following incident was a
common occurrence.   A planter in Amite County had furnished a yoke of oxen and a cart to a freedman who had four
children to help him on the farm.   Seeing him on his way
to the village one day with a small load of wood, and knowing that his little farm was rapidly going to grass, the planter
said to him, " How is this, uncle ? "   " Oh," he said, " I am
out of tobaccy, and am gwine to town to sell a load of wood."
His wife was housekeeping, and his four children had gone
a fishing.   His cows brought two calves, both of which starved
to death.

Another freedman in the same county, who as a slave
had managed fifteen laborers for his master, and who was
understood to be an intelligent overseer, rented a farm of
fertile bottom land, and with seventeen colaborers went into
the business of cotton planting for himself.   He bought two
mules, four horses, eight cows, a wagon, twelve hundred
pounds of bacon, a hundred and forty bushels of corn, borrowed four yoke of oxen, and obtained credit for $1000.
He made four bales of cotton, no corn, fodder, or vege-
tables.   Both mules and one yoke of oxen were dead at
the end of the year, and two of the horses were too
poor to stand alone; two were run off and sold; no rent
or debts were paid; and an additional debt of $500 was
incurred.   Although a negro might have a half interest in
the crop he was cultivating, if he was offered employment
for a day or two at a little more than the usual rates he
would leave his crop in order to earn a few dollars to spend
for trifles that would only please a child.   He exhibited the
same weakness in a far more pronounced degree for abandoning his work to attend political meetings.

Much of the legislation after the war was designed to encourage the flow of capital to the state, the establishment of
various manufacturing industries, and the building of railroads.   Some of the acts thus passed related specifically to
the publication of accurate crop reports; for the exemption
from taxation for a period of years of all factories established
in the state; for the encouragement of the growth of wool;
and for the encouragement of agricultural and mechanical
institutions, county and state fairs, etc.

II. RECONSTRUCTION OF THE POSTAL AND RAILWAY SERVICE

One of the first duties of reconstruction was the reëstablishment of the postal service in the late "insurrectionary" states. It will be remembered that upon the outbreak of hostilities, the United States postal officials in these states turned the funds and other property belonging to the Post Office Department over to the Confederate authorities or appropriated them to their own personal use. In February, 1861, the service was withdrawn from the South, it being impossible to continue it longer. As the territory passed under the control of the Union armies, a limited postal service was reëstablished for the exclusive use of the military forces of the United States, whenever the territory was held for any length of time. The President in his proclamations appointing provisional governors directed the Postmaster General to take steps to reëstablish the United States postal service in the South. Provisional governors were at once notified of the readiness of the department to appoint postmasters and mail contractors upon recommendation, and to put the mail on the railroads as soon as notified of their willingness to carry it.[1] Steps were also taken to recover the funds which had been turned over to the Confederate authorities or misappropriated at the beginning of the war. The amount thus due from former postmasters in Mississippi was about $34,000.[2] The claim of the delinquent postmasters that they should be credited with the amounts turned over to the Confederacy was not allowed. It appears that no effort was made to reorganize the service in Mississippi until November, 1865, when Mr. Kelly, a special agent of the department, came to Jackson, charged with the duty of arranging the necessary

[1] Report Postmaster General, 1865–1866, p. 12.
[2] *Ibid.* p. 107. The following amounts were claimed from the presidential offices in Mississippi : —

Aberdeen	.	.	.	.	.	$ 225
Canton	.	.	.	.	.	2556
Clinton	.	.	.	.	.	141
Columbus	.	.	.	.	.	1927
Holly Springs	.	.	.	.	.	1750
Jackson	.	.	.	.	.	3134
Natchez	.	.	.	.	.	6230
Vicksburg	.	.	.	.	.	3243

The total amount for all the Southern states was $341,000.

details. He called upon the people to recommend suitable persons to act as postmasters and make proposals for carrying the mail, assuring them that postal facilities could not be extended without the coöperation of the people. But the chief difficulty of restoring the service was due to the requirement that postmasters and mail contractors should take the iron-clad oath of July 2, 1862. Consequently, the opening of mail facilities proceeded at a rate that was exceedingly annoying to the inhabitants. The *Jackson Clarion* of January 7, 1866, complained that they had received no mail from the North for eight days, "and yet the people were loyal." As late as August 20 of the same year, only eighty-nine offices in the state had been "reconstructed," but one of which was in Hinds County.

The mail was carried by private contract between many towns for months after the collapse of the Confederacy. The *Clarion* urged the citizens to make an effort to find suitable persons who could take the oath, and if no such could be found, to get unmarried women appointed with the understanding that they were to appoint deputies to attend to the post offices. The same difficulties were met with in putting into operation the United States revenue laws. It was felt by the President and the Cabinet that the unpleasant duty of collecting Federal taxes from the impoverished people of the South should be performed by their own citizens. In view, therefore, of the difficulty of finding eligible Southern whites to serve as assessors and collectors, the President, in a way, dispensed with the test oath, and allowed it to be taken in a qualified form where the applicant was known not to have been a disunionist.[1] The same ruling was made with regard to postmasters and mail contractors. When Congress met, it adopted a resolution requesting the President to transmit the names of all persons who had been allowed to qualify by taking the oath in a modified form. Upon receipt of the information, Congress passed an act declaring vacant the offices held by such incumbents. In Mississippi, several of the assessors and collectors, and a majority of the postmasters, were compelled to surrender their offices. It was then ordered that the mails should not be delivered at any place where there was not a postmaster duly sworn according to the iron-clad oath.

The reorganization of the railway service upon "loyal principles" was another problem of reconstruction, but was

---

[1] Ex. Docs. 1st Ses. 39th Cong. No. 81, p. 5.

not attended with the same difficulties as in the case of the postal and revenue service. As the Union armies penetrated the Southern states, the railroads were seized as captured property, and held during the war and for some months after the cessation of hostilities, and used for military purposes. The seizures were made by the commanders in the field without reference to any other consideration than depriving the enemy of their use. They were destroyed or repaired and used as occasion required. The business of managing these roads became so great that a bureau styled "the Military Railroad Department" was created. In all, 42 southern railroads were thus seized, aggregating 2538 miles, and $45,000,000 were expended by the government in repairing and equipping them. In August, 1865, the President directed that they be turned over to their owners, and the management reorganized by the election of boards of directors whose loyalty should be established to the satisfaction of the commanding general. Each company was furthermore required to furnish satisfactory bonds that it would within a certain time pay the government a fair valuation for the rolling stock which it had supplied from Northern roads or had had especially manufactured for use on the Southern roads. Thus they became purchasers of government rolling stock to the amount of about $7,000,000. Practically none of the Southern roads were able to pay the several amounts as they fell due, and the radicals in Congress denounced the whole proceeding as a "complete surrender." The following exhibit shows the dates on which the several lines in Mississippi were seized for use as military roads, when they were restored, and their indebtedness to the government at the time of their restoration : [1] —

NAME.	WHEN SEIZED.	WHEN RESTORED.	INDEBTEDNESS TO THE U.S.
Memphis and Charleston	Feb'y, 1864	Sept., 1865	$474,496
Mississippi Central .	" "	Aug. 24, 1865	61,529
Selma and Meridian	" "	Aug. 25, 1865	142,870
Mobile and Ohio .	" "	" "	302,365
New Orleans, Jackson, and Great Northern	Jan. 30, 1863	June 30, 1865	——
Mississippi and Tennessee	——	——	102,460

[1] House Report, No. 15, 2d Ses. 40th Cong.; also Ex. Docs. *ibid.* No. 73.

The only one of these roads that had received a land grant from Congress was the Selma and Meridian, which, in 1856, had been given 171,750 acres.[1] On account of the aid which it gave the Confederacy, there was a strong sentiment among the reconstructionists in favor of forfeiting the grant. It appears, however, that no action was taken with that end in view.

So much for the reconstruction of the railroads from the political point of view. There was another very important aspect, namely, that of physical reconstruction. The condition of the roads in Mississippi was particularly unfortunate at the close of hostilities. They were creditors to the Confederate government to the amount of many millions of dollars for transporting its troops and supplies, all of which was, of course, lost. In the second place, they had paid large debts due to the state in Confederate currency under an act which was subsequently declared by the courts to be null and void. Consequently, these debts had to be discharged again, and in sound money. Worse than either of these misfortunes was the actual physical condition of the roads and their rolling stock. Nothing illustrates so well the desolation of the war as a picture of the several railway lines at the close of hostilities.

The Memphis and Charleston road extending across the northeastern corner of the state was taken actual possession of by the Federal army in 1862, and for three years it was a sort of picket line between the two armies, each of which seemed to try to outdo the other in inflicting destruction upon it. When the company was reorganized loyally, and its property restored, only a wreck of the former road existed. From Pocahontas to Decatur, a distance of 114 miles, it was almost entirely destroyed. Every bridge and trestle was gone, the cross ties were rotten, the depots and other buildings were in ashes, the water tanks were destroyed, the ditches filled up, the track covered with weeds and bushes, and forty miles of rails were burnt and twisted. Nearly all the locomotives and cars were destroyed, the machinery was beyond repair, and there was not a saw-mill left along the line.

The Memphis and Tennessee road, which runs from Grenada to Memphis, suffered quite as much as the Memphis and Charleston. Of the fifteen Howe truss bridges on its line in 1860, only three small ones remained at the close of the

---

[1] Ex. Docs. 1st Ses. 39th Cong. No. 101, p. 58.

war.   Two and a half miles of trestle, almost one-half of
the rolling stock, nearly all the water tanks, and two-thirds
of the depots were destroyed.   On the first of May, 1865,
but thirty of the one hundred miles of the road were in operation.   The work of reconstruction was begun without a
dollar in the treasury.   By the middle of June, trains were
running as far north as Senatobia, at which point passengers
for Memphis were transferred to horse cars.   Many enter-
prising Memphis merchants contributed money to aid in
repairing the road, in recognition of which their names were
placarded in the cars, and the friends of the road requested
to give them their trade.   By the end of the year 1865, it
was nearly reconstructed.   Freight depots had been built at
Memphis, Horn Lake, Cold Water, Como, Sardis, Batesville,
and Popes ; the Tallahatchie and Yazoo rivers had been
bridged; two and a half miles of trestle built; 100,000 new
cross ties laid; section houses, wood and water stations re-
placed; a good deal of track relaid; and a machine shop at
Memphis erected and equipped.   On January 3, 1866, the
first train went through from Memphis to Grenada.

The Mississippi Central railroad, extending from Canton,
Mississippi, to Jackson, Tennessee, was at the close of hostilities a mere wreck between Abbeville (near Oxford) and Grand
Junction.   But eight passenger coaches were left on the
road.   Bridges, depots, culverts, and most of the cross ties
were gone.   The machine shops at Canton and Holly Springs
were destroyed, and the company carried a debt of $1,500,000.
By the middle of June, 1865, trains were running between
Grenada and Oxford.   At the latter place, passengers for
points north were transferred to hand-cars, which constituted the chief means of conveyance between Oxford and
Holly Springs.   Both passengers and freight had to be transferred by boat across the Yazoo River at Grenada.   By September 20, all the bridges were completed to Holly Springs,
and by November 15, regular trains were running through
from Canton to Grand Junction.   Until June, 1866, however, there were only three locomotives in the service north
of Grenada.   The work of reconstruction was pushed rapidly,
and before the end of the year 1865, depots had been built at
Holly Springs, Oxford, Coffeeville, Winona, Vaiden, West
Durant, and Goodman, and a number of others were repaired.

The most important railroad in the state was the New
Orleans, Jackson, and Great Northern, now a part of the
Illinois Central, 206 miles in length, extending from New
Orleans to Canton, and built at a cost of $7,000,000.   It

was completed but a year or two before the outbreak
of the war, and was said to be the best equipped road in
the Confederacy. Its rolling stock was taken possession
of by General Lovell in April, 1862, but was subsequently
restored, and that part of the road between New Orleans and
Ponchatoula continued to be operated until the surrender of
the Confederate armies in 1865. A considerable portion of
the track in the vicinity of Jackson was destroyed by General Sherman in 1863. Some of it in the southern part of
the state was also destroyed by General Grierson. Consequently, that part of the road from Ponchatoula to Brookhaven, a distance of eighty-one miles, was not used after the
spring of 1863. Most of the bridges were destroyed, the
road-bed was covered with weeds, bushes, and briers, and
three-fourths of the cross ties were rotten. From Brookhaven to Jackson, a distance of fifty-five miles, the road,
though in a dilapidated condition, continued to be used with
the exception of about three miles south of Jackson. From
Jackson to Canton, the northern terminus, it was torn up
and the material destroyed. At the outbreak of hostilities,
this road was equipped with 49 locomotives, 37 passenger
cars, and 555 freight, baggage, and gravel cars. At the
close of the war, there were but one locomotive, three passenger cars, and six freight and baggage cars fit for use
between Jackson and Canton. Between Brookhaven and
Jackson there were but two locomotives, both badly damaged by fire, four box cars, and nine flat cars. Of all the
depot buildings and platforms attached, woodsheds, and
water stations, all of which were in good condition in 1862,
only those at Osyka, Magnolia, and Summit remained
standing in 1865, the rest having been destroyed from
time to time by the armed forces of the United States
or of the Confederacy. Not a dollar of available funds
remained in the treasury of the company when it was reorganized loyally in the summer of 1865. The new directors
set to work to reconstruct the road. Men were employed
to rebuild the bridges beginning at Ponchatoula. An agent
was sent to Washington to negotiate for rolling stock then
in possession of the government, and to secure contracts for
carrying the mail. General Beauregard was elected president, and by the middle of June, the road between Jackson
and Canton, with the exception of a mile at Jackson, was in
running order. Passengers for New Orleans, however, had
to travel by hand-car from Brookhaven to Ponchatoula, a
distance of eighty-one miles. In less than a year seventy-

eight bridges had been rebuilt, forty-two thousand cross ties laid, and a large amount of rolling stock acquired. By October 3, 1865, trains began to make regular trips from New Orleans to Canton for the first time since May, 1863.

The Mobile and Ohio was the chief railroad in the eastern part of the state. It was built largely by English capitalists, and was said to be one of the best equipped lines in the South. The last rail was laid just before the firing upon Fort Sumter. Upon the outbreak of hostilities it was taken possession of by the Confederate authorities, and used for the transportation of its men and supplies. At the end of the war, the Confederate government owed the road $5,000,000, none of which was, of course, ever paid. From Union City, Tennessee, to Okolona, Mississippi, a distance of 184 miles, all the bridges and trestles were destroyed. In the vicinity of Meridian, twenty-one miles of rails were bent and twisted by order of General Sherman, and all the bridges, trestles, and water tanks, as well as the rolling stock, were destroyed. The repair shops at Jackson, Tennessee, were destroyed, and all the tools and working materials carried away. The following comparative table shows the effect of the war upon the Mobile and Ohio railroad so far as rolling stock is concerned : —

	JAN., 1860.	MAY, 1865.
Locomotives in order	59	15
Locomotives out of order	0	38
Passenger cars	26	11
Freight cars	721	231

In this condition the road was restored to the company in May, 1865, upon the condition that government business should have precedence ; that all military orders should be obeyed; and that nothing should be construed as relieving the company from the pains and penalties imposed by the confiscation acts. The road was operated almost exclusively according to military orders, until all Confederate cotton captured by the United States was removed. By the middle of June, 1865, trains were running as far north as Okolona, and occasionally to Corinth.

The railroad from Vicksburg to Meridian was in no better condition, if as good, as the others. It suffered chiefly from the raids of Generals Sherman and Grierson.

Nothing illustrates better the spirit which animated the people of the South in their efforts to repair the losses of the war than the rapidity with which the railroads were reconstructed and put into operation. They seem to have showed few signs of discouragement at the disheartening picture which they were compelled to face upon the return of peace, but plunged into the work of reconstruction with the same confidence and enthusiasm with which they took up arms in the great contest which was destined to inflict incalculable ruin and misery upon them.

CHAPTER FIFTH

CONGRESSIONAL RECONSTRUCTION

I. THE NATIONAL INQUEST

ALTHOUGH the United States was able to suppress the "insurrection," it was unable to change the sentiments of the Southern people with regard to the righteousness of their cause. This was, to be sure, very natural under the circumstances, and nothing else should have been expected. The opinion was common, however, among the more radical politicians of the North, that the surrender of the Southern armies should be accompanied by an immediate surrender of their convictions on the subjects of slavery and secession, and an open profession of a warm attachment for the flag and government of the United States. For some time after the return of peace, the degree of this attachment was the subject of investigation by special committees and commissioners. Upon the result of these investigations, the government at Washington based its policy in dealing with the late seceded states. As to the manner of conducting the investigation, two different plans were followed. One was the despatch of special commissioners to the states in question, with instructions to take the testimony of representative leaders of all classes, and to observe personally the conduct of the people in their political, business, and even social relations. The other plan was the *ex parte* method by partisan committees. The one was the presidential plan, the other the congressional plan.

In pursuance of the presidential plan, three special commissioners in turn visited the South for the purpose of discovering whatever visible signs of "returning loyalty" there might be. The first of these was the general of the army, who had been the most conspicuous figure in the suppression of the insurrection; another was a major general, who possessed elements of statesmanship; and the third was a civilian, in whom the President reposed confidence. Each, independently of the other, visited the important towns and cities of the late Confederacy; had interviews with leading citizens, soldiers, and Confederate generals, travelled over the principal railroads, navigable rivers, and even in stage-coaches; called upon post and district commanders of the United States army and upon Freedmen's Bureau agents, and, when possible, procured written statements of their views. As a result of these investigations, the first commissioner, General U. S. Grant, reported that there was such " universal acquiescence " in the authority of the national government as to make the mere presence of a military force, without regard to numbers, sufficient to maintain order; that economy and the good of the country required that white troops should be employed in the interior of the country; that the presence of black troops demoralized the labor system by encouraging the freedmen to abandon the plantations and congregate about the military camps; that the people of the Southern states were anxious to renew their allegiance to the United States; and that they were earnest in wishing to do what was required by the government, provided it was not humiliating to them as citizens, and if such a course were pointed out to them, they would pursue it in good faith.[1]

Another commissioner, Carl Schurz, spent several weeks in the South, visiting, among other places in Mississippi, Meridian, Jackson, Vicksburg, and Natchez. With regard to Mississippi, he reported that the people had reorganized their government and were yielding obedience to the laws and Constitution of the United States with more willingness and greater promptitude than could reasonably be expected under the circumstances; that they evinced a laudable desire to renew their allegiance to the government, and to repair the devastation of war by a prompt and cheerful return to peaceful pursuits; that the demoralizing effects of the war had occasioned disorders in some cases, but they were generally local in character, and rapidly disappeared as the authority of the civil law was extended and sustained.[2]

Mr. Truman, the third commissioner, took a most rosy view of the situation. He declared that he looked to the disbanded regiments of the Confederate army with great confidence as the best and altogether most hopeful element of the South — the real basis of reconstruction and the material

[1] See Sen. Docs. 1st Ses. 39th Cong. No. 2, p. 106, for General Grant's report.   [2] See *ibid.* pp. 1–106, for General Schurz's report.

of worthy citizenship, and affirmed that there were few more potent influences at work in promoting real and lasting reconciliation and reconstruction than the influence of the Southern soldier. He said: " I know from actual observation that thousands of the rank and file and hundreds of their officers would gladly enlist in the United States army against any and all foreigners, particularly if they could serve under their old officers." He thought less than fifty of the leading politicians of the South still believed in the constitutional right of secession. He denied the report that Northern men were persecuted in the South, and declared that the freedmen were well treated by their late masters.[1]

The substantial concurrence of the commissioners in the opinion that the status in the South was such as to justify the readmission of the state to the Union, was highly gratifying to the supporters of the presidential policy, and was pointed to with pride as a vindication of their measures. The radicals, however, refused to accept this as a true picture of the situation, and General Grant's verdict in particular was criticised as a " whitewashing" report.[2] They rejected both the report and the testimony on which it was based. Whether there were objections to the manner in which the investigation was conducted, it does not appear. A new method of inquiry was accordingly devised. It consisted of a joint congressional committee on which the party of the South had one-fifth of the representatives. Considering the relative strength of the two parties in Congress, the committee can hardly be said to have been unfairly constituted. The testimony relating to Mississippi was taken by Hon. George S. Boutwell. He summoned such witnesses and asked such questions as his own sense of fairness dictated. No representative of the Southern party was present to cross-examine those whom he called. Mr. Boutwell held his examinations at Washington, and did not visit the scene of his investigations. Of the witnesses who were examined upon the condition of affairs in Mississippi, none were Democrats, and only two were citizens of the state. These were Governor Sharkey and Judge Hill. Of the other eight witnesses, three were major generals in the Union army, one a brigadier general, one a captain of a company of colored troops, one a United States treasury agent, one a revenue agent, and the other one said he was "engaged in ascertaining the amount of cotton in the Southern states for an association of

[1] See Sen. Docs. *ibid.* No. 43, for Truman's report.
[2] Burr's Life of Grant, p. 845.

New England manufacturers."[1] One of the witnesses, in reply to a question as to what opportunities he had enjoyed for observations in Mississippi, said that he had not been there for a year, except on a visit.[2] The congressional method was thus poorly devised for discovering "signs of returning loyalty." In this respect, it was well-nigh a failure. One of the witnesses gave his opinion that, with the exception of the northeastern part of the state, there was little loyalty to be found;[3] another thought there was an organization in the South for a renewal of the rebellion;[4] another declared that the Mississippians were the least loyal of any people in the South. Two of the witnesses affirmed that the condition of the freedmen was worse than in the days of slavery, which was probably true in the year 1865.[5] There was a concurrence of opinion among the witnesses who had served in the Union army, that without protection of Federal troops, Northern men in the state were in danger of violence. The complaint was also general among the witnesses that Northern men were not well received in Southern society, which was doubtless true in 1865, yet this was scarcely a proper subject for congressional investigation. It was certainly not a violation of the Thirteenth Amendment, under authority of which the investigation was made, and was not an evil for which there was any adequate legislative remedy. One of the witnesses professed surprise at never having met a Confederate who expressed regret or sorrow for anything except the failure of the Confederacy;[6] another saw few manifestations of good feeling toward the government;[7] another testified that Jeff Davis was cheered in "every conceivable way" by the people;[8] and another was horrified at meeting a rebel general who preferred Davis to Abraham Lincoln for the presidency.[9]

[1] Testimony of Warren Kelsey before the reconstruction committee, pt. iii. p. 1.
[2] Testimony of Warren Kelsey, *ibid.*
[3] Testimony of Edward Hatch, *ibid.* p. 4.
[4] Testimony of B. H. Grierson, *ibid.* p. 121.
[5] Testimony of J. H. Matthews, *ibid.* p. 47 ; and Warren Kelsey, *ibid.* p. 1.
The following explanation from the majority report of the reconstruction committee is significant : "To obtain the necessary information, recourse could only be had to the examination of witnesses whose position had given them the best means of forming an accurate judgment, who could state facts from their own observation, and whose character and standing afforded the best proof of their truthfulness and impartiality."
[6] Testimony of General Fiske, *ibid.* p. 32.
[7] Testimony of General Hatch, *ibid.* p. 4.
[8] Testimony of General Matthews, *ibid.* p. 4.
[9] Testimony of A. P. Dillingham, *ibid.* p. 116.

The failure to find the Confederate leaders in sackcloth and ashes was by no means conclusive proof of disloyalty. Nothing could have been more unnatural than for those who had made so many sacrifices for a cause whose rectitude they never doubted, to have suddenly changed positions, openly admitted their error, and asked forgiveness. That there should have been few healthy manifestations of good-will for the flag which the Southerners associated with all their woes, could hardly have been expected so soon after the smoke of battle. Men cannot, by laws and proclamations, be made to change their affections from one object to another in a moment, especially if the one has been an object of love and the other of hate. It was sufficient that in the summer of 1865 they took solemn oaths to obey the Constitution, and henceforth defend the flag of the United States. It was political intolerance to cite, as a proof of continued disloyalty, the admiration of the people for Davis, and their preference for Confederate leaders for positions of honor and trust. It was a subject of special complaint, and was cited as a further proof of disloyalty that Humphreys, an unpardoned Confederate brigadier general, was elected governor in 1865, over Judge Fisher, a non-combatant during the Civil War. The truth is, Humphreys was as much opposed to secession as his opponent, but, unlike the judge, he was unable to escape the snares of the conscript officer, had he wished to do so. Being a gallant soldier and a man of personal popularity, he easily defeated his opponent. With good taste, the people, in 1865, chose few original secessionists to offices of importance. All the members elected to Congress were Whigs, except one, who was a Union Democrat. All had originally opposed secession, but after secession became a reality, they could not avoid military service had they so desired. It was not dishonorable that the people were faithful to their leaders, and that the candidacy of any man who had been indifferent to the success of the Confederacy should be looked upon with disfavor. The sense of appreciation for faithful military service and skilful leadership was as keen in the South as anywhere. This was nowhere better illustrated than by the liberal appropriations made for the defence of Davis, and the setting aside of one-fifth of the state revenues to furnish maimed soldiers with artificial limbs. Few men were more unpopular in Mississippi in 1865 than Davis, yet the fact that he was the chosen chief of the Confederacy kept alive a feeling of attachment which the disasters for which he was largely responsible could not eradicate. As one man put it, " I don't like Jeff Davis, but he was our leader, and we would be mean creatures if, when he is reviled, we should not defend him." [1]

One of the subjects of investigation by the reconstruction committee was the alleged formation of historical societies in Mississippi. Governor Humphreys had, in February, 1866, suggested to the superintendent of army records the organization of a state historical society, and of local affiliated societies. The reason given was the rapid passing of many of the actors in the recent history of the state, that " one side of the story had been written, and the world's verdict had been rendered against the South and her people." [2] The purpose of the local societies was to gather historical data for the central society. General Grierson professed to have discovered in this an " organization for the renewal of the rebellion." The following is the testimony on the point : —

Mr. Boutwell : Have you seen an order [letter] purporting to have been issued by Governor Humphreys, advising the organization of historical societies in Mississippi ?
General Grierson : I have.
Q. Do you suppose that order to be genuine ?
A. I do.
Q. What is the purpose of these societies ?
A. One purpose is said to be to collect the records of distinguished soldiers in the Confederate service, and forward them to the state capitol for preservation.
Q. Do you know anything of the societies ?
A. No, sir.
Q. Do you know whether any were organized before you left ?
A. Yes, sir. I know of several.
Q. Do you know whether any of the people belong to them ?
A. I think they all belong to them, at least they give their aid and assistance in furnishing documents.[3]

What connection the organization of historical societies had with the loyalty of the people and the fitness of the

---

[1] Charles Nordhoff : Cotton States in 1875, p. 82.
[2] The letter is printed with the reconstruction testimony, pt. iii. p. 123.
[3] *Ibid.* p. 144. The character of this testimony well illustrates the practice of the *post bellum* Southern committees in inquiring into the domestic institutions of the people and their social habits and customs, their political opinions and prejudices. The constitutional right of Congress to enforce by appropriate legislation the Thirteenth Amendment would perhaps sanction an investigation of any alleged violation of that amendment, but there is no constitutional authority for such an investigation as the above, where there was no pretence that the amendment had been violated. The instructions of the reconstruction committee were to " inquire into the condition of the Confederate states, and report whether they were entitled to representation."

state for representation in Congress, does not appear from the report of the committee. The most probable explanation is, that in the opinion of the majority, the collection and preservation of historical data relative to alleged "Yankee depredations," was not conducive to loyalty.

The witness who was most competent to testify on Mississippi affairs, both from his wide acquaintance, his official relation, and his conservatism, was Governor Sharkey. He told the committee that the people had given up all idea of secession; that the secessionist party admitted that they had made a "most miserable failure," and that they felt sore over having involved the country in such terrible calamities; that the state government was in the hands of original Union men, with the exception of the supreme bench, which, he regretted to say, was occupied by secessionists;[1] that so far as obedience to the laws was concerned, the people were loyal, and were disposed to do the freedmen justice; that the recent legislation relative to freedmen violated the Constitution, which gave them the right to hold real and personal property; and that the military leaders had taken the oath of allegiance, were conducting themselves honorably, and were anxious to be restored to the Union. The governor declared that the freedmen had gone to work and were doing well, but that the chief obstacle to good feeling between them and the whites was the Freedmen's Bureau and the presence of negro troops. He was sanguine enough to believe that had these been withdrawn, he could have had a "perfect state of order" in two weeks after his appointment. In regard to the obligations incurred by the state government during the war, he said they had, with one or two exceptions, been repudiated; that the people were glad of an opportunity to be relieved of them, and he did not think that a dollar of the debt would ever be paid. The governor did not deny that much crime existed in the state, but he attributed it to the demoralization incident to the disbandment of the armies, and the collapse of civil government in some communities. Governor Sharkey's views as to returning loyalty, no doubt represented the opinions of the more intelligent and conservative citizens. After all, it is their opinions only that possess any historical value. On the whole, the conduct of the secession leaders

---

[1] The *Jackson Clarion* of April 26, 1866, took exception to some of Governor Sharkey's allegations on this point, and declared that the air of Washington City did not agree with him, and asserted that he had better return home before losing the confidence of the people who had intrusted him with so much.

showed modesty and good taste, though it will be granted that there were exceptions. For a time after the collapse of the Confederacy, they declined to make public addresses or take a conspicuous part in political movements. Ex-Senator Brown says he studiously avoided every act which might be construed as an attempt to interfere in matters with which a "proscribed rebel" had nothing to do.[1] Governor Clarke refused to address the legislature so long as he was a "prisoner of state under parole."[2] They were all willing to abandon the doctrine of secession, provided they might admit that it was good so long as it lasted. But as the arbitrament of the sword, if not the logic of the schools, had settled the question against them, they were willing to accept the result. This sentiment was expressed in an address at Vicksburg by a candidate for the office of Attorney General. He said: "In 1850, I opposed an attempt to break up the Union, and in 1860 I did the same. I travelled in Alabama and Mississippi to oppose the measure. But after the state did secede, I did all in my power to sustain it. I believed in secession while it lasted, but am now as good a Union man as exists, and am in favor of breaking down old barriers and making harmony and peace prevail."[3] A candidate for Congress expressed a similar opinion. He said: "In 1851, I was a delegate from Lauderdale County to the state convention and again in 1860. I was opposed to secession, and fought it with all my power; but after the state seceded, I went with it as a matter of duty, and sustained it until the day of the surrender, with all my heart and soul, mind and body."[4] The sentiment was unanimous in favor of the repudiation of secession, the acceptance of the result of the war, and the desire to be restored to the Union, although, they said, we cannot be expected to give up at once our convictions of right. Carl Schurz says sentiments like these were repeated to him hundreds of times in every state he visited, with some variation of language, according to the different ways of thinking, or the frankness or reserve of the different speakers.

Governor A. G. Brown represented a respectable minority in the view that from the day they laid their arms at the feet of the conqueror, they had no rights which he was bound to respect, and that it was absurd for a conquered people to talk of being degraded by submitting to the will of the conqueror.

[1] *New York Times*, Aug. 22, 1867.
[2] Letter in *New York Herald* of April 3, 1867.
[3] *Vicksburg Journal*, Sept. 19, 1865.
[4] Report of Carl Schurz, *supra*, p. 10.

He thought those who, like himself, were proscribed, had no legitimate reason for complaint.[1] At the same time, he did not believe that they were guilty of treason, inasmuch as one belligerent could not commit treason against another.[2] Few of the leaders who joined in the secession movement accepted the result of the war so unreservedly as did Alcorn, one of the United States senators-elect. He acknowledged that when he cast his vote for the ordinance of secession, he did so with the full understanding that it was an act of rebellion, and that he was liable to the penalties for treason.[3] He expected that his lands would be confiscated, and himself punished, but he was thankful that neither had happened, and that he had not heard of any individual who had been punished for treason.[4]

Chief-Justice Campbell, one of the most intelligent members of the Mississippi bar, and a former member of the Confederate Congress, said: " I think there never was a people more thoroughly subdued than the people of the South. They were sick and tired of war, wearied and worn out; with the destruction of the Confederate government and the abolition of slavery, all cause of enmity between the people of the United States had passed away, and I think the feeling of an overwhelming majority of our people was one of readiness to be faithful to the government." [5]

In June, 1866, the reconstruction committee made its report. The states lately in secession were declared to have been in a state of anarchy at the close of the war, without government or constitutions, and sustaining no political relations to the government of the United States; that Congress could not be expected to recognize as valid the election of representatives from disorganized communities; that Congress would not be justified in admitting such communities to a participation in the government of the United States without providing such constitution or other guarantees as would tend to secure the civil rights of all citizens of the republic, a just equality of representation, protection against claims founded in rebellion and crime, a temporary restoration of the right of suffrage to those who had not actively participated in the rebellion, and the exclusion from positions of public trust of a portion of those who had.

[1] Speech in *New York Times*, Aug. 22, 1867.
[2] Letter to *New York Herald* of April 3, 1867. Next to Davis and Quitman, Brown was the most influential of the secessionists before the war. His course after the war, however, was conservative.
[3] See his inaugural address, March 10, 1870.
[4] Address at Helena, 1869.
[5] Boutwell Report on Mississippi Elections, 1875, p. 938.

II. THE RECONSTRUCTION ACTS

The report of the majority of the congressional committee was accepted by the radicals as "an absolutely truthful picture of the Southern states at that time," and became the basis of the reconstruction policy finally adopted.[1] The late "insurrectionary" states were declared to be without legal governments, and without power to protect life and property. In order to insure these blessings, the states were grouped into military administrative districts, and placed under the authority of the United States. For convenience in administration, the local subdivisions were retained, and for the most part the machinery of the civil government was made use of, although declared illegal in the preamble of the act. The private law of the territory was not changed by the acts of Congress, but the military commanders were vested with full authority to modify or supersede it in their discretion. The duties of the district commanders were in general to maintain order, register the new electorate, and direct the movement for the reëstablishment of "republican" government. For the accomplishment of these ends, they were given absolute authority over life, liberty, and property, with the exception that death sentences should require the approval of the President. The existing state governments were to be deemed as provisional only, and in all respects subject to the paramount authority of the United States at any time to "abolish, control, modify, or supersede the same." The right of suffrage was conferred upon the freedmen, and withheld from a large class of whites.

It thus appears that the basic idea of the policy adopted was the duty of Congress to communicate a new political life to certain communities which had, by some act or other, put an end to their existence as states. Attempted withdrawal from the Union, and levying war against the United States, were alleged by the radicals to be the means by which the state existence was forfeited. Those who held to this view were undoubtedly inconsistent when they denied the validity of the ordinances of secession, as they generally did. Moreover, these ordinances had either been repealed or declared null and void, *ab initio*, by constituent assem-

---

[1] J. G. Blaine, Twenty Years of Congress, II. p. 9.

blies, and hence could have had no validity in 1867, if they ever had any.   Another view was, not that the states had by act of rebellion lost their membership in the Union, but that they had forfeited their right to be treated as states on an equality with the original members.   This would be a more rational view, were there any constitutional authority for a class of states in our Federal system not on an equality with the original states.   And even if it be granted that the Union is not one of equals, it cannot be seriously claimed that Congress, as an agent of the sovereign, could have the authority to establish the inequality and define its extent. This would be an exercise of constituent powers, while the creation of states and the delimitation of their spheres of activity is, under our system, an act of the sovereign, and not of the government.   Moreover, in assuming that the states were still in rebellion, that their governments were illegal, and that life and property were insecure, Congress seems to have gone to unnecessary lengths.   As a matter of fact, the commander-in-chief of the army and navy of the United States had more than a year before officially proclaimed the rebellion at an end, and there was probably not a Confederate soldier in arms against the government.   As for the alleged illegality of the state governments, it is sufficient to say that they were organized in the regular American way, and for the most part in accordance with constitutions and laws made before the passage of the ordinances of secession, and whose validity Congress never denied ; and made by men who, if they had forfeited their political rights by rebellion, had, nevertheless, received the executive pardon which absolved them from the legal consequences of their actions.   Moreover, these governments had been recognized by the chief executive as legal governments.   His right to do so seems to be well settled.[1]

The duty of the United States to guarantee " republican " government to the states was relied upon by Congress as a justification for its action.   The exact content of the term " republican " government had not been expressly defined in 1865.   By the well established principles of the public law of the United States, it may be said to have meant government by representatives, chosen by the political people.[2]   Judged by this test, the governments in the Southern states could hardly be said to have been unre-

---

[1] Luther *vs.* Borden, 7 How. 1.
[2] Cooley, Principles of Const. Law, p. 213.

publican. In Mississippi, certainly, all adult male citizens, with a few unimportant exceptions, were vested with the suffrage. This statement, of course, assumes that mere emancipation did not elevate the freedmen to citizenship. If the civil rights act of 1866 was a constitutional measure, it does not alter the case. The mere declaration of Congress that certain classes of persons within a commonwealth are citizens of the United States, does not invest them with the suffrage. If anything was more clearly established than another as a part of our public law in 1865, it was the principle that the definition of the electorate had been left by the sovereign to the several commonwealths. No attempt was made by the *sovereign* to alter that principle until 1868. Hence the action of the *government* in investing the late slaves with the suffrage in 1867, as well as its action in subverting the state governments, was one of doubtful validity. Able Southern jurists saw at once a possible escape from the "horrors" of reconstruction by a resort to the courts. The congressional policy had barely gone into operation in Mississippi, when a movement was set on foot to prevent its further execution. The method adopted was an application to the Supreme Court of the United States for a bill of injunction against the President and the district commander, to restrain them from enforcing the reconstruction acts. Ex-Governor Sharkey and Hon. Robert J. Walker appeared as counsel for the state. The bill which they asked permission to file declared that the attempt of a portion of the people to dissolve the connection between the state and the United States was null and void, and consequently the state was then, as it had always been, a member of the Federal Union, unimpaired and indestructible, and, being such, Congress could not constitutionally expel it from the Union.[1] The petitioners furthermore maintained that they had good reason to believe that Andrew Johnson, a citizen of Tennessee, in violation of the Constitution of the United States, and of the sacred rights of the states, would soon proceed, in pursuance of a mere ministerial duty against his own will,

[1] The *Jackson Clarion* of April 12, 1867, took exception to the allegation that secession was the work of a *portion* of the people of the state, and declared it to be untruthful—"a plea of not guilty to an act which is unjustly alleged to be a crime, and which all the world knows the state did deliberately commit." The editor declared it to have been the act of nineteen-twentieths of the people, and the attempt to throw the consequences upon a portion of the citizens violated the truth of history. "If their argument is true," he continued, "there is no hope for Mr. Davis."

to execute the said acts as though they were the law of the land. They alleged that the so-called reconstruction acts would in effect annihilate the state and its government, and render every citizen liable to deprivation of life, liberty, and property at the breath of a military commander, without the benefit of trial by jury, and without the observance of any of those requirements and guarantees by which the Constitution and laws protect the rights of the citizen. They further alleged that the duty of the President in the premises, being merely ministerial, was subject to the control of the courts.[1] The court refused to allow the bill to be filed on the ground that for reasons of expediency and policy the President should not be interfered with by the courts in the performance of his duties. No opinion was expressed as to the constitutionality of the reconstruction acts.[2] The petitioners then decided not to aim so high, and with others filed a bill against the Secretary of War, the general of the army, and the commander of the third district. The court in this case held that it had no jurisdiction over the subject-matter presented in the bill, and accordingly deemed it unimportant to examine the question as it respected jurisdiction over the parties defendant.[3]

Soon after this, a case involving the validity of the reconstruction acts came before the Supreme Court on appeal from a military commission sitting at Vicksburg. For a while, things looked gloomy for the reconstructionists, as there appeared to be no way by which the court could avoid a decision on the points involved. A decision in their favor would have been of great value to the party, but the risk of an adverse opinion was too great to be incurred. Consequently, after the arguments had been made, and while the case was under advisement, Congress with " unwonted celerity " passed an act depriving the court of jurisdiction in the particular case, and of all others of a similar character.[4] Thus perished the hopes of the opponents of the congressional policy. Every effort to have the Supreme Court pass upon the validity of the reconstruction acts failed either through evasion upon the part of the court or through the vigilance and

---

[1] The arguments of Sharkey and Walker fill five columns of the *New York Herald* of April 6, 1867. Walker's and Stanberry's arguments are printed in the *New York World* of April 13, 1867.

[2] Mississippi *vs.* Johnson, 4 Wall. 475.

[3] Georgia *vs.* Stanton, 6 Wall. 57.

[4] Ex parte McCardle, 6 Wall. 318 ; 7 Wall. 514.

activity of Congress in depriving it of jurisdiction in cases where the question was involved.

There was rumor of a movement to arrest the district commander in Mississippi by the local authorities, on a charge of treason against the state, and thus compel the courts to take cognizance of the case.[1] Steps were also alleged to have been taken to secure a mandamus to compel Congress to admit the representatives of the state to seats in that body. Reverdy Johnson, to whom application is said to have been made, was too good a lawyer to undertake the task of securing the mandamus. After the defeat of the constitution in 1868, proceedings in the nature of a *quo warranto* were instituted against General Ames, who was district commander and also provisional governor, requiring him to appear before the Circuit Court at Jackson to show by what authority he held the office and executed the duties of governor of Mississippi. But the attempt to oust the commander did not turn out successfully, and he continued in the discharge of his duties until the readmission of the state to the Union.

Although the validity of the reconstruction acts was never passed upon by the Supreme Court, their constitutionality was affirmed by the United States district judge in Mississippi in a *habeas corpus* proceeding.[2]

The same judge upheld the enforcement act, another measure which may be said to have constituted a part of the congressional policy.[3] The civil rights act does not appear to have come before the United States district court in Mississippi, although it was passed upon by the chief justice of the state, one of the "original secessionists" whose election to the bench had been the subject of Sharkey's lamentations before the reconstruction committee. The case was a *habeas corpus* proceeding instituted by a freedman who was in custody for carrying firearms in violation of a state law. The plaintiff alleged that the Thirteenth Amendment made him free, and *ipso facto* vested him with all the rights of a citizen under the Constitution of the United States, one of which was the right to bear arms. The chief justice thought otherwise, and held that the Thirteenth Amendment absolved the negro from slavery, but left his social and political status "to the developments of time and experience." Whether as a state judge it was within his province

---

[1] *New York Herald*, April 10, 1867.   [2] Ex parte McCardle, *supra*.
[3] Ex parte Walton *et al.* See Affairs in Insur. States, (Miss.) Vol. II. p. 985, for the text of the decision.

to declare an act of Congress null and void was a question which he said he had maturely considered, and was satisfied that it was his duty. "Under a solemn sense of official duty," he said, "I am therefore constrained to hold that the act of Congress in question is in contravention of the Constitution of the United States as to the matter now presented for my action, and is inoperative and void."[1] The decision no doubt reflected the prevailing opinion in the state, but the right of the judge in the premises was not seriously maintained by the bar, and, of course, the military authorities did not permit its enforcement.

In general, therefore, it may be said that whatever doubts may have existed as to the constitutionality of the congressional policy, it was carried out with great thoroughness, and with practically no interference from the courts.

III. MILITARY GOVERNMENT UNDER GENERAL ORD

Shortly after the enactment of the reconstruction measures, the President assigned General E. O. C. Ord to the command of the fourth military district, embracing the states of Mississippi and Arkansas, with headquarters at Vicksburg. General Ord was a native of Maryland, a graduate of West Point, commanded Sherman's right wing at Corinth, his left wing at Jackson, and was present at the surrender of Vicksburg. He was not, therefore, an entire stranger in Mississippi at the time of his appointment as district commander. On March 26, he issued a general order informing the people of his appointment, and a week later came to Jackson and spent several days as the guest of the civil governor, visiting and inspecting the public institutions, forming acquaintances with leading citizens, and gathering such information as would be of value to him in discharging the difficult duties which the reconstruction acts imposed upon him. He was waited on by many of the citizens who were pleased with his "firm but generous and judicious demeanor."[2] The *Jackson Clarion* assured him that all the people, both officers and private citizens, would "strive conscientiously to pro-

---

[1] The full text of the opinion is printed in the *New York Times* of Oct. 26, 1866.

[2] The *Clarion* of April 4 said that the district commander had made a favorable impression by his visit to Jackson. "He is," said the editor, "an educated officer of the old United States army, and who in fighting the battles of his government during the late war obeyed orders, and did what he doubtless believed to be his duty. The war having closed, he has no spirit of revenge or

mote the public peace and avoid collisions with the military power." This seems to have been the general feeling.

The district commander's duties were of a twofold character: first, the maintenance of peace and order; second, the registration of the new electorate and the direction of the movement for reëstablishment of civil government. In the discharge of the first class of duties, it was necessary, to some extent, to reconstruct the official organization which he found, to modify the private law so as to make it conform to the new order of things, and to detect and punish crime.

Shortly after General Ord assumed command, many of the civil officers, on account of the uncertainty as to what policy he would pursue, abandoned their offices, while some of the citizens hesitated or refused to pay taxes, in the belief that the collectors were not competent officials. The governor accordingly issued a proclamation informing the people that the reconstruction acts recognized the civil government, and that the relations and responsibilities of civil officers to the Constitution remained unchanged until the civil government should be superseded. Civil officers were informed that they would be held to a strict accountability for the performance of their duties, and all good citizens were admonished to assist the civil authorities in the maintenance of peace, to deal " justly and indulgently with each other in their political helplessness," and to offer no resistance to the military authorities except such as might be authorized by the courts. They were also directed to pay the taxes assessed upon them for the support of the civil government.[1] One of the first orders of the new commander was to authorize all competent civil officers to arrest and punish offenders against the laws, " so as to obviate as far as possible the necessity for the exercise of military authority under the reconstruction acts." [2] As his civil functions were limited chiefly to the maintenance of peace and order, he did not regard it necessary to instruct civil officers as to their duties when their functions did not relate to these subjects. He assumed, as a matter of course, that they would continue to perform their duties without authority from military headquarters.

partisan malice to gratify, and will strive to execute the law, under which he is acting, to the letter. Our people will ask no exemptions which are not accorded to their brethren of the other excluded states."

[1] *Jackson Clarion*, April 6, 1867.

[2] Correspondence Relative to Reconstruction, Sen. Docs. 1st Ses. 40th Cong. p. 144.

While the district commander was not specially authorized at first to remove civil officers, it was the spirit of the
reconstruction acts that vacancies should be filled with
" loyal " incumbents.   General Ord, therefore, notified the
people that no elections would be held to fill vacancies
until a registration of voters was made in accordance with
the reconstruction acts.   Civil officers of the state government were directed to inform him of all vacancies occurring,
in order that he might fill them.   Local officers were now
authorized to continue in the performance of their duties
until otherwise directed or until removed.[1]   In reply to a
telegraphic inquiry from the Secretary of War concerning a
report that he had threatened to disperse the legislature and
take possession of the public money, records, and other public
property of the state, General Ord said that he had made
no threats to depose any civil officer except for failure to do
impartial justice to persons accused of crime, and that he
contemplated no seizures of state property unless it was found
that the laws of Congress could not be enforced otherwise.
No civil officer, he said, had been displaced except in certain
cases where incumbents had been tried by military commissions and convicted.[2]   The unpleasant duty of removing
all the civil officers was imposed upon a later district commander.   Ord was, however, by the act of July 19, authorized to remove all disloyal persons in office, but the offices
were not actually declared vacant until February, 1869.   On
the 29th of July, he notified all state and local officers of the
special laws of Congress for the reorganization of the state
government on the basis of suffrage, without regard to color,
and informed them that any attempt to render nugatory those
laws by speeches or demonstrations would be regarded as a
sufficient cause for summary removal.[3]   Again they were
reminded that it was made the duty of the commanding general to remove from office all disloyal persons, and all who
used their official influence in any way to obstruct the proper
administration of the reconstruction measures.   This announcement was shortly followed by the removal of most of
the municipal officers of Vicksburg, in order to " secure an

[1] All the special and general orders of the military districts under the
reconstruction acts, together with the records of proceedings of military
commissions, have been collected, chronologically arranged, and bound by
General F. C. Ainsworth of the War Department.   The more important
orders, however, are printed in the Correspondence Relative to Reconstruction.
[2] Cor. Rel. to Recon., p. 138.   [3] Appleton's Ann. Cyclop. 1867, p. 576.

equal and just administration of the laws upon all alike, and to secure the best interests of the citizens thereof." Several local officers were also removed in Choctaw, Kemper, Holmes, Neshoba, and Washington counties. The aggregate number of removals by General Ord probably did not exceed twenty-five. The total number of appointments made by him was about seventy, all being for local offices.[1] The difficulty of finding suitable persons who could qualify made it necessary in some instances to leave the offices vacant. Thus, no person could be found in Leake County who possessed the necessary qualifications for the office of sheriff. A Northern man was appointed and sent to the county. Some of those who could take the oath were not disposed to defy public sentiment by accepting office under a "military despotism." One of Ord's appointees was I. T. Montgomery, formerly a slave of Jefferson Davis. He was made a justice of the peace, and was probably the first negro in the state to hold a public office.[2] There was no loud protest against Ord's policy toward the civil officers. He made as few removals as his sense of duty dictated.

General Ord's duties in the field of legislation related for the most part to police administration, the regulation of labor, and the status of freedmen. To "preserve health and prevent epidemics," non-resident persons were forbidden to congregate in towns. A weekly inspection of all garrisoned towns was ordered, and occupants were directed to keep their premises in order. Orders were also issued to prohibit the carrying of concealed weapons. The economic and social

---

[1] The following is a list of General Ord's appointments : —

Justices of the peace	13
Circuit clerks	2
Members board of police	12
Probate judges	3
Constables	4
Circuit judges	2
County administrators	5
Sheriffs	10
Aldermen	7
Mayors	7
Magistrates	2
County treasurers	1
Marshals	1
Recorders	1
Assessors	1
Total	71

[2] Montgomery was the only colored member of the Constitutional Convention of 1890, and is at present the mayor of Mound Bayou, Mississippi.

demoralization of the time, together with the general impoverishment, developed a widespread sentiment in favor of suspending or wiping out private debts. Accordingly, the military commanders in most of the districts were overwhelmed with petitions praying for the enactment of stay laws. General Ord was not able to withstand the pressure, and on the 12th of June, he issued an order staying and suspending, until the 30th of December, 1867, all proceedings for the sale of land under cultivation, or of the crops, stock, implements, or other material used in tilling such land, in pursuance of any execution or writ, where the debt was contracted prior to January 1, 1866. All interferences under color of legal process with tenants in cultivating the growing crops was forbidden, except where the crops had been hypothecated for money or supplies.

The purpose of the order was alleged to be to "secure to labor its hire or just share of the crops, and to protect debtors and creditors from the sacrifices of property by forced sales" in the then impoverished condition of the country. Occasional orders were issued to stay executions in individual cases. Sheriffs, by another order, were directed to exempt from seizure and sale by distress for rent, all property exempt from execution or attachment by the terms of the homestead exemption act of Mississippi.

Sub-district and post commanders were ordered to seize all distilleries that did not pay the legal taxes assessed on them, and sell their property for the benefit of the poor. It was alleged that corn, so much needed by the poor, was being illicitly made into whiskey.

A considerable part of General Ord's legislation related to the freedmen. He issued an order congratulating them that they now held a common interest in the general prosperity of the state, but at the same time he reminded them that prosperity did not depend so much upon how they voted, as upon how they labored and kept their contracts. He informed them that the most important duty devolving upon them in their new condition was to make provision for the support of themselves and their families. They were admonished not to neglect their business to engage in political discussion, but to continue to comply with their contracts, and thus avoid the threatened famine. They were assured that at the proper time for them to have their names registered as voters they should be informed through the proper channels.

Orders were then issued at different times to prevent discrimination against them in the administration of the laws.

Thus, it was ordered that whipping or maiming as a punishment for crime, misdemeanor, or other offence should be prohibited. All civil officers were forbidden to collect any tax on freedmen as a class, that was not imposed upon all persons without distinction of race or color. Such a tax was alleged to be inconsistent with the civil rights act.

Another order required agents of the Freedmen's Bureau to investigate all charges against landholders for driving off freedmen with a view to withholding from them their arrears of wages. The removal of all crops was forbidden until the shares of laborers were ascertained and assigned to them. Post commanders were directed to investigate all complaints made by persons who claimed to have been persecuted by the civil authorities for opinion's sake, and to forward to headquarters a full report of the same, together with the testimony and affidavits taken in the course of the investigation. An order of September 10 directed all persons within the state, who had voluntarily exiled themselves since April, 1865, to report in person or in writing at the headquarters of the commanding general within thirty days. Another, informed overseers of the poor that every neglect to provide for colored paupers would be a dereliction of duty. Another, directed that persons indicted for criminal offences, and who were willing to make affidavit that during the war they were in the Federal service, and for that reason could not get justice in the civil courts, might transmit the papers in the case and the names of witnesses to headquarters, for trial by military commission.

The large amount of theft in General Ord's district seems to have claimed a good deal of his attention. One of the most common offences of this kind was the stealing of seed cotton, the demand for which made its sale an easy matter. To diminish the amount of this traffic, General Ord enacted that it should be a military as well as a civil offence, and therefore triable by military commission, and that no person after June 1, 1868, should be permitted to purchase country produce without a license from the mayor in incorporated towns, and from a member of the county board in country districts. Heavy penalties were prescribed for violations of the order.

Another offence of this kind was horse stealing. For the suppression of it, General Ord adopted rather drastic measures. He refused to allow the civil courts to take jurisdiction of such offences, but tried them before military commissions constituted by himself. Post commanders were directed to despatch forces of mounted men in search of such thieves, upon receiving reliable information that a theft had been committed in the neighborhood of their respective posts.   Civil authorities were requested to hand over to the military officials such offenders of this class as were in their custody.   All good citizens were urgently requested to coöperate with the commanding general in his efforts to break up the "nefarious trade," by giving full and explicit information, and by volunteering to act as guides. He asked for permission to imprison in the Dry Tortugas such thieves as were sentenced by military commission, believing that the moral effect would be wholesome.   The permission was granted with certain restrictions, and a number of persons were thus punished.

General Ord's interference with the civil authorities does not seem to have been very general, although he occasionally exercised his power in a way that led to loud complaints. The legislature was in session when he assumed command, and although he did not disperse it as he did the Arkansas legislature, such of its acts as were not conducive to the success of the congressional policy, as he understood it, were not permitted to be enforced.   Thus, he suspended all action that had been taken in Scott County for the removal of the courthouse until an election could be held by the qualified voters under the reconstruction acts.   Verdicts of juries and judgments of courts in a few instances were set aside or modified.   His interference with the judicial authorities led the chief justice to resign his position.[1]   The other members of the court followed his example shortly thereafter.

The freedom of the press and of speech was tolerated only to a limited extent.   An "unreconstructed" white man in Newton County was tried before a military commission and given ninety days' hard labor at the Dry Tortugas for allowing himself in the heat of passion to say that if it were in his power he would blow the old government to atoms, that the registration of negroes was a "humbug," and that no true Southern man could or would take the oath.   Another man was given two years for "insulting the flag."

Two Vicksburg editors were tried before a military com-

---

[1] In his letter of resignation, the chief justice declared that the character and dignity of the court could not be maintained, since its powers must be held and exercised in subordination to the behests of a military commander. "The conduct of the commanding general," said he, "is such an invasion of the legitimate powers of the judiciary as to place it in a condition of military duress in which I cannot seem to acquiesce by acting under it." Davis, Rise and Fall of the Confederacy, II. pp. 753–754.

mission for publishing libels against each other. The most noteworthy instance of General Ord's interference with the press was the well-known case of Colonel McCardle, the editor of the *Vicksburg Times*. Colonel McCardle took occasion to severely criticise the general's course in particular, and the congressional policy in general. On November 13, 1867, a squad of soldiers under the command of a lieutenant filed into the *Times* office, arrested the editor, and sent him to the headquarters of General Gillem, where he was confined in a military prison. Shortly thereafter, he was brought for trial before a military commission upon the charge of denouncing General Ord as a usurper and a despot, with defaming the character of a certain agent of the Freedmen's Bureau, and with advising voters to remain away from the polls on the occasion of the election to ascertain whether a convention was desired to secure the readmission of the state.[1] These specifications were a part of the general charge of impeding the execution of the reconstruction laws. The prisoner applied to the United States Circuit Court for a writ of *habeas corpus*. The writ was issued, and Colonel McCardle was given a hearing by Judge Robert A. Hill, who held that the question presented involved the constitutionality of the reconstruction acts, in pursuance of which the prisoner had been arrested. He decided that those acts were constitutional, that the powers vested in the commanding general had not been transcended by him, and that the prisoner was subject to arrest and trial before a military commission without indictment or jury. He was accordingly remanded to the custody of the military authorities. He appealed to the Supreme Court of the United States under the act of February 5, 1867, authorizing appeals in such cases, and upon entering into his recognizance of $1000 conditioned for his appearance before that tribunal, he was released.[2] Before a decision could be reached Congress passed an act depriving the court of jurisdiction of the case.

The following is a complete list of the cases tried by military commissions during General Ord's administration, together with the name of the place where the offence was committed, and the punishment in each case : [3] —

[1] The following well-known army officers constituted the commission that tried Colonel McCardle : General Gillem, General Pennypacker, Major John Power, Major Lynde Catlin, Major S. S. Sumner, and Major D. G. Swain.

[2] Ex parte McCardle, 7 Wall. 506.

[3] This list is compiled from "The Special and General Orders of the Fourth District."

	Offence.	Where committed.	Punishment.
1	Larceny of a horse . .	Adams County . .	2 years' imprisonment in the penitentiary.
2	Larceny of a horse . .	Yazoo County . .	6 months' imprisonment.
3	Larceny of a horse . .	Adams County . .	1 yr. (colored offender).
4	Larceny of a horse . .	Claiborne County .	1 yr. (col'd offender).
5	Larceny of a horse . .		
6	Larceny of a horse . .	Oktibbeha County .	6 mo. (col'd offender).
7	Larceny of a mule . .	Lauderdale County,	2 yr.
8	Larceny of a mule . .	Warren County .	1 yr.
9	Larceny of a mule . .	Marshall County .	2 yr.
10	Larceny of a mule . .	Washington Co. .	Acquitted (col'd offender).
11	Larceny of a horse . .	Hinds County . .	1 yr. (col'd offender).
12	Larceny of a horse . .	Hinds County . .	Acquitted.
13	Robbery	Noxubee County .	Acquitted.
14	Larceny of a horse . .	Issaquena County .	1 yr. (2 col'd offenders).
15	Murder of a negro . .	Panola County . .	10 yr.
16	Rape and subornation of perjury	Kemper County .	Acquitted.
17	Larceny of a horse . .	Lowndes County .	2 yr.
18	Larceny of a mule . .	Monroe County .	3 yr. (col'd offender).
19	Larceny of two mules .	Marshall County .	5 yr.
20	Larceny of a horse . .	Amite County . .	1 yr.
21	Larceny of a horse . .	Carroll County . .	4 yr.
22	Larceny of a horse . .	Madison County .	3 yr. (col'd offender).
23	Disloyal utterances and deterring negroes from registering	Newton County .	3 mo. at the Dry Tortugas.
24	Larceny of a horse . .	Adams County . .	2 yr. (col'd offender).
25	Larceny of a horse . .	Jefferson County .	2 yr. (col'd offender).
26	Assault on negro . . .	Warren County . .	2 yr.
27	Larceny of a horse . .	Lee County . . .	6 mo. (col'd offender).
28	Larceny of a horse . .	Copiah County . .	Acquitted.
29	Larceny of a mule . .	Warren County . .	Acquitted.
30	Larceny of a mule . .	Grenada County .	Acquitted.
31	Assault on negro . . .	Marshall County .	2 yr.
32	Assault on negro . . .	Marshall County .	3 yr.
33	Larceny of five mules .	Yazoo County . .	5 yr. hard labor at Dry Tortugas.
34	Selling pistol to soldier .	Warren County .	6 mo. and fine of $200.
35	Larceny of a mule . .	Simpson County .	1 yr.
36	Larceny of three horses,	Pike County . . .	5 yr. at Dry Tortugas.
37	Larceny of twelve horses,	Warren and Hinds counties . . .	5 yr. at Dry Tortugas.
38	Larceny of a horse . .	Claiborne County .	5 yr. at Dry Tortugas.
39	Larceny of a horse . .	Claiborne County .	Acquitted.
40	Larceny of a mule . .	Jefferson County .	2 yr. at Dry Tortugas.
41	Burglary and robbery .	Pike County . . .	7 yr. and 2 mo. at Dry Tortugas.

It is well to remember that in all these cases the offenders were civilians, and in no way connected with the military service. In no case was there a presentment or indictment by a grand jury, although the accused was furnished with a written copy of the charges against him ; nor was there a trial by a jury of the vicinage, nor were the well-established forms of judicial procedure followed ; yet, according to the proclamation of the President, the rebellion had come to an end more than a year before, and the courts, both state and Federal, were open and in the full and unobstructed discharge of their accustomed functions. Every effort to have the Supreme Court of the United States pass upon the validity of such proceedings in the South was defeated, sometimes by methods of questionable propriety. Trial by military commission in a Northern state where the courts were open was held to be unconstitutional.[1]

Next to the McCardle case, the most notable instance of a trial before military commission in Mississippi was that of E. M. Yerger, editor of the *Jackson News*. He was charged with slaying Lieutenant Colonel Crane of the United States army and acting mayor of Jackson by military appointment. He was arrested by the military authorities, and taken before a military commission presided over by Brigadier General R. S. Granger. His counsel protested against the authority of a military tribunal to try him, alleged that he was a citizen of Mississippi not in the service of the army or navy of the United States, and consequently, the civil courts of the state were competent to deal with him on the regular indictment by a grand jury. The objections were overruled, whereupon Yerger applied to the Circuit Court of the United States for a writ of *habeas corpus*, which was granted. The court decided that the imprisonment was lawful, and ordered that the prisoner be remanded to the custody of the military authorities, to be held to answer the charges brought against him. To obtain release from imprisonment Yerger asked for a writ of *certiorari* to have the case taken to the United States Supreme Court for review, and for a writ of *habeas corpus*. October 25, 1868, the chief justice gave his decision, affirming the power of the court to issue the writ, but gave no opinion as to the power of a military commission to try

[1] Ex parte Milligan, 4 Wall. 2, 120. Attorney General Hoar, in an opinion of May 31, 1869, held that the district commander in any state undergoing reconstruction might take a man from the civil power and try him before a military commission, and according to martial law, even though neither party was in the military or naval service of the United States.

a civilian in time of peace without a jury and without indictment by a grand jury.[1] The hearing on this all-important question was postponed until the next term of the court. Before the case was reached, the military government of the state had come to an end, and Yerger was handed over to the civil officers for trial. Thus, what would have doubtless been an interesting and important decision was avoided.

Such, in brief, was the administration of General Ord, so far as his first class of duties was concerned. There were local charges that he abused his powers and was an irresponsible despot, but it does not appear that he violated the spirit of the reconstruction acts, although it will be admitted that he might have administered them with less rigor and severity.

IV. REGISTRATION OF THE NEW ELECTORATE

The chief political duty of General Ord was to make a careful registration of the new electorate, as defined by the reconstruction acts. To protect the registration officers from interference while in the discharge of their duties, he made liberal requisitions upon the War Department for troops, and organized a large number of parties of mounted men to assist in the work of registration.[2] On the 15th of April, he appointed by special order a board of four military officers, who were charged with the duty of dividing the state into a convenient number of election districts for the purpose of facilitating the work of registration. It was also made the duty of this board to examine and recommend applicants for the position of registrar, and in order to procure suitable persons, the board was directed to correspond with the "most prominent and reliable Union men of the state." That none but "loyal" men should be appointed, the board was directed to make a record in each case, giving fully the

---

[1] Ex parte Yerger, 8 Wall. 85.

[2] The following was the strength and distribution of the military force in the state at the time of the registration : —

STATION.	STRENGTH.	STATION.	STRENGTH.
Vicksburg	269 men	Pass Christian	80 men
Brookhaven	80 "	Grenada	256 "
Meridian	83 "	Columbus	161 "
Jackson	242 "	Holly Springs	162 "
Winchester	77 "	Corinth	167 "
Woodville	77 "	Yazoo City	77 "
Natchez	86 "		

reasons for recommending the applicant.[1]   A board of three registrars was appointed for each county.   Each appointee was required to subscribe to and file in the office of the commanding general an oath that he had never voluntarily borne arms against the United States ; that he had never given aid, countenance, counsel, or encouragement to persons engaged in armed hostility thereto ; and that he had never sought, accepted, or attempted to exercise the functions of any office whatever under the authority or pretended authority in hostility to the United States, nor yielded a voluntary support to any such authority.   Of course, few of the native whites could take this oath.   As a consequence, General Ord's registrars were for the most part freedmen, military officers, and ex-Union soldiers who had settled in the state since the close of the war.[2]

The first board of registrars was appointed by special order on April 24.   Other appointments followed in quick succession, until the 30th of May, when the last registry board was completed.[3]   They were directed to select suitable offices and begin at once the registration of the electors. The several counties were to be divided into a suitable number of precincts, each of which was to be visited by the registrars in person after giving five days' notice, and they were to remain sufficiently long at each precinct to enable all qualified voters to register.   Each person registered was to be furnished with a certificate showing that he was a legal

[1] Gen. Orders No. 9, Cor. Rel. to Recon. p. 147.   The following was the detail for the board : General Alvan C. Gillem, Colonel Joseph R. Smith, Major O. D. Greene, Major Charles A. Wikoff.

[2] In an early report to General Grant, Ord announced that he purposed to visit each county and make his appointments only after personal interviews with applicants.   He also declared his intention of selecting two of the three election judges in each county from the late volunteer forces, and the third member from "loyal" residents, when such could be found.   In his first report, he expressed the opinion that there were few such persons in the state, by which, of course, he meant there were few who could take the iron-clad oath.

[3] The names of the registrars appointed by General Ord, together with the special orders issued to each board, are to be found in the Correspondence Relative to Reconstruction, pp. 148–190.   The expenses of registration were very large, on account of the elaborate machinery provided for the purpose. On July 9, before the work of registration was half completed, the Paymaster General informed Secretary Stanton that a further appropriation of $245,539 was needed for the completion of reconstruction in the fourth district.   He said : " If General Ord's registrars estimated for to July 1 should be continued on duty to July 31, there should be added to the above expenses for that month $159,781, and if continued to the end of August, $319,562."   Of the original appropriation of March 30, 1867, $97,222 had been used in the fourth district.   Report of Secretary of War, 1867, p. 260.

voter under the reconstruction acts.   Pending the decision
of the Attorney General as to who were disfranchised, registrars were to give the strictest interpretation to the law,
and exclude every person about whose qualification there
might be any doubt.   Any person so excluded, who might,
under the subsequent decision of the Attorney General, be
entitled to vote, would be duly informed and permitted to
register.

On the 10th of June, a circular of instructions to registrars
informed them that they had no power to decide in doubtful
cases upon the question of qualification or disqualification,
but must register all persons who were willing to take the
required oath, although it might be evident that the applicant was perjuring himself.   It was the opinion of the commanding general that the applicant must determine upon his
own responsibility, and at his peril, his ability or disability.
Registrars were, however, directed to report promptly to
headquarters for investigation by a military commission all
cases in which there was reason to believe that persons disqualified by the reconstruction acts had taken the oath.
They were urged to use every possible means to ascertain
the antecedents of doubtful applicants, and to warn them of
the penalty fixed by the reconstruction acts to the crime of
perjury.   If, however, the applicant insisted upon being registered, he must be given a certificate marked "reported for
investigation."[1]   General Ord transmitted a copy of these
instructions to General Grant for his approval.   In the letter of transmission, he expressed the opinion that the position
he had taken in regard to registration accorded with the
intent of the reconstruction acts, and that with the certainty
of trial before a military commission, few disqualified persons
would have the boldness to take the oath.[2]   General Grant at
once replied that he entirely dissented from the views of General Ord, and it was his opinion that registrars should use
every means to prevent disqualified persons from registering,
and to that end, they should be empowered to administer oaths
and examine witnesses.[3]   In a subsequent circular, registrars
were instructed to act in accord with the views of General
Grant on this point, and Congress, by the act of July 19,
made his instructions the law of the land.   It provided
further that no person should be entitled to vote by reason
of any executive pardon or amnesty.

[1] Cor. Rel. to Recon. p. 142, Circular of June 10.
[2] *Ibid.* p. 141, Letter of June 15.   [3] *Ibid.* p. 143, Despatch of June 23.

The work of registration began early in June. The registrars, accompanied by soldiers, clerks, and assistants proceeded from precinct to precinct. Only males twenty-one years of age, who had resided in the state one year, and who could take an oath of which the following was the substance, were entitled to be registered as legal voters : that the applicant had never been a member of any legislature, nor held any executive or judicial office and afterward engaged in rebellion against the United States, or had given aid or comfort to its enemies; that he had never taken an oath as a member of Congress or as an officer of the United States, or as a member of any state legislature, or as an executive or judicial officer of any state, to support the Constitution of the United States, and afterward engaged in insurrection against it, or gave aid or comfort to its enemies.[1] These stringent requirements in effect disqualified most of the prominent and influential white citizens, for there were few of that class who had not at some time held a petty office. They had all served the cause of the Confederacy.

In the meantime, the work of registration was going on. General Ord was able to telegraph General Grant June 15 that registration was progressing satisfactorily in thirty-five counties.[2] By the first of July, he reported that the work was going on in all the counties.[3] In a number of places, the

---

[1] Reconstruction act of March 23. The provisions of this oath in effect extended the disfranchisement beyond the requirements of the act of March 2, inasmuch as neither conviction, judgment of a court, nor any express legislative act was required to establish the fact of disfranchisement. Opin. of Stanberry, Attorney General, May 24, 1867. There was a difference of opinion as to the meaning of the phrase, "executive and judicial officers of a state." It was the opinion of the Attorney General that members of the secession convention, and all persons who during the war acted in an official capacity, where the duties of the office necessarily had relation to the support of the Confederacy, were intended to be included in the disqualifying clause. Officers whose duties were simply the preservation of order and the administration of the law did not come within the purview of the act. Such, for example, were militia and municipal officers, commissioners of public works, directors of state institutions, of banks, and of other corporations. Conscripts and slaves forced into the Confederate service were not to be taken as persons who had engaged in the rebellion. Mere acts of charity, where the intent was to relieve the wants of the Confederate soldier and not in aid of the cause which he represented, did not disqualify, although organized contributions of food and clothing for the general relief of persons engaged in the rebellion, and not of a mere sanitary character, were acts which disqualified. Voluntary contributions to the Confederacy in the form of loans and the purchase of its bonds or securities likewise worked disqualification. Opinion of June 12, 1867. The act of July 19 defined "executive and judicial officers" as being all civil officers created by law for the administration of any general law of the state or for the administration of justice.

[2] Cor. Rel. to Recon. p. 141.   [3] *Ibid.* p. 144.

whites were charged with deterring the negroes from registering.   The report was spread abroad that the purpose of registration was to enable the government to impose a tax upon the negroes, and to require military service of them.   By an order of June 29, bureau agents were directed to visit every important plantation within their reach, and instruct the freedmen upon the subject of registering and voting, and to correct any mistaken ideas that they might have, and report to headquarters the names of all persons interfering with the work of registration.   Only one individual seems to have been punished on this account.

Early in September the work was completed, with the following result : [1] —

White voters	.	.	.	.	.	46,636
Colored "	.	.	.	.	.	60,167
	Total	.	.	.	106,803

Of the sixty-one counties, thirty-three had negro majorities. The ann   ncement of the result greatly surprised the whites. The negro majority was far in excess of the estimates made by the newspapers, and showed that the negroes were not becoming extinct as rapidly as the census of 1866 seemed to indicate.   The result showed, moreover, the thoroughness with which General Ord had executed the reconstruction acts and settled the question as to whether the negro was interested in politics.   It revealed, too, as nothing else had done, the real political situation in which civil war and reconstruction was fast placing the whites.   It was now plain that the management of their political affairs, which they had come to look upon as theirs of right, must soon pass to their late slaves, together with white strangers from other states.   Many declared that the state was no longer a fit habitation for white men, and some prepared to emigrate to other countries.   Those who went in advance, however, made such discouraging reports that it was decided that negro suffrage was preferable to a life of exile.[2]

As the holidays approached, rumors of a negro insurrection disturbed the peace and quiet of the state.   Again the

---

[1] These figures do not include the registration in Bolivar, Covington, and Tunica.   The population of Bolivar and Tunica was overwhelmingly black. The counties with the largest colored majorities were Adams, Carroll, Claiborne, Hinds, Issaquena, Jefferson, Lowndes, Noxubee, Warren, Washington, and Yazoo.

[2] *De Bow's Review*, 1867, p. 537.

negroes had conceived the notion that Christmas would bring a distribution of the lands among them. Accordingly, they refused to make contracts for the ensuing year, or to leave the plantations where they lived. The indications of an armed outbreak became so numerous that the civil governor, Mr. Humphreys, on December 9, issued a proclamation reciting that communications had been received from different portions of the state expressing serious apprehensions that " combinations and conspiracies " were being formed among the blacks to seize the lands unless Congress should arrange a plan of distribution by January 1. It appears that complaints had been made to General Ord, which complaints were referred to Governor Humphreys for his coöperation with the military authorities. The proclamation of December 9 warned the blacks that if they entertained any such hopes, they had been grossly deceived. The governor told them plainly that the first outbreak against the peace and quiet of the state would signalize the destruction of their cherished hopes and the ruin of their race. The day before General Ord turned over the command of the fourth district, he instructed General Gillem, commander of the sub-district of Mississippi, to ascertain what white men were advising the freedmen to take up arms and seize the lands, and to inform the leading freedmen that there was no intention upon the part of Congress to take the lands of planters for the benefit of their former slaves, that the government already had plenty of land in Mississippi for freedmen, and they could settle upon it whenever they chose to do so. General Gillem accordingly issued a proclamation informing them that they would be required to earn their support during the coming year, and those who were able to work, and would not, would render themselves liable to arrest and punishment as vagrants. The coöperation of all civil officers was invoked to secure the enforcement of the order.

V. PARTY POLITICS IN 1867

The registration being complete, General Ord made ready for an election to determine whether the electorate, as now constituted, was in favor of a constitutional convention for the purpose of reëstablishing civil government and restoring the state to the Union, or whether they preferred to remain under military rule and without representation in Congress. An election to settle this question was ordered to be held on

the first Tuesday in November.   Delegates to the convention
were to be chosen at the same time.   On September 26, the
commanding general issued an order regulating in detail
the manner in which the election was to be conducted.   The
election at each precinct was to be held by a registrar, a
judge, and a clerk, who were to receive $6 per day for their
services.[1]   Only those who could subscribe to the iron-clad
oath were qualified to serve as election officials.   Each ballot was to have written on it the words " for a convention,"
or " against a convention," and also the names of the delegates voted for.   No returning officer was allowed to be
a candidate at this election.   The commanding general announced that he would exercise to the fullest extent the
powers vested in him to punish all cases of fraud and violence.   If it appeared that a majority of the votes cast were
in favor of a constitution, the names of the delegates would
be officially announced, and orders issued for the assembling
of the convention.   The excitement incident to the approach
of the first election in the state in which colored voters participated, led the commanding general to adopt stringent
measures to preserve the peace and secure a fair election.
Sub-district commanders were directed to cause all bar-rooms
and saloons to be strictly closed on occasions of political
meetings.   All persons making inflammatory speeches to
freedmen, or endeavoring to endanger the public peace by
exciting one class against another, were to be reported to
headquarters.   In pursuance of this order, a man was tried
before a military commission at Vicksburg for an alleged
attempt to deter registrars from their duties, and inducing
freedmen not to register by telling them it was the design
of the government to enroll them for service in a foreign
war.   He was convicted and sent to the Dry Tortugas for
imprisonment.   The assembling of armed bodies of citizens
under any pretence whatever was forbidden.

[1] General Ord's action in appointing freedmen as judges and clerks of the
election was the subject of great protest by the *Vicksburg Herald*.   That
journal said : " We hoped this shameful humiliation would be spared our
people, at least until the freemen of Mississippi decide whether they will submit to negro equality at the ballot box or elsewhere.   General Ord has heretofore exhibited a wisdom in his administration which has been highly
approved by the people, but we doubt not the lovers of peace throughout the
country will condemn the order as injudicious, if not insulting, to that race
whom God has created superior to the black man, and whom no monarch can
make his equal.   The general commanding cannot surely have forgotten that
the negro has no political rights conferred on him by the state of Mississippi,
although he is given the privilege by a corrupt and fragmentary congress to
cast a ballot in the coming farce dignified by the name of election."

As these reconstruction movements proceeded, a difference of opinion arose among the whites as to the proper course for them to pursue in the premises.   On the 15th of October, a state convention of "constitutional Union men" was held at Jackson, and it adopted resolutions urging all persons in sympathy with them to abstain from participation in the election of delegates to the reconstruction convention. In an address of December 12, they declared that the policy of Congress had reduced the people to utter ruin, and had contrived for them the perpetuity of negro rule, which meant that the Southern states were foredoomed to become African provinces, in which they and their children were to be held in negro subjection.   The supporters of this party purposed to take no part or lot in the proceedings by which such a condition of things was to be inaugurated.[1]   They took the view that inasmuch as the government was being reëstablished on principles abhorrent to their traditional ideas of popular government, and by those who had shown so little consideration for their welfare, their interests could be best subserved by abstaining from all participation in the work of reconstruction, and by permitting the state to remain under military rule.   As the call for the reconstruction convention required the approval of a majority of the registered voters, they could easily defeat it by refusing to vote.   Although the call for a convention of those who held to these views had been published in every county, and the people urged to send delegates, only six or eight counties responded.   The *Clarion* said this proved beyond doubt that the people were in favor of reconstruction.

The other party, which consisted of a respectable minority of the leading politicians and editors, took the position that it was the duty of the whites to register, vote for a convention, and in every possible way assist in the reconstruction of the state.   They saw clearly that there was no escape from negro domination, and that a policy of sullen inactivity would only increase the prejudice of the radicals in Congress, to whose power they were undoubtedly subjected.[2]   An acceptance of the reconstruction policy as cheerfully as their

[1] Their address is published in the *New York World* of Jan. 4, 1868.
[2] The *Jackson Clarion* of June 21, 1867, said : " The belief that negro suffrage can be averted by voting down a convention is a miserable, bald, and stupid delusion, and will soon run its course."   The *Kosciusko Chronicle* declared that if the question of a convention was defeated, another reconstruction act would be passed disfranchising nineteen-twentieths of the whites, and the state would be reorganized by the negroes, and those few whites who could take the oath.

pride would permit could not make their situation any the worse, and it would perhaps be the means of securing concessions from the radicals in Congress. Their support was, of course, not to be an outspoken advocacy of the reconstruction measures, but a hearty acquiescence. Some of the leading politicians of the state who supported this view were ex-Senator Brown, Mr. Barksdale, editor of the *Jackson Clarion*, and Judges Watson, Campbell, and Yerger.[1] Brown acknowledged the right of Congress to dictate terms to them, and he was willing to "make the best of it."[2] As for negro suffrage, he would not oppose it as an original proposition if it was done at the right time, by the right men, in the right way.[3] He was ready to "meet Congress on its own platform and shake hands."[4] Judge Campbell said he was in favor of accepting the reconstruction acts of Congress, for he felt that the people were in the power of the Federal government. "I agreed," he said, "with Mr. Barksdale, who favored a prompt acquiescence on the part of our people, and to make the most of the situation and form an alliance with the negroes politically by a full recognition of their rights to vote and hold office, acquire ascendency over them, and become their teachers and controllers instead of allowing the Republicans to do so." He thought the policy of the Democratic party drove the negroes to band together under the lead of the Republicans.[5] Ex-Governor McRae, Fulton Anderson, and others, advised every man who could to take the oath and vote for delegates to the convention. The foremost advocate of this policy was the *Jackson Clarion*, a Democratic paper. As early as the 16th of May, it advised the whites to register, vote, and otherwise aid in the work of reconstruction. The same issue of the *Clarion* published a list of twenty-two papers that had come out in favor of reconstruction. The editor affirmed that the policy of inactivity had no advocates in the state, and that "multitudes," who were at first inclined to take no part in reconstruction, had come over to its support. A state central reconstruction club was formed at Jackson, and counted among its members the two most eminent members of the Mississippi bar, Wiley P. Harris and William Yerger. Upon

[1] See editorials in the *Jackson Clarion* of Aug. 1 and 2, 1867, in which the duty of the whites is stated.
[2] Letter in *Jackson Clarion*, Jan. 6, 1869.
[3] Letter in *New York Herald*, April 3, 1867.
[4] *New York Tribune*, Feb. 11, 1869.
[5] Testimony in Boutwell Report, p. 937.

their advice, local affiliated clubs were formed in many communities.

The most advanced reconstructionist among the prominent whites was General Alcorn.   Inasmuch as there was no hope of escape from the power of the radicals, he proposed to form an alliance with them in order to secure terms.   He proposed to " vote with the negro, discuss politics with him, sit, if need be, in council with him, and form a platform acceptable to both, and pluck our common liberty and prosperity from the jaws of inevitable ruin."   With a platform guaranteeing to the negro all his rights as a citizen, generous provision for the education of his children, and the possession of a homestead, Alcorn believed that the white people would be able to hold their old positions as advisers of the negro race. With such an alliance, they would be in a position to " open negotiations " with the dominant political party of the North, with a view to securing the abolition of the cotton tax, the reconstruction of the levees, and the restoration of political rights.   Northern hatred of the Democratic party, he said, made it useless to continue to affiliate with that party.[1]

In the meantime, a new political party was being organized in the state.   On the 10th of September, it held a convention at Jackson.   This was the first Republican convention ever held in the state.   About one-third of the delegates were freedmen, the others were election registrars, bureau agents, and Northern men who had recently taken up their abode in the state.   They adopted a platform endorsing all the principles of the national party, and declared that the Mississippi Republicans would " keep step with it in all the progressive political reforms of the age."   They endorsed the congressional plan of reconstruction, and promised to use their best efforts in extending the benefits of free education to every child in the state, and to give the ballot to every man not disfranchised for crime, including treason. They declared that they would never recognize any distinction based on race or color.

" Two things are clear," said a newspaper correspondent who reported the proceedings, "first, the negro vote is in the majority ; second, it will be controlled by a few white men."[2] The *Clarion* found something in the action of the convention to be hopeful for.   It said: " Whatever may be thought of their platform, it is clear that if they get control of the

---

[1] See his address to the people, in the *New York Times* of Sept. 2, 1867.
[2] *New York Herald*, Sept. 25, 1867.

convention, it commits them against imposing disabilities and proscriptions beyond the requirements of the reconstruction acts. They have heartily adopted the congressional plan, and cannot go beyond it." The judgment of the *Clarion* proved to be unsound.[1]

The election to settle the question of a convention was held in the latter part of November, and the reconstructionists won by a large majority. The following was the result :

Registered voters	139,327
Votes cast	76,016
For a convention	69,739
Against a convention	6,277

The votes in favor of a convention were not only a majority of those cast, but a majority of the registered votes. The great mass of the whites took no part in the election, but allowed it to go by default. In pursuing this course, they made a great mistake. As a result of their refusal to participate in the election, the radicals secured a large majority of the delegates in the convention.[2] On December 10, the commanding general issued an order from Holly Springs, declaring that inasmuch as a majority of the votes cast were for a convention, it would assemble as already directed in a general order of December 8.

On the 28th of December, General Ord was directed to turn over his command to General Alvan C. Gillem and proceed to San Francisco and assume command of the Department of California. His incumbency as military commander of Mississippi covered a period of about nine months. From the standpoint of the reconstructionist, his administration was a thorough success, being vigorous in character, and in

[1] Among the delegates to this convention, and who were therefore among the founders of the Republican party in Mississippi, were George C. McKee, Jonathan Tarbell, R. W. Flourney, J. S. Morris, J. L. Wofford, L. W. Perce, H. R. Pease, and the Rev. James Lynch, colored. During the organization of the convention, Pease moved that the word " colored " be added to the name of each negro delegate, whereupon Lynch moved to amend so that the color of each delegate's hair be added, also. Both motions were laid on the table.

[2] Relative to this election, a Vicksburg paper said : " We urge every decent white man, every honorable gentleman of the Caucasian race to avoid General Ord's election as he would pestilence and prison." After the election, it said : " We are gratified to be able to announce that at the courthouse yesterday, the only place open to the whole people, there were cast the votes of eight persons only. We tried to get the names of the interesting sneaks who voted, but failed, though we are ready to pay a dollar for the name of each."

accordance with strict military methods. It was distinctly a military administration of military law, and therefore the sphere of civil liberty was reduced to a minimum. There were loud protests against the severity of his rule, and upon his own request, it is said, the President removed him and appointed as his successor a commander whose Southern sympathies led him to mitigate to a great extent the rigor of military rule which had been established.[1]

VI. MILITARY GOVERNMENT UNDER GENERAL GILLEM

General Gillem assumed command of the fourth district January 9, 1868. He had already been in command of the sub-district of Mississippi since the inauguration of the congressional policy, and was therefore, like his predecessor, not an entire stranger in the state. General Gillem was a native of Tennessee, a personal friend of President Johnson, had distinguished himself for gallantry in the Union army, and had taken a leading part in the reorganization of Tennessee.

At the time he assumed command of the fourth military District, the Twenty-fourth and Thirty-fourth regiments of infantry, together with two companies of cavalry, constituted the military force in the state. The troops were posted at Vicksburg, Meridian, Jackson, Natchez, Grenada, Columbus, Holly Springs, Corinth, Durant, Brookhaven, and Lauderdale. On account of the excitement incident to the election and the apprehension of collisions between the white and black races, four companies of infantry were brought from the Department of the Cumberland in June.[2]

There was a marked improvement in the economic condition of the state during Gillem's administration. The cotton crop had been almost a total failure in 1867, employers being unable to meet their obligations either to laborers or merchants from whom they obtained their supplies. There was much suffering among the poorer whites and the negroes. Both races appealed to General Gillem, who was then a sub-

[1] General Ord died of yellow fever at Havana in 1883. The order of the War Department announcing his death, concluded as follows : "As his intimate associate since boyhood, the general commanding [Sherman] here bears testimony of him that a more unselfish, manly, and patriotic person never lived." Powell's Officers and Soldiers, p. 27.
[2] Report Secretary of War, 1868–1869, p. 523.

district commander, for assistance.   General Gillem believed that the relief asked for would be an actual injury, and so he declined to advance provisions to either.   He urged the farmers to plant extensively, and the freedmen to enter into contracts for the following year, assuring both races that each would be held to a strict compliance with their agreements.   Finding that they would receive no aid from the government, all went to work, and an abundant crop was made, the first since 1860.   The system of labor so deranged at the close of the war, had, in a measure, adjusted itself to the changed conditions.   The whites had become convinced that free negro labor could be made profitable ; the negroes, on the other hand, had come to believe that there was no desire on the part of the whites to reënslave them or cheat them out of their earnings.   General Gillem reported that there were few complaints during his administration from either laborers or employers.

There was also an improvement in the political condition of the state, and a relaxation of the rigors of military rule. Gillem's first official act was to restore to the civil courts jurisdiction in cases of horse stealing, and, in fact, of all cases whatsoever, except in a few instances, where, from excitement or prejudice on account of race, politics, or "local animosities" it was believed that justice could not be secured.   In such cases the military tribunals were to continue to have jurisdiction.   Certain of his predecessor's orders giving to the military tribunals jurisdiction of cases involving disputes over the division of crops among employers and employees, and of cases between debtors and creditors were revoked, except where the Freedmen's Bureau had jurisdiction by act of Congress.   These cases were now to be cognizable by the civil courts.   He also used his pardoning power rather freely to relieve from imprisonment many persons convicted of crime by General Ord's military commissions.   The cases of all persons who were in confinement awaiting trial on the charge of horse stealing were directed to be investigated at once by post commanders, and reports made of those cases which, in their judgment, would receive impartial justice at the hands of the civil authorities.   Such cases were to be turned over to the civil courts "with the least possible delay."   General Ord's order requiring licenses to sell country produce after sunset was revoked, and so were his orders imprisoning several Vicksburg editors for libel against one another.   A number of General Ord's appointments were also revoked.

As will appear from the following exhibit, comparatively few cases were tried by military commissions during Gillem's administration, and there were still fewer convictions: —

OFFENCE.	WHERE COMMITTED.	PUNISHMENT.
1. Illegal collection of fines and obtaining money under false pretences (bureau agent). . .	De Soto County	"Guilty, but acquitted."
2. Murder	Warren "	Five years' imprisonment.
3. Murder of a freedman .	Hinds "	Acquitted.
4. Larceny of a horse . .	Lowndes "	Acquitted.
5. Murder	Panola "	Acquitted.
6. Robbery and assault with intent to kill (soldiers)	Grenada "	Ten years' imprisonment.
7. Bribery and illegal charges for service (bureau agent). . .	Panola "	Dishonorable discharge from army. Ten months' imprisonment and fine of $50.
8. Theft (U. S. soldier) .	Grenada "	Two years' imprisonment.
9. Larceny of a mule . .	Tishomingo "	Five years' imprisonment.
10. Assault on a freedman	Graysport	Acquitted.
11. Assault with intent to kill	Jeffers'n County	Three years' imprisonment.
12. Murder of a private soldier	Lincoln "	Acquitted.
13. Assault with intent to kill (colored offender)	Grenada "	Acquitted.
14. Larceny of two mules .	Tishomingo "	Five years' imprisonment.
15. Larceny of 400 lbs. meat	Choctaw "	Acquitted.
16. Larceny of two swine .	Choctaw "	Acquitted.
17. Riot	Choctaw "	Acquitted.

There were also comparatively few cases of interference with the civil authorities during General Gillem's administration. In one case, he ordered a change of venue, in another case, he suspended for investigation a chancellor's decree, in another, he declared a private sale of property void, and in another, he detailed an army officer to investigate the question of the removal of a County courthouse. By another order he directed that a special tax on guns and pistols in Washington County be reduced so as to conform to the tax levied in other counties, and in another case, he suspended the collection of the levee tax. With a view to diminishing crime, he forbade the carrying of concealed weapons, under heavy penalties, and to settle disputes between employer and employees, he made provision for boards of arbitration. In the absence of legislative sessions, it devolved upon him to make regular appropriations for support of the state institutions.[1] So far as reconstructing the official personnel of the civil government was concerned, it may be said that General Gillem removed a few more officers than his predecessor, due chiefly to the pressure which Congress brought to bear upon the district commanders. The mayor of Jackson was removed for failure to enforce law and maintain order, and an army officer was appointed to act in his stead. The circuit and probate clerks of Madison County were removed for using their positions for "political purposes." Sheriffs, probate judges, district attorneys, and justices of the peace were removed in several instances. On account of these removals, and on account of a good many resignations, the power of appointment was exercised considerably more than by his predecessor. The total number of civil appointments made by General Gillem aggregated about two hundred and thirty.[2]

There were during Gillem's incumbency few complaints from freedmen or white men, such as had occupied the time of the courts, agencies of the Freedmen's Bureau, and the "arbitrary boards" established by General Ord. Gillem says there was not a single complaint from the sub-district of Vicksburg, containing a large population of whites and blacks. His theory was to interfere as little as possible with the civil authorities, and to restrict the sphere of the military power to its legitimate function, that of preserving the peace. He reported at the end of the first year of his administration that the courts of record almost without exception had performed their duties impartially, although some of the minor courts were not so fair. The civil authorities, he said, did what lay in their power to maintain order and enforce the law.[3]

[1] At different times he appropriated sums aggregating $32,560 for the Lunatic Asylum, $13,551 for the University, and $500 for the Penitentiary.

[2] The following is a list of General Gillem's appointments: —
Three judges of the High Court of Errors and Appeals, 2 circuit judges, 7 probate judges, 2 district attorneys, 21 sheriffs, 15 mayors, 14 assessors, 12 circuit clerks, 3 probate clerks, 3 county treasurers, 4 magistrates, 56 aldermen, 28 justices of the peace, 20 constables, 5 marshals, 3 recorders, 3 coroners, 24 members Board of Police, 6 school trustees.

[3] Report Secretary of War, 1838–1869, p. 506. It was his opinion that the great defect in administering justice lay, not in the courts, but in the impracticability of detecting crime and arresting criminals. The majority of the crimes were committed at night by persons in disguise whom their victims were unable to recognize.

The extent of General Gillem's authority under the reconstruction acts subsequently came before the state Supreme Court. It arose over an act of his in setting aside the decision of a board of arbitration made adversely to the claim of a negro, satisfactory evidence having been submitted to the general that undue advantage had been taken of the negro's ignorance. Objections were taken to the authority of the district commander, but his action was sustained by the Circuit Court held by Judge Tarbell, a Northern man. The Supreme Court reversed the decision of the lower court. The two justices who concurred in the decision held that while very large discretion had been vested in the district commander so far as political questions were concerned, and in the maintenance of peace and order, absolute power over person and property had not been conferred upon him. They denied that the military commander could set aside and vacate the judgment of a court in a civil case. From this decision Justice Tarbell, who had in the meantime been appointed to the Supreme bench, dissented, and affirmed that the military commander was the source of all power, authority, and law ; and that he could annul the constitution or code, either wholly or in part, or he could make law by his military fiat as he pleased, and that in the exercise of the power vested in him, he could displace the judge, and hear and determine the case himself. " By no refinement of reasoning, therefore," he continued, " can we escape the fact that there existed in the state in 1868 a pure undisguised military government, and the military force was not kept there simply as a police force, a sort of comitatus to preserve the peace, but it was sent there to govern as well." [1] Tarbell's view was certainly justified by the actual practice of the commanders, if not by the spirit of the reconstruction acts ; whether it was justified by the Constitution of the United States is not quite so clear.

VII. THE RECONSTRUCTION CONVENTION OF 1868

The important political event of General Gillem's administration was the session of the reconstruction convention, locally known as the " Black and Tan " convention. It assembled at Jackson January 9, just two days before General Gillem assumed command of the district. Viewed from

---

[1] Welborne *vs.* Mayrant, 48 Miss. 653.

the standpoint of both its personnel and its policy, it deserves to be ranked as the most remarkable political assemblage ever convened in Mississippi. General Ord, who had brought it into existence, fixed the number of delegates at one hundred, and apportioned them in such a way, it was charged, as to give the reconstructionists a large majority. Thus thirty-two of the sixty-one counties of the state had negro majorities, and were given seventy delegates, while the twenty-nine white counties were given but thirty.[1] This was the first political body in Mississippi in which the negro race was represented, there being seventeen colored delegates returned. With the exception of the colored ministers,[2] they were without education, and none of them had ever before held public office. There were but nineteen conservatives in the convention. The so-called "carpet bag" element had twenty odd representatives, nearly all of whom had been soldiers in the Union army. There were twenty-nine native white Republicans, derisively called "Scalawags." Four of the Northern born Republicans had lived in the South before the war, and two of them had served in the Confederate army. Among the more prominent ex-Union soldiers in the convention were General Beroth B. Eggleston, a native of New York, but who had enlisted as a private in an Ohio regiment; Colonel A. T. Morgan, of the Second Wisconsin Volunteers; General W. S. Barry, formerly commander of a negro regiment raised in Kentucky; General George C. McKee, formerly a practising attorney at Centralia, Illinois, and a graduate of Knox College; Major W. H. Gibbs, of the Fifteenth Illinois infantry; Judge W. B. Cunningham, of Pennsylvania; and Captain E. J. Castello, of the Seventh Missouri infantry. These were among the founders of the Republican party in Mississippi, and were more or less prominent in the politics of the state down to 1876.[3]

---

[1] The following inequalities were computed from a table giving the population of each county (see Appleton's Ann. Cyclop., 1868, p. 517). There were 106,000 registered voters (before the revision). Apportioning 100 delegates among these would give a ratio of 1 delegate to 1100 voters; yet Tippah County with 901 votes had two delegates; Panola with 1233 had two; Holmes with 877 had two and one floater with Madison; Washington with 2231 had three, and Tishomingo with 3273 (nearly all white) had only two.

[2] One authority says the number of colored preachers was eight, the most prominent being J. Aaron Moore of Meridian, now a blacksmith at Jackson, Mississippi, C. W. Fitzhugh, and T. W. Stringer, the latter a Northern man who went South with the Freedmen's Bureau. He sat for Warren County.

[3] The subsequent careers of some of the members of the "Black and Tan" convention are full of interest. Five met violent deaths. Caldwell, after-

The convention was called to order January 7, by Mr. Mygatt, a Northern man who had lived in the state before the war, and who had supported the cause of the Confederacy in a feeble way until the surrender of Vicksburg, shortly after which he renewed his allegiance to the United States. Upon taking the chair, he delivered a harangue in which he reminded the delegates that the long-looked-for hour had at last come, — "the hour," said he, "for which our registrars have so long toiled, the hour that all loyal men have labored to hasten, but which a disloyal press has striven to prevent." "This hour," he said, "brings to a close a period of Mississippi history."[1] Eighty-three members answered to their names, one of whom (Orr of Harrison) failed to produce official evidence of his appointment. The committee on credentials reported that in the matter of contested seats it belonged to the commanding general to determine who were elected, and who, therefore, were entitled to seats.

General Eggleston was elected president of the convention, and Thad P. Sears, late of the Federal army, was chosen secretary. There was also a large corps of employees and hangers-on, for some of whom it must have been difficult to find any duties.[2]

The first task of the convention was to fix the compensation of the delegates and employees, and provide for raising the necessary means, for it will be remembered that the

wards senator (colored) from Hinds, was, with his brother, assassinated on the streets of Clinton in December, 1875. He had been charged with participation in the Clinton "Massacre"; Combast was hung by the Kuklux in Sunflower County ; Orr was shot at Pass Christian ; Fawn was shot in the courthouse at Yazoo City ; Fred Parsons, defender of Governor Ames in his impeachment trial, was found dead in a water-hole, having been murdered by unknown persons. The Northern members, almost without exception, left the state after the "revolution" of 1875.

[1] Convention Journal, p. 3.

[2] The following is a partial list of the thirty employees of the convention, and the per diem of each, where the amount is ascertainable from the journal : —

One reporter at $15 per day ; 1 secretary at $15 per day ; 2 assistant secretaries at $10 each per day ; 1 sergeant at arms, $10 ; 2 assistant sergeants at arms, $5 each ; 1 printer ; 1 warrant clerk ; 2 enrolling clerks ; 1 reading clerk ; 1 minute clerk ; 1 auditor ; 1 treasurer ; 1 auditing clerk ; 1 chaplain at $10 per day ; 1 postmaster at $8 per day ; 1 hall porter at $4 per day ; 4 pages at $2.50 each ; 2 doorkeepers at $5 ; 1 woodchopper at $2.50. There was also a number of committee clerks with salaries ranging from $5 to $15 per day. The employment of a regular chaplain was exclusively a reconstruction innovation. Every one of the employees was either a Northern white man or a negro, "men of known loyalty," as they were called. A resolution offered by a native white Republican that some of the clerkships be given to loyal Southern men was voted down. — Journal, p. 30.

expenses of the convention were to be defrayed by the state, and not by the United States. On the first day of the convention, one member had the temerity to propose that "in order to expedite business and quicken consciences" each delegate be required to pay his own expenses. His motion was of course laid on the table, and a committee was appointed to arrange a schedule of salaries. The committee reported an ordinance fixing the compensation of members at $20 per day. This, however, was thought to be too large, and it was accordingly reduced to $10 per day and forty cents per mile while travelling to and from the capital.[1] Perhaps less than a dozen of the delegates who voted for the compensation ordinance were owners of real estate in Mississippi. This was said to be the "long-looked-for hour" to which the chairman of the committee on compensation had alluded in his address already mentioned, the hour for which "loyal" men had so long toiled, and a "disloyal" press striven to prevent. Never had a legislative body or a state convention in Mississippi placed so high an estimate upon the value of its services. And what seems almost incomprehensible, there was a feeling that they had a legitimate right to exploit the taxpayers to any extent they pleased. To protest against such a schedule of salaries was treason and disloyalty.[2] Upon the passage of the compensation ordinance, an indignant Democrat offered a resolution declaring that inasmuch as a large and influential class had been disfranchised, and a large class who had never been citizens were enfranchised, a majority of the delegates on the floor were not entitled to their seats, and therefore the assembly was illegal and not entitled to compensation. This resolution was voted down with a whoop and amid cries of expulsion. He did not despair, however, and after regaining his composure, offered another resolution, to the effect that after the expiration of twenty days, no delegate should receive over $5 per day for his services. His language was denounced as insulting to the convention, and a resolution was introduced asking him to withdraw and pay his own expenses. The resolution further directed that he be cen-

[1] Some of the delegates drew as much as $240 on account of mileage. The average seems to have been about $160.

[2] It should be said, however, that on account of the depreciated state of the currency, the compensation was not as great as it appears. Members were paid in state warrants worth sixty-five or seventy cents on the dollar. It should also be said that the scale of compensation for members was but little higher than that fixed by the Democratic legislature in 1865.

sured and granted a leave of absence for fourteen days.[1]   A committee was then appointed to ascertain if any member was opposed to reconstruction, or had declared the convention unconstitutional, or did not regard its acts as valid.

The convention was extravagant in other particulars. The Secretary of State was requested to furnish delegates with stationery.   He replied that he had none on hand, and no means with which to procure any.   A committee of three was appointed to provide stationery for the convention.[2] They sent an agent to New Orleans to purchase a supply. The amount of his bill was $1458.80.[3]   This supply was soon exhausted, and additional quantities were purchased of a local firm.[4]   The delegates also seem to have had a lively appreciation of the value of keeping posted on current events.   They made ample provision for supplying themselves with daily newspapers, those of the reconstruction type, of course, being given the preference.[5]   A no inconsiderable sum was spent in sending telegrams to Washington, and in sending committees to various places, especially to Vicksburg to consult with General Gillem.   Having got a taste of office, the members of the convention now made an effort to oust every official in the state from his position. About the third day after the organization of the convention, General Barry moved the appointment of a committee of seven to memorialize " our noble Congress " to confer on the conven-

[1] Convention Journal, p. 35.
[2] Ibid. p. 16.
[3] Ibid. p. 36.   The largest items were, 105 reams paper, $897.80 ; 2400 writing pens, $39 ; 900 penholders, $18 ; 150 inkstands, $42 ; 650 lead pencils, $80 ; 26,000 envelopes, $195.   There were, in addition, large quantities of ink, blotting paper, erasers, mucilage, fasteners, etc.
[4] The total sum paid the local firm for stationery, as far as can be ascertained from the journals, was $468.47.
[5] Each delegate was allowed five copies of any daily paper that he might select.   One member favored making the number twenty ; another thought fifty was not too large.   So far as can be determined from the journal, the following amounts were appropriated for newspapers : for the

Jackson Pilot	$ 44.
Times	85.
Vicksburg Journal	1783.
Memphis Bulletin	8.
Clarion	1123.53
Vicksburg Herald and *New Orleans Republican*	139.60
Vicksburg Republican	120.
Memphis Post	68.
Avalanche	3.
Vicksburg Chronicle	296.
Total	$ 3670.13

tion power to declare all civil offices vacant, and vest the appointment of the new incumbents in the convention, in order that all the said offices might be filled by men of "known loyalty" to the United States government.[1] The *Clarion* said this was the "coolest piece of audacity" that had come to its notice, and that if the scheme was consummated, it would do more than anything else to concentrate the opposition of the people against the entire work of the convention, and surely lead to its rejection.   Fifteen conservatives protested against sending the memorial to Washington, and affirmed that the government of the state was not in the hands of rebels; that the civil officers had not neglected to protect life, liberty, and property of loyal men; that there were not enough competent men in the state who could take the iron-clad oath; and that the convention was assembled to make a constitution, and had, therefore, no jurisdiction in the premises.   The convention refused to allow the protest to go upon the records, and decided by a vote of fifty to nineteen that "it be wrapped in brown paper and returned to the gentleman from Marshall." The orthodox test of loyalty, in General Barry's opinion, was straight-out radicalism.   That the state should be handed over to his party, was a matter of supreme importance, and he insisted that the consideration of his motion be made the special order of the following day.   It was lost by only a small majority.[2]   It became so manifest that one of the purposes of the convention was to secure the offices, that Judge Watson made an attempt to checkmate the radicals by an ordinance declaring delegates ineligible to any office of trust or profit under the state, should it be reorganized in accordance with Barry's measure.   His resolution was voted down by a large majority.[3]

The convention had been in session several weeks before it seems to have dawned upon the delegates that the establishment of a constitution was the purpose for which they

[1] The memorial declared that " the loyal people of this state require your immediate aid to remove obstructions impeding the actions of their representatives; that the loyal men of the state have accepted in good faith the reconstruction laws, and are laboring to institute a civil government that shall recognize and protect the liberties of the citizens; that the state is under a civil government organized in 1865 by not more than one-third of the white men who were authorized to vote by the President's proclamation, rebels in name, in heart, in head, in policy, indeed in all respects save open hostility. All this has been borne by the faithful Union loyalists with a calm defiance and unaltering devotion to country, to liberty, and to the Union; and now this rebel sentiment has culminated on the floor of this convention by a member in a report averring that this body is an unauthorized assembly."

[2] Convention Journal, p. 14.   [3] *Ibid.* p. 15.

were assembled. They remained in session but three hours per day, apparently adopted no methods for expediting business, in fact, exhibited no inclination to speedily conclude their labors and secure the readmission of the state at as early a date as possible. The greater part of the first week was consumed in effecting an elaborate organization and arranging the compensation schedule.

The next subject to engage their attention was the invention of some scheme for the support of the colored people in their idleness. There were many freedmen who still clung to the delusion that the government intended to make a division of the lands among them. Their refusal to labor or make contracts resulted in reducing large numbers of them to poverty. One of the first acts of the convention was the appointment of a committee of five to investigate and report what *legislation* was needed to afford adequate relief and protection to the state and citizens thereof.[1] The committee reported early in February that they had made a careful examination and found that there existed nearly all over the state an " alarming " amount of destitution among the laboring classes and, to some extent, among other persons " strangers to labor and economy." They were inclined to fix the number at thirty thousand, although they believed that to be a low estimate. They thought the number of those in " straitened and needy circumstances " could be safely set down at not less than forty thousand; that only eleven counties were free from distress and suffering, and in nearly all the rest, there was more or less destitution, and in some, it bordered on actual starvation. They recommended that the poll tax collected in the several counties be placed at the disposal of a commissioner selected by the convention, and applied to the relief of destitute persons in their respective counties.[2]

The resolution was adopted, and a committee sent to Vicksburg to ask General Gillem to issue the requisite order. But the commanding general, knowing that the report was greatly exaggerated, and being further convinced that the convention did not possess powers of general legislation such as were involved in the appropriation of a poll tax and the appointment of a committee to distribute it, refused to

---

[1] Convention Journal, p. 18. The convention throughout its entire session refused to be bound by the well-established principle of American public law that a constituent assembly does not possess powers of ordinary legislation.

[2] The report is printed in the Report of the Secretary of War for 1868, p. 613.

comply with their request.   At the same time, he assured
the committee that he had thoroughly investigated the subject of destitution throughout the state, and, as assistant commissioner of the Freedmen's Bureau, he had the means and
would employ them in relief of such destitute persons as
really required assistance ; that he had instructed the officers
and agents of the bureau to procure employment for all who
were able and willing to earn a support ; and that the aged,
decrepit, and orphans would be cared for in hospitals and
asylums.   General Gillem was satisfied that the demand for
laborers exceeded the supply, and if destitution existed, it was
due to the unwillingness of the negroes to labor.   He said
he was constantly receiving letters requesting aid in hiring
laborers.   He declared that the very day on which the committee interviewed him, five hundred negro men with their
families could have procured labor at the office of the bureau
in Vicksburg, and that free transportation would have been
furnished every laborer to the point where he was wanted.
He accompanied his reply with official reports of bureau
officers to show that there was no legitimate reason for destitution, if it existed.[1]   In view of this, he said he deemed
it " inexpedient " to direct so large an amount of the revenue
of the state to the object specified, when there were no funds
in the state treasury, and when the state penitentiary, lunatic
asylum, and other institutions were being supported at the
expense of the United States.[2]

It was charged by the Democrats that the extraordinary
solicitude of the convention for the colored people was a
political move to secure their support at the next election, at
which nearly all the delegates expected to be candidates.[3]

---

[1] See Convention Journal, p. 226, for report of Colonel J. W. Scully,
U. S. A., dated Vicksburg, February 18.   The colonel declared that the
destitute condition of the freedmen was mainly due to their refusal to work
for wages.   "They insist," said he, " that upon the adjournment of the convention, the lands will be divided among them, and until then they can live
without work."   See also *ibid.* p. 227, for report of Lieutenant Merritt Barber,
dated Vicksburg, February 12.   He says persons from Tennessee and points
in Mississippi had visited Grenada (headquarters of his sub-district) for the
purpose of procuring laborers, offering excellent terms, without being able to
secure a single one.   The bureau agent at Panola reported that he had more
applications for laborers than he could fill.   The Holly Springs agent reported
the same, and declared that the laborers of his district had received all their
wages for the last year, and that not an instance of destitution had come to
his notice.

[2] General Gillem's letter declining to issue an order directing sheriffs to
reserve the poll tax is found in the Convention Journal, p. 223; also in the
Report of Secretary of War, 1868–1869, p. 614.

[3] See speech of Senator James B. Beck, appendix to Globe, 41st Cong. p. 257.

Failing in this scheme, the convention turned its attention to the invention of other "relief" measures. A committee was early appointed to frame an ordinance for the "relief of the people of Mississippi from their pecuniary embarrassments." In the opinion of the convention, this could be successfully accomplished by means of stay laws or abolition of all debts. The commanding general was accordingly requested to order tax collectors to suspend the collection of all taxes which might have been assessed against freedmen prior to January 1, 1868.[1] Another provided for the abolition of all debts, contracts, and judgments that had been incurred or made prior to April 28, 1865.[2] This measure was actually adopted, and a committee appointed to confer with General Gillem and request him to issue the order for its enforcement. Again, the general refused to coöperate with the convention. He respectfully referred them to the homestead and bankrupt laws, and suggested that with the allowances and exemptions provided by these, no family was threatened with starvation, present or prospective, by allowing the law to take its course.[3]

Again, a committee of five was appointed to proceed to Vicksburg and urge the commanding general to issue an order forbidding all officers and trustees from making further sales of property, except for wages or mechanical labor, until further orders from him. Again, the general informed them that the law under which the convention was assembled did not vest them with general powers of legislation, and that, moreover, such action would be "detrimental" to the interests of the people of the state. He declined to issue the order.[4]

The commanding general was next requested to furnish from the public funds the necessary means to enable all persons known as "refugees" to return to their former homes, from which, it was alleged, they had been dragged by the slave trader and sold in Mississippi as slaves, and for lack of

---

[1] Convention Journal, p. 70.

[2] Report Secretary of War, pp. 608, 609. This was of course in violation of the Constitution of the United States, Art. I. Sec. 10, par. 1.   Mr. Railsback, a radical preacher from Bolivar County, offered a resolution for the incorporation of an "article" in the constitution for suspending, for a period of ninety-nine years, all legal proceedings for the collection of all debts, of whatsoever kind, incurred before the passage of the ordinance of secession. It was laid on the table.

[3] Appleton's Ann. Cyclop. p. 506.

[4] Letter to Hon. George A. Stovall, H. Mis. Docs. 3d Ses. 40th Cong. p. 69 ; also Report Secretary of War, 1868-1869, p. 609.

means had never been able to return.[1] Others, they said,
had been induced by promises of liberal compensation for labor
to leave their families and friends, and were now " cast on
the cold charities of the world without money, and far from
friends who might be able to afford them temporary relief."
To General Gillem this appeared to be another scheme for
exploiting the treasury, and he respectfully declined to comply with the request, alleging that there was no legal authority for expending the public funds for such a purpose.[2]
Congress was now asked to set aside for distribution to the
colored people through the Freedmen's Bureau one-half of
the Federal cotton tax collected in the state.[3]

On March 7, the convention adopted a resolution requesting General Gillem to issue an order directing the restoration of property alleged to have been unlawfully taken from
colored persons, on the ground that property accumulated by
them while in a state of slavery belonged to their masters.
It was also alleged that the courts did not protect them in
their lawful rights.   Gillem at once informed the convention that he was charged by the reconstruction acts with
protecting all persons in their rights, and any instance
brought to his notice where persons, without regard to race
or color, were deprived of their property, should receive
his prompt attention.   He declined to issue the desired
order.[4]

The convention in the meantime was instituting an in-
quisitorial investigation into the affairs of the civil governor,
Mr. Humphreys.   In the first week of the convention, a
committee was appointed to investigate and report on
the charges made by Governor Humphreys, in his proclamation of December 9, relative to the apprehended negro
insurrection.[5]   The committee reported that it had spent
some time "hunting up information," and had found that
there was no just cause for issuing the proclamation, that
it was a libel on the people of Mississippi (the colored people,

---

[1] This report is signed by Moore, Stringer, and Fitzhugh, all colored
ministers. Report Secretary of War, p. 611.

[2] Convention Journal. The commanding general informed the convention that it had been his custom, as assistant commissioner of the Freedmen's
Bureau, to furnish children with transportation to parents or relatives desir-
ing to take charge of them, and also destitute persons who were likely to
become a charge on the government, to places where employment might be
obtained, or where they might be provided for by friends. Further than that,
it was imprudent to extend the practice. He declared that it would take
$1,000,000 to transport the negroes of Mississippi to their places of birth.

[3] Journal, p. 70.

[4] Report Secretary of War, p. 632.   [5] Convention Journal, p. 30.

of course), and the governor was requested to furnish the
convention with "more specific information" in regard to
the reports which constituted the basis for his action.   In
a sarcastic reply, the governor said that he presumed the
convention did not admit that it had any constitutional
right to require him to account for his administration of
civil government in Mississippi.   He acknowledged, however, the right of the people to petition for redress of
grievances, and the correlative duty of civil officers to furnish, when respectfully requested to do so, such information
as pertained to the welfare and happiness of the people.   This
proclamation, he said, had been issued at the urgent request of
General Ord, from whom he received all the information then
in his possession, except a few letters from private citizens.

General Gillem declined to furnish the convention with
the sources of information, believing it would be a breach of
faith to do so, and would result in no public good.[1]   The
governor's course in another matter had aroused the opposition of the convention.   It will be remembered that
the ladies of Baltimore had contributed supplies for the
relief of the destitute of Mississippi, and had sent their
donations to Governor Humphreys to be distributed.   It
appears that the whites were almost wholly the beneficiaries
of this benevolence.   When the convention met, one of its
first acts was the appointment of a committee to inquire
into the distribution of all funds received by the state
treasurer or other state officers from various towns, cities,
or private individuals in the Northern states, for the relief
of the destitute in the state, and to demand of the governor an itemized statement of the receipts and disbursements of such funds during his term of office.   Upon
receiving the request, the governor at once replied that he
had received no such funds.   He said, "those who have
intrusted me, as their private agent, with the distribution
of their charities, have neglected to instruct me to account
to your body, and your committee have failed to furnish me
with any evidence that the donors have given you any authority to make the inquiry proposed.   As these donors may regard their charities as their own private matters, and may
object to having the names of the beneficiaries made public,
I must respectfully decline to comply with the request of

---

[1] H. Mis. Docs. 3d Ses. 40th Cong. affairs in Mississippi, p. 71.   See
also Report Secretary of War, pp. 629–632, for the correspondence between
General Gillem and the convention on this subject.

the committee, until authorized to do so by the donors, at which time I will cheerfully exhibit the proper vouchers."[1] This ended the matter.

The convention did not enter actively upon the discharge of its main duty until provision was made for defraying its enormous expenses. While the United States government had borne the expense of registration and election, it was left to the state to provide the means for the support of the convention. Various revenue schemes were suggested. One of these provided for the levy of a tax of $2.50 on every voter in the state for this purpose.[2] Another scheme provided for the issue of state warrants, to be made receivable in payment of taxes and other dues to the state. Still another provided for a committee of three, to confer with the President of the United States, and represent the " true state of affairs " in Mississippi, and request from the United States government a loan of $100,000 for the use of the convention.[3] A resolution was finally adopted instructing the finance committee to frame an ordinance for levying a tax upon the real and personal property of the state.[4] This, of course, shifted the burden to the shoulders of those who received so little consideration at the hands of the convention. Those whom members referred to as the " loyal " people of the state did not contribute enough to pay the doorkeepers and pages of the convention.

On the 26th of January, the chairman of the finance committee called on the commanding general at his headquarters and asked whether, in the event of the adoption of an ordinance for the levy and collection of a special tax on the real and movable property of the state, the civil authorities would be prevented from collecting the tax either by forcible resistance, or injunction, or other judicial process.[5] The chairman was informed the same day that the civil authorities would not be prevented from collecting the taxes by forcible resistance, and any ordinance made in conformity with the reconstruction acts under which they were assembled would be recognized as legal.[6] With this assurance, the convention proceeded to enact an elaborate revenue measure, consisting

---

[1] H. Mis. Docs. 3d Ses. 40th Cong. affairs in Mississippi, p. 71.

[2] Convention Journal, p. 31. The number of registered voters at the June election was 139,327. This plan would have produced $348,317.50. The motion was made by a white Democrat for obvious reasons. The scheme was, of course, rejected.

[3] *Ibid.* p. 238.   [4] *Ibid.* p. 125.

[5] H. Mis. Docs. 3d Ses. 40th Cong. condition of affairs in Mississippi, p. 71.

[6] Report Secretary of War, 1868, p. 586.

of thirty-six sections, and imposing a tax on auction stores, distilleries, livery stables, coal yards, carriage factories, bounty
agents, gunsmiths, banks, exchange brokers, street venders,
express and telegraph offices, grist-mills, cotton gins, ferries,
bridges, turnpikes, billiard tables, photograph galleries, in-
surance agencies, etc.   The ordinance reads like a war revenue measure.   Even the press did not escape,[1] nor the
railroads, although exempt by statute from taxation until
1874.[2]   Every bale of cotton in the state was taxed fifty
cents.   In addition, a special tax equivalent to one-third of
the state tax was levied upon all real and movable property.[3]

Immediately after the passage of this ordinance, a committee of tax payers called on General Gillem and protested
against its enforcement, declaring it to be in conflict with
the reconstruction act under which the convention was assembled.   That act authorized the convention to lay a tax
on the property of the state for the purpose of defraying the
expenses of the convention.   The commanding general declined to take any action, but suggested that they appeal to
the United States district court, as the construction of a
Federal statute was involved.   Judge Hill was then applied
to for an injunction to prohibit the collection of the tax.
He declined, without examining into the merits of the bill,
to interfere, on the ground of lack of jurisdiction.   They
then applied to one of the state circuit judges, who granted
the injunction.   On February 12, the convention passed a
resolution reciting the action of the state courts in enjoining
the collection of the tax and the opposition of the people in
public meetings and through the press, and requested General Gillem to publish an order forbidding interference by
the courts, and directing the people to pay.[4]   General McKee
was appointed to wait upon the commanding general and present the resolution.   This he did on the 13th of February.
Gillem's reply was delayed until the 19th.   He then informed
the convention that after a careful examination of the ordinance, he was convinced that many of its provisions were in
violation of the reconstruction act; that they had not re-

---

[1] The amount imposed on each daily newspaper was $50 ; on each tri-
weekly, $30 ; on each weekly, $20 ; on each job printing office, $25.

[2] Five of the roads were assessed $200 each ; three, $50 each ; and the
others $10 each.

[3] The ordinance is published in the Report of the Secretary of War, pp.
616–620.

[4] The commanding general was requested to "answer immediately."
They had now been in session more than a month without having received
any compensation.

stricted themselves to levying a tax on property, but had taxed persons, privileges, and franchises ; had, in fact, made some of their taxes retrospective in effect; and, moreover, had assumed the legislative power of creating a new system for the collection of the tax, through collectors unknown to the laws of the state, and from whom no bonds were required ; and also a special treasurer to receive and disburse the money collected.[1]   It was General Gillem's opinion that the tax would net an income of $300,000, although the convention claimed to need only $100,000.[2]   The convention was informed that the additional state tax levied by the twenty-seventh article of the ordinance seemed to be in conformity with the reconstruction act, and he would afford them every facility in collecting it.   The others he declined to enforce. He recommended that sheriffs be intrusted with the collection of the tax, and the state treasurer with the disbursement of the funds.[3]

On the 27th of February, the convention adopted another revenue ordinance.   It levied a general tax, equal to fifty per cent of the state tax for 1867, upon all property ; a special tax of one and one-half per cent on the value of stock belonging to all dry goods stores, groceries, drug stores, and all other personal property of whatever nature ; and fifty cents on every bale of cotton in the state.[4]   Sheriffs were authorized to make the collections.   This was acceptable to General Gillem, and he issued an order directing the sheriffs to proceed with the collection, though he extended the time of collection from ten to thirty days.[5]   Soon after the publication of this order, the commanding general received a communication from the president of one of the railroads, protesting

---

[1] Section 17 provided for at least one collector in each county, who was to receive as compensation for his services five per cent of all money collected. The collectors were given extraordinary powers.   They were authorized to administer certain oaths, and if not satisfied with the statement of the person as to the amount of his sales, the collector might assess and collect whatever seemed to him just.   There was no limit to the exaction which he might make.   Only five days' notice was to be given to the tax payer.   The property of the delinquent was to be sold on three days' notice.   Gibbs, a carpet bagger, had made an effort to get through an ordinance exempting all officers from making bonds.

[2] The convention seems to have anticipated this, as provision was made for investing the surplus in U. S. Bonds.

[3] The text of his letter to McKee is printed in the Report of the Secretary of War, pp. 621, 623.

[4] The ordinance is printed in the Report of the Secretary of War, p. 625.

[5] Ibid. p. 625.   The convention was afterward convinced that even this extension did not allow sufficient time for the collection of the tax, and requested, by resolution, that it be extended from April 6 to August 1.

against the assessment of the tax on his road, on the ground
that it was exempt by law from taxation until 1874.[1] General Gillem referred the communication to the judge advocate and to the attorney general of the state, both of whom
gave opinions that the tax was illegal, the exemption being
a vested and chartered right.[2] The High Court of Errors
and Appeals had also taken this view.[3] General Gillem
accordingly issued an order directing sheriffs not to collect
the tax on railroads. The convention then appointed a
committee to confer with the general on the subject. They
called on him May 15, at Vicksburg ; insisted that the convention had the same power to tax property in Mississippi
that Congress had ; that it did not recognize any state law
or chartered rights granted by the legislature, and that if
the collection of the tax, estimated at $50,000, was not
enforced, it would be necessary for the convention to delay
its contemplated adjournment, or meet again in about ten
days to provide for the deficiency thus caused, which would
involve a much heavier expense. General Gillem says he
was convinced that the convention was exceeding its powers
and violating the national Constitution. As for the delay
of the contemplated adjournment, he did not think it had
sufficient legal force to require refutation. He therefore
declined to enforce the tax on railroads, but assured the
convention that he would enforce the collection of any tax
which might be levied in conformity with the acts of Congress, and that sheriffs who had failed to collect the tax
already levied should be directed to do so at once.[4] A list
of delinquent counties was reported to him, and he at once
issued an order informing the sheriffs of those counties that
a failure to collect the taxes would be considered a failure
to faithfully execute the duties of tax collector, as required
by their bonds. The taxes were paid reluctantly, of course,

---

[1] An act of Feb. 27, 1854, had exempted from taxation for twenty years
the fixtures and property of the S. W. Air Line Extension R. R. Co., and
extended its benefits to all railroad charters granted before the passage of the
act as well as all granted thereafter.

[2] See Report of Secretary of War, pp. 635, 637, for their opinions.

[3] So R. R. Co. *vs.* Mayor and Alderman of Jackson, 38 Miss. p. 334.

[4] Report of Secretary of War, p. 641. The *Jackson Clarion* of April 13
contains a strong appeal to General Gillem to " call a halt " upon schemes of
the convention. It said : " In the name of a long-suffering, tax-ridden, and
patient people, we appeal to him for relief. The people are not permitted to
right their own wrongs, else they would not ask for help. Goaded almost to
desperation, they appeal earnestly to the commander to see that the law is
no longer wantonly and deliberately violated for purposes of insult and
pelf."

and the convention seems to have had ample funds to meet its enormous expenses.

After having been in session more than a month, discussing schemes for the "relief" of "loyal" people, endeavoring to adopt a tax ordinance that would be acceptable to General Gillem, and in passing various resolutions relating to state sovereignty, and explanatory of the principles of government as they understood them, a motion was carried for the appointment of a committee of fifteen, to prepare a constitution for the state, and to report in three days.[1] A resolution to adopt the old constitution with the changes made necessary by the abolition of slavery was laid on the table. It was determined that the new constitution should have as little in common with that of 1865 as possible. The subject receiving the greatest attention was the qualifications for office and suffrage. The discussion on these topics began in February, and continued until the latter part of April. A strong effort was made by the minority to secure the adoption of a provision that would exclude from the franchise the great mass of ignorant blacks. After the report of the franchise committee, a long and acrimonious debate took place, during the course of which many personalities were indulged in.[2]

The franchise article was adopted by a large majority on the eighty-sixth day of the convention, whereupon twelve of the white delegates resigned their seats and returned to their homes. They were followed by two others on the succeeding day.[3] "They are," said the *Clarion* of April 17, "a

---

[1] On the forty-fifth day the convention began holding night sessions. On the sixty-sixth day Aaron Moore offered a resolution that as the convention was composed of majors, generals, captains, lawyers, ministers, farmers, planters, and blacksmiths, they ought to go to work and frame a constitution, and go home to their constituents. It was unanimously adopted. It was not until the convention had been in session one hundred and eleven days that they consented to the adoption of a resolution that after a certain date (May 15), the per diem of members should cease. Journal, p. 687.

[2] At one point the bitterness became so great that personal altercations and fights were of common occurrence. The president of the convention was assaulted in front of the capitol building by a Democratic delegate. Other fights occurred. A majority of the members on both sides went armed.

[3] Journal, p. 541. The vote on the franchise article was 44 to 25. For some weeks the Democratic members had taken little part in the proceedings. They felt that they were out of place, and consequently remained away. Their absence was the subject of criticism by the Republicans. On the 13th of February, Captain Castello moved the appointment of a physician to inquire into the health of the absent members. It was charged that they were engaged in writing articles for the newspapers, defamatory of the convention, and otherwise impeding the work of reconstruction. Journal, p. 273. One delegate was expelled for drunkenness and for publishing an article impugn-

noble band whose names will long be remembered by their countrymen."

By the franchise article as finally adopted, applicants for registration were required to take and subscribe to the test oath prescribed by the reconstruction acts, and swear further that they admitted the civil and political equality of all men.[1] No person was eligible to office who, as a member of the legislature, had voted for the call of the secession convention; or who, as a delegate to any such convention, had voted for or signed the ordinance of secession; or who had given voluntary aid, countenance, counsel, or encouragement to persons engaged in armed hostility to the United States; or who had accepted or attempted to exercise the functions of any office, civil or military, under any authority or pretended government, authority, power, or constitution within the United States hostile or inimical thereto, except all persons who had aided reconstruction by voting for the convention; or who had continuously advocated the assembling of it and should continuously and in good faith advocate the acts of the same.[2] Members of the legislature and state officers were required to make oath that they had never, as members of any convention, voted for or signed an ordinance of secession, or, as members of any legislature, voted for the call of any convention that passed such an ordinance.[3] Many other resolutions, generally with long preambles, were adopted. One declared all acts of the convention of 1865 null and void; another changed the name of Davis County to Jones, and the name of the county seat from Leesburg to Jonesboro, and the name of Lee County to Lincoln;[4] another provided for the appointment of a committee of fifteen to take into consideration the propriety of moving the capital from Jackson to Kosciusko.[5] Other ordinances forbade forever the adoption of any property qualification for office or the adoption of any property or educational qualification for suffrage;

ing the motives of members. The Democratic members fell to making light of the convention, and offered various resolutions to bring it into contempt. One such began with the preamble : "We the carpet baggers and scalawags of Ohio, Vermont, Connecticut, Maine, Africa," etc. Another moved that the "whole convention go down to Pearl River and drown itself." Journal, p. 209. After the twelfth day, newspaper reporters were excluded for designating negro members as "colored," and for refusing to prefix "Mr." to their names.

[1] Section 3, Art. 7.   [2] Section 5, Art. 7.   [3] Section 26, Art. 12.
[4] Convention Journal, pp. 133, 145.
[5] *Ibid.*, p. 646. The committee reported in favor of continuing the capital at Jackson until 1875, after which it should be removed to Kosciusko, a village situated then twenty-five miles from the nearest railroad.

forbade slavery or involuntary servitude in the state otherwise than in punishment for crime; denied the right of
any state to withdraw from the Union on account of any
real or supposed grievances; forbade the making of any
distinction among the citizens in reference to the possession, enjoyment, or descent of property; prohibited the
abridgment of the right of all citizens to travel on public
conveyances; and recommended to Congress the removal
of the political disabilities of one hundred and thirty
persons.[1]

This was the chief work of the "Black and Tan" convention. After having been in session one hundred and fifteen
days, it adjourned May 18.[2]

The cost of making the constitution and securing its adoption was at least a quarter of a million dollars. The per
diem of the delegates aggregated $116,150. The pay of the
large number of employees and hangers-on probably raised
the amount to $150,000;[3] $28,518.75 was paid to four
newly established Republican papers to print the proceedings.

The amount was distributed as follows: —

Mississippi State Journal	$13,924
Vicksburg Republican	6,910
Meridian Chronicle	5,428
Mississippi Pilot	2,255

This does not include the cost of printing the large journal of nearly 800 pages, nor the cost of publishing the con-

---

[1] Relative to this memorial, one of the radicals wrote Speaker Colfax,
saying : " We need these men to fill certain positions in the party, and to labor
for its success, and it is of great importance to *us* that their disabilities be
removed so that the reward of loyalty may be seen and felt. They have all
done us great service, and are still at work fighting valiantly side by side with
the best and truest radicals of the party. We want them for office." H.
Mis. Docs. 2d Ses. 40th Cong. No. 34.

[2] The following comparative table shows the number of days for which
each of the several constitutional conventions in Mississippi, except that of
1817, was in session : —

Convention of 1832	29 days.
Convention of 1861	23 days.
Convention of 1865	11 days.
Convention of 1868	115 days.
Convention of 1890	71 days.

[3] The Appendix to the House Journal of 1870, pp. 125–178, contains a list
of the convention warrants that had been cashed up to September 1. There
were 3071 warrants, amounting to $130,886.13. The cost of the constitu-
tional convention of 1890 was $53,760, exclusive of printing. It does not

stitution and ordinances in the local papers, nor the cost of printing 20,000 copies for distribution. Items like the following appear on the pages of the Journal : —

For printing constitution, *Summit Sentinel* . . . . $	481
For printing constitution, *Corinth News*	400
For printing constitution, *Grenada Sentinel*	245
For "services as public printers," Gens. Dugan and Stafford .	30,337

In addition to the expenditures on account of the convention must, of course, be reckoned the cost of revising the registration lists twice, and of holding two elections before the constitution was finally ratified. As will be seen later on, the expenses under these two heads were very large, and were defrayed out of the state treasury.

Before adjourning, the convention made elaborate provision for submitting the constitution to the people. The 22d of June was selected as the day on which the election should begin. It was to be continued through such period as the commanding general might direct, in order that every voter should have an opportunity to express his preference. Provision was made also for an election at the same time of state officers, members of the legislature, and members of Congress. The legislature to be chosen was to meet on the second Monday after the official promulgation of the constitution, and proceed at once to ratify the Fourteenth Amendment. Until this was done, that body was to have no power of legislation, nor were members to receive any compensation for their services. Another notable provision was the appointment of a committee of five from the members of the convention to have general supervision of the arrangements for holding the election, to ascertain the result, and make proclamation thereof. This committee was empowered to sit during the adjournment of the convention, and exercise all powers "necessary to carry into effect the purposes of the reconstruction acts." It was authorized to appoint three commissioners for each county to attend the election, be present at the counting of the votes, and forward the result to the chairman.[1] The committee of five was empowered to

appear from the Journal the amount expended on the latter account. The expenditures on account of the convention of 1865 amounted to $14,050.

[1] These commissioners were to receive $6 per day and their expenses, to be paid out of the convention fund. This added vastly to the cost of the convention. It is the testimony of certain of General Gillem's election inspectors that in numerous instances these commissioners rented offices when there were vacant rooms in the courthouses which they might have used.

reconvene the convention in the event of the rejection of the constitution.

VIII.   PARTY POLITICS IN 1868

The day after the adjournment of the convention, that is, May 19, General Gillem issued an order reciting the authority under which the convention had been called, and announced that its labors were now terminated, and the constitution of government would be submitted to the registered voters of the state for their ratification or rejection, beginning on June 22, and continuing until every elector had had an opportunity to cast his vote.   Electors were to vote "For the Constitution" or "Against the Constitution," and also, upon the same ballots, for state officers and representatives in Congress. Commencing fourteen days before the election, the several boards of registration were to meet at the county seats in their respective counties, and after having given reasonable public notice, were to proceed to revise the registration lists for a period of five days.   All additions and removals were required to be reported to headquarters.

In order to secure as nearly as possible a full expression of the people, it was ordered that the election should be held at each precinct under the direct supervision of the board of registration.   Each county was to be divided into three equal portions, to each of which was assigned a registrar, who, with a judge and a clerk of his own appointment, was to be held responsible for the conduct of the election.   They were to provide themselves with ballot-boxes, locks, and keys, and after giving timely notice by means of hand-bills, were to proceed from precinct to precinct, holding the election on consecutive days, when the distance between precincts would permit.   Detailed instructions were given for opening and closing the polls, examining certificates of registration, inspecting, locking, and sealing ballot-boxes, etc.   Registrars were to begin at the most remote precinct and proceed toward the county-seat, at which place an election was to be held under the joint supervision of all the registrars for the benefit of any voters who might not have had an opportunity to vote in their precincts.   Judges and clerks of election were to be selected by registrars, preferably from among the residents

They continued to draw pay for days after the election.   The expenses of these 165 commissioners must have aggregated $10,000, assuming that the expense of each was about $60.

of their respective districts, if competent persons of eligibility were available. They were required to take and subscribe to the iron-clad oath of July 2, 1862, a copy of which was to be transmitted to headquarters and kept on file in the office of the acting assistant adjutant general. Careful lists of all registered voters who did not vote were to be kept and forwarded to headquarters. None but registered voters were allowed to challenge the right of others to vote. Sheriffs were to be held responsible for preservation of order, and were directed to appoint a sufficient number of deputies for each precinct. As additional safeguards for insuring peace, each judge, registrar, and clerk was empowered to make arrests; and all public bar-rooms, and other places at which intoxicating liquors were sold, were ordered to be closed on election days. The carrying of firearms or other deadly weapons in the vicinity of the polls was strictly prohibited. Registration judges and clerks were forbidden to stand as candidates for any office, and all army officers and bureau agents were prohibited from electioneering, speaking, or endeavoring to influence voters, although they might instruct freedmen in regard to their rights as electors. The commanding general announced that he would exercise to the fullest extent the powers vested in him to secure a fair election, and he warned all persons against attempts to abridge the right of electors by contracts.[1] On the following day, he announced, by general order, the names of the registrars for the several counties.[2] An active army officer or an ex-Union soldier was placed on each registration board. The other two members were usually native Republicans, although occasionally a Democrat was appointed. Appointees were directed to report at once their acceptance, and to subscribe to and forward to headquarters a copy of the test oath.

A week later, the commanding general issued another order detailing ten army officers to serve as inspectors of election, one for each of the ten districts into which the state was divided.[3] It was made their duty to visit the boards of registration in their respective districts, and ascertain by close inquiry and examination whether the registrars fully understood their duties, and to furnish them such information and instruction as might appear to be necessary. They were required to make detailed reports to headquarters of the

[1] See Report of the Secretary of War, 1868–1869, pp. 645–648; also H. Mis. Docs. 3d Ses. 40th Cong. No. 53, p. 75.

[2] *Ibid.* p. 649; *ibid.* p. 79, where names of registrars are given.

[3] Report Secretary of War, p. 651.

progress of registration in each county, and to make minute inquiry into the nature of the services performed by registrars, in order to be able to form correct judgments as to the reasonableness of their accounts. Furthermore, they were to give particular attention to the cost and means of transportation and the rental of offices for registrars.

When it was found that improper persons had been appointed, they were to recommend removals and nominate their successors by telegraph. They were authorized to give orders in the name of the commanding general, and to keep him constantly informed of the progress of the election.[1] Registrars were also directed to travel throughout their subdivisions during the nine days intervening between the close of the registration books and the beginning of the election, and give general and thorough notice of the time at which the election would be held in each precinct. The commanding general urged upon registrars the most rigid economy, and informed them that whenever their accounts were deemed excessive they would be disallowed.[2]

On June 12, he issued a circular designating one person in each county to take the election returns and records of registration boards to Vicksburg.[3] Other circulars directed that the polls should be open two days instead of one in the fourteen largest towns of the state; authorized duplicate certificates in certain cases; and directed inspectors to fill vacancies in registration boards in certain contingencies.[4] The constitutional convention having provided for the election of state officers, representatives in Congress, and members of the state legislature, a circular was issued May 28, defining the congressional and state senatorial districts and apportioning representatives in the legislature.

On the 15th of June, General Gillem announced through a general order that commanding officers of stations, posts, or detachments would be held responsible for the preservation of peace and good order during the election, and directed that detachments be sent to such places as might be deemed necessary, to protect all classes in the right of voting.[5] Five additional companies of troops were brought from the Department of the Cumberland to aid in maintaining peace. These, with the troops already in the state, amounted to thirty-two companies, and were distributed at sixty-three points. Gen-

[1] Report Secretary of War, p. 655.   [2] Ibid. pp. 654, 655.
[3] The circular is printed in ibid. p. 661.   [4] Ibid. pp. 658-659.
[5] Gen. Orders, No. 8, ibid. 134.

eral Gillem asserts that in every instance in which it was
reported that fears of disturbance or interference with elections was apprehended, regardless of the source from which
the report emanated, troops were sent to the locality, in order
to insure peace and prevent intimidation.[1]

Nothing illustrates so well the thoroughness of the congressional policy of reconstruction as the regulations for
registering the voters and conducting the elections. Every
possible precaution to prevent fraud and unfairness seems to
have been taken by the district commander. It is difficult
to see what more could have been done.

The policy of the convention had hardly been determined
when the friends and opponents of the constitution began to
marshal their forces for the contest that was evidently preparing. The Republican state convention met at Jackson,
February 5, less than a month after the meeting of the reconstruction convention. There were about 175 delegates
present, the majority of whom were members and hangers-
on of the reconstruction convention. The leading candidates
for the gubernatorial nomination were General Eggleston
and Mr. Musgrove, both Northern men, and Judge Alderson,
a native Republican. General Eggleston was nominated. He
was a native of Saratoga County, New York, and claimed the
distinction of having received the surrender of Atlanta. The
other nominees were also Northern men, with two exceptions.
The negro race was completely ignored, although a strong
appeal was made in behalf of the Rev. Mr. Stringer for a place
on the ticket. "Two things are noticeable," said the *Clarion*,
in regard to the action of the radical convention: "first,
the imported stock out-distanced all competitors; second,
Sambo was left out." The negroes, who constituted ninety-
nine one-hundredths of the Republican voters, were naturally
not pleased with this sort of recognition, and some of them
protested loudly. One of these was the Rev. Mr. Fitzhugh,
a well-educated negro from the North, and a member of the
reconstruction convention. He published a letter in the
Woodville Republican of August 1, 1868, in which he informed
his race of the action of the state convention in refusing to
recognize their claims, and of his belief that it was the
intention of the white Republicans not to permit colored men
to hold office. He accordingly urged them to join hands with
the Southern whites and "bid defiance" to the carpet bagger.
These men, he said, "garbed in the disguise of friends to us,

---

[1] Report Secretary of War, p. 74.

are impostors, and will cause more blood to be spilt than the Union is worth." He announced his withdrawal from the Republican party, believing it to be "ruinous to the Union, and an enemy to the black race."[1]

After some wrangling, the convention endorsed General Grant for President, and adopted a platform pledging its adherence to the Republican party, declared in favor of equal rights to all, and "unwavering fidelity" to the Union, and announced that it would stand by these principles, and never lower the standard of Republicanism. The convention also nominated presidential electors, all except one of whom were "carpet baggers."

The opponents of the constitution began to bestir themselves even earlier than the reconstructionists. On the 8th of January, the day after the assembling of the reconstruction convention, the *Jackson Clarion* published an urgent call for a convention of "white citizens," to meet on the first Monday in February, to "take into consideration our situation, and determine our future course." It pleaded for a union of all white men as the only means of preventing the ratification of a constitution which, it apprehended, would embody the "worst elements of radicalism." "We need and pray," said the *Clarion*, "for such a body. It is no time for pique, petulance, or preference. It is no time for personalities, or for narrow, purblind selfishness."

On the 16th of January, a convention of conservatives was held at Jackson, and a platform of principles adopted. They styled themselves the Democratic White Man's Party of Mississippi, and declared that the "nefarious design of the Republican party to place the white men of the Southern states under governmental control of their late slaves, and degrade the Caucasian race as the inferiors of the African race, is a crime against the civilization of the age which needs only to be mentioned to be scorned by all intelligent minds, and we, therefore, call upon the people of Mississippi to vindicate alike the superiority of their race over the negro, and their political power to maintain constitutional liberty." Nothing worried the leaders of this party so much as the fear of division among the whites, such as existed the year before. The January convention, in dropping the name of the party (Constitutional Union), under which the campaign was conducted in 1867, was the subject of considerable opposition upon the part of the more conservative opponents of the con-

---

[1] The letter is printed in the *New York Herald* of Aug. 18, 1868.

stitution. The *Clarion* of January 18, in a strong appeal for
unity of action said: " Fellow-citizens, let there be no strife
among us in this solemn hour. We are all Constitutional
Union men, we are all Democrats, let us unite with one
heart and one mind."

On the 19th of February, what seems to have been the
regular state convention of the Democratic party was held at
Jackson. It was largely attended, and was in session three
or four days. There was a considerable difference of opinion
among the delegates as to the proper course to pursue, although
the *Clarion* said there was no difference of principle. They
endorsed the action of the January convention, and adopted a
long platform severely arraigning the radicals, and declaring that the only hope for the restoration of constitutional
liberty lay in the defeat of the constitution.

They denied that the state had ever been out of the Union,
and affirmed that the convention then in session assuming
to frame a constitution of government for Mississippi, was
assembled without constitutional authority, the delegates not
being elected by the qualified voters of the state, but by
negroes destitute alike of the moral and intellectual qualifications required of electors in all civilized countries, combined with a small minority of white adventurers from other
states; that the acts of the latter class demonstrated them
to be the enemies of the people of the state, who had constituted it from its territorial infancy to the present time; that,
under a fraudulent pretence of framing a constitution, they
were wickedly conspiring to disfranchise and degrade the
people, and rob them of their liberty and property, to destroy
their political and social status, and, finally, to place them
under the yoke of a negro government.

The convention appointed a committee of five to prepare
and publish an address to the people of the state "explanatory of the views and principles which govern the Democratic party." April 27, the address was issued. It called
upon the people for renewed activity to defeat the radical
constitution. A plan of organization was submitted to the
county associations for their acceptance. It appealed to all
lovers of liberty to assemble and organize, and prepare for
the great contest before them. There was a registered majority of seventeen thousand to be overcome, but with eternal
vigilance and activity it could be done.

On the 12th of May, the convention was reassembled to
determine more definitely what action should be taken at the
coming election. The February convention had neither

nominated state officers, presidential electors, nor decided
whether it would be expedient to take any part in the election on the constitution. Their first thought was to defeat it
by "sullen inactivity," but the action of Congress in providing that a majority of the votes cast at the election would
be sufficient to ratify the constitution spoiled this plan. The
reassembled convention therefore nominated a state ticket,
and advised that an effort be made to defeat the constitution
by outvoting the Republicans. It made no difference which
way the election went, their nominees for state offices would
never be installed into office, for if the constitution was
defeated, there could be no state officers, and if it was ratified,
the Republican nominees would, of course, be elected. Officers
were nominated, therefore, with no expectation that they
would ever be called upon to serve, but as a means of rallying the voters. The executive committee was empowered to
nominate presidential electors in the event the state was
permitted to take part in the presidential election. General
Gillem was appealed to for permission to take part in the
choice of electors, but he informed the chairman of the
Democratic executive committee that he had no authority to
order such an election. The state, therefore, took no part in
the presidential election of 1868.

As the proscriptive character of the constitution became
more generally understood, the opposition of the whites
increased. Every man who had given counsel or encouragement to a Confederate soldier was to be debarred from office.
It was provided, however, that these proscriptive clauses
should not apply to those who had aided reconstruction by
voting for the convention, or who had continuously advocated
its assembling, or who had in good faith advocated all its
acts. Simple acquiescence in their work of proscription and
disfranchisement, however sincere, was not sufficient; but
continuous and outspoken advocacy of acts which the commanding general had to suppress as palpable violations of
law and justice was necessary to secure to the most intelligent and virtuous citizen rights accorded to the most ignorant
of his former slaves. The franchise clause was almost equally
obnoxious to the whites. The applicant for registration was
required, in the first place, to make oath that he was not
disfranchised by the reconstruction acts. This in itself
excluded a large and influential class. He was, moreover,
required to make oath that he believed in the political and
civil equality of all men. Removal of political disabilities
imposed by the reconstruction acts was not valid in Missis-

sippi until the act of Congress should be concurred in by the state legislature. This constitution thus practically denied the power of Congress to remove political disabilities without the consent of the state legislature. There were, besides the so-called proscriptive features of the constitution, other objections. The next governor, who, it was well understood, would be General Eggleston, was made a veritable autocrat. He was to have the appointment of all judges, supreme and circuit, all chancellors, all militia officers, and all county, district, and precinct officers. The present incumbents were to be removed by him within thirty days, and his power of appointment was to continue until the legislature should provide by law for the election of such officers.[1] Other objections were the provision for mixed schools and the increased expense of administering the government under the new constitution. Relative to the proscriptive features of the constitution, the *Clarion* asserted that if adopted it would disfranchise twenty or thirty thousand citizens of the state, and that not more than one thousand whites would be able to hold office, vote, serve on juries, or teach in the public schools.[2] "Such a picture," it said, "is shocking, and is an outrage on humanity, an impious desecration of religion, and a declaration of outlawry against the virtue and intelligence of the state — a decree of exile against her white citizens, for they could not live under such a government."[3] Although a negro majority of nearly twenty thousand had to be overcome, a determined effort was made to do it. Early in the campaign, J. Z. George addressed an open letter to the people, advising them to arouse from their lethargy and organize for the election. The letter was widely published, and the suggestions contained in it were acted upon. The *Yazoo Banner* called upon the young men to organize for the "impending struggle." The *Clarion* endorsed the appeal, declared that the cause which they represented was as holy as any that ever gave strength to the arm of man or inspiration to the heart, and appealed to the young men to organize not only into "clubs" but into "vigilance committees" and "committees of correspondence" and "enter at once upon the work with

[1] One of the best informed men of the state at the time estimated that the number of civil officers which would come within the purview of the provision would aggregate 2160 ; the number of militia officers, 6450, making a total of over 8000 offices, which it was expected would be distributed among the friends of the convention. Appendix, 41st Cong. p. 25. Testimony of Judge J. W. C. Watson.

[2] Issue of June 25, 1868.

[3] Issue of January 22, 1868.

all the zeal of their generous and unselfish natures." "They ought," the editor said, "to have a club at every precinct, and move in solid column when the final day of the struggle comes."[1] Again it called upon the people to hold regular meetings and appoint canvassers, and in all their movements "be firm, discreet, and resolute."[2] "With such exertions, we know," said the hopeful editor, "that the constitution can be defeated, and oh, how great will be the reward!"[3]

The campaign that ensued has certainly never been surpassed in enthusiasm and determination except by the great contest of 1875. The student who reads the local newspapers of the time cannot fail to find abundant evidence that the whites were aroused as they had never been before. The address of the state executive committee covered an entire page of the *Clarion*, and was kept running in its columns during the whole campaign. The same paper, of May 29, contained announcements of thirty-six Democratic mass meetings, at one or more of which every speaker of note in the state was billed for an address. In Rankin County alone sixteen mass meetings were held during the first week in June. Such was the political campaign of 1868. Just before the election began, the attention of the people was diverted by another event, namely the supersedure of General Gillem and the appointment of General Irwin McDowell in his stead.

IX. THE REMOVAL OF GOVERNOR HUMPHREYS AND THE APPOINTMENT OF GENERAL AMES

Having completed elaborate preparations for holding the election, General Gillem, by direction of the President, turned over the command of the fourth district to General Irwin McDowell, who ruled Mississippi from June 4 to July 4.

During his brief administration, he issued but five general orders, only one of which has any historical importance. That was an order for the removal of the civil governor, Mr. Humphreys, and the attorney general, Mr. Hooker. The reason alleged for the displacement of these officials was their opposition to the reconstruction acts. The specific charge was activity in the campaign against the constitution. Brevet Major General Adelbert Ames, lieutenant colonel of the Twenty-fourth Infantry, was appointed provisional

[1] Issue of April 7, 1868.   [2] Issue of April 15.   [3] Issue of May 12.

governor.   Captain Jasper Myers, United States army, was
detailed to perform the duties of attorney general.   On
February 9 following, the Secretary of State was also removed, and Mr. Warner, late of the Federal army, was
appointed in his stead.   The new appointees were directed
to repair without delay to Jackson, and enter at once upon
the discharge of their respective duties.   They were to
receive no further allowances than as officers of the army.
General Ames proceeded at once to Jackson, informed Governor Humphreys of his appointment, and expressed a desire
to be notified of the time when it would be convenient to
receive him for the purpose of carrying out the order.
Governor Humphreys delayed his answer nearly a week,
and then informed General Ames that he regarded the
attempt to remove him as a usurpation of the civil government of Mississippi, unwarranted and in violation of the Constitution of the United States ; and that he had telegraphed
the President, and was authorized to say that the executive
disapproved the order making the removal.   " I must, therefore," he concluded, "in view of my duty to the constitutional rights of the people of Mississippi, and the disapproval
of the President, refuse to vacate the office of governor, or
surrender the archives and public property until a legally
qualified successor under the constitution of Mississippi is
appointed."   On the following day, Colonel Biddle, commanding the military post at Jackson, made a formal demand
upon Mr. Humphreys for the governor's office, and being
refused, sent a detail of soldiers into the state house to take
forcible possession.   The governor called in several persons
to witness the seizure of the office and the ejection of the
chief executive, in order that the world might know, he
said, that he yielded only to " stern, unrelenting military
tyranny."   Upon his return to the office, from which he
had temporarily absented himself, he was ordered to halt
at the point of the bayonet, and was not permitted to
enter.[1]

The removal of the governor and attorney general was
the subject of loud protest by the Democratic press.   The
Vicksburg Times gave the following account of the affair

[1] Lowry & McCardle, Hist. of Miss. p. 380.   Relative to Humphreys' refusal to surrender, the *Clarion* of June 23 said : "Let the general now exhibit
his army in front of the Capitol in a time of peace. Let him open his batter-
ies and charge with his bayonets. Let him enter by force the office of the
governor. Let him bivouac as did Grant in the executive mansion. There
let him play Bombastes Furioso ; there let him strut the hero and ape the
wise man ; there let him issue the victor's bulletin."

which represented the view of the less conservative Democrats : —

The First Act of Our New Despot — Shoulder-Straps in the Executive Mansion

" General McDowell has signalled his appearance in Mississippi by removing and attempting to degrade two of the ablest and purest officers of which any state can boast.   For this act of tyranny, insolence, and outrage on the part of our new-fledged despot, General McDowell has neither apology nor the shadow of excuse.   It is a gross, wanton, and outrageous exercise of unbridled power of brute force which is as disgraceful as it is indefensible."

The executive mansion was taken possession of in a similar manner.   For some days after the ejection of Governor Humphreys from the executive office, his family was permitted to occupy a part of the official residence jointly with General Ames.   But the course of political events was not satisfactory to General Ames.   Accordingly, he addressed a letter to Mr. Humphreys informing him that since his appointment as provisional governor he had found good cause to change his mind in regard to the joint occupancy of the mansion, and that he desired it to be vacated at as early a date as possible.   Mr. Humphreys at once replied that the executive mansion was built by the tax payers of Mississippi only for the use and occupancy of their constitutional governors and families ; that at the recent election, the qualified voters, both black and white, had unmistakably expressed their desire for his continuance in the use and occupancy of the mansion ; and that, moreover, such occupancy could not obstruct the administration of the reconstruction laws.   He therefore respectfully declined to vacate the mansion until a legally qualified successor should be elected under the constitution and laws of the state.   General Ames grew impatient at a correspondence that seemed destined to be protracted indefinitely, and on July 10 wrote : " You entirely ignore the reconstruction acts and the action taken by those empowered to act under them.   I recognize no other authority.   The feeling entertained not only by me, but by others, not to cause you any personal inconvenience has, through your own action, ceased to exist. This controversy about the mansion can only terminate as indicated in my letter of yesterday."   This ended the corre-

spondence.[1]   Colonel Biddle was called upon to do the
rest.   Accordingly, on July 13, he addressed a note to Mr.
Humphreys informing him that the mansion must be vacated.
The note was delivered by Lieutenant Bache, who, with a
guard detailed for the purpose, proceeded to execute the
order.

He notified the governor of his purpose, and expressed
a desire to avoid all unpleasantness toward him and his
family, but added, " If you desire for political purposes to
have a military pantomime, it shall be carried out with
all the appearance of a reality without actual indignity."
There could be but one termination to this controversy.
The governor and his family were marched out between the
files of guards, leaving General Ames in possession.

General McDowell made but a single change in General
Gillem's arrangements for holding the election.   Three days
before the beginning of the election he issued an order
directing that the election should be continued for an additional day at each county seat, exclusively for the benefit of
those who had lost their certificates of registration.[2]

X. THE REJECTION OF THE CONSTITUTION

The result of the election was a surprise to both parties.
On the 10th of July, General Gillem, who had, in the meantime, been restored to the command of Mississippi,[3] announced
by general order that 56,231 votes had been cast for the constitution, and 63,860 against it.   He announced further that
four of the five members elected to Congress were Democrats,[4]
that Humphreys had defeated Eggleston for governor by a
majority of over 8000, and that of the 138 members of the
legislature, the Democrats had secured 66.[5]

[1] The correspondence continued through a period of more than a week.
It is printed in Appleton's Ann. Cyclop. for 1869 under article " Mississippi."

[2] Gen. Orders No. 24, H. Mis. Docs. 3d Ses. 40th Cong. No. 33, p. 93.

[3] Relative to the restoration of General Gillem to his old command, the
Clarion of July 2 said : " Another ' fraud ' has been perpetrated at the
expense of radicalism.   General Gillem is again in command.   Let the people rejoice.   The clouds of apprehension will soon be dispelled.   The rays of
law, liberty, and order are brightly beaming."

[4] All the Republican nominees for Congress were Northern men.   George
C. McKee was the only successful candidate on the Republican ticket.

[5] The legislature contained about a dozen negro members, but one of
whom was a senator.   This was the Rev. Mr. Stringer of Vicksburg.   See
Report of Secretary of War, 1868, pp. 590–603, and H. Mis. Docs. supra,
for the election returns as reported by General Gillem.

In officially reporting the result of the election, General Gillem alluded to the charges of fraud made by both parties, but expressed the belief that the election had been as free from intimidation and fraud as was possible to secure under existing circumstances. As the defeat of the constitution involved the continuation of military rule, he said he felt it to be his duty to call the attention of Congress to the difficulty of finding competent persons to fill vacancies in the state and local offices. He accordingly recommended the modification of the act of July 19, 1867, so as to render eligible to office persons who were qualified voters.[1] The election inspectors seem to have concurred in the view of Gillem that there was as little fraud and intimidation as could have been expected under the circumstances.[2] The announcement of the result was somewhat disconcerting to the radicals. The prospect of being excluded from the offices filled them with gloom. Without despairing, however, they set to work to have the election declared a Republican victory. The committee of five appointed by the convention to ascertain the result and make proclamation thereof, now called upon the commissioners whom they had appointed to attend the polls, to make detailed reports of their observations. The committee, after investigating these reports, announced that fraud had been practised in various counties. A sub-committee was then appointed to confer with the commanding general and request him to make an investigation. This he declined to do.[3] The committee of five then determined to make the investigation for itself, and to withhold its proclamation until the result was known. Without waiting, however, for the investigation, they made a long report to the reconstruction committee two days before the election registrars had completed their returns, with the intent, it was

---

[1] Report of Secretary of War, p. 603.

[2] One of the inspectors reported instances in which negroes were threatened with the vengeance of the Kuklux and with discharge from employment if they did not vote the Democratic ticket. On the other hand, he knew of two well-authenticated cases of negroes who were threatened with being taken to Vicksburg in irons, sent to Cuba and sold into slavery, should they fail to vote the radical ticket. The men who made these threats stated that they had "orders" from the headquarters of the fourth military district. These influences deterred the negroes from voting, "bothered" them, as they expressed it, so that not more than half the colored vote was cast.

[3] General Gillem told the reconstruction committee at Washington that he investigated all the reports of fraud that came to his notice, both before and after the election, and that in each case he sent troops to the locality under an officer with directions to make an investigation. H. Mis. Docs. *supra*, p. 60.

charged, of forestalling Gillem's report.   They charged that
threats and intimidations had been resorted to to such an
extent in some counties that election commissioners had
been unable to discharge their duties ; that in others, a reign
of terror was inaugurated for the purpose of deterring
colored men from voting ; that social proscription, threats
of discharge from employment, resolutions refusing to countenance in any manner those who voted for the Republican
ticket, and publishing the names of negro voters as enemies
to the white people of the state were some of the means used
by the Democrats to carry the election.

The committee asked leave to call attention to the fact
that in most of the counties of the state the offices were held
by "disloyal" persons, and Congress was memorialized to
afford "adequate relief" as soon as possible.   The report
concluded with the announcement that prominent men would
visit Washington at the earliest possible moment to "confer
with the proper authorities in regard to the condition of our
state."

After making this report to Congress the committee
of five proceeded to make an elaborate investigation.   It
had rooms at the Capitol, was supplied with stationery at
the expense of the state, and the members received $10
per day for their self-imposed services.[1]   The committee was
overwhelmed with communications and reports from disappointed office seekers throughout the state, giving accounts
of fraud and outrage which were alleged to have come under
their observation.   Hundreds of depositions, most of which
were signed with marks, were taken and are published as a
part of the documentary evidence on the subject.[2]   The committee sat with closed doors and took the testimony of a
large number of negroes who made their way to Jackson
from different parts of the adjacent country.   The Democrats were not permitted to take any part in the investigation, either to cross-examine witnesses or to offer testimony
in rebuttal.[3]   Ever since the defeat of the constitution,

---

[1] General Gillem did not particularly fancy the idea of an investigation
by this committee.   They had insisted upon having three commissioners of
their own appointment present at each polling place, and he had yielded to
their demands, although the reconstruction acts required that the election
should be conducted by officers or persons appointed by the commanding
general.

[2] H. Mis. Docs. *supra*, pp. 136–299.

[3] The chairman of the Democratic executive committee addressed a communication to General Gillem suggesting that as a matter of obvious justice
and propriety the Democrats should have an opportunity of cross-examining

the radicals had entertained the hope that Congress would afford them the "relief" asked for in their address of July 8, by declaring the constitution ratified, spite of Gillem's report to the contrary. For a number of days before his report was made public, persons claiming to represent the committee of five hung around the rooms of the reconstruction committee at Washington, urging it to recommend Congress to declare the constitution ratified. On July 24, the House passed a bill to reassemble the convention and frame a new constitution, but the Senate rejected it.

After an investigation continuing through a period of about four months, the chairman of the committee, on November 3, issued a pompous proclamation from "the rooms of the committee of five, of the Mississippi constitutional convention," reciting at length the reconstruction acts, the calling of the convention, and the adoption of the ordinance providing for a committee, and concluded as follows: " Now, therefore, by virtue of the authority vested in the said committee of five, I, as chairman of the said committee, after a careful examination of the reports made by the commissioners appointed to hold said elections, and after a patient and diligent investigation of the affidavits and statements of many other citizens of the state in reference to the conduct of said elections, do proclaim and declare the constitution thus submitted to have been duly ratified and adopted by a majority of the legal votes cast at said election, and the Republican state ticket duly chosen and elected at the same time; and I do further declare that the elections held in the counties of Copiah, Carroll, Chickasaw, De Soto, Lafayette, Rankin, and Yallobusha, on account of threats, intimidations, fraud, and violence practised in said counties, to be illegal and void." He further declared that two of the five Republican candidates for the Fortieth Congress had been elected instead of one as returned by Gillem's registrars. He even declared that five Republicans had been elected to the Forty-first Congress, although it does not appear that an election was held for the choice of members to that Congress. He also declared and proclaimed that a large number of Democratic senators and representatives, reported by General Gillem as having been elected, were chosen through

and producing witnesses on their own behalf. The general was urged to issue an order so directing, but refused. The refusal of the committee to allow Democrats to hear the testimony led to an altercation between the committee and a party of whites.

fraud.[1] The audacity of the proclamation shows the desperation to which they were reduced. There was not a shadow of authority for the extraordinary action of the chairman. The proclamation had little effect, however, for it remained with Congress to determine the status of Mississippi. The rejection of the House bill of July 24, to reassemble the convention, did not dampen their ardor. A movement for a state convention of Republicans to take action on the subject was set on foot. It met at Jackson, November 25, memorialized Congress to declare the constitution ratified, drew up a long address with a statement of some of the causes of their "present embarrassment," and appealed to Congress for "speedy and permanent relief." The address charged that since the suppression of the rebellion a large class of people in Mississippi, in "defiance of the authority and regardless of the wishes of Congress, had rejected in contempt all terms of restoration, and had assumed the right to dictate the terms under which they would condescend to be readmitted to the Union."

The address then took up the matter of the late election, and declared that it had been carried by "bribery, threats, misrepresentation, fraud, violence, and murder."   By way of criticism of General Gillem, the address declared that it had been a cause of great embarrassment to the "loyal" people of Mississippi that "disloyal" persons had been continued in office, and their opposition to reconstruction thereby encouraged.   The address concluded with a fervent appeal to Congress to declare the constitution in force, and the Republican ticket elected.

A committee of six persons from the state at large, and two from each of the five congressional districts, was appointed to proceed to Washington and lay before Congress the address and urge the readmission of the state.[2] This committee is commonly known as the committee of sixteen.[3] In the meantime, the Republicans throughout the state were

[1] The full text of the proclamation may be found in H. Mis. Docs. *supra*, pp. 18, 19 ; also in the appendix to the Globe, 40th Cong. p. 259.

[2] The address is printed in full in H. Mis. Docs. 3d Ses. 40th Cong. No. 53, pp. 261-263. It is signed by R. W. Flourney, Alston Mygatt, George F. Brown, W. H. Gibbs, G. W. Van Hook, T. W. Stringer.

[3] The following are the names of the committee of sixteen. For the state at large: R. W. Flourney, Jonathan Tarbell, A. Alderson, Alston Mygatt, E. Stafford, and F. Hodges. First district, U. Ozanne, J. L. Alcorn ; second district, W. W. Bell, J. G. Lyons ; third district, George F. Brown, G. W. Van Hook ; fourth district, T. W. Stringer, H. W. Barry ; fifth district, E. J. Castello, W. H. Gibbs.

holding mass meetings and local conventions, adopting resolutions and addresses to Congress.   Such a meeting was
held at Corinth, December 8, with Major Gillenwaters of the
United States army in the chair.   Resolutions were adopted
declaring that, in view of the financial condition of the state,
and the "distraction" to the various industrial pursuits consequent upon a heated political canvass, another election
would be detrimental to the peace and quiet of the state,
and should Congress refuse to readmit her, the best interests
of the people would be subserved by giving the state a provisional government.[1]   The Republicans of Lauderdale
County held a mass meeting at Meridian, December 28, and
adopted similar resolutions.   Congress was urged to readmit
the state and declare the Republican ticket elected.[2]   On the
following day, a meeting of the Washington County Republicans was held at Greenville, and resolutions were adopted
appealing to Congress to admit the state to the Union in
accordance with the proclamation of the committee of five.[3]
The Republicans of Wilkinson County assembled at the Union
League hall at Woodville, January 2, and adopted resolutions of the same tenor.[4]   On the 16th, the Scott County
Republicans assembled at Hillsboro, declared the late election to be an "echo of terrorism"; that even the soldiers
sent to their protection publicly expressed a desire to shoot
"radicals and negroes"; and that the result was a wicked,
damnable fraud on the freedom of election, and this was
known by General Gillem.[5]   The Rankin County colored
Republicans recommended another constitutional convention.   They expressed a desire to cultivate kind relations
with their white friends, invited the whites to join with
them in these sentiments, and announced their intention
to support capable and honorable men who were identified
with the country.[6]   Resolutions such as the foregoing
were adopted by Republican mass meetings in nearly
every county of the state.   They were all published in
the Republican journals of the time, and copies transmitted to the committee of sixteen at Washington, to
be in turn laid before the reconstruction committee of
Congress.

[1] H. Mis. Docs. *supra*, p. 251.   [3] *Ibid.* p. 253.   [5] *Ibid.* p. 269.
[2] *Ibid.* p. 252.   [4] *Ibid.* p. 269.   [6] *Ibid.* p. 234.

XI. THE MISSISSIPPI QUESTION IN CONGRESS

The struggle over the constitution was now transferred to Washington. Shortly after the meeting of Congress in December, the committee of sixteen arrived on the scene, and for many weeks badgered members of Congress, and urged them to put no faith in Gillem's report, but to declare the constitution ratified or to revive the convention. They went individually before the reconstruction committee and gave their testimony. The chairman of the committee of five recited at length his conference with General Gillem, and the latter's refusal to make an investigation; affirmed that the committee of five had a right to make arrangements for holding the election, and to appoint commissioners to be present at the polls; and expressed his conviction that a large number of the members elect of the legislature would not be able to take the oath of office required by the reconstruction acts. On December 16, ex-Governor Sharkey appeared before the committee, and testified that, so far as he knew, the election was conducted as fairly as any he had ever seen; that many of the negroes of the state voted voluntarily with the Democrats; that there was a state of good feeling between the races; and that while the negroes demanded the right of suffrage for themselves, they had no desire to deprive white men of the right. It was his opinion that the constitution was defeated fairly, and if another was submitted with the proscriptive clauses stricken out, it would be ratified.

General Gillem testified as to the precautions he had taken to insure a fair election, and declared that he had investigated every report of fraud and intimidation brought to his knowledge. In regard to the charge that sheriffs and soldiers had electioneered against the constitution, he informed the committee that most of the sheriffs were loyal men appointed by himself and General Ord. As for the soldiers, he said not twenty of them had been enlisted in the state, but that they were Northern men. If, therefore, they voted against the constitution, as they had a right to do, it afforded additional evidence of the obnoxious character of that instrument. He gave it as his opinion that the defeat of the constitution was due to its proscriptive character, as it was unreasonable to suppose that men would vote to disfranchise themselves, and if a constitution had been framed in accordance with the reconstruction acts, it would have been adopted by a large majority. He denied emphatically that his administration of affairs in Mississippi was animated by a spirit of opposition to the reconstruction acts and the policy of Congress, and claimed that the opposition to his course had been confined to disaffected persons, who failed to get appointments, and others whom he had declined to allow to enter upon the discharge of their official duties, because they could not give the requisite bonds.   Then there were others, he said, whose schemes of plunder he had thwarted.   These persons found fault with his administration, and desired his removal.

Another important witness before the reconstruction committee was Hon. J. W. C. Watson, an old-line Whig who had canvassed the state against secession in 1860, but who, upon the passage of the ordinance, could not persuade himself, as he says, to go against his blood and kindred, and so went earnestly into the contest on the side of the Confederacy, and did all he could, consistently with the rules of civilized warfare and of Christianity, to advocate its cause.   He was a member of the Confederate senate from 1863 until the close of the war, a member of the reconstruction conventions of 1865 and 1868, from which latter he resigned when it became evident that the majority intended to frame a constitution, the effect of which would be to disfranchise the more influential whites, and render them ineligible to office.   When the constitution was submitted to the people, he canvassed the northern part of the state against it.   He was satisfied that had the convention gone no further than the requirements of Congress, the constitution would have been adopted by a large majority.   The white people of the state, he said, were still opposed to negro suffrage, but with no further disfranchising provisions than were actually required by Congress, it would have been accepted.

On the 24th of March, the committee of sixteen called on President Grant, congratulated him on his election, thanked him for removing Gillem, and asked his influence in the enactment of a bill to readmit the state in spite of the rejected constitution.   The President told them that the matter was in the hands of Congress, but it appeared to him that the most feasible way to settle the question was to resubmit the constitution, in such a way as to enable the electors to vote on the obnoxious clauses separately.[1]   While the radical Republicans were besieging the President and members of

---

[1] The *New York Herald* of March 25, 1869, contains an account of the interview between President Grant and the committee of sixteen.

Congress to have Gillem's election set aside, and themselves installed into office, a committee of conservative Republicans were bestirring themselves at Washington to defeat the policy of the "Eggleston Clique." They styled themselves the representatives of a "very large, respectable, and influential portion of the Republican party," and in an address to the reconstruction committee protested against the attempt of the radicals to have the constitution forced upon the people against their will. They recommended Congress to declare all the offices vacant, provide for the appointment of a provisional governor with power to fill the vacancies, divest the constitution of its proscriptive features, and resubmit it to the people for ratification.[1]

About the same time a committee of Democrats, among whom were ex-Governor Brown and Judge Simrall, waited upon the President and appealed to him to use his influence with Congress to defeat the radical programme. The venerable justice, who is one of the few survivors of those who were prominently connected with the events above described, thus speaks of his mission to Washington: "When we reached Lynchburg, we learned from the papers that the reconstruction committee of the House would close its hearing that day. We telegraphed the committee to hold the matter open until we arrived. Our request was granted, and we had a full and patient hearing by the committee. During our stay in Washington, the senators and prominent members of the House seemed anxious to confer with us at their houses. We had no difficulty in discussing the matter with any we desired to see. We had two interviews with General Grant: first, at the war office, and afterward at the executive mansion at night, the latter meeting having been arranged by Mr. Dent, the President's brother-in-law. At this interview, several members of the committee of sixteen were present, and at the President's suggestion, two on each side were heard. General Grant gave no intimation by word or expression of countenance what impression had been made. At its conclusion, the President took from a table a printed copy of the constitution and referred to the several clauses relating to the elective franchise and said, in substance, that these proscriptive clauses should not be there, that they would be a continual source of discord and

[1] Some of the leaders of this party were A. Warner, A. C. Fiske, Judge Jeffords, J. L. Wofford, and Frederic Speed. They were all Northern men except one, and were more or less prominent in the politics of the state.

disorder, provocative of riots and bloodshed, perhaps, between the races.

"Turning his thoughts to the remedial aspect, he said, in effect, that he had been down in Mississippi, and knew something of the conditions; that the people were poor and had not fully recovered from the effects of the war; that he could, through the commanding general, order the same convention to reassemble, but they might not improve the matter; or he could have another convention called, but that would be expensive.

"Addressing himself to the governor and myself, he asked how it would do to submit the constitution to another vote, first striking out the objectionable clauses. Governor Brown and I consulted, and replied that to us that seemed the shortest way out of the trouble, and we believed it would be satisfactory to our people. In a short time, the suggestion was adopted by the government, and on the second vote these clauses were, by a very large majority, stricken out. If credit is due to any one, it is to President Grant, for the result attained."

In the meantime, Congress was giving its attention to the question of the status of Mississippi. Bills for the readmission of the state were successively introduced by Bingham and Beck in the House, and Boutwell and Payne in the Senate. Nothing however came of these efforts, and the Fortieth Congress ended March 4, 1869, with the question still unsettled.[1] The matter was at once taken up by the Forty-first Congress, which assembled early after the adjournment of the Congress.

On the 19th of March, Mr. Butler introduced a bill to provide for the organization of a provisional government for Mississippi. On the 24th, the chairman of the committee on reconstruction, who happened to be Mr. Butler, reported back his bill with the recommendation that it pass. The bill provided that for the "better security of persons and property in Mississippi," the convention should be authorized to forthwith assemble upon the call of the president thereof, and upon his failure to make the call within thirty days, the commanding general should be authorized and required to do so.[2] The reassembled convention was to have power to

[1] See Globe, 2d Ses. 40th Cong. pp. 1143, 1227.
[2] Appendix to Globe, 1st Ses. 41st Cong. p. 74. The president of the convention was at that moment in the lobby endeavoring to have the constitution declared in force. There was not the remotest probability that he would refuse to call the convention together. He would have been only too glad for an opportunity do so.

appoint a provisional governor, and to remove and appoint registrars and judges of election.[1] The constitution thus framed was to be submitted to the people within ninety days after the adjournment of the convention.[2]   Mr. Beck, a Democratic member of the reconstruction committee, and the leader of the opposition, at once took the floor and proposed an amendment to the Butler bill, vesting the appointment of the provisional governor in the President of the United States, instead of in the convention.   General Butler, in a set speech on the 24th of March, defended his bill, and explained its meaning section by section.[3]   Beck replied to him on the same day, pointing out in his speech the objections to the bill, and defending his own amendment.   He wished the power to appoint a provisional governor vested in the President, because he said he had infinitely more confidence in him than he had in the convention, believing that the President would use his power to secure a free and fair election, whereas he knew the convention would not permit either.

Discussion of the Butler bill continued through several days. On the 31st, Mr. Farnsworth of Illinois offered a substitute, providing that the commanding general should be empowered to submit the constitution again to the qualified voters, and that the objectionable clauses should be submitted separately, and if defeated, they should be stricken out of the constitution.   Another feature of the substitute provided that the sections relating to the appointment of chancellors and judges should be so changed as to require those officers to be elected by the people.[4]

Mr. Farnsworth followed up his substitute with a speech in defence of the same.   It seemed to find favor with members, and was, no doubt, a better measure than the Butler bill.   Discussion on the measure continued off and on for several weeks.   On March 31, Mr. Dawes of Massachusetts spoke at length in favor of postponing further consideration

---

[1] Dawes, Butler's colleague, in speaking of this bill, said he would as soon leave the choice of the warden of the state prison at Charlestown to the convicts themselves as to leave the choice of a provisional governor to the Mississippi reconstruction convention. Globe, 1st Ses. 41st Cong. p. 14 (Appendix).

[2] Ibid. p. 253.

[3] General Butler said Eggleston had accepted the surrender of Atlanta, and he would accept the surrender of Mississippi if he was appointed provisional governor.   He frankly admitted that "good politics" required compliance with the schemes of the radicals.   He said : " Now if you do not reconstruct Mississippi, you cannot get a loyal legislature [and consequently two 'loyal' senators] ; you cannot pass the Fifteenth Amendment, and with it you lose half a dozen Northern states."   Ibid. pp. 16, 17.

[4] Globe, ibid. 398.

of the Mississippi question until the next session, on the ground that life and property would be safer in the state the longer it remained under military rule.[1]

On the 1st of April, further consideration of the bill was postponed until the first Monday of December.[2] On April 8, 1869, General Butler reported from the committee on reconstruction a bill modelled after Farnsworth's substitute.   It authorized the President of the United States, at such time as he might deem best for the public interest, to submit the constitutions of Mississippi, Virginia, and Texas to a vote of the people, and at the same time submit to a separate vote such provisions as he might choose.   In the event of ratification, the legislature was required to assemble at the Capitol on the fourth Tuesday after the official promulgation of such ratification.   The commanding general was empowered to suspend all laws that he might deem unjust and oppressive to the people, this power to be subject to the approval of the President, and to terminate upon the assembling of the legislature.[3]   This last provision was directed principally against the poll-tax law in Mississippi, and several laws concerning the collection of debts, which laws, the Republicans alleged, were unjust and oppressive.   Mr. Paine objected to the bill, which authorized the President to submit the constitution to the voters, and at the same time submit separately the obnoxious clauses.   He therefore offered a substitute, authorizing the President to submit the constitution, in the first place, as a whole, and then submit it with the objectionable provisions stricken out.[4]   The same day the bill passed the House by a yea and nay vote of 125 to 25.[5]   It was immediately sent to the Senate, where it was read twice, and ordered printed without reference to a committee.   The following morning the bill was called up and read, when Mr. Morton offered an additional section, providing that before the states in question should be admitted to representation in Congress, their several legislatures should be required to ratify the Fifteenth Amendment.[6]   This section became the subject of an animated discussion, and was opposed by Republicans and Democrats alike.   Senator Trumbull declared that in imposing this new condition, the government was breaking faith with those states, inasmuch as Congress had already given its solemn pledge that they should be readmitted upon the performance of certain conditions.   He desired to know of

---

[1] Globe, 1st Ses. 41st Cong. p. 408.
[2] *Ibid.* p. 437.
[3] *Ibid.* p. 633.
[4] *Ibid.* p. 634.
[5] *Ibid.* p. 636.
[6] *Ibid.* p. 653.

senators when this thing of imposing conditions upon the
late insurrectionary states was to end. " Suppose," said he,
" they comply with this requirement, then are they to be told
at a subsequent session of Congress that there is something
else to be done before they can be admitted to representation." Morton was urged not to press his amendment, as it
was unnecessary, and might lead to a protracted debate and
delay their contemplated adjournment on the following day.
The Indiana senator said he regarded the amendment as
being of the utmost importance, and would rather see the
bill fail than to have it pass without the additional section.[1]
After a short but spirited debate, Morton's amendment
passed the Senate by a yea and nay vote of 30 to 20.[2] The
bill with the Morton amendment, together with several
unimportant verbal amendments, passed the Senate by a vote
of 49 to 9. Later, on the same day, the House, under a suspension of the rules, concurred in the amendments of the
Senate, after which it adjourned, leaving the Mississippi
question in the hands of the President and the people of
the state.

XII. MILITARY GOVERNMENT UNDER GENERAL AMES

On the 4th of March, 1869, the man who had placed General Gillem in command of Mississippi, and who had sustained
him in his opposition to the policy of the radicals, passed
from the presidency to private life. On the following day,
the order went forth for Gillem's removal. This was the
first victory of the committee of sixteen. There was a general manifestation of regret by the whites over the removal
of General Gillem, and it was openly declared that the reason for the President's action was the incapacity of the general to serve political ends. However this may be, it was
certainly unfortunate for the political repose of the state.[3]

---

[1] Globe, p. 654.
[2] Ibid. p. 656.
[3] Ex-United States Senator Fowler, in an unpublished memoir of General
Gillem, says he not only possessed high qualities as a soldier, but also elements of statesmanship ; that he always deprecated the invasion of the civil
power by the military, never forgetting that he had risen from the ranks of
the people, and must confide the destiny of his children to their hands ; that
his work in Mississippi was greatly complicated by the errors of a predecessor,
and that the material interests of the state and the general tone of society
assumed an improved aspect after he became commander. He subsequently
served as commander of the Department of California, took part in the
Modoc War, and died in 1875.

General Gillem's successor in Mississippi was General Adelbert Ames, who, it will be remembered, had been acting-civil governor since July 15, 1868, by appointment from General McDowell.   General Ames was a native of Maine and a graduate of West Point.   He was brevetted major general for gallantry and meritorious conduct in the Civil War, and in 1868 was sent to Mississippi with the rank of lieutenant colonel in the Twenty-fourth Infantry.   He was but thirty-three years of age when he became provisional governor, had never held a civil office, and was without training in the civil law.   His administration as provisional governor seems to have been characterized by moderation and tact.   His appointment, therefore, as district commander was favorably received.   The *Hinds County Gazette* extended him a " cordial welcome," and promised to " most gladly support him in every honest effort to give a good administration." Barksdale of the *Clarion*, who had better opportunities for knowing him, said : " The appointment should be acceptable to the people.   In the discharge of the duties of provisional governor, General Ames has commanded the respect and won the esteem of all classes." [1]   The new commander assumed control by issuing the following brief order : —

HEADQUARTERS 4TH MILITARY DISTRICT,
VICKSBURG, March 17, 1869.

GENERAL ORDERS }
    No. 14.   }

　　　　　In compliance with paragraph No. 55, current series, headquarters of the army, adjutant general's office, the undersigned hereby assumes command of the 4th Military District.

ADELBERT AMES,
Brevet Maj. Gen. U.S.A.

Shortly after assuming command, the headquarters of the district were removed from Vicksburg to Jackson for his convenience as provisional governor.   In the two capacities of civil governor and military commander, there were few limitations upon his power.   According to his own testimony, his power as military governor gave him supremacy in Mississippi, and he allowed no law to stand in his way when he felt that it was a hindrance to the execution of his policy.[2]   His authority embraced the whole municipal

---

[1] *Clarion* of March 11, 1869.
[2] Boutwell Report on Miss. Elections, 1876, p. 17.

power of the state. It included the rights of person and property, the assessment and collection and disbursement of taxes, the apportionment of representatives in the legislature, and the control of elections through the appointment of registrars, judges, and inspectors, and by prescribing the time, place, and manner of holding them. At the time he assumed command, there were about one thousand troops in the state.[1] These were employed, he says, for ordinary routine duty, and in making expeditions for the purpose of "arresting lawless characters guilty of murder or other serious offences." He reported that a few men, "supported by public opinion," committed murders and outrages, and the civil authorities were unequal to the task of bringing them to justice; that neither injured parties nor their friends often undertook to aid the civil or military authorities, and if so, with reluctance; and that offenders were often secretly concealed or otherwise shielded by the people.[2] His charge that public sentiment supported criminals in their lawlessness was repelled by the press as a base "calumny upon the fair name of the state." His report was the subject of much unfavorable comment, and cost him not a little of the confidence and respect which he at first enjoyed.

The removal of Gillem was not the only victory scored by the committee of sixteen. It will be remembered that they had represented to Congress that all the offices in the state were in the hands of rebels and disloyal persons. Congress was therefore urged to declare all offices vacant, and order them filled with "loyal" men. A joint resolution was accordingly adopted, declaring that all persons holding office in Mississippi, who could not take and subscribe to the oath of July 2, 1862, should be removed, and the vacancies filled by the district commander with persons who were able to take the oath. This practically vacated all the civil offices in the state, for not one in a hundred of the incumbents could take the oath required. The resolution went into effect February 16, 1869, and was not to apply to those whose disabilities had been removed by Congress. On the 23d, a gen-

---

[1] The following exhibit shows the strength and distribution of the military force of the state during his administration : —

POST.	STRENGTH.	POST.	STRENGTH.
Ship Island	280 men	Natchez	59 men
Jackson	209 "	Lauderdale	60 "
Grenada	173 "	Corinth	86 "
Vicksburg	129 "		

— Report Secretary of War, 1869, p. 160. [2] *Ibid.* p. 99.

eral order to carry into effect the joint resolution was issued by the commanding general. The order declared that all incumbents whose disabilities had not been removed, and who had not qualified under appointment from headquarters were directed to take and subscribe to the oath at once, and forward the same to headquarters. Those who could not take the oath were directed to retain custody of all books, papers, and other property belonging to their respective offices, and transfer them to their successors when they had qualified and were ready to enter upon the discharge of their duties. The work of turning out the "rebels" now began in earnest. Nearly every civil officer in the state, from governor down to the pettiest constable, was removed. Three days after the promulgation of the general order mentioned above, General Ames made his first batch of appointments.[1] General Ames's order book shows that scarcely a day passed during the remainder of his term on which a special order was not issued removing certain persons from office, and appointing their successors. He removed nearly all the state officers, and hundreds of county and local officers. At the same time he appointed 60 sheriffs, 72 circuit and probate judges, 3 judges of the criminal court, 16 prosecuting attorneys, 70 county treasurers, 120 circuit and probate clerks, 60 county assessors, 50 mayors, 220 aldermen, 385 justices of the peace, 165 constables, 370 members of the board of police, 40 coroners, 20 surveyors, 25 city marshals, more than 300 election registrars, and a large number of minor officials, such as school commissioners, city collectors, superintendents of the poor, county attorneys, trustees of state institutions, etc.[2] All appointees were required to furnish the proper bonds and take and subscribe to the iron-clad

[1] Special Orders, No. 59, dated March 26. By this order the state treasurer, Mr. Echols, was removed, and Captain Myers of the ordnance department of the army was detailed to perform the duties of the office. By the same order, the probate judges of Madison and Scott counties were removed, and two Northern men appointed to succeed them. A Northern man was appointed circuit clerk of Madison, and two Northern men were appointed sheriffs of Lowndes and Yazoo counties.

[2] These statistics are tabulated from a printed volume entitled, Special Orders of the Fourth Military District, which General Ames kindly placed in my hands. It contains 283 special orders, being all that were issued from Jan. 2 to Dec. 31, 1869. The majority of them relate to the removal and appointment of officers. The others relate to special duties of army officers, boards of survey, trial of offences by court martial and military commissions, movements of troops, registration of voters, and management of elections. Of the orders in this volume General Gillem issued fifty, General Ames the others.

oath, and forward a copy to the acting assistant adjutant general at headquarters.   They were then furnished with written authority by the commanding general to enter upon the discharge of their duties.   As few of the native whites of respectability could take the oath, General Ames found it next to impossible to get competent persons to fill the offices. Being a stranger in the state, he was compelled to follow the recommendations of those who, doubtless, deceived him in many instances.   He says he did the best he could under the circumstances.   He was charged by Congress with appointing only persons who could take the iron-clad oath, and if there were few respectable whites who could do it, making it necessary, therefore, to appoint freedmen and white strangers from the North, the blame should properly attach to Congress and not to him.   No man unaccustomed to civil pursuits, and unacquainted in the state, could have selected two thousand honest and competent officials out of a body of citizens from which the more intelligent and influential were excluded.   Some of the Northern men appointed by General Ames were competent and worthy officials.   That they were not always cordially received in the communities to which they were sent was due chiefly to the Anglo-Saxon instinct for home rule.   The action of Congress in handing the local governments over to the former slaves of the whites, together with a few strangers from other parts of the country, may have been necessary to the congressional policy of reconstruction, but it certainly complicated the problem by increasing the animosities and passions of the time, inflicting corrupt and expensive government upon the inhabitants, and producing other causes which resulted in persecution, fraudulent elections, and finally revolution.[1]

The course of General Ames in reconstructing the official organization with only those who were known to be his political supporters was the subject of loud protest.   He did not scruple to remove the "loyal" appointees of Gillem and Ord, when it became known that they were not his supporters. The removal of the sheriffs of De Soto, Claiborne, Clay, Calhoun, and Hinds counties were cases in point.   In some

---

[1] Of the twenty-five appointees of General Ames who subsequently became the most prominent Republican politicians in the state, not one had ever held office there before, eight were colored, while all of the white appointees except four were Northern men who had come to the state since the war.   One of these appointees became governor, one United States Senator, one lieutenant governor, two justices of the Supreme Court, two representatives in Congress, one attorney general, while the others were judges, sheriffs, members of the legislature, and county officers.

of these instances, the new appointees had never been in the counties to which they were sent, and made their bonds in other parts of the state.   In another instance, he removed a justice of the Supreme Court whom he had four months before recommended to the President for appointment as United States district judge.   It was alleged that the judge in question had ceased to be a party adherent of the commanding general.   He summarily dismissed the state printers who had been elected by the legislature, and appointed in their stead the editor of a Republican sheet lately established.   None of his removals, it was said, showed so much the prejudices of the commander as his dismissal of a highly respected Presbyterian minister from the governing board of the asylum for the blind.   The same was said of the removal of a prominent banker from the board of directors of the Illinois Central railroad.   The United States attorney for the Southern district resigned his position, and gave his reason in a published address that he was unwilling to be identified with an administration " whose acts in Mississippi he could not approve." The officer in question was a Northern man, and one of the founders of the Republican party in Mississippi.[1]   The *Pilot*, the organ of the Republican party, said, that General Ames had made mistakes in some of his appointments was apparent, but that he would in due time rectify them.   But what called forth greater criticism was his apparent disposition to shield such of his appointees as turned out to be dishonest in their official relations.   Thus his appointees to the offices of probate judge and sheriff in Rankin County were convicted of official crimes and sent to jail.   The commanding General is said to have sent over a detachment of troops, which forcibly opened the jail, took the prisoners out, and a soldier with musket in hand escorted the judge to the court house, and opened and adjourned the court.   The offenders were then given an opportunity to leave the state, which they lost no time in making use of.[2]

Complaints were loud among the whites that General Ames went to an unreasonable extent in his interference with the freedom of the citizens and with the actions of the civil authorities. Professor Highgate, a negro teacher in Madison County, and

---

[1] *Clarion*, Aug. 17, 1869.   In a letter to the President, he said General Ames's course had been marked by a " tyrannical exercise of power utterly antagonistic to the reconstruction acts."   " I should be false to the party if I longer retained the office to which you have appointed me."

[2] *Jackson Clarion*, Oct. 9, 1873.   See also Lowry and McCardle's History of Mississippi, p. 382.

an ex-Union soldier, presumed to criticise somewhat severely
the conduct of the military authorities in the Rankin County
affair already described.   For this he was arrested and made
to stand on a barrel with his hands tied behind him and
his mouth gagged from 9 A.M. to 4 P.M.[1]   By the commander's direction, twenty-five or thirty white men in Copiah
County were somewhat arbitrarily arrested and imprisoned,
for political purposes, it was charged.[2]   Two tax collectors in Choctaw County were " arbitrarily " dealt with, and
an official in Yallobusha was arrested and imprisoned " without authority of law." [3]   Commanders of posts at Jackson,
Vicksburg, Corinth, Natchez, Lauderdale, and Grenada were
forbidden to obey any writ of *habeas corpus* issued by a
Federal court for the release of prisoners in their custody,
the purpose being to prevent the testing of the legality of
arbitrary arrests by the military authorities.   The *Clarion*
of August 24 called it a " high-handed measure," and
said it was evidence of the " malignant and despotic temper " with which they were ruled in time of peace.   The
legislature had made liberal provision for supplying maimed
Confederate soldiers with artificial limbs, and had exempted
such persons from the payment of a poll tax.   By a general
order of April 14, General Ames forbade the further use
of money for this purpose, and directed that the poll-tax law
should be applied to disabled Confederates the same as to
other persons.   He ordered furthermore that the poll tax
should be reduced in amount on account of its alleged
oppressiveness to the non-property-holding class.[4]   One of
the most important enactments of General Ames was an
order, of April 29, 1869, declaring freedmen to be competent
jurors.[5]   There was of course a great outcry against the
order, quite as much as against the admission of negro testimony to the courts, but, as the *Clarion* said, nobody was
surprised.   The *Clarion* advised its readers to take a " practical view of it, and treat it as they would any other matter of

[1] Highgate's affidavit setting forth these facts is published in the *Clarion*
of Aug. 31, 1869.
[2] Lowry and McCardle, History of Mississippi, p. 382.
[3] *Clarion*, Oct. 9, 1873.
[4] Relative to this order the *Aberdeen Examiner* said : " No one blames
General Ames for his late order, as it reduces the poll tax from $4 to $1.50 ;
for though it was the only tax collected from the mass of the freedmen, it was
exorbitant, and the boy of twenty-one who owned nothing save the scanty
suit that defended him from the blast was mulcted in as large an amount for
the benefit of the revenue as the man of fifty-five with his section of fraudu-
lently assessed land."
[5] Report Secretary of War, 1869–1870, p. 100.

concern." While the editor regretted that persons so incompetent as the freedmen were to try issues involving life, liberty, and property, he was satisfied that the white citizens infinitely preferred service with them to association with the lower class of "carpet baggers" who had been appointed of late.[1] The state Democratic executive committee urged every white man who was summoned to do jury duty to be careful to attend, without fail, and "aid the inexperienced to discharge the new trusts confided to them."[2] For this act, and others of a similar kind, General Ames says the colored people sent him to the United States Senate.[3]

There being no legislature to provide for the support of the state institutions, General Ames by military order appropriated various sums for this purpose.[4] Other orders were issued for extending the time allowed by law for tax assessors to complete and deliver their rolls ;[5] for extending the time of collection by distress and sale of personal property in a number of counties ;[6] for extending the time allowed by law for tax collectors to make their settlements with the auditor ; for constituting courts martial ; for constituting military commissions ; for setting aside injunctions and other processes of the civil courts ;[7] for annulling the proceedings of a magistrate's court and ordering a new trial before the county judge ; for directing the circuit court of Clarke County to dismiss a case pending before it, and prohibiting the said court from entertaining jurisdiction of it in the future ; for directing that all proceedings in the circuit court of Lauderdale County in the case of the Selma and

---

[1] Issue of April 29, 1869.   [2] *Ibid.*

[3] "In order that the whites should know that colored men were not slaves, and in recognition of their loyalty, I gave them office and put them in the jury box, and relieved them from unjust and oppressive legislation of their masters, for which a successful and grateful party sent me to the senate." Speech of General Ames on the Enforcement Act, U.S. Senate, May 20, 1872. Globe, 42d Cong. 1st Ses. p. 520.

[4] On the 1st of March, he directed that $10,000 be drawn from the treasury for the support of the Lunatic Asylum ; $10,000 on May 4 ; $10,000 on June 22 ; $10,000 on August 25 ; and $10,000 on December 7. May 25, $1200 was thus appropriated for repairs on the Asylum for the Blind.

[5] The beneficiaries of this order were the assessors in fourteen counties only.

[6] Twenty in all.

[7] By Special Order No. 232, dated Nov. 1, 1869, an injunction granted by Judge James M. Smiley of the Chancery Court of Claiborne County restraining the board of aldermen of Port Gibson from carrying into effect an ordinance creating the office of city weigher, was set aside. By Special Order No. 1, of Jan. 3, 1870, an injunction issued by the circuit court of Marshall County to restrain a certain individual from keeping a feed and sale stable on the public square of Holly Springs, was likewise set aside.

Meridian Railroad Company be vacated, that the sheriff be directed to release all rolling stock held by virtue of any process of said court, and that the said property be exempted from seizure by virtue of any authority from the courts of Mississippi.

Although General Ames interfered more or less with the civil authorities, he seems to have left the courts to exercise jurisdiction over criminal offences, except crimes against freedmen and Union men. The following is a list of the cases tried by military commissions during his administration : —

OFFENCE CHARGED.	WHERE COMMITTED.	PUNISHMENT.
Killing of a freedman .	Newton County	Acquitted.
Arson and larceny . .	Newton County	Acquitted.
Murder of a freedman .	Warren County	Acquitted.
Murder of a freedman .	Warren County	Acquitted.
Conspiracy to murder a teacher	Adams County	One year's imprisonment.
Killing of two mules . .	Claiborne County	Acquitted.
Robbery and assault . .	Claiborne County	Ten years' imprisonment (two negroes).
Carrying pistol and resisting military officer .	Lee County	Acquitted.
Forgery	Lee County	Two years' imprisonment.
Assault on U. S. soldier .	Marshall County	Two years' imprisonment.

The most notable of these cases was the alleged conspiracy of four young men in Adams County to murder the teacher of a negro school. They were charged with taking him from his house and demanding the revelation of the password to the Loyal League. Upon his release they maltreated him somewhat barbarously. Under the state law, this offence was only a misdemeanor, and was not punishable by imprisonment in the penitentiary. Their counsel, Judge Simrall, sued out a writ of *habeas corpus* before the United States district judge, and based his argument for their discharge on the ground that the reconstruction acts did not repeal the state laws, and that the military tribunals were only substitutes for the state courts, and could not improvise a penalty as could a court martial. The judge agreed with him, and discharged the prisoners. The military authorities obeyed the mandate, and discharged the prisoners from custody. The military authorities thereafter invariably conformed to that interpretation of the acts of Congress.

XIII.   PARTY POLITICS IN 1869.   THE CONSTITUTION
RATIFIED

On the 13th of July, 1869, President Grant issued a proclamation designating Tuesday, November 30, as the day on
which the constitution should be resubmitted to the electorate.

He directed that the three proscriptive clauses, together
with the provision forbidding the loaning of the state's credit,
should each be submitted to a separate vote.   Each voter
who favored the ratification of the constitution without the
above provisions was directed to indicate his will by voting
"for" the constitution.   Those who favored the rejection of
the constitution were directed to vote "against" it.   Each
voter was also allowed to cast a separate ballot for or against
the objectionable provisions.[1]   Soon after the publication of
the proclamation, preparations for the campaign began.   The
white Republicans were still divided into a conservative and
a radical wing, the negroes for the most part affiliating with
the radical contingent.   The conservatives made the first
move.   Early in June a circular was sent to prominent politicians in various parts of the state, who were known to be
in sympathy with the conservative movement, inviting them
to meet at Jackson on the 23d for the purpose of "taking
steps to promote the general interests of the state."   Those
who signed the call had been conspicuous in the opposition to
the committee of sixteen, and they styled themselves "Members of the National Union Republican party of Mississippi."
In their address they said : "Believing that our state should
be reconstructed in accordance with the acts of Congress
and the principles enunciated by General Grant, and that
toleration, liberality, and forbearance will command respect,
inspire confidence, restore harmony, and bring peace and
prosperity, we ask the aid of every patriotic citizen in the
state, be he white or black, high or low."   The proposed
convention of conservatives met at Jackson pursuant to the
call, and was presided over by Mr. Wofford, an ex-Confederate soldier, but a Republican in politics, and at the time
editor of a Republican paper published at Corinth.   The
convention made ready for the coming campaign by the
appointment of a state executive committee, and the adoption of a platform of principles, but adjourned without mak-

[1] Richardson, Messages and Papers, Vol. VII. pp. 16, 17.

ing any nominations. Their platform expressed "unfaltering devotion " to the National Union Republican party, and declared that the failure of the reconstruction convention by its proscriptive measures to restore the state to the Union had rendered its supporters unworthy of the respect and confidence of the voters of Mississippi. The conservatives endorsed the Fifteenth Amendment, deprecated all attempts to impose further disabilities than the Constitution and laws of the United States required, and voted a resolution of thanks to the President and Congress for rejecting the constitution. The executive committee was authorized to issue an address to the people declaratory of the principles of the new party, and to issue a call for a state convention to nominate candidates for office.

The radical Republicans held their first state convention on July 2, and adopted a platform of seventeen resolutions in which they likewise expressed " unfaltering devotion " to the National Union Republican party with which they professed to be in full sympathy ; declared in favor of an impartial' and economical administration of the government ; full and unrestricted right of speech to all men at all times and places ; unrestrained freedom of the ballot ; a system of free schools ; a reform of the " iniquitous and unequal " system of taxation and assessments which discriminated against labor ; declared that all men without regard to race, color, or previous condition of servitude were equal before the law ; recommended a removal of political disabilities as soon as the "spirit of toleration now dawning upon the state " should be so firmly established as to justify Congress in taking such action; declared in favor of universal amnesty, universal suffrage, and encouragement of immigration ; endorsed the administration of President Grant ; expressed confidence in and admiration for General Ames, and eulogized Congress as the assembled wisdom and expressed will of the nation. This convention, like that of the conservatives, organized the party for the approaching election, and adjourned without nominating a state ticket.

It now remained to see what action the regular democracy would take. It was apparent from the outset that there was little hope of success for them, especially if they entered the contest under the name and banner of the regular party. A movement was therefore inaugurated for the organization of a conservative party, which, though opposed to the policy of the radicals, was in favor of ratifying the constitution

:ninus the so-called proscriptive provisions.   Ex-Governor
Brown, in a letter to the *Clarion* of April 22, outlined a
policy which was favorably discussed by several leading
newspapers, and was endorsed by mass meetings of conservatives in different parts of the state.   He proposed an acceptance of the Fifteenth Amendment ; a guarantee of the civil
and political rights of the freedmen ; no " partisan " opposition to the administration of General Grant ; " hostility to
men who had come to the state for the purpose of making
mischief, and hearty good will to all who came in good faith
to share the fortunes of the Southern people."   His platform
had much in common with that of the conservative Republicans, and soon negotiations were entered into for a union of
the two parties on the basis of a common opposition to the
radicals.   The conservative Democrats signified their willingness to support acceptable candidates of the National Union Republican party.   Early in May, the conservative press
of both parties brought forward the name of Judge Louis
Dent, a brother-in-law of General Grant, as a suitable candidate to head the state ticket against the radicals.   Judge
Dent was not an absolute stranger to the people of the state,
having been a government lessee of " abandoned " land in
Coahoma County during the later years of the war, and, in
fact, was a resident of the county at the time of the election
of General Grant to the presidency.   Upon the inauguration
of the President, he was invited to make his home at the
White House, where he was living at the time his name was
suggested for the governorship.[1]   His chief claim upon the
democracy of Mississippi was the use of his influence with
the President against the schemes of the committee of sixteen during its sojourn at Washington.

Soon after the adjournment of the National Union Republican convention in June, certain members of the executive
committee proceeded to Washington to get the formal permission of Judge Dent to use his name before the nominating convention in September.   He expressed entire approval
of the platform, and readily gave the desired permission.[2]

[1] Judge Dent was born in St. Louis, emigrated to California with General
Kearney in 1846, and there married a daughter of Judge Baine, late of
Grenada, Mississippi.   He practised law in Sacramento and San Francisco,
was an unsuccessful candidate for Congress, and a member of the first con-
stitutional convention of California.   Two of his uncles, Benjamin and
George, had lived in Mississippi during the territorial period.

[2] The following is a copy of Judge Dent's letter : —

WASHINGTON, D.C., July 9, 1869.

GENTLEMEN : Your communication of this date requesting permission to
place my name before the National Union Republican Party is at hand.   In

The proposed nomination of Judge Dent met with favor among the conservatives of both parties. The *Clarion* of August 5 published an address signed by more than one hundred prominent Democrats, calling upon the people to support the ticket of the National Union Republican party as the only means of defeating the radicals. The same paper of August 7 gave the names of thirty-three newspapers favoring the "conservative movement." It was agreed, therefore, among the leaders of the Democratic party not to put out a ticket, but to support Judge Dent.

They issued an address declaring that the adoption of the constitution was not an issue, the only question being as to the character of the candidates. The present basis of reconstruction was, they said, as fair as could be hoped for. The address called attention to the advantages of being again admitted to the Union, and thus putting an end to the "gigantic military despotism with its terrible humiliations and oppressions, under which they had so long languished and suffered." "With readmission to the Union," they said, "the blessings of peace and civil government would return, and capital and labor would flow into the state." The address concluded, "No true Mississippian, worthy of that honor and name, can think for a moment of adhering to the radical party as it exists in the state of Mississippi. From them we have received nothing but cruel tyranny, unjust persecution, and a degree of oppression unequalled in the sad history of conquered nations." The question of calling a state convention to nominate a regular ticket was carefully discussed by the state executive committee. On September 9 the committee announced that it was inexpedient to nominate a state ticket. The people were urged to meet in county conventions, organize a Dent party, nominate candidates for the legislature, and enter upon the campaign at once. There were many Democrats, however, who were unwilling to sacrifice their party name, and in a measure their political principles, by supporting for governor a man

reply, I beg to assure you that if I can in the least be instrumental in restoring the state of my adoption to her normal place in the Union and securing to her a good local administration, you have permission to use my name for any position within the gift of the National Union Republican Party of your state.

With great respect, I have the honor to be your obedient servant,

LOUIS DENT.

The platform adopted at your convention at Jackson on the 23d of June last I most heartily approve and endorse.

To MESSRS. J. L. WOFFORD,
     EDW. A. JENCKS,
          WILLARDS.

who was not a *bona fide* citizen of the state, and whose politics were scarcely known to the people.

In response to a call issued by several Democratic newspapers that were opposed to the "Dent Movement," a convention attended by a small number of delegates was held at Canton, October 20. They adopted resolutions declaring that the Democratic party would retain its organization intact, that it had not been, nor could by any competent authority be committed to the support of either wing of the Republican party; that they had no advice to offer to the people of Mississippi as to the course proper for them to pursue in the present contest, but as for themselves, they proposed to remain firm in their devotion to the great doctrine of state rights, and leave the responsibility for the establishment of a Republican party in Mississippi to rest where it properly belonged. The convention further resolved that in view of the dissensions existing among the people, a result due to the "manœvures" of politicians, it was deemed inexpedient for the Democratic party to put a state ticket in the field during the present campaign.

The chief purpose, of course, in nominating the brother-in-law of the President was to get the support of the national administration. At the time Judge Dent's name was proposed, no one doubted that the President would lend his support to the conservative party whose policy he had seemed to favor on the "Mississippi question." The *Clarion* of August 10 announced that the President "unquestionably desired the success of the Dent ticket, though delicacy forbade his active interference." A few days later the publication of the following letter destroyed the hopes of the conservatives : —

LONG BRANCH, Aug. 1, 1869.

DEAR JUDGE: I am thoroughly satisfied in my own mind that the success of the so-called Conservative Republican party in Mississippi would result in the defeat of what I believe to be the best interests of the state and country, that I have determined to say so to you (in writing of course). I know or believe that your intentions are good in accepting the nomination of the conservative party. I would regret to see you run for an office and be defeated by my act; but as matters look now, I must throw the weight of my influence in favor of the party opposed to you. I earnestly hope that before the election there will be such concessions on either side in Mississippi as to unite all true supporters of the administration in support of one ticket. . . . I write this solely that you may not be under any wrong impression as to what I regard, or may hereafter regard, as my public duty.

Personally I wish you well, and would do all in my power proper to be done to secure your success, but in public matters personal feelings will not influence me.[1]

With kindest regards, yours truly,

U. S. GRANT.

With this discomforting letter ringing in their ears, the state convention of the National Union Republican party assembled at Jackson September 8 to nominate a state ticket. Three hundred and twenty delegates representing forty counties were present. The " Dent Movement" had progressed too far to be abandoned, in spite of the assurance of the President that his support should be given to the radicals. Dent was accordingly nominated for governor. He was brought into the convention hall, where he made a speech accepting the nomination. His politics were unknown, and he allowed all parties to remain in blissful ignorance of his views on democracy and republicanism.[2] The ticket was framed with a view to catching the vote of the conservative negroes, should there prove to be any. The *Clarion* early in the year had advised the selection of colored delegates to the local and state conventions, and to a limited extent the advice was followed. In the state convention there were three colored candidates for the nomination for secretary of state. Thomas Sinclair of Copiah County succeeded in carrying off the honor. He had few qualifications for the position, and was the first negro ever nominated for a state office in Mississippi. The remainder of the ticket was divided between the Democrats and

---

[1] Judge Dent made a spirited reply to the President's letter, in which he asked if it was reasonable to suppose that people having the free choice of their representatives would elect a class of politicians whose conduct had made them peculiarly obnoxious. This, he said, was the charge made against the radicals, not because they had fought in the Union army, or because they were men of Northern birth and education, for many of them were with the conservatives, or because they were Republicans, for their opponents were among the first to advocate civil and political equality of all men, but because of their policy of proscription, a policy that has made them objects of peculiar abhorrence. A continual advocacy of proscription in time of profound peace was calculated to lead to a black man's party and a war of races. He concluded: " To this class of men whom you foiled in their attempt to force upon the people of Mississippi the odious constitution rejected at the ballot box, you now give the hand of fellowship, and spurn the other class, who, accepting the invitation of the Republican party in good faith, came *en masse* to stand upon its platform and advocate its principles."

[2] The *Grenada Sentinel*, a Whig journal, said: " We are not advised of Judge Dent's antecedents on whiggery or democracy, but we are willing to go for him on the faith we have that Baine would never have consented for a daughter of his to marry a Democrat."

Republicans.   The nominees for lieutenant governor, auditor, and treasurer were ex-Union soldiers, while the nominees for attorney general and superintendent of education were native Democrats.   The *Clarion* of September 11 announced that the ticket would receive its warmest support, inasmuch as the triumph of the party meant the "triumph of peace, justice, and liberty."

On September 30, the nominating convention of the radical Republicans met at Jackson.   Early in the year the *Okolona News* (Republican) demanded that Eggleston should be "shelved" in the race for governor, on account of the conspicuous part he had taken on the committee of sixteen in its efforts to have him declared governor in spite of the election of Humphreys.   This view seems to have been widespread.   He was accordingly set aside, and J. L. Alcorn, a native Republican, received the nomination.   Captain R. C. Powers, a Northern man and an ex-Union soldier, was nominated for lieutenant governor.   He was at the time sheriff of Noxubee County by military appointment from General Ames.

The colored race, which had been so completely ignored the year before, received a little more consideration at the hands of this convention.   They were permitted to furnish the nominee for secretary of state, and their choice was the Rev. James Lynch, an eloquent mulatto preacher from Indiana.   The nominee for auditor was Mr. Musgrove, an ex-Union soldier from Illinois.   H. R. Pease, a late Federal captain from Connecticut, was nominated for superintendent of education.   The nominees for the other two offices were native whites.   The ticket as constituted, therefore, contained three white "carpet baggers" three "scalawags," and one representative of the colored race.   An equitable distribution of the higher offices among these three classes was one of the chief problems of reconstruction politics, and was an element that could never be safely left out of consideration.[1]   General Ames was present at the radical convention, and informed them that they had his sympathy, and should have his support.

The campaign now began in earnest.   Dent was prevailed upon to come to Mississippi early in September and enter

---

[1] Thus in 1870 we find Alcorn governor and Ames and Revels United States senators ; in 1875 we find Ames governor and Alcorn and Bruce in the Senate, in each case the Northern Republicans, the Southern Republicans, and the colored race being represented in one of the three greatest offices within the gift of the party.

into the canvass at once.   The *Clarion* of September 14 announced appointments for him at forty-three places. Alcorn made his opening speech at Hernando, August 20. His speech was confined chiefly to abuse of the Democratic party, for which he seems to have had the most profound contempt.   He drew a gloomy picture of the state under Democratic rule, accused the conservatives of attempting to deceive the negroes, warned them not to believe the representations of the Democrats, denied that the whites were law-abiding, and brought forward statistics in support of his charge.   Dent challenged him for a joint discussion, and they met for the first time at Grenada early in October.   The *Clarion* said it was a field day for the National Union Republicans.[1]   This however does not appear to have been the fact. Alcorn's readiness as a stump orator gave him a decided advantage over his adversary, who was unaccustomed to this style of campaigning.   Judge Dent's chief weapon was his sarcasm.   As a member of the secession convention, Alcorn is alleged to have boasted how he expected to move upon the Federal Capital.   He did not, however, participate in a single battle, or receive a single wound.   Dent turned this to good account, and pictured Alcorn returning from the war he had helped to inaugurate, " covered all over with honorable wounds." [2]   The judge devoted much of his time in an effort to convince his hearers that he was a *bona fide* citizen of the state.   He declared that his "whole soul was enlisted in the great agricultural and commercial interests of Mississippi, and their resuscitation and development."[3]

In the meantime, the district commander was making ready for the election.   On October 14, a military order was issued by General Ames directing that the election be held on November 30 and December 1, in pursuance of the President's proclamation.   The same order contained detailed instructions for the revision of the registration lists, the general management of the election, and the making of the returns.   On November 5, he issued another order appointing the registrars.[4]   " To the end that the laws might

[1] Issue of October 5.

[2] The *Aberdeen Examiner*, in speaking of a joint discussion between the two candidates at Aberdeen, said : " We had expected in Judge Dent a modest declaimer who would say his piece and gracefully retire, but we were most agreeably surprised to find in the conservative champion a most able and eloquent debater and orator, one worthy to cope with any man upon the stump whom we have listened to since the war."

[3] *Clarion*, Aug. 12, 1869.

[4] Special Orders, No. 234.   The pay of registrars, over one thousand in number, was $5 per day and their expenses.   The work of registration con-

be fairly and justly executed," it was ordered that two white and two colored persons of different political parties should be selected by the board of registry in each precinct to challenge the right of any person to be registered who in the opinion of the person challenging was disqualified from voting. Many other elaborate provisions were made for securing a correct registration and a fair election. Every possible precaution with this end in view seems to have been taken. The commanding general announced that if fraud was committed at the polls, or voters intimidated, a new election should be held. On the 6th of November, an order was issued detailing forty-nine army officers to serve as election inspectors. They were for the most part captains and lieutenants of the Sixteenth Infantry. In general, an inspector was assigned to each county. They were to visit boards of registry, and instruct them in regard to their duties, and exercise general control of the work of registration, observe closely the manner in which the election was held, and report to headquarters. They were authorized to give orders in the name of the commanding general, and were instructed to keep him advised in advance upon probable occurrences likely to affect the result of the election.

The election for the most part passed off quietly. There were small "riots" in Sunflower, Newton, and Hinds counties, which the *Clarion* said were due to "radical intimidation." The constitution was ratified almost unanimously,[1] but the so-called proscriptive sections submitted separately were rejected by overwhelming majorities.[2] The Dent

tinued through a period of five days, the election continued two days, and it required several days to complete the returns. The five presidents of registry boards in each county were allowed pay for three days extra. The president of the board of canvassers in each county was allowed $5 per day and his expenses for bringing the returns to Jackson. Presidents of registry boards received allowances for ballot boxes, stationery, and room rent, and a deputy sheriff at each precinct was allowed $5 per day during the election. The total cost of registering the voters and holding the election could not have fallen far short of $100,000.

[1] The vote for the constitution was 113,735 ; against it, 955.

[2] The vote in favor of retaining the disfranchising provision was 2206 ; against it, 87,874. The vote in favor of the disqualifying provision was 2390 ; against it, 87,253. The section requiring all state officers and members of the legislature to make oath that they had never served as members of any secession convention, voted for or signed any ordinance of secession, or as members of any legislature voted for the call of any secession convention, was rejected by a vote of 88,444 to 2170. But one of the clauses submitted to a separate vote was ratified. That was the provision forbidding the loan of the state's credit. The results, herewith given, are taken from the official report of General Ames, contained in General Orders, No. 60. Appleton's Ann. Cyclop. gives the vote in favor of the constitution as 105,223.

ticket was defeated by a majority that was truly discomforting to the Democrats who supported it. Alcorn received 76,143 votes as against 38,133 cast for his opponent. Almost the solid colored vote was cast for the radical ticket. Twenty-eight of the sixty counties had colored majorities. Alcorn carried all these, together with fifteen counties having white majorities. All the candidates for Congress on the Dent ticket were likewise defeated, and a straight Republican delegation consisting of three Northern men and two natives was returned.[1] The legislature elected was overwhelmingly Republican. The Senate consisted of thirty-six Republicans and seven Democrats ; the House of Representatives contained eighty-two Republicans and twenty-five Democrats. No local officers were chosen at this election, the appointees of General Ames holding over for two years longer, that is, until the fall of 1871, when the first general election for all county and local offices since reconstruction was held.

In announcing the result of the election, the *Clarion* said nobody was surprised. In the first place, the national administration had sustained the district commander in his " unscrupulous measures to carry the election by fraud and violence."[2] In the second place, a large number of whites, which the *Clarion* estimated at about 15,000, were disfranchised,[3] and in the third place, the voters in many white counties had remained away from the polls. For example, in Lauderdale and De Soto counties, 1300 white voters took no part in the election, the number was 1500 in Tishomingo, 1000 in Tippah, and 200 in Rankin.[4] A Franklin County pastor suggested a day of thanks and prayer to God, who, he said, had permitted the radicals to get control of the state, for the reason that the whites had forgotten him.[5]

---

[1] The following were the members elected : First district, George E. Harris ; second district, J. L. Morphis ; third district, H. W. Barry ; fourth district, George C. McKee ; fifth district, Legrand W. Perce. Harris was a native of Tennessee, and a Whig before the war. He became a Republican in 1867, and was living at Hernando at the time of his election to Congress. The same may be said of Morphis, who resided at Pontotoc. Barry was a native of New York, served in the Union army, rose to the rank of brevet brigadier general, and was a delegate in the reconstruction convention. He served three terms in Congress, and died in Washington in 1875. McKee was a native of Illinois, a graduate of Knox College, and a brigadier general in the Union army. He was a delegate in the reconstruction convention, and represented the Vicksburg district in Congress from 1870 to 1876. In legal and forensic accomplishments he was the ablest of the " carpet baggers " in Mississippi. Perce was a native of New York, and an ex-Union soldier. Harris and Perce are the only survivors of the Mississippi delegation in the Forty-first Congress.   [2] Issue of Dec. 21, 1869.   [3] Issue of Dec. 2, 1869.
[4] Issue of Dec. 11, 1869.   [5] *Ibid.*

The *Clarion* said there was one gratifying reflection upon the result, namely, the state would be readmitted to the Union, and the right of the people henceforth to hold their own elections free from military interference and the right of self-government were in sight.   While a radical state administration would unquestionably, the editor thought, prove a "serious affliction," the prospective advantages alluded to would be infinitely preferable to military government under General Ames.[1] The chief questions of interest were whether Alcorn would appoint a good judiciary, and whether he would retain his office or abandon it to "adventurers." Relative to the first question, the new governor announced that he would appoint judges "learned in the law, and whom society would not presume to ignore." On the second question he was painfully silent.

On December 20, General Ames issued an order reciting the act of Congress under which the constitution had been resubmitted, the proclamation of the President relative thereto, and his own duty of announcing the result. He declared that the Alcorn ticket had been elected, including those members of the legislature whose names were therewith published. The legislature was directed to meet at Jackson, January 11, 1870.

On December 23, he issued the following order : —

HEADQUARTERS 4TH MILITARY DISTRICT,
DEPARTMENT OF MISSISSIPPI,
JACKSON, MISS., Dec. 23, 1869.

SPECIAL ORDERS, }
   No. 277.   }

The following named persons are hereby appointed to office in the state of Mississippi : —

Jas. L. Alcorn, Governor.

Jas. Lynch, Sec'y of State, *vice* Henry Musgrove, whose resignation is hereby accepted.

Henry Musgrove, Auditor of Public Accounts, *vice* Thos. T. Swann, whose resignation is hereby accepted.

Joshua S. Morris, Attorney General.

Appointees must file with the proper officers such bonds and other recognizances as may be required by the statute laws of Mississippi, and take and subscribe to the oath of office prescribed by the Act of Congress of July 2, 1862.

By command of
BREVET MAJ. GEN. AMES,
WM. ATWOOD, *Aide-de-Camp.*

[1] Issue of Dec. 2, 1869.

Although order No. 277 was issued as a "command," Alcorn refused to accept the appointment. He informed General Ames that, coming as it did from the military authorities, and subject for its support to the military power, the fitness of things forbade his acceptance, while he held in immediate prospect the position of civil governor by that sanction most acceptable to his instincts as an American citizen, that of popular choice.

CHAPTER SIXTH

THE FREEDMEN'S BUREAU

ONE of the institutions of reconstruction was the Freedmen's Bureau. In view of the importance which was attached to it by the reconstructionists, it has been thought worth while to devote a separate chapter to its history and operations in Mississippi. As the Union armies, in the spring of 1863, moved down the Mississippi Valley to begin the siege of Vicksburg, many of the planters abandoned their plantations and fled before the approach of the enemy, leaving the growing crops standing in the fields. The slaves, tempted by the promise of freedom, or terrified by the policy of the Confederate military commanders in transporting them to less exposed parts of the country to prevent their capture, went over in great numbers to the Federal lines, gathered about the camps, or followed in the wake of the army. As a result of this exodus from the plantations, General Grant had fifty thousand freedmen in his camps along the Mississippi River shortly after the fall of Vicksburg.[1] To provide subsistence for the new "contrabands" was a problem that for a time greatly embarrassed him. His first recourse was a call upon benevolent and philanthropic people of the North for contributions of clothing and other necessaries to relieve the government of what appeared to be an insupportable burden. At the same time, he sent the Rev. Mr. Fiske, chaplain and superintendent of contrabands, to the North, to personally solicit supplies for the same purpose. In the meantime, plans were in preparation for the employment of the freedmen. In August of the preceding year, while General Grant was in North Mississippi, the President had directed him to seize and use any property that he might need for the prosecution of the war, and to employ as many negro laborers as he might deem advantageous for military purposes.[2] By an order of August 10, 1863, it was directed that at all posts where slavery had been abolished, camps

---

[1] Report of Secretary of War, 1869–1870, Vol. I. p. 497.
[2] Official Records, Series III. Vol. 3, Serial No. 124, p. 397.

should be established for freed people out of employment, and that superintendents should be detailed to distribute rations among them. It was ordered, furthermore, that they should be employed as far as possible on the public works, in gathering the crops on the abandoned plantations, or hired to the planters. It was made the duty of provost marshals to see that every negro within the jurisdiction of the military authorities was employed by some white person or sent to the camps for freedmen. Planters were permitted to make contracts with them for wages by the month, or, in the case of families, by the year, the employer in each case obligating himself to furnish food and clothing to the laborer and support the infirm members of the family. The rate of wages was fixed at an amount equal to one-twentieth of the value of the crops, and employers were required to give bond for kind treatment and proper care of their employees.[1]

The abandoned plantations were seized by the government and leased to private persons, who employed the freedmen to gather the crops. The harvest for 1863 was small on account of the early abandonment of the growing crops, and it proved impossible to gather all on account of Confederate raids which scattered the negroes, and so terrified them that they could not in many instances be induced to remain.[2] In some places where the plantations were abandoned, the negroes left behind asserted a sort of squatter claim, and gathered the crops on their own account. One such family was reputed to have thus gathered twenty-four bales of cotton, and sold it for $250 per bale. The scheme seemed to meet the approval of the President, and he announced that the occupation of the abandoned plantations and the employment of the freedmen thereon might be considered as the settled policy of the government.[3] Accordingly, preparations on a large scale were made for leasing the plantations for the following year to such "loyal" persons as would obligate themselves to employ the contrabands. The whole matter was under the supervision of General Lorenzo Thomas, who was assisted by three subordinates styled "commissioners for leasing plantations."[4] In the latter part of October, General Thomas issued an elaborate code of regulations for the government of lessees. It was stated that the property of disloyal persons belonged of right to the United States, and might be taken possession of

---

[1] *New York Times*, Aug. 30, 1863.   [2] *New York Herald*, Jan. 3, 1864.
[3] Official Records, Series III. Vol. 4, p. 124.
[4] They were Judge Field of Natchez, Colonel Montague of Vicksburg, and Judge Dent of Goodrich Landing.

and leased to loyal citizens.   Owners of "undoubted loyalty," who had been so from the beginning, were allowed to retain their plantations, but where a doubt existed, they were permitted to do so only upon condition that the owner in each case should take for a partner some "loyal" citizen.   It was announced that the primary object of this requirement was to line the banks of the Mississippi with a loyal population so as to secure the uninterrupted navigation of the river.   The commissioners were overwhelmed with applications for lease-holds, for the price of cotton was phenomenal ($250 per bale), the land fertile, and labor cheap.   From far and near the applications came, many from Northern men, who knew little of the methods of cultivating the cotton plant.   One newspaper correspondent informed his Northern readers that the country would undoubtedly be filled with "loyal" men by the first of April following.   A few fortunes were made by the lessees of abandoned plantations, but the failures far outnumbered the successes.   One lessee invested $13,000 in a crop and sold the product for $135,000.   One correspondent thus figured out the profits to be made in a single year:—

For purchase of stock, implements, supplies, and labor.	.	$ 14,000
Sale of eight hundred bales of Cotton .	. . . .	160,000
Net profits	. . . .	$146,000

"There are few places in the North," said the writer, "where so large a return can be made from so small an investment."[1]   And he was doubtless correct.

The lease was usually in the form of a permit, which granted to the lessee the right to "use, farm, and enjoy" the possession of a certain plantation until January 1, 1865.   He was required to take and file an oath of allegiance to the United States, to pledge himself to employ a certain number of able-bodied freedmen at $7 per month, to care for the infirm of the family, to furnish them with a specified amount of provisions, and not to inflict corporal punishment on any employee.   The consideration which the government was to receive was $4 for each bale of cotton, and 5 cents for each bushel of corn produced.   The utterance of a disloyal word at any time terminated the lease and all the privileges which it carried.[2]   General Thomas estimated that about 160 plantations would be leased in 1864.   General Sherman opposed the "plantation system," as he called it,

---

[1] Natchez correspondent, *New York Herald*, Jan. 3, 1864.
[2] These regulations are printed in the Official Records, Series III. Vol. 3, Serial No. 124, p. 939 ; also in the *New York Herald* of Dec. 31, 1863.

on military grounds.   He declared that it would be impossible to cultivate these abandoned lands on account of their
proximity to the territory under Confederate jurisdiction.[1]

In May, 1864, an order was issued to protect lessees from
alleged raids of guerillas.   It was directed that whenever a
government lessee was robbed, the commander of the nearest
military post should send a sufficient force to seize from
disloyal persons property enough to indemnify the injured
lessee.   If crops belonging to a lessee were destroyed or
injured, crops of the same kind belonging to disloyal persons
in the neighborhood would be seized and harvested for the
benefit of the lessee.   If any lessee should be killed, an
assessment of $10,000 was to be levied on all disloyal per-
sons residing within thirty miles of the place occupied by
the lessee, and appropriated for the benefit of his family.[2]

In the spring of 1864, a more elaborate code of regulations
was adopted by the treasury department for the management
of abandoned property.   Provision was made for the establishment of a home farm in each special treasury agency, to
be set apart for the colonization of such freedmen as preferred
to cultivate land on their own account.   Each colony was to
be under the supervision of a superintendent.[3]

The site selected for the home farm in Mississippi was a
peninsula known as the Davis Bend, near Vicksburg.   This
piece of land is shaped by a sweep of the Mississippi River
toward the west for six or eight miles, and then back again,
making the neck about a half mile in width.   This narrow
stretch was fortified and defended by a regiment of negro
soldiers.   The bend consisted of ten thousand acres of fertile
land, most of which was comprised in the plantation of
Jefferson Davis.   When Farragut's fleet steamed up the river,
in 1863, it stopped long enough to allow the marines to go
ashore and destroy or carry away everything of value.[4]   The
slaves had already been sent away to Edwards Station, where
Grant freed them shortly afterward.   But the land still
remained as fertile as ever, and General Dana " consecrated
it as a home for the emancipated."   The order setting it apart
for this purpose declared it to be a "suitable place to furnish
means and security for the unfortunate race which he [Davis]
was so instrumental in oppressing."   All persons not connected with the military service were directed to leave the

1 Official Records, *supra*, p. 224.
2 *New York Times*, May 27, 1864.
3 Treasury Regulations for the Third Special Agency.
4 T. W. Knox in *New York Herald*, Dec. 28, 1863.

plantation by January 1, 1865, after which no white person would be allowed there without written permission. And thus, it was said, the "nest in which the rebellion was hatched has become the Mecca of freedom." [1] It was to be restored, of course, at the close of hostilities, if the owner could furnish satisfactory proof of undoubted loyalty throughout the war.

The method of leasing the plantations was to a considerable extent modified from time to time. Freedmen employed on them were not to be enlisted as soldiers. Provost marshals were stationed in the neighborhood of leased plantations to "see that justice and equity were observed in all relations between employers and freedmen." One school at least was to be established for colored children in each police district. To prevent demoralization of the freedmen by the presence of negro troops, the latter were forbidden to visit the plantations, while the former were prohibited from leaving their places of employment. Employers were required to register the names of employees in the office of the nearest provost marshal, and laborers were expected to render ten hours of "faithful and honest" labor every day, for which they were to receive "healthy rations, comfortable quarters, clothing, fuel, medical attention, instruction for their children, and $10 per month in cash," one-half of which was to be forfeited in case of indolence, insolence, and disobedience. In case of stubbornness, the offender was to be turned over to the provost marshal, who had plenary powers in all matters connected with the labor of freedmen.[2]

This was the status of the problem when Congress turned its attention to the establishment of a more adequate and systematic method of caring for the freedmen. On the 1st of March, 1864, the House passed a bill to establish a "Bureau of Freedmen's Affairs." The Senate modified it, the House refused to concur, and Congress adjourned without taking further action on the subject. At the ensuing session, the matter was again brought forward, and on the 2d of March, 1865, a bill was agreed to by both Houses, and was signed on the same day by the President. On the following day, Congress adjourned without making an appropriation for the support of the bureau. However, the revenues from abandoned lands and the proceeds from the sale of confiscated property were sufficient to partially meet the demands of the

---

[1] *New York Times*, Dec. 4, 1864.
[2] Order of March 11, 1864. Official Records, *supra*, pp. 166–170.

bureau, and it was accordingly organized and put into operation. General O. O. Howard, commander of Sherman's
right wing in the army of the Tennessee, was decided upon
by President Lincoln for the head of the bureau. The
assassination of the President, however, occurred before he
had sent in the nomination, but Mr. Johnson, knowing his
wishes in the matter, promptly appointed General Howard.
The head of the bureau in Mississippi was styled an "assistant
commissioner;" and the first incumbent was Colonel Samuel
Thomas. The state was divided into three sub-districts, each
of which was under the supervision of an "acting assistant
commissioner." At first the organization was as follows: —

I.   The Northern District . .   Lieutenant Colonel R. S. Donaldson.
II. The Southern District . .   Major George D. Reynolds.
III. The Western District   . .   Captain J. H. Webber.

These were officers of negro regiments. There were in
addition to the commissioners a state superintendent of education, an assistant adjutant general, an assistant inspector
general, a surgeon-in-chief, and a large corps of local agents
and teachers.[1] The character and strength of the organization
varied from time to time. In December, 1865, there were
fifty-eight local agents and sixty-seven teachers in the service
of the bureau in Mississippi. It appears also that at one time
there were nearly a hundred medical officers and attendants
in the service. The agents were all military officers, and
the number exceeded those of any other state except Virginia,
which had eighty-four.[2] In 1866, the organization consisted
of eight districts, each under the supervision of two or more
military officers, the senior officer in each district being styled
a sub-commissioner.[3] In 1868, the organization consisted of
twenty-four sub-districts under the supervision of seven
officers of the regular army, eight officers of the reserve,
and eight civil officers.[4] The number of local agents at this
time does not appear from the reports. In March, 1865, the
headquarters of the bureau were removed from Memphis to
Vicksburg, where they remained until the bureau was abolished in 1869.

On the 3d of August, 1865, General Slocum, commander

[1] Ex. Docs. 1st Ses. 39th Cong. No. 69, p. 167.
[2] Report of the commissioner, *ibid.* No. 11, p. 36.
[3] Sen. Docs. 2d Ses. 39th Cong. No. 6, p. 95.
[4] At this time there were 141 commissioned officers, 412 agents, and
348 clerks in the entire service of the bureau in the South. Report Secretary
of War, 1869–1870, p. 497.

of the Department of Mississippi, issued an order calling attention to the recent act of Congress for the establishment of the Freedmen's Bureau, and directed all military authorities, who held abandoned property of any kind, to turn it over at once to the officers of the bureau, together with all funds or other property held for the benefit of freedmen. All officers were directed to familiarize themselves with the law establishing the bureau, and to aid in executing in good faith the Emancipation Proclamation.[1]

Officers were instructed to inform colored people that they had a right to visit the bureau officers for advice, information, and protection whenever they thought they were wronged; that whenever the state laws or courts did not afford them justice by admitting their testimony in cases in which they were interested, they must apply to the nearest bureau office for advice; and that they were now free and entitled to wages for their labor, but that freedom did not mean the right to live without work at other people's expense. The freedmen were advised to be patient, to behave themselves and not show spite toward their former masters, to form lawful and regular marriages, and to regard the marriage contract as sacred. Their attention was called to the advantages of education, and they were informed that teachers would be sent among them as soon as possible.[2]

Again, they were informed that, as soon as possible, officers would be detailed to visit every locality in the state, while others would be stationed at places of importance for the purpose of enforcing the laws of Congress and the proclamations of the President; to see that they were secured in their freedom and allowed a fair compensation for their labor; to impress upon them the nature of their new relations and obligations; and to inform them that the government did not intend to support them in their idleness.[3] Planters were urged to visit the bureau officers and by personal inquiry learn of its organization, obtain copies of all orders and circulars, and communicate the contents to their neighbors.[4] Every effort seems to have been made to establish relations of harmony between the bureau and the civil authorities, and to secure the coöperation of the latter. The efforts in this direction were attended by a large measure of success, particularly under the later administration of the bureau.

[1] *New York Times*, Aug. 18, 1865.
[2] Report of the commissioner, Ex. Docs. 1st Ses. 39th Cong. No. 69, p. 155.
[3] *Ibid.* p. 150.   [4] *Ibid.* p. 159.

In general, the duties of the bureau were to supervise
and manage all subjects relating to freedmen and refugees.
One of these was to enforce the Emancipation Proclamation.
As early as August 1, 1863, General Grant had called upon
the people of Mississippi to acknowledge the freedom of the
negroes, and enter into labor contracts with them.[1]   His
recommendation was regarded about as seriously as his order
relative to the abandonment of cotton by its owners.   Those
slaves, however, who came into his lines were given their
freedom so far as the military commander in prosecution of
the war could do so.   The *Philadelphia North American* estimated that at the time the above-mentioned order was issued
there were 155,140 negroes in Mississippi who had been set
free by the "administration or the events of the war."   No
owner, however, considered his slaves legally free, and of
course, did not treat them as such, except when under military
compulsion.   With the surrender of the Confederate armies,
the various post commanders issued proclamations declaring
the slaves to be free, and admonishing owners to treat them
as such.[2]   The freedmen were advised to remain at home, but
the advice was not generally taken.   They congregated in
the larger towns to such an extent that it became necessary
in some instances to order them back to the plantations by
military force.   Thus at Columbus the commander issued an
order reciting that freedmen in great numbers were "revelling
in idleness," and that they must "retire to their homes or seek
employment elsewhere."   They were given ten days to find
employment.[3]   They were ordered out of Natchez in a similar
manner.   In August, 1866, all negroes in Vicksburg without
visible means of employment were informed by General Wood
that they must leave at once.   In June, 1865, General Osterhaus ordered that vagrancy among the negroes must not be
permitted, that they must be put to work, and the issue of
rations "closely watched."

A circular of July 9, 1865, instructed the agents of the
bureau in Mississippi to use all practicable means of making
public the proclamation of the President, in order that the
negroes might know that they were free.   Agents were
directed to assemble them where possible, read the proclamation, and use every effort to familiarize them with its contents.
They were furthermore advised to place printed copies in
the hands of colored ministers, who were requested to read it

---

[1] *New York Times*, Aug. 30, 1863.   [2] *Ibid.* June 11, 1865.
[3] *New York Herald*, July 10, 1865.

to their congregations.[1] Subsequently it was charged that "combinations" existed among white persons for the purpose of retaining control over their former slaves. Accordingly, bureau officials were directed to take immediate steps for the arrest and trial by military commission of such persons. A sufficient cavalry force was to be placed at the disposal of the officer, to enable him to make the arrest. Agents were urged to use greater exertions in making public the substance of the Emancipation Proclamation.[2] These instructions were followed by another circular in August, which charged that the continued reënslavement of the negro was leading to "abuses of the gravest character," and the assistant commissioner declared that "the thing must stop." He reminded the whites that emancipation was a fact, although some of them were refusing to recognize it as such; he discoursed upon the importance of observing good faith toward freedmen, and of treating them with kindness; and declared that the "old appliances" of slavery must be abandoned entirely.[3]

The bureau continued the policy of leasing the abandoned plantations and of establishing colonies for freedmen, although there were some minor changes of methods, for example as regards the form and amount of rent which the government received.[4] The amount of land leased by the bureau varied from time to time. In 1865, the amount was 59,280 acres of land and 52 town lots.[5] After the issue of the President's amnesty proclamation, great pressure was brought to bear upon the military authorities by owners to secure the restoration of their lands. The bureau announced its determination to reject all applications for the restoration of such lands as came strictly within the definition of "abandoned" property. Not even a full and absolute pardon from the President would be accepted as entitling the owner to a restoration. The most perfect evidence of constant loyalty

[1] Ex. Docs. 1st Ses. 39th Cong. No. 69, p. 150. [2] Ibid. p. 168.
[3] Ibid. p. 159. The Natchez Courier of July 22, 1865, contains an editorial deprecating the action of certain whites in attempting to make the negroes believe that they were still slaves. Every employer was urged to explain to his employees that they were free, that labor was honorable, and idleness a crime.
[4] Thus a circular of Nov. 14, 1865, declared that the previous method of leasing lands had failed to secure to lessees the protection necessary to the full realization of the benefits of their contracts. It was therefore ordered that leases be so modified as to require lessees to pay two cents per pound for all cotton produced, in lieu of one-eighth, as stipulated in the existing contracts.
[5] Ex. Docs. 1st Ses. 39th Cong. p. 6.

throughout the war — evidence which could not be established by a simple oath — would alone entitle the owner to his property.   The President, however, overruled the policy laid down by the bureau officials, and by an order of July 1, 1865, directed that all abandoned property in the possession of the bureau should be restored to its owners upon presentation of a special pardon from himself or a copy of the amnesty oath properly signed and authenticated.   This order was censured by the radicals, who clamored for the confiscation of rebel land and its division among the freedmen.[1]   On the 12th of September, a circular was issued prescribing detailed instructions for the restoration of abandoned property.   The land under cultivation by the freedmen was to be held by the bureau until the growing crops were gathered, unless owners were willing to make full compensation for labor already performed.   By the first of December, Colonel Thomas reported that he had restored ninety plantations in Mississippi, aggregating forty-five thousand acres of land, and one hundred business houses and lots, and that there still remained in the possession of the bureau thirty-five thousand acres and forty-two pieces of city property.[2]   By the first of November, 1867, all property in the possession of the bureau had been restored to its original owners.[3]   Confiscated land was not so promptly restored.   The bureau continued to lease or colonize it.   In addition to the Home Farm colony at Davis Bend, already mentioned, other colonies were established at Camp Hawley, a short distance north of Vicksburg, at De Soto Landing, and at the village of Washington near Natchez.   The land occupied by these colonies was divided up into small farms, tenant houses were erected, and a system of self-government in one instance was put into operation.   The Davis Bend colony at one time contained 1750 freedmen who are alleged to have cleared $160,000 in 1865.   The Camp Hawley colony cultivated 700 acres and produced 223 bales of cotton.   This colony came out in debt.   The Home Farm colony, in 1865, produced 234 bales, at an actual profit of about $25,000.[4]

---

[1] Report of the commissioner, Ex. Docs. 1st Ses. 39th Cong. No. 11, p. 4. General Howard proposed that in restoring abandoned property, those who owned more than $20,000 worth should be required to convey in fee simple to each head of a family formerly held in slavery, a homestead varying in extent from five to ten acres.

[2] Sen. Docs. 1st Ses. 39th Cong. No. 27, p. 30.   The plantation of Joseph Davis adjoining that of his brother Jefferson was not restored until Jan. 1, 1867.   He was allowed rent, however, from Mar. 20, 1866, amounting to $8000.

[3] Report of Secretary of War, 1867–1868, pp. 621, 660.

[4] See Sen. Docs. 1st Ses. 39th Cong. No. 27.

One of the undertakings of the bureau was to provide free transportation for "refugees" or those who, declining to support the cause of the Confederacy, were compelled to move away at the outbreak of the war, and those who had followed the Federal army to other parts of the country. This policy seems to have been attended with great abuses. The commissioner issued an order announcing that free transportation should be restricted to cases where humanity demanded the return of the refugee.[1] Four thousand and thirty-one Mississippi refugees were beneficiaries of this provision; 1946 were free negroes.[2] The rest were white deserters from the Confederate army, stragglers, aliens, and Northern men who were living in the state at the beginning of the war. In addition to the refugees included under this head, free transportation was furnished to 307 teachers and agents of missionary societies in the North. The total expenses on this account were, for Mississippi, $312,424.

A larger task than the above was to provide for the immediate wants of the large class of freedmen alleged to be destitute. To furnish them with medical attention, nine hospitals and two dispensaries were established in Mississippi. A surgeon-in-chief, twelve medical officers, and seventy-nine assistants were employed at one time in the work.[3] During the first year of its operations, 5716 patients were treated.[4] During the summer of 1865, 182,899 rations were furnished to freedmen in Mississippi.[5] They were alleged to be in destitute circumstances, although the commissioner says in his report of December 1, 1865, that no necessity existed why a single freedman should be out of employment, and that 50,000 more laborers could be profitably employed if they could be obtained.[6]

By direction of General Howard, no rations were issued to freedmen in Mississippi after August 26, 1866, except in case of the sick in regularly organized hospitals, and refugees in actual want.[7] The number in both of these classes seems to have been considerable. Thus from September 1, 1866, to June 1, 1867, nearly 5000 freedmen received hospital treatment, and during the same period 99,842 rations were

---

[1] Report of the commissioner, Ex. Docs. 1st Ses. 39th Cong. No. 11, p. 16.
[2] Charles Truman relates that while at Selma, Alabama, in 1865, he saw large numbers of negroes, "refugees," making their way back to Mississippi. They had followed Sherman's army to Georgia.
[3] Report of the commissioner, *supra*.
[4] Sen. Docs. 1st Ses. 39th Cong. No. 27, p. 31.
[5] *Ibid.* pp. 30, 40.   [6] *Ibid.* p. 43.
[7] Sen. Docs. 2d Ses. 39th Cong. No. 6, p. 95.

issued.   This was partly due to the failure of the crops, on
account of which widespread suffering existed in the state.
Congress came to the aid of the bureau, and authorized the
Secretary of War to issue through the bureau supplies of
food to prevent starvation and extreme want to any and all
destitute persons.   From May to September, 1867, provisions
were issued to more than 12,000 persons, of whom about 5000
were white.[1]   Large quantities of supplies were also contributed by benevolent persons in the North.

Another duty which the bureau assumed was that of
extending the advantages of education to those whom the
fortune of the war had made free.   At first, chaplains of
colored regiments were put to teaching.   Schools were established by missionary societies and benevolent associations.
Upon the organization of the bureau, a systematic plan of
negro education was adopted.   A state superintendent of
education was appointed to exercise general supervision
over the schools.   Sub-commissioners were directed to set
apart the necessary accommodations, and to make provision
for the employment of teachers.[2]   During the first year of its
existence the bureau established sixty-eight schools in Mississippi, with an enrollment of 5271 pupils.[3]   The teachers
were for the most part from the North, were furnished free
transportation on account of the bureau, and were usually
paid by missionary societies.   The United Presbyterian body
at one time had fifteen teachers at Vicksburg and Davis
Bend.   The Freedmen's Aid Commission, the American
Missionary Association, the Indiana and Ohio Friends also
supported schools in Mississippi.   The opposition to negro
schools led the commissioner to publish a circular on October 24, setting forth at length the advantages of educating
the freedman, and the unwisdom of keeping him in ignorance.[4]   He advised that no schools be established in any
place where a bureau agent was not stationed.   He furnished the names of twenty-two places where he said it
would be "safe and expedient" to open freedmen's schools.[5]
Public sentiment soon underwent a change, and many planters
established schools on their places, donated school sites to

---

[1] Report Secretary of War, 1867–1868, pp. 621, 660.
[2] Ex. Docs. 1st Ses. 39th Cong. No. 69, p. 155.
[3] Sen. Docs. 1st Ses. 39th Cong. No. 27, p. 31.
[4] The *Vicksburg Herald* said: "These unscrupulous agitators who appoint
themselves in the name of the North to come down here and tell the negro
what he ought to do if the government does not do this or that, ought to be
shipped back to their homes and warned not to return again."
[5] Ex. Docs. 1st Ses. 39th Cong. No. 69, p. 160.

the freedmen, or contributed money for the erection of schoolhouses.[1]

One of the most useful functions of the Freedmen's Bureau was the assistance which it afforded in the readjustment of the labor system. In order to prevent dishonest employers from taking advantage of the freedman's ignorance to inveigle him into oppressive contracts, it was ordered that all labor agreements should be made in writing, and copies of the same filed with the nearest sub-commissioner, whose approval was necessary to their validity.[2] The chief objection to this requirement was the inconvenience to which it put the employer, and the likelihood of injustice resulting from the unfamiliarity of the agent with the value of the different kinds of labor in the South.

No complaint was more general among the whites than that the bureau encouraged the negroes in their idleness by taking them under its care and dispensing rations to them. The complaint was certainly not without foundation, and yet the higher officials of the bureau constantly used the vast influence which they possessed with the freedmen, to induce them to form labor contracts and to adopt habits of thrift and industry. It will be remembered that the freedmen for the most part refused to make contracts for the year 1866, in the belief that the lands would be distributed among them.[3] Colonel Thomas issued circular after circular admonishing the negroes that complaints were being made to him that they could not be induced to labor, and that as laborers they were unreliable. In order to encourage them to seek employment, he offered to furnish free transportation to any freedman who found it necessary to go to another part of the state in order to find employment. On the 31st of December, 1865, he issued a circular reminding them that the time had come when it was highly important that they should make contracts for the ensuing year, in order that crops might be produced for their support. They were urged to familiarize themselves with the forms of law, cherish a respect for its commands, and regard their contracts and obligations as

[1] See Report Secretary of War, 1867–1868, p. 621; also, report of John M. Laughton, inspector of schools, *New York Times*, Aug. 9, 1867.

[2] Ex. Docs. 1st Ses. 39th Cong. No. 69, p. 168.

[3] When the Fifty-fifth United States Colored Infantry was mustered out at Jackson in February, 1866, not one of them could be induced to enter into a labor contract. Charles Truman, *New York Times*, Feb. 4, 1866.

A Northern traveller says an intelligent freedman in Mississippi told him that he considered no man free who had to work for a living. *New York Herald*, Oct. 2, 1865.

sacred. Every effort seems to have been made to impress upon them a sense of their obligations to society and to civil government. A general order of the same date made it the duty of bureau agents to see that freedmen were properly contracted with; to act as their next friend, by affording them advice on all matters relating to contracts; and to make full reports to headquarters of all attempts to deal unjustly with them.[1] Again, on the 2d of January, 1866, Colonel Thomas published an address to the freedmen of the state, telling them that he was their lawful protector and adviser, and to some extent responsible for their conduct.[2] Again he reminded them of the necessity of entering into contracts for the ensuing year, informed them that he had received many complaints charging them with not living up to their contracts, but working as they pleased, and deserting their crops when they knew that the employer would lose all. " The time has come," he said, " when you must contract for another year's labor. I wish to impress upon you the importance of doing this at once. You know that if a crop of cotton is raised, the work must be begun soon, and hands employed for the year." Continuing, he said, " I hope you are all convinced that you are not to receive property of any kind from the government, and that you must labor for what you get like other people. As the representative of the government, I tell you that your conduct is very foolish, and your refusal to work is used by your enemies to your injury." He told them that the vagrant laws were right in principle, and he could not ask the civil authorities to allow freedmen to remain idle and depend for their subsistence upon begging or stealing. In regard to their professed fear of entering into written contracts, he said : " Some of you have the absurd notion that if you put your hands to a contract you will somehow be made slaves. This is all nonsense, made up by some foolish, wicked person. Your danger lies exactly in the other direction. If you do not have some occupation, you will be treated as vagrants, and made to labor in the public works."

Colonel Thomas time and again gave the freedmen sensible advice like the above. In view of the great influence which army officers exerted upon the freed people, there can be little doubt that such addresses were productive of good results.

During the winter of 1865–1866, Colonel Thomas made a

[1] Ex. Docs. 1st Ses. 39th Cong. No. 27, p. 36.
[2] Sen. Docs. 1st Ses. 39th Cong. No. 27.

tour of investigation through the state to ascertain, as he said, how the freedmen were being treated by the whites, what they were doing, and the general effect of the return to civil law. Among the towns visited by him were Jackson, Meridian, Lauderdale, Macon, Columbus, Aberdeen, Okolona, Corinth, Holly Springs, Grenada, and Canton. He said he made it his object to converse with mayors, magistrates, and other civil officers, together with the most influential freedmen. Upon the completion of his tour, he reported that the bureau "was working in perfect harmony with the state government and the department commander"; that freedmen had for the most part contracted with their old masters, had gone to work, and showed a disposition to live up to their contracts; that, on the whole, they were treated better than could be expected; that their freedom was generally recognized by the white people, who had undergone a change of feeling toward them; that the praises of the freedman were being sounded everywhere for his readiness to work and his general good conduct, there being few crimes among them greater than petty larcenies; that the vagrant laws were not being enforced in any of the towns, there being no necessity for it; and that the demand for labor exceeded the supply.[1]

The most notable political function of the bureau was to "afford protection and justice" to the freedmen. In General Slocum's order of August 3, 1865, announcing the establishment of the Freedmen's Bureau, he directed that all legal controversies between white and colored persons should be adjudicated by the bureau, so long as the testimony of freedmen was excluded from the civil courts. But at the same time, he directed that military officers must not remove from the custody of the civil authorities any freedman charged with larceny or other misdemeanor, where the court was willing to concede to the negro offender the same privileges as were granted to whites. He declared that it was not the purpose of the government to screen negro criminals from just punishment, nor to encourage them in the idea that they could escape the penalties of crime, but simply to secure to them the rights of freemen.[2] The policy of removing civil cases to bureau tribunals was extremely objectionable to the whites, and was vigorously protested against by the civil authorities. On several occasions, the forcible removal of

[1] Sen. Docs. 1st Ses. 39th Cong. No. 27, p. 43.
[2] *New York Tribune*, Aug. 18, 1865.

white offenders from the custody of the civil officials created
not a little excitement. One of these was the case of Joseph
Jackson, who was charged with the murder of a negro in
Washington County, the only witness to the act being a
black man, whose testimony was not admitted to the court.
Jackson was taken from the custody of the civil authorities,
and in pursuance of orders from Washington, tried before a
military commission.[1] That the authority of the bureau
officials was sometimes abused, appears from the following
case. A master was before the court of Madison County,
charged with maltreating an apprentice. Colonel Donaldson, sub-commissioner of the bureau, undertook to instruct
the circuit judge as to what he should do in the premises.
This communication was referred to Governor Humphreys,
who sent it to the major general commanding, with a letter
in which he pointed out the fact that so far as the differences
in the law of apprenticeship were concerned, the advantages
were with colored children. " Why the legislature has discriminated thus in favor of the freedmen is," he said, " not
for the executive to inquire into; but to avoid collision between the military and civil authorities, it is important for
the civil officers to know with certainty whether these laws
are to be nullified." The matter ended with a letter from
Colonel Thomas to Lieutenant Colonel Donaldson, in which
he said: "Nothing but the most convincing proof that the
child was inhumanly treated should have caused you to take
any step for his release, and then only after the refusal of
the judge of probate to release him on the presentation of
the facts as they were before you. It is the policy of the
bureau to recognize the civil power of the state to the fullest
extent, and to infuse into the minds of the freedmen respect
for the civil officers and government under which they must
live at no distant day. It is not desired to nullify any state
law, but to soften the application of those parts that may
seem oppressive, and to interfere for the protection of freedmen only in individual cases, when local prejudices may
cause the executive or judicial officers of the state to deny
the freedmen the rights which we are here to secure them.
If you will examine the decision of Judge Campbell attached
to this paper, you will see that he is willing to give the law
an interpretation that is liberal and just. It would be wrong
for the bureau to assume any attitude that would injure this
officer's influence. It is my opinion that the larger number

[1] *New York Tribune*, Aug. 18, 1865.

of the judges of the state would render the same decisions, and that only isolated cases occur where the law is interpreted oppressively. It is but treating them with due respect to make an effort to correct an evil through them, before any other method is adopted. You will see on reflection that it was not proper to write a letter of instructions to any officer of the civil government. You will, therefore, in the case of Charles Pitard, write a letter to the judge of probate at Canton, Mississippi, saying that you withdraw your letter of instructions." [1]

A conflict between the bureau authorities and the civil power occurred in Copiah County in November, 1865. An officer of the bureau had been arrested by the sheriff on a warrant, issued by a magistrate, for assault and battery upon a citizen. The officer defied the sheriff, but was finally arrested and lodged in jail. He refused to give bond for his appearance at the next term of the circuit court, although it is alleged a number of persons offered to make his bond. The military authorities decided to release him, and a detachment from the Fifty-eighth Colored Infantry took him from the jail and arrested the deputy sheriff who executed the warrant. Governor Humphreys telegraphed the facts to the President, and asserted that the civil authorities were being defied by the military. The President at once directed General Osterhaus to cause the release of the deputy sheriff, and ordered that no more interferences of this kind be permitted. The commander who was responsible for the affair was relieved of his command. [2]

The possibility of conflicts between the bureau and civil authorities was diminished by the arrangement between Governor Sharkey and Colonel Thomas, in which it was agreed that negro testimony should be admitted to the courts, and military interference should cease. The arrangement was so generally carried out in good faith by the judicial authorities that all Freedmen's Bureau courts were discontinued November 1, 1865. [3] All further interference by the bureau officials in any manner with the execution of the state laws or judicial proceedings were henceforth forbidden. On account of the ignorance and poverty of the freedmen, however, provision was made for assisting them in the prosecution of their cases in the courts. They were advised as to their rights at law,

[1] Goodspeed's Memoirs of Mississippi, Vol. II. p. 26.
[2] Jackson correspondent *New York Daily News*, Nov. 16, 1865; also *New York Tribune*, November 25.
[3] Ex. Docs. 1st Ses. 39th Cong. No. 69, p. 159.

and were aided by professional counsel. Sub-commissioners were directed to appear before the courts in behalf of colored litigants, advise them as to the merits of their cases, and of the best mode of procedure, and to see that witnesses were suitably instructed in regard to the nature and responsibility of oaths.[1]   A Northern attorney was employed to act as special counsel for freedmen who had cases before the courts. He reported, December 1, 1865, that he had defended freedmen in nineteen cases and had sworn out writs of *habeas corpus* for their benefit in seventeen instances.[2]   He was satisfied as to the judicial integrity of the judges, and did not think that a white jury would knowingly convict an innocent freedman.

With the surrender of the judicial functions of the bureau, it was announced that the vagrancy laws might be enforced, and convicted parties put to work on the public roads or handed over to the bureau authorities, who would undertake to find employment for them; that no more marriage licenses would be issued by bureau officials, except upon refusal of county clerks to issue them; and that no further regulations would be made concerning the price of labor.[3]

Several changes were made in the administration of the bureau in Mississippi. Colonel Thomas's administration was marked by numerous conflicts between the military and civil authorities, and his course was the subject of constant complaint by the whites. He was superseded, early in 1866, by General Thomas J. Wood, whose administration seems to have been an improvement over that of his predecessor. There were fewer collisions with the civil authorities, and the general tone of society assumed a more settled condition. He reported that the whites were "acting nobler than could be expected of them," that they manifested a disposition to obey the laws and become loyal citizens, and that he and the civil government worked in perfect harmony.[4]   General Wood turned over to the civil authorities all complaints of crime except in a few extraordinary cases. In all such cases, he said, substantial justice had been done the negro, and offenders punished. In the beginning of the year, he advised the freedmen to form labor contracts, but refused to enforce the state law absolutely requiring them to contract. His administration was the subject of favorable comment by the

---

[1] Report of the commissioner, Ex. Docs. 1st Ses. 39th Cong. No. 69, p. 173.
[2] Ex. Docs. 1st Ses. 39th Cong. No. 27, p. 36.
[3] *Ibid.* No. 69, p. 173.
[4] *New York Times,* Feb. 4, 1866.

whites.[1] He was succeeded, in January, 1867, by General Alvan C. Gillem, who was the last assistant commissioner. The offices of district military commander and assistant commissioner of the bureau were consolidated in 1867.

Congress, in July, 1868, directed that the bureau be withdrawn from the several states, and its operations, with the exception of the education and bounty divisions, be discontinued after January 1, 1869. Freedmen were reminded that they must now look to the civil magistrates for protection of their rights, and that supplies of food, clothing, medicines, free transportation, and assistance in making contracts must soon cease.[2]

The chief objection of the Southern white man to the bureau was that it established a sort of espionage over his conduct. He could not enter into a contract with a freedman, no matter how advantageous the terms might have been to both, without the approval of a bureau agent whose headquarters were perhaps fifty miles away, and who perhaps knew little of the value of the consideration he was called upon to approve. If a colored employee neglected his crop, and the employer discharged him, the employer was almost sure to be arrested and brought before a Freedmen's Bureau court. Police regulations intended to check the demoralization of the freedmen, and compel them to work, were often construed as attempts to deprive them of their newly acquired rights. Being released from the effects of the old slave laws that prevented them from assembling at night, they now seemed to be possessed of the belief that it was unrepublican not to wander about and hold meetings of different kinds. The attempts of the civil authorities to restrain this new propensity were not generally allowed to be enforced.

In June, 1866, Generals Steadman and Fullerton visited the state as special commissioners to investigate the affairs of the bureau.[3] They spent more or less time at Meridian, Columbus, Corinth, Grenada, Jackson, and Vicksburg, where they had personal interviews with all classes of the inhabitants. They reported that only here and there had the bureau accomplished any good. The chief objection, they said, was not due to the conduct of the higher officials, but to

---

[1] The *Vicksburg Herald* said : " So high does he stand in the estimation of our people, that it would be fortunate for the country if the administration of the Freedmen's Bureau could have such an enlightened and excellent officer as General Wood in every state. See also the Report of Generals Steadman and Fullerton, *Chicago Tribune*, Aug. 10, 1866.

[2] Report Secretary of War, 1869–1870, Vol. I. p. 497.

[3] Their report is printed in the *New York Times* of July 7, 1866.

the subordinates, "who had the idea that the bureau was established simply for the freedmen." [1]

[1] The *New York Times* of Oct. 5, 1866, contains a letter from I. T. Montgomery, an intelligent negro at Davis Bend, and the first of his race to hold a public office in Mississippi, complaining of the dishonesty of the bureau agents in charging excessive fees for their services. The only instances of official dishonesty among the subordinate officials which I have been able to find was the case of an agent in Rankin County, who was convicted of malfeasance by a military commission and sentenced to the penitentiary. See H. Mis. Docs. 3d Ses. 40th Cong. No. 53, p. 240.

Another agent in De Soto County was dismissed by General Gillem for imposing illegal fines and for collecting money for a negro woman and refusing to pay it over to her. *Ibid.* p. 194.

CHAPTER SEVENTH

The Reëstablishment of Civil Government

I. THE FINAL ACT OF RECONSTRUCTION

THE reconstruction legislature, the body which was to perform the final act in the work of congressional reconstruction, so far as the duty of the state was concerned, met at Jackson, January 11, 1870, in pursuance of the orders of the commanding general. It was the first meeting of a legislative body in the state since the inauguration of the congressional policy of reconstruction, the legislature elected in 1868 having never been convened on account of the defeat of the constitution to which it owed its existence.

In personnel as well as in politics, the first reconstruction legislature differed widely from any law-making body that had ever assembled in the state. In the first place, it contained nearly forty colored members, most of whom were slaves up to the close of the war.[1] Not one of them had any legislative experience, some of them had almost no conception of their duties as lawmakers, while a goodly number were unable to read and write, and were compelled to attach their signatures to the legislative pay rolls in the form of a "mark."[2] There were, on the other hand, some very intelligent negroes in the legis-

---

[1] As far as I am able to determine, the following is a list of the colored members in the lower House : —

Charles P. Head, Peter Borrow, and Albert Johnson of Warren ; Henry Mayson and C. F. Norris of Hinds ; J. F. Bolden of Lowndes ; John R. Lynch and H. P. Jacobs of Adams ; Edmund Scarborough and Cicero Mitchell of Holmes ; Dr. J. J. Spellman of Madison ; William Holmes of Monroe ; Isham Stewart, Nathan McNeese, and A. K. Davis of Noxubee ; John Morgan and Dr. Stites of Washington ; W. H. Foote of Yazoo ; Ambrose Henderson of Chickasaw ; M. T. Newsom of Claiborne ; Emanuel Handy of Copiah ; Merrimon Howard of Jefferson ; J. Aaron Moore of Lauderdale ; David Higgins of Oktibbeha ; C. A. Yancey and J. H. Piles of Panola ; H. M. Foley and George W. White of Wilkinson ; C. M. Bowles of Bolivar ; Richard Griggs of Issaquena ; and George Charles of Lawrence.

[2] My authority for this statement is a letter from Senator Pease, who was at the time state superintendent of education.

lature, this being particularly true of the ministers of the gospel, of whom there were about one dozen in the lower House. In the Senate there were five colored members, three of whom were ministers.[1]

Nothing illustrates better the extent of the revolution than the fact that some of the wealthiest counties of the state were represented wholly by men who a few years before were negro slaves. Thus Warren, of which Vicksburg is the chief place, was represented in the House and Senate by four negroes. Hinds, the county in which the state capital is located, had two negro representatives and one negro senator; Adams, of which Natchez is the county seat, — a county standing first in the history of the state for its ancient aristocracy, its wealth and culture, was represented in the lower House by three negroes, and in the Senate by another; the large wealthy county of Washington, of which Greenville is the chief town, had two colored representatives and one colored senator; the great county of Noxubee, in the eastern part of the state, noted for its fertile prairie farms and well-to-do planters, was represented by three negroes; Holmes, Panola, and Wilkinson, all large and wealthy counties, had two colored representatives each, while a good many others had one each. In addition to this element, there was a sprinkling of "carpet baggers," for the most part ex-Union soldiers, who had recently settled in the state.[2] These two elements, together with the "scalawags," or native white Republicans, constituted a large majority, and thus easily outvoted the representatives of the class which had hitherto held the political power of the state. They controlled the organization of the legislature, shaped the legislation, and established the public policy of the state. The House organized by electing to the speakership Dr. Franklin, a "carpet bagger" from New York. He sat for the county of Yazoo. Immediately after the completion of the organization, General Ames, in his capacity as provisional governor, sent in a message requesting immediate consideration of the Fourteenth and

[1] The colored senators were Rev. H. R. Revels of Adams; Rev. William Gray of Washington; Rev. T. W. Stringer of Warren; Charles Caldwell of Hinds; and Robert Gleed of Lowndes. Revels became a United States Senator, Gray a brigadier general of state militia, and Caldwell was killed shortly after the Clinton riots in 1875.

[2] The "carpet baggers" in this legislature who subsequently figured prominently in the politics of the state, were W. H. Gibbs from Illinois; A. Warner from Connecticut; A. T. Morgan from Wisconsin; A. G. Packer from New York; O. C. French from Ohio; W. B. Cunningham from Pennsylvania; W. H. Warren from Massachusetts; and H. W. Lewis from Ohio.

Fifteenth Amendments.   They were promptly ratified by large majorities.[1]

This completed the reconstruction of Mississippi, so far as the duty of the state in the premises was concerned.   In performing this final act the duty of the legislature was ministerial only.   It was made an absolute condition precedent to the reëstablishment of civil government and admission to representation in Congress.   General Ames informed the members that they were entitled to no compensation, and that they had no power to enter upon general legislation, until this act had been performed.

It devolved upon the legislature at this session to choose three United States senators, — one for the full term beginning March 4, 1871, and two for unexpired terms.   For the full term, Governor-elect Alcorn was chosen almost unanimously.   For the unexpired terms, General Ames and the Rev. Hiram R. Revels (colored) were chosen.[2]   Senator Revels went to Mississippi during the war as the chaplain of a negro regiment.   He enjoyed the distinction of being the first colored man to secure a seat in the United States Senate, and strangely enough was chosen to fill the unexpired term of Jefferson Davis.[3]   The more sentimental of the radicals saw in this the fulfilment of a prophecy which Davis is alleged to have made to Simon Cameron upon the former's withdrawal from the Senate in 1861, namely that in all probability a black negro would be sent there to take his place.[4]   After ratifying the constitutional amendment and electing United States senators, the legislature adjourned to await the action of Congress.

[1] The Fourteenth by a vote of 23 to 2 in the Senate ; and by a vote of 87 to 6 in the House.   The Fifteenth was ratified by the Senate unanimously ; in the House but one vote was cast against it.

[2] General Ames received all the Republican votes in the Senate and 72 in the House, as against 19 for Lowry, Democrat.   Revels was brought in and elected as a " dark horse," General Eggleston being the leading candidate in the beginning of the contest.

[3] Dr. Revels was born in North Carolina, removed to Indiana in early life, where he attended a Quaker seminary and became a Methodist minister and a teacher.   At the outbreak of the war he was engaged in pastoral work at Baltimore, but at once entered the Federal service and assisted in the organization of two negro regiments.   He followed the army to Jackson, Mississippi, and aided in the administration of the Freedmen's Bureau.   At the close of the war, he settled at Natchez and became a presiding elder and a member of the state Senate, which position he was holding at the time of his election to the United States Senate.   Since 1873 he has lived at Holly Springs.

[4] *New York World*, March 4, 1870.

II. READMISSION TO THE UNION

The state having fulfilled every condition of the reconstruction acts, and of the act under which the constitution had been resubmitted, every consideration of good faith required its speedy admission to the Union on an equality with the original states.   On the 3d of February, 1870, General Butler, from the committee on reconstruction, reported a bill for this purpose, and asked that it be put immediately upon its passage, it being the same in substance as the bill to readmit Virginia, which had already been fully discussed.[1]   This bill provided for the readmission of the state upon the condition that before any member of the legislature should take his seat, or any officer of the state should enter upon the discharge of his duties, he should take and subscribe to the following oath, a copy of which was to be deposited with the Secretary of State for permanent preservation : " I do solemnly swear that I have never taken an oath as a member of Congress or as an officer of the United States, or as a member of any state legislature, or as an executive or judicial officer of any state to support the Constitution of the United States, and afterward engaged in rebellion against the same, or given aid or comfort to the enemies thereof, so help me, God."   The provision did not apply to those whose political disabilities had already been removed by Congress.[2]   Additional conditions were : first, that the constitution should never be amended so as to deprive any citizen of the right to vote ; second, that it should never be lawful for the state to deprive any citizen of the United States, on account of race, color, or previous condition of servitude, of the right to hold office under the constitution and laws of the state ; third, the constitution should never be amended so as to deprive any citizen of the United States of the benefits and privileges of the public schools.[3]   Mr. Beck offered as a substitute for the Butler bill a simple resolution for the unconditional readmission of the state.   The substitute was rejected, and the Butler

---

[1] Globe, 2d Ses. 41st Cong. pt. i. p. 1013.

[2] Most of the prominent Republicans of the state had already secured the removal of their disabilities.   By a concurrent resolution of January 15, the disabilities of 139 such persons were removed.   Most of them were officers elect, and the resolution was passed to enable them to qualify.   Among them were Judges Simrall, Orr, and Peyton, and Hon. J. S. Morris, Hon. J. L. Morphis, and George E. Harris.

[3] Globe, 2d Ses. 41st Cong. pt. i. p. 1173.

bill passed on February 3, by a yea and nay vote of 136 to 56.[1] In the Senate, the bill was referred to the judiciary committee, of which Mr. Trumbull of Illinois was chairman. On February 10, the committee reported back the bill with the recommendation that the preamble, together with all the conditions prescribed for the readmission of the state, be struck out, and that a simple resolution be adopted providing for the readmission of the state to representation.[2] This was the same as Beck's substitute. Every requirement of Congress had been complied with. A constitution in harmony with the reconstruction acts had been framed and ratified almost unanimously. The Fourteenth and Fifteenth Amendments had been ratified by votes approaching unanimity. State officers, members of the legislature, and representatives and senators in Congress had been elected and were waiting to enter upon the discharge of their duties. Notwithstanding this, there were men in Congress who desired to impose unreasonable conditions upon the people of the state, or keep them under military rule. Butler in the House and Morton in the Senate were the leaders of this party. They demanded the reimposition of the old proscription features of the constitution which had been overwhelmingly rejected at the polls in 1869. They went even further, and imposed restrictions which, in effect, deprived the state of its equality with the original members of the Union. One of the conditions imposed by the Butler bill denied to the state the power of changing its organic law in certain particulars. Nothing could have been more contrary to the spirit of the Federal Constitution.

The debate over the readmission of Mississippi continued at intervals for a period of two weeks, when Senator Sherman, on February 17, gave notice that unless a vote was reached very soon, he intended to antagonize other public measures with the Mississippi bill. On the same day, the recommendation of the judiciary committee was rejected by a vote of 32 to 27, and the main bill, as it came from the House, passed by a vote of 50 to 11.[3] It was signed by the President on February 23. And thus, after having been excluded, to all intents and purposes, from the Union for a period of five

[1] Globe, 2d Ses. 41st Cong. pt. i. p. 1014.
[2] On January 31, Senator Morton had introduced a bill to readmit Mississippi. On February 1, Senator Conkling introduced a similar bill. Both were referred to the Committee on Judiciary, but were indefinitely postponed, as the subject-matter was covered by the House bill.
[3] Globe, supra, p. 1364.

years, during three of which it was treated as conquered territory, and held under military government, the state was restored to the Union, but with conditions annexed which very
materially impaired its sovereignty, and left it far from being
on an equality with the original states of the Union. It is the
essence of a Federal system that the distribution of powers
among the constituent members shall be the act of the sovereign, and not of the government. Congress, in assuming the
power to deprive the state of the right to change its constitution of government in certain particulars, arrogated to itself
sovereign powers, and had it been able to enforce its commands, the principle of the Federal system would have been
destroyed, and a league *inter disparates* left in its place.
Some of these limitations have been disregarded, and no one
doubts that the others may be set aside in the same way.
This is one of the numerous instances of the utter break-
down of the reconstruction policy.

Upon receipt of information that the President had approved the Mississippi bill, Mr. Henry Wilson presented the
credentials of Senator-elect Revels, and requested that they
be read and that he be sworn in. The Senator's credentials
bore the signature of Adelbert Ames, who styled himself
Brevet Major General U. S. A. and Provisional Governor of
Mississippi. They certified that Revels had been duly elected
a Senator of the United States by the legislature on January
20, 1870, for the unexpired term begining March 4, 1865, and
ending March 4, 1871. Immediately after the reading, Senator Saulsbury of Delaware raised an objection to the reception
of such evidence, and declared that the certificate of a military
officer was not such evidence as was required by law ; that General Ames, who styled himself provisional governor, was not
the true executive of Mississippi; that another person elected by
the legal voters of the state in accordance with the laws and
constitution, was the rightful governor, and the person whose
signature was required by act of Congress to be attached to
the credentials of senators elect. Senator Stockton offered a
resolution to refer the credentials of both Ames and Revels to
the judiciary committee with instructions to inquire and
report whether either or both had been citizens of the United
States nine years, and whether the former was not, for several
years prior to and at the time of his election, a commanding
officer in the army of the United States. This resolution was
discussed on the 24th and 25th of February, after which it
was rejected. A motion to administer the oath of office to
Senator Revels was then carried by a vote of 48 to 8, where-

upon he was escorted to the desk by Mr. Wilson and sworn in.[1] The day on which Senator Revels took his seat, Mr. Robertson presented the credentials of General Ames. They were referred to the judiciary committee.[2] On the 18th of March, Senator Conkling, from the committee, reported back a resolution that General Ames was not eligible to a seat in the Senate of the United States. Senator Conkling took occasion to say that had the question been one of sentiment, an adverse report could have commanded no support, but that inasmuch as the general had gone to Mississippi under military orders, and remained there in obedience to the same, he could not be considered a citizen of the state at the time of his election.[3]

The debate on the resolution was able and lengthy, extending through a period of several weeks. The chief supporters of General Ames were Senators Morton, Boutwell, Edmunds, and Sherman. Bayard and Thurman led the opposition. Much was said in regard to the form of the credentials which General Ames presented. They were as follows: —

I, Adelbert Ames, Brevet Major General U. S. A., Provisional Governor of Mississippi, do hereby certify that Adelbert Ames was elected United States Senator by the legislature of this state on the 18th day of January, 1870, for the unexpired term which commenced on the 4th day of March, 1869, and which will end on the 4th day of March, 1875.

In testimony whereof, I have hereunto set my hand and caused the great seal of the state of Mississippi to be affixed this 25th day of January, 1870.

A. AMES,
Brevet Major General U. S. Army,
Provisional Governor of Mississippi.

Although there was no evidence of irregularity or illegality in thus certifying to his own election, it was, to be sure, an

---

[1] Globe, 2d Ses. 41st Cong. pt. ii. p. 1568. It was said that the demands of poetic justice required that Senator Revels should be given the selfsame seat which Jefferson Davis had occupied, but it appears that Davis's seat was held by a Senator from Kansas who declined to surrender it.

[2] *Ibid.* p. 1542.

[3] *Ibid.* p. 1568. The *Jackson Clarion* preferred Revels to Ames as a Senator. In the issue of Jan. 20, 1870, it said Revels was a citizen of the state and a registered voter, and would expect to return to Mississippi after the expiration of his term, while General Ames did not have the slightest idea of ever again being within her borders after crossing the Tennessee line on his journey to Washington.

anomalous proceeding for a military commander, with the
vast power which he exercised, to declare himself elected to
the United States Senate. Nothing just like this had occurred
in the history of the United States. It was charged that he
had made use of his influence over the legislature to secure
his election.[1] There is no evidence that General Ames was
not regularly and legally elected by the legislature, over which
he undoubtedly wielded great influence. But there can be
little doubt, on the other hand, that he was guilty of bad taste
in becoming a candidate, in view of the relationship which he
sustained. It was discreditable to him and the profession
in which he had honorably distinguished himself, that his
sense of propriety and his conviction of right did not lead
him to take another course. He owned no real property in
the state, paid little or no taxes for the support of the government, knew little of the state and its needs ; in fact, was a
stranger to the people, and had little respect for their tastes,
habits, and prejudices. He was summoned before the judiciary committee and asked as to his intention of making Mississippi his permanent residence at the time he became a
candidate. He replied: " Upon the success of the Republican party in Mississippi, I was repeatedly approached to
become a candidate for the United States Senate. For a long
time I declined. I wrote letters declining. A number of
persons visited this city [Washington] to find arguments by
which I might be influenced to become a candidate. I hesitated, because it would necessitate the abandonment of my
whole military life. Finally, for public and personal reasons,
I decided to become a candidate and leave the army. My
intentions were publicly declared and sincere. I even made
arrangements almost final and permanent with a person to
manage property I intended to buy." [2] He declared that it
was doubtful if he would have remained in the state and
made it his home had he failed of election to the Senate.[3]
The action of the Senate was hastened by a joint resolution
of the legislature, passed March 24, declaring it to be the
solemn judgment of that body that Senator Ames's election
was regular and legal, and requesting his immediate admis-

---

[1] One of these charges was that he had placed the colored members of the
legislature under obligations to him by inviting them to a champagne party ;
another, that he had threatened to withhold their *per diem* in case of his
defeat ; another, that General Grant wanted him chosen, and that the state
would fail of readmission in the event of his failure to secure a seat in the
Senate. The charges do not seem to have been taken seriously. See Speech
of Garrett Davis, Globe, 2d Ses. 41st Cong. pt. ii. p. 2168.
[2] *Ibid.* p. 2125.   [3] *Ibid.* p. 2130.

sion.[1] The report of the committee that he was not an inhabitant of the state at the time of his election, and was not,
therefore, eligible to a seat in the Senate, was rejected on
April 1 by a vote of 40 to 12.   He was escorted to the desk
by Mr. Morrill, and sworn in.[2]   Neither Ames nor Revels possessed any of the qualities of the representative in the American sense of the term, and it was certainly straining a tech-
nicality to say that General Ames was a *bona fide* resident
of the state.   He regarded himself as the special representative of the colored race, whose rights he had upheld while
military governor.[3]

The state having been admitted to the Union, and Alcorn
having qualified as civil governor, General Ames turned over
the government to him, and passed from the army into the
United States Senate.   In thus exchanging a military career
for a civil one, he committed, according to his own admission,
the fatal error of his life.   General Orders No. 25, dated
February 26, 1870, recited the facts relative to the readmission of the state to the Union, and announced that the command hitherto known as the fourth military district had
ceased to exist.

III. THE INAUGURATION OF A CIVIL GOVERNOR

It will be remembered that after ratifying the Fourteenth
and Fifteenth Amendments and electing United States senators, the legislature adjourned to await the action of Congress.
On the 8th of March, it reassembled, the state having in
the meantime been readmitted to the Union.   On the 10th,
Mr. Alcorn, the first Republican civil governor, was inaugurated, and received the "crown of civil government from the
hands of the conqueror."   His inauguration marked the close
of military rule under which the state had existed for years.
Government by military commanders, provost marshals, and

---

[1] Globe, 2d Ses. 41st Cong. p. 2314.

[2] *Ibid.* p. 2349.   Among the twelve senators who voted against seating
him were Conkling, Schurz, Edmunds, and Trumbull.

[3] He said: "I found, when I was military governor of Mississippi that a
black code existed there, that negroes had no rights, and that they were
not permitted to exercise the rights of citizenship.   I had given them the
protection they were entitled to under the laws, and I believed that I
could render them great service.   I felt that I had a mission to perform
in their interest, and I hesitatingly consented to represent them and unite
my fortune with theirs."   Testimony before Boutwell Committee, March
28, 1876, p. 17.

military commissions was no longer to exist. Legislative
enactments were to take the place of "general orders," and
the decrees and judgments of the courts were no longer liable
to be suspended by military commanders.   The troops were
withdrawn from the state, with the exception of small detachments at two or three of the larger towns, and the civil
authorities were left to perform their duties uninterfered with.
A large part of the governor's inaugural was of a personal
character.   He spoke of his attachment to the state of Mississippi, of his long identification with the people, of his solicitude for their welfare; he told of the sacrifice of conviction
which he had made in joining in the "madness which had
plunged the state into ruin"; and spoke apologetically, as
he was so often wont to do, of his course in voting for the
ordinance of secession, and of his hearty acceptance of the
legal consequences which attached to his action.   "Secession," he said, "I have ever denounced as a fallacy."   "In
casting my lot with my own people in the late war, I did not
seek justification behind logical subtleties.   When I said in
the secession convention, 'the Rubicon is crossed, I join the
army that moves to Rome,' I spoke not as a sophist, after the
fashion of Calhoun, but as a rebel, after the fashion of Cæsar.[1]
I took the step in full view of the fact that it was one of
simple rebellion.   In the exercise of the right of revolution, I
accepted all its risks with my eyes open to the fact that those
risks included, in both law and fact, the penalties attaching to
treason.   And during even the first hour of defeat, when I
lay with my people crushed under the heels of thundering
armies, I accepted the fact that one end of the rope around
my neck and around their necks had been grasped by the
hands of a triumphant conqueror."

Few of the ex-Confederates were so ready as Alcorn to
acknowledge that their action was rebellion, or openly to
advocate the reconstruction policy.   The majority of the
leaders advised cheerful acquiescence in, and obedience to, the
reconstruction measures, but the advice was not based on any
assertion that the measures were either wise or expedient.
Alcorn was almost alone in basing his action as a secessionist
on the right of revolution rather than on an inherent legal
power of a state to withdraw from the Union, and by force of
arms to maintain the separation permanently.   He was equally

---

[1] Relative to this declaration the *Jackson Clarion* of March 11, 1870, said
it would have been nearer the truth, in view of Alcorn's military record, if he
had said he was a soldier after the fashion of Falstaff.

alone among the prominent secessionists in the view that the
penalties which attached to his action were those of treason,
the common view being that as belligerents they were legally
incapable of committing treason against the United States.
Whether Alcorn's views were the result of honest convictions
or of policy there is a difference of opinion.   He seems to
have been sincere in his professions.   Of his attachment to
the people of the state, founded on long residence and identification of interests, there can be no doubt.   He declared in
his inaugural that he was a Southern man in heart and soul.
"My affections," he said, "my interests, my habits of thought,
identify me indivisibly with the people of the South.   The
conqueror of the armies in which one of my sons won a
major's star, and another a martyr's crown, is no more a subject of love with me than with any other Southern soldier.
The military government which I have the happiness to bow
out of the state was no more a subject of pleasure to me than
it was to any other Mississippian whose blood glows as mine
does with the instincts of self-government."   With regard to
their new relation, and the hopefulness of the future, the
governor said: "The Union has brought us back, pardoned
children, into its bosom.   It bids us go forward this day to
the reconstruction of a government on the ruins left by our
own madness.   Restored to our lost place in the sisterhood of
states by the grace of the nation, that grace has brought us
back an equal among sovereigns.   Erect and free, Mississippi goes forward now to work out her destiny in a fellowship of states, the peer of the proudest."   He declared it to
be the duty of the government under the new régime to
extend its protection and encouragement to all the citizens
of the state, black as well as white.   He announced emphatically that the state government during his administration
would expend a large part of its energies and revenues in
educating the poor white and colored children of the state.
Those who were charged with setting in motion the machinery of civil law were advised to "gauge every project of legislation in the light of severe economy."   The hope was
expressed that those "who were disposed to violate the law,
and persecute other citizens," would abandon their evil ways,
and thus save the expense of maintaining an armed militia.
He asserted positively that so long as he was governor, all
citizens, without respect to color or nativity, should be
"shielded by the law as with a panoply," and where necessary, the militia should be called out and the people brought
to a sense of their obligations to society.   Slavery, he said,

was dead, and the ballot box, the jury box, and the offices of the state must be thrown open to the honest and competent without distinction of color. Relative to his obligation to the colored people for their political support, he said: "In the face of memories that might have separated them from me as the wronged from the wronger, they offered me their confidence, offered me the guardianship of their new and precious hopes with a trustfulness whose very mention stirs my nerves with emotion. In response to that touching reliance, the most profound anxiety with which I enter my office as governor of this state is that of making the colored man the equal, before the law, of every other man — the equal, not in dead letter, but in living fact."[1] He asserted that the wealth, intelligence, and social influence of the state were, to a large extent, arrayed against the spirit of the laws enacted to secure these rights, consequently, the judges must be in hearty accord with the policy of reconstruction. Before closing his inaugural address, he took occasion to pay his respects to the Democratic party, whose theories, he said, were a "system of brilliant fallacies, and whose speedy dissolution was a consummation to be devoutly wished for by every patriot in the land."

Much uncertainty existed in the minds of the whites as to whether Governor Alcorn would abandon his office for a seat in the United States Senate and leave the government in the hands of the "carpet baggers." Public meetings were held in a number of places, and resolutions adopted calling upon him not to resign his office.[2] It was said that with all of Alcorn's radicalism he was a large property owner, and was disposed to economy in the administration of the government, and that his transfer to the Senate would mean the removal of the only restraint upon those not inclined to economy. Notwithstanding these representations, he resigned the office of governor on the 30th of November, 1871, and passed into the Senate as the successor of Dr. Revels, who now became president of the new university for colored students. His transfer to the Senate was said to be a political move by the "carpet baggers," who desired a free hand in the state.[3] Whatever the facts of the case may be, if Alcorn was disposed to economy

---

[1] Relative to the position of the class of poor whites before the war, the governor said, "Thousands of our worthy white friends have ever remained to a great extent strangers to the helping hand of the state." The *Clarion* regarded this as a fling at the Democratic party.

[2] *Jackson Clarion*, Nov. 8, 1870.

[3] Lowry and McCardle's Hist. of Miss. p. 226.

in the administration of the state government, his influence does not seem to have counted for much, for the state expenditures during his own term were as great if not greater than during the term of his successor. In thus exchanging the governorship for a place in the Senate, Alcorn was not hampered by the embarrassment that confronted Ames in 1874, for the lieutenant governor, instead of being an unpopular colored man, was a worthy and honorable white man, and although an ex-Union soldier, he was a *bona fide* resident of the state, an extensive planter, and a conservative Republican in his politics.[1] Few of the " carpet baggers " won the respect and confidence of the native whites to such an extent as did Governor R. C. Powers.

IV. REORGANIZATION UNDER THE RECONSTRUCTION CONSTITUTION

The organization of civil government under the reconstruction constitution did not differ materially from the antebellum type. It was more democratic, in that all distinctions on account of color were forbidden, as well as all property qualifications for jury service, and all property and educational qualifications for suffrage. It was more democratic, perhaps, in requiring less rigorous qualifications for office, especially as regarded residence in the state. This constitution, moreover, has the distinction of being the only one in Mississippi ever submitted to the electorate for approval or rejection. The absolute prohibition upon the legislature as regards loaning the credit of the state, was a new and admirable provision, and was of great service later on. Under the new constitution as compared with the old, the powers of the governor were greater, salaries in general were higher, and offices were more numerous. An additional source of expense was a sub-

[1] Governor Powers's experience as a reconstruction sheriff in Mississippi convinced him, he says, that the reconstruction policy was little less than a " national crime." In a letter to me, he says : " Over and above the wickedness of the Kukluxism and fraud and intimidation that were resorted to to overthrow the congressional plan of reconstruction, there was a cause inherent in the plan itself, and it was abandoned by its authors on this account. Had the plan of reconstruction been based on sound principles of statesmanship, its friends would have stood by it, and the long train of evil and suffering that resulted from it would have been avoided. Without justifying any of the crimes that were committed to overthrow reconstruction, it is eminently proper that the historian who writes for future generations should point out the crime concealed in the so-called congressional plan itself."

sidized press. The reconstructionists seem to have made no attempt to change the type of local institutions which they found in Mississippi, although there was an effort here and there to inject into the administration new ideas, as illustrated in the public school system, immigration bureau, etc. The doctrine of *laissez faire* was not so scrupulously followed as it had been in the days prior to the war. No complaint was more general than that the reconstructionists governed too much, and the charge was certainly not without foundation. The official organization which they established was considerably more elaborate than that which obtained before the war. They provided for a lieutenant governor, a commissioner of immigration and agriculture, a state superintendent of education, a state board of education, a state board of equalization, a state printer, district printers, special treasury agents, and increased the number of judges threefold. They did not abolish outright the system of private law which they found in force, but through the Constitution reënacted, subject to modification or repeal by the legislature, all laws not passed in furtherance of secession and rebellion.[1] Those about which there was doubt were left to the action of the courts. Many of those reënacted by the constituent assembly, however, were repealed or modified by the legislature, so that, by 1875, an entirely new, but not a very different, system of law had been built up. Much of the new legislation was no improvement on that which was displaced; some of it was certainly unnecessary, but the belief seems to have been general among the reconstructionists that they were legislating for a totally different order of things, and for a new people, hence the necessity for a new system of law.

The chief task of the first legislature, after reconstruction, was to organize the system of "Republican" government, established in pursuance of the acts of Congress. One of the first measures provided for the organization of the new judicial system. The old county probate courts were superseded by a system of chancery courts, twenty in number, each to be held by an officer styled a chancellor, appointed by the governor, with the advice and consent of the Senate, for a term of four years. A term of the court was to be held in each county four times a year. The only qualification required of the first incumbents was residence in the state six months. Another new feature of the judicial machinery was provision for a chancery clerk in each county. He was to be elected

---

[1] Constitution, Art. XIV. Sec. 2.

by the people, and was to serve four years.   All business remaining undisposed of in the probate courts was transferred to the new chancery courts.[1]

Fifteen circuit courts were established, each to be held by a judge appointed by the governor, by and with the advice and consent of the Senate, for a period of six years.   Court was to be held three times a year in each county, and the first judges were not required to be residents of the state.[2]   The old High Court of Errors and Appeals was superseded by a Supreme Court consisting of three justices appointed in the same manner as the circuit judges and chancellors, for a term of nine years.[3]   Compared with judicial establishment before the war, this was rather an elaborate organization.   It proved to be unnecessarily so, and was modified slightly by the Republicans, and largely by the Democrats after their restoration in 1876.

The judges appointed by Governor Alcorn were, for the most part, Southern men, who, like himself had affiliated with the Republican party since its organization in Mississippi in 1867.   The practical impossibility, however, of finding competent Southern Republicans for high judicial stations, compelled him to appoint several Northern men and some Democrats.   On the whole, it was a judiciary of fair ability.   The judges seem to have been men of official integrity, although there were several whose lack of legal training prevented them from securing the respect of the bar.   One of these was notoriously incompetent, and was induced to resign his office.[4]   The justices of the Supreme Court appointed by Governor Alcorn were, H. F. Simrall, E. G. Peyton, and Jonathan Tarbell.   Simrall and Peyton were both old citizens of the state, and the latter was an active supporter of the Republican party.

---

[1] Constitution of 1868, Art. VI. ; Act of May 4, 1870.

[2] *Ibid.* Act of April 22, 1870.

[3] *Ibid.* Act of April 2, 1870.

[4] The chancellors appointed by Governor Alcorn were J. M. Ellis, O. H. Whitfield, W. G. Henderson, A. E. Reynolds, G. S. McMillan, D. P. Coffy, J. J. Hooker, E. Stafford, E. G. Peyton, D. N. Walker, Wesley Drane, T. R. Gowen, Edwin Hill, E. W. Cabiniss, Austin Pollard, Thomas Christian, De Witt Stearns, J. F. Simmons, Samuel Young, and Theodoric Lyon.

The circuit judges appointed by him were J. M. Smiley, M. D. Bradford, W. M. Hancock, B. B. Boone, G. C. Chandler, A. Alderson, Uriah Millsaps, Robert Leachman, J. A. Orr, O. Davis, C. C. Shackleford, E. S. Fisher, Jason Niles, W. B. Cunningham, and George F. Brown.   Less than half a dozen of these were "carpet baggers."   Alcorn desired to appoint Southern white men to all the offices, but was unable to withstand the pressure of the colored politicians and the "carpet baggers."   The appointment of Judge Tarbell was dictated by the Republicans of Northern birth, Alcorn's favorite being Judge Niles of Kosciusko.

Both were jurists of high repute, and during the passions and animosities of the time, they continued to enjoy the confidence of both political parties. The same may be said of Justice Tarbell, an ex-Union soldier from New York, who at the close of the war settled in Scott County, and in 1869 became probate judge by appointment from provisional governor, General Ames. Judge Tarbell belonged to the better class of "carpet baggers," was a man of fair ability and extraordinary industry, a ready and voluminous writer, as his opinions show, but he lacked experience and knowledge of the state jurisprudence when he went upon the bench.[1] Peyton and Tarbell were the only Republicans that ever occupied seats on the supreme bench of Mississippi. Their successors have all been Democrats, and so were their predecessors, with the exception of an occasional Whig in the ante-bellum period. The local judiciary, consisting of two or more justices of the peace in each supervisor's district, was reconstituted, and its jurisdiction largely increased. The first incumbents were to be appointed by the governor, and were to have jurisdiction in civil cases where the amount in controversy did not exceed $150, and concurrent jurisdiction with the circuit courts in cases of assault and battery, petit larceny, insult and trespass, attachments, actions of replevin, etc.[2] The extension of their jurisdiction in civil matters from cases involving $50, the limit before the war, to $150, and the increased amount of petty judicial business after the war, made the justice's courts an important part of the judicial machinery of the state. The system of county courts established in 1865 was abolished, and the cases pending before them were transferred to the circuit and justice's courts.[3] The old county board of police was superseded by the board of supervisors, an institution that differed only in name from that which it displaced.[4] County organizations were not generally disturbed, although in one or two instances there was a change of names where the old name perpetuated memories which the radicals did not particularly cherish.[5] A number of the large counties were reduced in area, and six or eight new ones were created and

---

[1] The late Justice L. Q. C. Lamar of the United States Supreme Court says Tarbell was esteemed in Mississippi as an upright judge, and his reputation for integrity was unquestioned. See *Mag. of Am. Hist.* Vol. 18, p. 424. After the overthrow of the Republicans and the expiration of his term, he removed to Washington, where he died several years ago. Simrall is, at the present writing, the only survivor. He is in his eighty-fourth year.

[2] Laws of 1870, p. 80.   [3] *Ibid.* p. 87.   [4] *Ibid.* p. 81.

[5] For example, the substitution of Jones County for Davis County, Lincoln County for Lee County, and Ellisville for Leesburg, etc.

given good loyal names, such as Lincoln, Sumner, Colfax, Union, etc. One of the reforms of the democracy after its restoration was to find new names for some of these counties.[1] There was a shifting of county seats in a number of instances, although this does not seem to have had any political significance. A reapportionment act was passed which had the effect of depriving ten " white " counties of separate representation in the legislature, they being consolidated with other counties to form large legislative districts.[2]

Much of the legislation of the time related to the erection and repair of state institutions which had either been destroyed during the war or had fallen into decay. The state university was reorganized by the removal of the board of regents and the appointment of a new board. An investigation was instituted, with a view to the removal of the state capitol from Jackson.[3] Congress was memorialized to remove the disabilities of all citizens of the state who had not been so relieved, and to grant the state two millions in money and five million acres of land to aid in the restoration of the levees. Provision was also made for the codification of the laws.[4]

Civil rights measures naturally constituted a no inconsiderable part of the legislation of this period. All laws relative to free negroes, slaves, and mulattoes, as found in the Code of 1857, and the laws constituting the so-called " Black Code," were declared to be forever repealed. It was also declared to be the true intent and meaning of the legislature to remove from the records of the state all laws of whatever character, which in any manner recognized any natural difference or distinctions between citizens or inhabitants of the state, or discriminations on account of race or color.[5] All distinctions among citizens in drawing, selecting, or summoning petit or grand juries were forbidden.[6] It was made unlawful for any person or corporation controlling railroads, steamboats, or stage-coaches to discriminate in any manner against any passenger, and the law imposed a penalty

[1] This was the case with Sumner County, which was changed to Webster, and Colfax, which was given the name of Clay.

[2] Testimony of J. F. Sessions, Kuklux Report, p. 207. The operation of the act is well illustrated in the cases of Wayne and Warren counties. The former, a " white " county, had no separate representative, while the latter, with a large black majority, had five, the fifth being given for a fraction of seven hundred people. [3] Laws of 1870, p. 618.

[4] The commissioners appointed in pursuance of this act were J. A. P. Campbell, A. R. Johnson, and A. Lovering, all Democrats.

[5] Laws of 1870, p. 73. [6] *Ibid.* p. 88.

not exceeding $5000 on any conductor who should attempt to compel any passenger on account of race or color to occupy a particular part of the conveyance.[1] The right of negroes to seats in theatres, without respect to the particular location of any seat, was upheld by the state Supreme Court.[2]

The first session of the first reconstruction legislature in Mississippi was the longest in duration of any in the history of the state. It continued from January 11 to July 21, with the exception of the month of February and a week in March. The Democrats allege that few or no attempts were made to expedite business, and the allegation was not entirely without foundation. The whole body of Democratic legislation was overhauled, and little of it was thought worthy of retention.[3] The increase of the citizenship and the somewhat chaotic condition of the laws incident to the great revolution no doubt increased the necessities for legislation. This should, therefore, be taken into consideration in framing an intelligent estimate of the comparative cost of government before and after the war. The expenses of the legislative department were nearly three times those of 1865.[4]

A session of six months in 1870, however, was not sufficient to reorganize the state government and enact sufficient legislation for the needs of the state, and accordingly the legislature met again January 3, 1871. During the recess four members had died, among the number being the speaker, Dr. Franklin, of Yazoo County. The House organized by the election to the speakership of Mr. H. W. Warren, a white man lately from Massachusetts. He sat for Leake County. The colored Republicans, although in the majority, were not at this time so demoralized by their greed for office that a black skin was an indispensable qualification for the speaker who presided over their deliberations. Accordingly they consented to the election of a "loyal" white man. Subsequently, their views of the rights of the colored race in this respect were modified.

<hr/>

[1] Laws of 1870, p. 104. Upon request of Governor Alcorn the presidents of the several railroads in Mississippi met the colored members of the legislature at the executive mansion for the purpose of settling, if possible, the question of equal rights on the railroad trains without recourse to legislative action. The colored members demanded that orders be issued to all conductors to grant equal privileges to all passengers without respect to race or color. The railroad managers offered to provide separate cars with equal accommodations. The negroes rejected the proposition, whereupon Alcorn lectured them upon their refusal, and plainly told them that a law embodying their demands could not be enforced without bloodshed. *Clarion*, Feb. 17, 1871.
[2] Donnell *vs.* the State, 48 Miss. 661. [4] Auditor's Report, 1871, Doc. G.
[3] The total number of acts and resolutions passed was 325.

The governor in his annual message commended the legislation of the previous session, and declared that when it was remembered that many of the members had lately been "inducted into freedom," and that few had ever sat in a deliberative assembly, their work showed a moderation and wisdom highly creditable.   He indulged in some sarcastic allusions to the character of the customary ante-bellum executive message to the legislature, asserted that the "speculative statesmanship of the South, having had its day and its result," he would not follow precedent and devote himself to the principles of government but to questions which more directly concerned them.   He advised the legislature that as their "rights in the territories had occupied the attention of previous legislatures, somewhat in excess of wise policy," they should devote themselves to the more practical work of gathering up and rebuilding whatever those abstractions may have left of their rights at home.   He informed the legislature that he had not accepted the facts of reconstruction without more or less misgivings, but to satisfy himself of the wisdom of the policy of Congress, he had instituted a series of investigations into the capacity of the colored people for "well-ordered freedom." The results of his inquiries into the marriage relations of the blacks were in the highest degree encouraging to the reconstructionists.   Both the constitutions of 1865 and 1868 dignified those of the colored race who had cohabited together by giving them the legal status of husband and wife.   It had been feared that the negroes would continue the practice of cohabitation without taking out marriage licenses.   Quite the reverse, however, proved true. The dignity of marriage by a minister rather appealed to the negro's sense of pride.   It implied a sense of equality with the whites which they were not slow to appreciate.   The result was that the proportion of marriages among them after 1865 was nearly as large as among the whites.[1]   From this the governor felt satisfied that the colored people were striv-

---

[1] The following results are tabulated from the investigations in thirty-one counties: —

| CLASS | POPULATION IN | MARRIAGE LICENSES ISSUED | | | | | |
	1860	1865	1866	1867	1868	1869	1870
Whites	189,645	2708	3129	2829	2546	2655	2204
Blacks	239,930	564	3679	3524	2802	3584	3427

ing " to rise to the moral level of their new standing before
the law, to the extent of a strict adherence to the formularies
of sexual proprieties." A recent act of the legislature raising
the fee for marriage licenses from one to three dollars was
criticised as a " blow not only at the virtue of the poor whites,
but at the successful organization of the colored people on
the basis of a free civilized society."

Governor Alcorn affirmed that the results of his investigations established the general good faith of the freedmen with
regard to their marital relations. Unfortunately, however,
there were so many exceptions to this during the early years
of their freedom that the condition of society did not present
a very hopeful aspect. But the provision for public schools,
the multiplication of the number of ministers, and the increase of religious institutions vastly elevated their sense of
the sanctity of the marriage contract. In no respect did the
colored race show greater signs of improvement than in the
increase of their religious organizations. In twenty-five counties the number of churches built by the negroes increased
from 105 in 1865 to 283 in 1870, while the number of ministers increased from 73 to 262.

With regard to industrial pursuits, there were the same
evidences of progress. In seventeen counties the number
of shoemakers' shops owned by the negroes increased from
21 in 1865 to 63 in 1870, and the number of blacksmith shops
from 40 to 113.

Along, however, with the industrial progress of the negro,
went an enormous increase in the amount of crime, which
Governor Alcorn thought showed a " degree of barbarism
truly shocking." [1] Much of this Governor Alcorn attributed
to the " barbarous practice " of carrying deadly weapons,
which was almost universal among both races in the South
at this time. He recommended drastic legislation to prevent
this " outrage on civil society."

The most important legislation of 1871 related to the lease
of the penitentiary and the encouragement of railroad building. The provision for the lease of the penitentiary was the
subject of much censure by the Democrats.[2] The act to
encourage railroad building provided that any railroad com-

---

[1] In a letter to the *New York Tribune* Governor Alcorn said 124 murders
had been committed in the state from April, 1869, to March, 1871. In a despatch to Senator Ames in April, 1871, he said the auditor's books showed
48 murders within the last three months, and there were known to be 15
cases not reported. *Clarion*, April 11, 1871.

[2] Testimony of J. F. Sessions, Kuklux Report, p. 208.

pany which would construct twenty-five miles of road within the limits of the state and have it equipped and in good running order by the first of September, 1872, should receive from the state the sum of $4000 per mile for each mile so constructed.[1]   The stock which the state held in the various railroads of the state was donated to the New Orleans, Jackson, and Great Northern railroad.   The amount was about $250,000.   It appears that when the charter was first granted to the road, it was upon condition that the company was to build a branch from Canton to Aberdeen by way of Kosciusko, otherwise the charter was to be forfeited.   Upon the expiration of the period named, the extension had not been made, and the charter consequently fell.   The legislature at this session renewed the charter, required the company to complete the branch to Kosciusko within two years, and to Aberdeen within five years. The same act surrendered to this road all railroad stock held by the state, provided the people living along the line would contribute $7500 per mile.[2]   The measure was opposed by all the Democratic members, except those who lived on the line of the proposed extension, as a piece of unnecessary extravagance and favoritism.[3]   The Republicans, on the other hand, contended that unless state aid was given to the road it would go into bankruptcy, and the state would lose all its stock.[4]

On the 13th of May the legislature adjourned, having been in session since January 3, making a total legislative session of ten months and a half in 1870 and 1871.   The Republican members asserted that the legislative needs of the states called for long and frequent sessions ; the Democratic members asserted that the per diem method of compensation was the true reason.[5]

---

[1] Laws of 1870, p. 745.   Under this provision the Ripley Railroad Company became entitled to $81,000 from the state.   The auditor acting upon the advice of the attorney general declined to issue the warrants for the amount.   It was charged that upon receiving a bribe of $6000 the attorney general withdrew his objections — a joint committee of the legislature upon investigation reported that the "robes of the attorney general were tainted." See *Clarion* of March 20, 1873.

[2] Laws of 1871, p. 177.

[3] Testimony of J. F. Sessions, Kuklux Report, p. 213.

[4] Testimony of O. C. French, *ibid.* p. 22.

[5] The compensation was $7 per day and 20 cents per mile going to and from the seat of government.   After an agreement to adjourn had been reached, four members drew up a long protest, declaring that they ought not to abandon their posts ; that it was their duty to work "diligently and considerately, deliberately, dispassionately, moderately, and without too much haste."   See House Journal of 1871, pp. 823–826.

CHAPTER EIGHTH

The " Carpet-Bag " Régime

I. THE ELECTION OF GENERAL AMES AS CIVIL GOVERNOR

In 1873, the year of the state election, General Ames was serving in the United States Senate. In this field, he achieved no particular distinction.[1] He was a member of the committee on military affairs, and introduced a number of measures affecting the army, one of which had in view the opening of all branches of military service to colored people and the abolition of all distinctions therein on account of race or color. He made an ineffectual attempt to have Hon. Robert A. Hill, United States district judge, removed from office in order to secure the position for a friend. The reason alleged for his action was that Judge Hill's Southern sympathies prevented him from impartially enforcing the Kuklux Act.[2] The only measure which Senator Ames supported with any marked ability was the bill to extend the provisions of the Kuklux Act. This he did in a set speech on the 20th of May, 1872, devoting much of his time to a defence of the " carpet bagger " in general, and of himself in particular. He declared with pride that he had fought his way to Mississippi during the war by his

---

[1] General Ames acknowledges that he was little " versed in civil affairs." See Globe, 1st Ses. 42d Cong. p. 570. He writes me under date of Jan. 17, 1900: "I am frank to confess that I was poorly equipped for the position of senator. While in the Senate I devoted myself mainly to the Southern question." Relative to his abandonment of the army for a civil career, he says: "That I should have taken a political office seems almost inexplicable. My explanation may seem ludicrous now, but then it seemed to me that I had a mission, with a large M. Because of my course as military governor, the colored men of the state had confidence in me, and I was convinced that I could help to guide them successfully, keep men of doubtful integrity from control, and the more certainly accomplish what was every patriot's wish — the enfranchisement of the colored men and the pacification of the country."

[2] General Ames subsequently admitted that he had been misled as to Judge Hill, and always regretted his action. Letter to Attorney General of the United States, Correspondence of Governor Ames, 1874, p. 48.

own right arm, through much blood and over many battle-
fields, and asserted that he had a right to go there and to
stay there.[1] This was in reply to an attack by his new colleague, Senator Alcorn, who had now entered the Senate as
the successor of Senator Revels. Alcorn was an old resident who had emigrated to Mississippi from Illinois many
years before the war.[2] He was a wealthy planter of fine
personal appearance, a man of inordinate vanity, somewhat
imperious in disposition, and, as the debates show, possessed
some forensic ability. He had served a few weeks in the
state militia during the war, in whose cause he had little
faith, and to the success of which he gave but a lukewarm
support.[3] He had been an old-line Whig in politics, but
voted for the ordinance of secession, an act for which he
never ceased to apologize. After the enactment of the
reconstruction measures, he joined the Republican party,
believing it to be the duty of the whites to accept unreservedly the policy of Congress and, if possible, get control of the
negro vote ; but having a substantial interest in the state,
and being a popular stump orator, and an ex-slaveholder, he
succeeded in gaining in a large measure the confidence of
the native whites, which General Ames was never able to
do. General Ames's attempt to dispute with Senator Alcorn
the leadership of the party in Mississippi called down upon
him the hostility of his colleague, who denounced him in the
Senate in the most unmeasured terms, and otherwise treated
him with an air of contempt.[4] In a speech on the Kuklux
bill, delivered May 20, 1872, Senator Alcorn charged General Ames with having taken advantage of his position " to
seize a senatorial toga before taking off his military coat."
He said : " My colleague is not connected with my state by
any of the ties that make up the reality of the representative.
He is not a citizen of Mississippi. He has never contributed
a dollar to her taxes. He is not identified with her to the

[1] Globe, *supra.* Appendix, p. 393.

[2] General Ames said of him : " My colleague went from a free country
earlier than I did. He is one of the natives. He is one of the high-toned,
chivalric gentlemen of the state. On the other hand, I am simply from
Yankeedom." Globe, *supra*, p. 393.

[3] He is reported as saying that he rejoiced when the flag of the Confederacy fell. *Clarion,* July 3, 1869.

[4] General Ames had been in Mississippi but a short time before the breach
occurred between him and Alcorn. In a letter of March 30, 1871, to C. F.
Norris, a colored member of the legislature, Ames charged Alcorn with not
protecting the negroes, but allowing them to be killed by " tens and hundreds," and with " gaining power and favor from the democracy at the price
of blood, and that, the blood of his friends."

extent of even a technical residence." The mutual hostility
of the two senators ended in an appeal of each to the Republican party of the state for an indorsement of his course.
Each became a candidate for governor. Ames succeeded in
securing the regular nomination of the party, receiving five
times as many votes as Alcorn in the convention. Alcorn's
adherents bolted and nominated a state ticket in opposition
to Ames. The nominees were about equally divided between Northern and Southern Republicans. The ticket contained the name of one colored candidate, the Rev. T. W.
Stringer, a member of the legislature from Adams County.
Alcorn at once challenged Ames to meet him in debate at
Jackson, but the general, knowing that as a stump orator
he was no match for the "Sage of Coahoma," declined, on
the ground that Alcorn was not a regular nominee of any
political party.[1] In a public speech at Jackson August 29,
Alcorn announced his candidacy and his platform. He gave
an account of his record in the Senate, told the negroes that
he had secured for them the right to ride in railroad cars
with white people, declared that he had appointed many
good men to office, and some bad ones, also, and denounced
Senator Ames as the most vindictive man in Congress.[2]
Ames received the almost unanimous support of the negro
voters, who were grateful to him for his course as military
governor. He was, likewise, the choice of the "carpet-bag"
element, which was not very strong numerically, but potent
in influence. Alcorn was supported for the most part by
the native white Republicans and by the Democrats, who had
no regular ticket in the field, the Democratic state convention
at Meridian having declared it "inexpedient" to make a
nomination, meaning thereby that it was useless to do so.
As between the two Republican candidates, they preferred
Alcorn as the lesser of two evils, and therefore gave him a
feeble support. The result was the election of Ames by a
large majority.[3] On the ticket with Governor Ames were
the names of three negroes, A. K. Davis, for lieutenant

---

[1] *Jackson Clarion*, Sept. 4, 1873.
[2] *Ibid.*
[3] The exact vote was Ames, 69,870 ; Alcorn, 50,490. As early as the 16th
of January, 1873, the *Hinds County Gazette* predicted that Ames would be
the next governor of Mississippi, and that Ham Carter (colored) would be
lieutenant governor, and eventually governor, as Ames would be chosen to
the Senate after a short term as chief executive. The *Jackson Clarion* of
May 15, 1873, said Ames was the favorite for governor against all comers.
The *Prairie News* (Republican) said his nomination was essential to the success of the party.

governor; James Hill, for secretary of state; and T. W. Cordoza, for superintendent of education.

The belief among the colored voters that they had not secured their proper share of the state offices in 1870, led them practically to establish a "color line" before the next election. In the state convention of 1873, they demanded that at least three of the seven state offices should go to colored men, and the Warren County delegates are alleged to have mounted the desks in the convention hall, and with pistols drawn declared that one of the three candidates must come from Vicksburg.[1] Their argument was that colored men did the voting and were, therefore, entitled to the offices.[2]

They were strong enough numerically to enforce their demands, and as the state superintendent of education, a white "carpet bagger" of undoubted competency, happened to be a resident of Vicksburg, he was set aside for a negro whose chief qualification was the color of his skin. It was a common remark that this marked the beginning of the downfall of Governor Ames in Mississippi. Davis and Cordoza hung like millstones about his neck, and by their dishonesty, incompetency, and bad counsel, which he too often accepted, did much to make the administration odious in the eyes of the whites.[3] The colored secretary of state

[1] *Columbus Free Press* of Aug. 7, 1875 (a Republican paper edited by two Northern gentlemen, Lewis and Bliss). "Let him dispute it who will," this paper declared, "it is no less true that there are in the Republican ranks, scores of colored men who are just as determined to establish a color line and run nobody but colored men for office, as there are of white men who are bent on establishing a white line." "This policy has finally brought the Republican party, not only of the South but of the nation, up to the very verge of destruction." General Ames writes me that this charge was, no doubt, true. He says, "The demands of the colored delegates for state offices seemed to be irresistible, especially for lieutenant governor."

[2] The *Vicksburg Plaindealer*, a radical sheet published by a negro, declared that McKee, Pease, Wells, and other white men had always insisted on holding the offices, while the colored men did the voting, but that "this thing had played out."

[3] Cordoza, at the time of his nomination, was under indictment for larceny at Brooklyn, New York. A copy of the indictment is printed in the *Jackson Clarion* of Aug. 13, 1874. It is signed by Benjamin F. Tracy, United States District Attorney for the eastern district of New York. Charles Nordhoff, a staff correspondent of the *New York Herald*, relates that while in New Orleans, some one, knowing that he was interested in schools, gave him a letter of introduction to Superintendent Cordoza. On asking for him in Jackson, he was told that the superintendent had gone to Vicksburg to look after an indictment that had been found against him. When he himself went there, he found that Cordoza was not merely indicted, but, as an indignant Republican put it, he was "shingled" all over with indictments for embezzlement and fraud, and likely to go to the penitentiary if justice was done.

was a competent officer, and succeeded in escaping the impeachments of the democracy in 1876.

II. THE INAUGURATION OF THE AMES ADMINISTRATION

The inauguration of Governor Ames took place January 22, 1874. It is the testimony of his political opponents that he made a favorable impression upon those who witnessed the inaugural ceremonies.[1] Many such expressed their intention of supporting him in his determination, publicly declared, to give the people of Mississippi an honest and economical administration.[2] They knew little of the new governor. Few, in fact, had ever seen him except as a uniformed commander setting aside the verdicts of their juries and the decrees of their courts. To the great mass of the people he was known only as the cruel " Yankee " who had put the " nigger " in the jury box, removed their governor, and ejected his family from the mansion. He now stood before them in civilian dress as their civil governor, and in his inaugural address pledged them that, as far as lay in his power, they should have an administration marked by economy and reform.[3]

The legislature elected in 1873 was overwhelmingly Republican, and was otherwise the most interesting of the post-bellum legislative bodies in Mississippi. Politically, the Senate was composed of twelve Democrats and twenty-five Republicans ; the House had thirty-six Democrats, seventy-seven Republicans, and several Independents. The Senate contained nine colored members and nine white " carpet baggers." In the House, there were fifty-five colored, and sixty white members, the " carpet-bag " element having fifteen representatives. Adams County was represented in the Senate by a dull but honest colored minister ; in the House, by three colored members of little education, and by a white ex-Union soldier from Ohio. Hinds, the county in which the state capital is located, had an illiterate negro senator, and three negro representatives. Noxubee, one of the largest counties of east Mississippi, had an extremely

---

[1] Letter of George E. Harris to President U. S. Grant, Report Sen. Sub. Committee on Mississippi elections, 1876, p. 591.

[2] Governor Ames said shortly afterward that he intended to make Mississippi the exception among the reconstructed states, and wanted it to escape the condition of South Carolina and Louisiana. Correspondence for 1874, p. 66.

[3] Inaugural Address, Jan. 22, 1874.

black and ignorant senator. He was, however, honest, and had been a member of the legislature continuously since 1868, and was not even retired by the "revolution of 1875." In the House, Noxubee was represented by one negro and two white men, both of whom were Republicans. Warren, the county of which Vicksburg is the chief city, had as senators a negro and a Northern white man ; in the House, Warren had three representatives, all negroes. Lowndes had a negro senator of little education, but of some natural ability, a good speaker, and a man of considerable wealth. He had been a slave up to the close of the Civil War. Lowndes was represented in the House by two negroes and one white Republican. Marshall and Chickasaw had negro senators. Wilkinson, Bolivar, and Washington, large river counties, were each represented in the Senate by negroes of fair intelligence. Yazoo County had three negro representatives ; Holmes, three ; Marshall, three ; Panola, Jefferson, Lowndes, Madison, Rankin, Washington, and Issaquena, two each ; while many other counties had one each. There were a number of whites of poor ability, some of whom were Democrats, some Republicans.

The legislature met in January, and the House organized by the election of a negro member named Shadd, from Adams County, to the speakership. In the first reconstruction legislature, the colored members consented to have a white man preside over their deliberations, but afterward, as long as they were in power, with a temporary exception in 1873, a black skin was an indispensable qualification for the office of speaker, another illustration of their greed for political power.[1] It is not to be supposed, however, that all the colored speakers were men of ignorance and incompetency. Hon. John R. Lynch, the speaker in 1872, was a notable exception. He presided over the deliberations of the House

---

[1] Relative to the course of the colored members in this legislature, a prominent Democrat writes me as follows : " In my opinion, if they had all been native Southern negroes, there would have been little cause of complaint. They often wanted to vote with Democrats on non-political questions, but could not resist the party lash. The majority of whites of both parties exhibit the same weakness." With a few exceptions, the colored members took little part in the work of legislation, although some of the principal chairmanships were held by them. They were inclined to interrupt the proceedings with motions and points of order, were particularly sensitive on the subject of civil rights, and often objected to Democratic measures on the general assumption that their purpose was the abridgment of the privileges of the negro race. Frequent objections were made to the conduct of newspaper reporters in designating the negro members as "colored," and refusing to prefix "Mr." to their names.

with dignity and impartiality, a fact to which his political opponents bore testimony upon his retirement.[1] He was a slave at the close of the war, became a justice of the peace by appointment from General Ames in 1869, and in 1873, was elected to Congress, where he served two terms. He presided over the Republican national convention in 1884, and is at present a paymaster in the United States army. He is one of the most intelligent men of his race, is conservative in his views, and distinctly Caucasian in his habits.

Governor Ames followed up the promise made in his inaugural address with a special message on the subject of the state's finances, in which he recommended several reforms. Taxes were higher at this time than ever before in the history of the state, having increased from one mill on the dollar in 1869 to fourteen in 1874.[2] The credit of the state was impaired, and the annual expenses of the government exceeded by one-fifth the receipts, while state paper was hawked about the streets and sold at from 20 to 40 per cent discount. The governor recommended a return to a cash basis, which he said would save the state 25 per cent in the cost of administering the government, or at least $300,000 annually. He recommended also that appropriations be cut down 25 per cent. He declared with truth that there were opportunities for curtailment in every branch of the government; that $50,000 could easily be saved in the cost of administering the judiciary, without impairing its efficiency, by a modification of the law relative to the compensation of jurors; and that the expense of maintaining the university and supervising the public schools might be reduced in like manner. He said : " The average cost of the legislature per day is $1800. The annual sessions are long drawn out, the average cost of a sixty days' session being over $100,000, aside from public printing." He recommended a change in the per diem mode of compensation for the legislature, provision for equalization of assessments through-

---

[1] At the close of the session, the House presented Speaker Lynch with a gold watch and chain. Upon motion of a prominent white Democrat, a resolution was adopted thanking him for his " dignity, impartiality, and courtesy " as a presiding officer. The *Clarion* bore testimony to his impartiality as a speaker in the following words : " His bearing in office had been so proper, and his rulings in such marked contrast to the partisan conduct of the ignoble whites of his party who have aspired to be leaders of the blacks, that the conservatives cheerfully joined in the testimonial." Issue of April 24, 1873.

[2] Report of W. H. Gibbs, state auditor, 1875.

out the state, and begged for the earnest support and coöperation of the legislature in his effort to bring about financial
relief.[1]

These recommendations were undoubtedly wise and practicable.   They do credit to the governor who made them.
They do not sound like the utterances of a "carpet bagger"
bent on peculation and plunder.   They rather indicate that
Ames had some knowledge of the needs of the state and
some interest in its welfare.[2]   Soon after the meeting of the
legislature, an able and respectful address drafted by a state
convention of taxpayers was laid before the two Houses.
The address called attention to the alleged abuses of the
state government, its wastefulness and extravagance, compared the expenses of administering the government before
and after the war, and contained a number of recommendations looking toward economy.[3]   But the legislature to
which these recommendations were addressed did not seem
to favor reform.

Early in the summer, Governor Ames, according to his
custom, went North to spend his vacation, leaving the negro
lieutenant governor in charge of the government.   The governor remained away from the state one and a half or two
months, during which time Davis proved conclusively that
the office of lieutenant governor is something more than an
empty honor if only the incumbent is given a chance.[4]   A

[1] Special message to the legislature, p. 4.

[2] A prominent Democrat, who was a member of the legislature in 1874 and
subsequently Speaker of the House, writes me that Governor Ames was undoubtedly more favorable to economy and reform than was the majority of
this legislature.

[3] This address is printed in full in the Boutwell Report, p. 450 *et seq.*; in
the Report of the Senate Sub-Committee on Mississippi Elections, p. 848–854;
and in James Lynch's Kemper County Vindicated, Appendix.   Hon. George
C. McKee, a Republican member of Congress from Mississippi at the time,
declared this to be the "ablest paper" he had seen in Mississippi for years.
He warned the members of the legislature that there was no fear of cutting
too deep.   "The evil," said he, "is too enormous.   The petition of the tax-
payer's convention should be heeded."   See Report of Senate Sub-Committee, p. 601.   The Democratic tax-payers were not the only persons to
protest against the heavy burdens imposed by the state government.   On the
16th of October, the day before the meeting of the legislature, the Jackson
Republican Club unanimously adopted a series of resolutions deprecating
"the heavy burdens under which the people of Mississippi are now groan-
ing," and declared that they could be safely reduced without impairing the
efficiency of the government.   They respectfully petitioned the legislature to
abolish annual sessions, reduce by one-half the number of circuit judges
and chancellors, reduce the expenses of printing at least $75,000 annually,
and appropriate nothing for the support of the militia.

[4] Davis had somewhat exaggerated ideas of the importance of the lieutenant governor in the administration of the government.   He expected the

breach had already occurred between the governor and the
lieutenant governor, the latter, according to the opinion of
the governor, having gone over to the "sore heads."

Lieutenant Governor Davis, upon assuming control, at
once discharged the employees about the capitol and appointed his friends to their places. He then dismissed the
governor's private secretary, and next proceeded to appoint
chancellors for several judicial districts, although Governor
Ames, foreseeing the occurrences of these vacancies during
his absence, had already made provision for filling them
before leaving the state. Davis held that the governor
could not legally make appointments before the vacancies
had actually occurred, but in this view was not sustained by
the attorney general.[1] Governor Ames, upon returning to
the state, at once revoked the appointments made by Davis,
and recommissioned those whom he had formerly appointed.
This was one of the grounds of his impeachment. Another
way in which the lieutenant governor made good use of his
opportunities was by dispensing pardons to his colored
friends who languished in the county jails or penitentiary,
or who were under indictment and likely to be sent there.
From June 15 to July 25, Davis issued twenty-three pardons, commutations, and remissions of forfeiture. Governor
Ames was again absent for a month in the autumn, during
which time the lieutenant governor granted thirty-four
pardons, six remissions of forfeiture, and six commutations
of sentence.[2]

The following is the record of both the governor and the

governor to call him to the executive chair when the latter was away from
the capital, no matter how brief the absence. On one occasion, Governor
Ames had gone to the Gulf coast, his route taking him across the corner of
Louisiana. The lieutenant governor was highly offended because he had not
been called to Jackson to assume the government, and telegraphed a friend
in New Orleans inquiring if Governor Ames was in that city. Upon
receiving an affirmative answer, Davis proceeded to the office and ordered
the governor's private secretary to open the door and make out commissions for some friends whom he desired to have appointed to office.
The door was shut in his face, and the alleged insult became the subject of some interesting correspondence between the governor and the
lieutenant governor. See correspondence of Governor Ames, 1874, p. 7.
Governor Ames's continued absence from the state was the subject of
great complaint.

[1] Opinion in *Jackson Pilot*, July 11, 1874.

[2] Jan. 1, 1875, Governor Ames writes Davis : " Sir : Pardons having been
issued by you while acting governor of Mississippi in the enclosed list of sixty
cases, and not being in possession of your reasons therefor, I am unable to
report the same to the legislature as required by law. Will you please state
in writing your reasons for pardon in each case ? " Correspondence of
Ames, 1875.

lieutenant governor for the first year of the administration, namely, from January 22, 1874, to January 4, 1875 : —

Pardoned out of the penitentiary	Ames, 18	Davis, 32
Pardoned out of the county jails	" 9	" 4
Pardoned before trial	" 0	" 17
Commutations	" 5	" 6
Remissions	" 4	" 6
Total	" 36	" 65

It will be seen from the foregoing exhibit that a number of pardons issued by Davis were granted to criminals before trial — a practice which Governor Ames declares to have been abhorrent to his sense of justice, and one to which he never resorted. It was proved to the satisfaction of the legislature in 1876 that Davis accepted a bribe of $800 for pardoning a criminal sent up from Lowndes County for murder. For this he was removed from office. It should also in this connection be said that Governor Ames himself did not entirely escape from the charge of abusing the pardoning power.[1]

One of the chief subjects of criticism against the administration of Ames was his course in regard to the judiciary. At the time of his election, twenty circuit judges and as many chancellors constituted the judiciary of Mississippi. They were appointed by the governor with the advice and consent of the Senate, the former for six years, and the latter for four.[2] It thus happened that the terms of all the chancellors appointed by Governor Alcorn in 1870 expired during the spring and summer of 1874. Instead of nominating their successors for the confirmation of the Senate, in anticipation of the vacancies, while that body was in session, Governor Ames waited until after its adjournment, and then nominated and commissioned the new chancellors with the intention, it was charged, of controlling them by removing those whose decisions and actions were not in accord with his own views.

[1] Almost his last official act as governor of the state was the issue of a pardon to Alex. Smith on March 11, 1876. Smith was sent to the penitentiary for life for the crime of rape. The grant of a pardon in this case constituted the twenty-second article of impeachment. It charged that pardon was issued upon representation made by two of the governor's personal friends who had no knowledge of the facts, and to whom it was alleged Smith paid $3000 for using their influence with the executive. Smith was prosecuted by a Republican district attorney and sentenced by a Republican judge. Impeachment Testimony, pp. 49, 50.   [2] Constitution, 1868, Art. VI.

In short, he purposed to hold their appointments over them
in terrorem, and make the judiciary "subservient to his corrupt and partisan purposes, and thereby destroy its independence."[1] In pursuing this course, Governor Ames seems
to have brought down upon himself not only the criticism
of the Democrats, but of the more respectable Republicans
as well.[2] His action was, to say the least, a violation of the
spirit of the Constitution, which required the advice and consent of the Senate to judicial appointments. Moreover, every
consideration of courtesy to the Senate and for the proprieties of official life required him to consult that body. To
this should also be added the consideration of expediency,
for his acquaintance with the bar of the state was very
limited and recent.

During the absence of the governor from the state in July,
the terms of four of the chancellors expired, and, as already
noted, Davis appointed their successors, completely ignoring
the appointments made by the governor before his departure.
The governor's action in revoking Davis's appointments was
characterized by the Democratic legislature of 1876 as
"wilful, corrupt, and unlawful," and intended to "corrupt, degrade, and control the judiciary of the state."[3] The
circumstances do not seem to justify the view taken by the
legislature that the governor was guilty of a "high official
misdemeanor" in revoking Davis's appointments. It will
hardly be contended that the spirit of the Constitution
intended to confer the appointment of the most important
state officers upon the lieutenant governor when there was
no question as to the capacity of the governor in the premises. Making provision a few days in advance for filling
vacancies, which he knew would occur during his temporary
absence from the state, should hardly be construed as a violation of the Constitution, although it may be admitted, as
charged, that his action was for "the purpose of advancing
the interests of his party."[4]

Another instance in which the governor was charged with

---

[1] Impeachment Testimony, p. 32.

[2] Hon. J. S. Morris, ex-attorney general, and one of the leaders of the
Republican party, said: "He [Ames] refused, contrary to the advice of all
the intelligent Republicans of the state, to send in his nominations, although
the Senate was in session and waiting for more than three weeks, and finally
adjourned and went away. He then appointed the chancellors *ad interim*,
and claimed and exercised the right to remove them at pleasure, according to
their absolute and abject obedience to his sovereign will." Letter to *New
York Herald*, Jan. 7, 1876.

[3] Impeachment Testimony, pp. 38, 39.   [4] *Ibid.* p. 104.

"degrading" the judiciary was in allowing "with his permission, assent, connivance, and assistance," a certain chancellor and a certain district attorney to exchange offices.[1]
The facts in regard to the affair are these: The chancellorship was held by a young lawyer of some prominence,
while the district attorney was an elderly gentleman to whom
the prosecution of criminals for perquisites was distasteful.
The chancellor preferred the active and stirring duties of the
public prosecutor, while the district attorney longed for
the more quiet and sedate duties of the bench.   Each preferred the office of the other, and there can be little doubt
that each was better suited for the place of the other.
They agreed to resign and ask the governor to appoint them
to the offices which they desired.   They did resign, and he
complied with their wishes.   No complaint of incompetency
or unfitness was alleged against either.   As the governor
had the undoubted right to accept their resignations and
reappoint them to other offices, it hardly seems fair to charac-
terize his action as a "high crime" or a "misdemeanor," nor
does the charge of "tampering" with the judiciary in this
instance seem to be well founded, in view of the excellence
of the change.[2]

The governor's course in another case was the subject of
much criticism, and substantiates the charge that his purpose
in withholding the nomination of the chancellors from the
Senate was to control their decisions.   In January, 1874,
the sheriff elect of Yazoo county, one A. T. Morgan, was
brought before a chancellor whose appointment had never
been confirmed by the Senate, upon the charge of killing his
predecessor in the sheriff's office.   After hearing the case,
the chancellor remanded Morgan to prison without bail.
He was subsequently removed to Jackson for safe keeping.
Morgan was a strong personal friend of Governor Ames,
who was displeased at the action of the chancellor in refusing him bail, and in not allowing the Republican coroner sufficient time to qualify as Morgan's successor.   He accordingly
revoked the appointment of the chancellor and appointed
another in his stead, who thereupon released Morgan on

---

[1] Impeachment Testimony, p. 31.
[2] It was the opinion of the circuit judge of the district, a man who had the
confidence and respect of both political parties, that the exchange was an excellent one, and conducive to the public good.   It should also be said that the
district attorney was overwhelmingly reëlected by popular vote, and the
chancellor unanimously confirmed by the Senate, Democrats and Republicans
all voting for him.   Report Minority Impeachment Committee.

bail,[1] the legislature in the meantime having passed a special act allowing a second writ.[2]   It was alleged that the release of Morgan was the consideration for the appointment, and was one of the specifications in the general impeachment charge against the governor of attempting to control the judiciary for partisan purposes.   In regard to Morgan's legal right to bail, there was a difference of opinion among the best lawyers of the state.

Another specification in the general charge against the governor of seeking to control and degrade the judiciary was the alleged attempt to influence a decision of Chancellor Peyton.   Peyton was another one of the chancellors appointed during the recess of the Senate.   Before the meeting of the legislature, and consequently before his appointment had been confirmed, a case was brought before him to enjoin the state treasurer from paying to the Vicksburg and Nashville Railroad Company certain moneys, amounting to nearly $350,000, belonging to the university.   These funds had been loaned the railroad by act of the legislature in 1873.   The governor, being dissatisfied with the sufficiency of the securities provided by the act and offered by the railroad company, and prompted only by a desire to protect the state against loss, brought suit against the railroad by way of injunction.   So far, the zeal of the governor for the welfare of the state was in the highest degree commendable. Chancellor Peyton, after hearing the argument, decided that the injunction should be dissolved.   The governor was again displeased with the decision of one of his chancellors, and refused to send Peyton's name to the Senate when it met, although he had been serving nearly a year.   While the case was pending, it was suggested at a conference of the leading Republicans held in the executive mansion, that the governor have a talk with the father of the chancellor, the venerable chief justice of the state, and induce him to advise his son as to the law, and if possible have the injunction granted.   Accordingly, the chief justice was sent for, whereupon the governor expressed disappointment at the course his son had seen fit to pursue, alleging, among other things, that he would not suffer his rulings to go upon the records, in consequence of which, the case could not be appealed to the Supreme Court.   The chief justice was indignant at what he believed to be an attempt on the part of the governor to influence the action of his son in rendering a decision, and

---

[1] Impeachment Testimony, p. 79.   [2] Acts of 1874, p. 22.

informed him in language rather severe that his son would not permit himself to be controlled by any person.   Chief Justice Peyton was himself a Republican, was a jurist of high standing in the state, and highly approved the governor's zeal in wishing to protect the interests of the state.[1] Governor Ames always asserted that his motives in this affair were misconstrued.   He declares that he had no intention of influencing the decision, but simply wished to show the chief justice how the case had been conducted by his son.[2]

The most serious and well-founded complaint against the course of Governor Ames in regard to the judiciary was that he appointed incompetent men to judicial positions.[3] Several of the chancellors appointed by him were not even members of the bar, were ignorant of both law and practice, had never conducted a case in court, and did not know a plea in bar from a demurrer.[4] They secured promises of appointment, stood the examination, obtained licenses to practice, and were nominated to the Senate.[5] Others already had licenses before appointment, but they had no standing at the bar.   One of these appointees was notoriously unfitted for a judicial position, and besides was under charge of forgery at the time of his appointment.   He was a licensed attorney, but had no practice, and depended upon several little offices, such as superintendent of education, United States commissioner, etc., for his support.   Against the protests of men of high character, he was appointed during the recess of the Senate, and served about eight months.   When the legislature met, the governor could not get his nomination through the Senate, although there were only nine Democrats in that body.[6]   Another judicial appointee was a practising physician at the time of his

[1] Impeachment Testimony, p. 54.

[2] Minority Report Impeachment Committee.   In a letter to General Butler under date of Feb. 10, 1875, Governor Ames said : " It is a matter of little political significance, but my duty demands that I should save the third of a million to the state if I can."   Correspondence, p. 128.

[3] Article XV, impeachment charges.

[4] Letter of George E. Harris, Attorney General, to U. S. Grant, Boutwell Report, p. 591.

[5] The law required applicants for admission to the bar to be examined by the circuit judge, or a committee appointed by him.   The examination was a mere form.   The candidate was usually taken aside and asked a few questions, after which the committee reported favorably to the judge, testifying to the moral character and competency of the candidate, who was thereupon granted a license.

[6] On this point see sworn statements of J. W. C. Watson, Boutwell Report, p. 982 ; and J. M. Stone, Impeachment Testimony, p. 152.

appointment, and supported himself by several paltry offices. He was almost wholly unlearned in the law. There were others equally unfitted. The articles of impeachment charge the governor with "wilfully and corruptly" nominating these men for "partisan purposes." I am unable to find any evidence of a "corrupt" motive. That they were appointed for partisan purposes is more nearly the truth. It has long been a practice in the United States to make appointments to office for partisan purposes. The truth is, he could hardly have done better without sacrificing his party connections, for, according to his own testimony, there were few Republican lawyers in the state, the bar being almost wholly Democratic.[1] Governor Ames's field of choice was further restricted by his practical refusal to appoint members of the bar who affiliated with the Alcorn wing of the party. Consequently, a considerable proportion of his appointees were Northern men. It was also necessary in some cases to appoint chancellors to districts in which they were not resident.[2] The importance and responsibility of the office of chancellor under the constitution of 1868 were such as to require men of judicial training and integrity. Their courts had full common law chancery jurisdiction. Their writs and processes extended throughout the state, and to all causes, without limitation of the amounts involved. They had jurisdiction of all orphans' affairs, the estates of minors, dower of widows, etc., the business of which was enormous after the war. Moreover, the business of the court was largely *ex parte*, so that an incompetent or corrupt chancellor could do a vast amount of injury. They had also certain political functions, such as the appointment of election registrars and the public printers for their respective districts. It was for these latter reasons deemed highly important that the chancellors should be of the proper political faith.

Notwithstanding the allegations of incompetency made against the judicial appointees of Governor Ames, it must be said in his favor that the proportion of judgments reversed by the Supreme Court upon appeal from decisions of his chancellors was smaller than under his predeces-

---

[1] Letter to the Attorney General of the United States. Correspondence of 1874, p. 46.

[2] Thus, June 1, 1874, he wrote an applicant that he could not appoint him chancellor of the district in which he resided (it was in the northern part of the state), but that he might have a chancellorship in one of the southern districts. Correspondence, p. 65.

sor, Governor Alcorn.   Of the 33 cases appealed from
decisions of his appointees in 1874–1875, only 8, or 25 per
cent, were reversed; while in the two years preceding, of
328 cases appealed, 107, or 33 per cent, were reversed.   In
1859–1860, of 266 cases appealed, 107, or 36 per cent, were
reversed.[1]

The criticism of the governor's course in regard to the
judiciary does not apply to the circuit courts or to the
Supreme Court.   He appointed no circuit judges, these having been appointed by Alcorn in 1870, and their terms, being
six years, did not expire until 1876.[2]

III.   LOCAL GOVERNMENT UNDER REPUBLICAN RULE

Under the reconstruction constitution the sheriff, both
on account of the large emoluments which he received and
the political powers which he wielded, was the most important county official.   He controlled to a large extent the
selection of the trial juries, appointed one of the three election registrars, and collected the state and county taxes.
Much of his compensation consisted of fees and perquisites
for services, which were numerous during the reconstruction
period.   The fees of the office amounted to as much as $20,000
per year in some of the counties, in others $15,000, while
perhaps the average was not far below $5000.   With the oppor-
tunities which the sheriff had for speculating in warrants, he
was sometimes able to amass a snug fortune, and at least one
sheriff was alleged to have secured a seat in the United States
Senate by cashing at par the depreciated warrants of the
members of the legislature.[3]   He could, of course, use the
warrants in settling his accounts with the auditor.[4]   Where

[1] Certificate of clerk of Supreme Court, Minority Report of Impeachment
Committee.   It is the testimony of some of the governor's political opponents, that the majority of the judges appointed by him were personally good
men of fair ability and competency.   A few were jurists of high standing.

[2] The following are the names of the chancellors appointed by Governor
Ames: W. G. Henderson, G. S. McMillan, O. H. Whitfield, E. Hill, E. Staf-
ford, E. G. Peyton, R. Boyd, J. J. Dennis, C. A. Sullivan, W. D. Frazee,
C. C. Cullens, L. C. Abbott, J. N. Campbell, P. P. Bailey, Thomas Walton.
William Breck, H. R. Ware, R. B. Stone, E. H. Osgood, Hiram Cassidy, Jr.
Six of these were reappointments.   They were all Republicans, but less than
one-half were Northern men.

[3] The author is personally acquainted with a gentleman now living in a
Northern city who was sheriff of a Mississippi county in 1870.   His fees, he
says, amounted to $20,000 per year.   By dealing in warrants he accumulated
a fortune, after which he returned to the North to enjoy his wealth.

[4] The *Clarion* of April 12, 1876, contains the names of thirty-six colored
members whose warrants were cashed by the sheriff in question.

the colored voters were in the majority in a county, the
office was often held by a negro, though more generally by
a Northern white.   Few of the colored incumbents were
competent to perform the duties of the office; in fact,
they seldom made any attempt to perform them.   The office
was usually farmed out to white deputies, with whom the
emoluments were shared.   De Soto County for four years
had a negro sheriff who, it was alleged, could neither read
nor write, and who did not pretend to have any conception
of the duties of his office.   Issaquena in 1876 had a negro
sheriff who was serving his fourth term.   The fees of the
office, he says, amounted to $3000 per year.[1]   Jefferson
County had a negro sheriff for three terms.   Hinds, Bolivar,
Coahoma, Claiborne, Warren, and Washington, had negro
sheriffs at one time or another between 1870 and 1876.   The
office in Washington County was worth $15,000 per year.[2]   It
could not have been worth much less in the others mentioned.
Many were the difficulties which Republican sheriffs-elect
experienced in their efforts to furnish the bond required by
law.   In some cases they were unable to qualify, but as the
boards of supervisors were generally of the same political
party, their bonds were usually approved.   No complaint
was more general among the whites than that bonds made by
non-residents and colored men with little or no real estate,
were approved by these boards.   Now and then a Republican
sheriff was found missing or short in his accounts, leaving
behind a worthless bond.[3]
   The assessor, like the sheriff, was a high-salaried official,
but did not wield as great political powers.   Like the sheriff,
also, his compensation was in the nature of fees, being a certain percentage of the value of the property assessed.   The
increase in the cost of assessing the taxes was a standing complaint of the whites.   In 1855, the expenditures
under this head were $9980; in 1868, they were $27,638; in
1871, they were $118,158.   Governor Alcorn, in a special

[1] See his testimony, Boutwell Report, pp. 589, 596.
[2] Testimony of S. W. Ferguson, *ibid.* p. 1470; also testimony of H. P.
Putnam, *ibid.* p. 1446.
[3] I have been unable to verify the charge that many of the Republican
sheriffs and treasurers turned out to be defaulters.   A "carpet-bag" sheriff
of Holmes County was alleged to be a defaulter to the amount of $51,000; a
"carpet-bag" treasurer of Panola County was said to be short in his accounts;
a "carpet-bag" sheriff of Pike County disappeared with a large sum.   No
trace of him has ever been discovered.   Whether he was robbed and murdered, or whether he fled the state, is a question about which there is a difference of opinion.   The colored sheriff of De Soto was alleged to be a defaulter
for $13,000.   A radical sheriff of Leake County was under similar charges.

message to the legislature in 1871, charged that the assessor in Warren County was receiving a salary of $8000 per year. The state auditor in 1875 estimated that the assessor in Warren would receive $4900; the assessor in Hinds, $4500; in Adams, $4000; in Washington, $4360.[1] The Taxpayers' Convention, in January, 1875, petitioned the legislature to fix the compensation of the assessor, so that it would not exceed $1500 per year, but the prayer was not granted.

The other county offices, with the exception of those of the circuit and chancery clerks, cannot be said to have yielded unreasonable fees. They were not usually sought after by the colored politicians to the same extent as the office of sheriff, although occasionally we find a county with a negro treasurer, as in the case of Yazoo in 1875, or with a negro superintendent of education, as in the cases of Bolivar, Wilkinson, Washington, Issaquena, and a few other river counties where white Republicans were scarce. At one time, the superintendent of Bolivar was B. K. Bruce, who resigned to become sheriff of the county, and who eventually became United States Senator and register of the treasury. Now and then a negro politician had the boldness to accept the office of county clerk, the duties of which he was never able to perform. De Soto County had in 1874 a negro circuit clerk who, it was alleged, could neither read nor write. Warren County had a colored chancery clerk in 1870, and a colored circuit clerk. Both were men of intelligence, but proved to be dishonest officials. Yazoo County in 1874 had colored circuit and chancery clerks. Claiborne County had a colored circuit clerk in 1875.

Perhaps the most important local officials under the reconstruction constitution were the boards of supervisors and the justices of the peace. Their importance was due chiefly to the work of rebuilding or repairing bridges, public buildings, etc., destroyed by the war, and to the vast amount of petty offences over which the justices exercised jurisdiction. In the Southern type of local government, the county board is a legislative and administrative body of great responsibility. It assesses and disburses the taxes, has supervision of roads and highways, selects juries, awards county contracts, examines and determines upon the sufficiency of official bonds, negotiates loans, and in the river counties appoints the levee commissioners. It was alleged, with more or less truth, that in

[1] House Journal, 1875, p. 44.

many counties these officials were incompetent.   In some instances the board was composed entirely of illiterate negroes. Although their duties necessitated calculation and computation, there were instances in which no member could do the smallest operation of arithmetic, and their highest mark of erudition was the ability of the president to sign his name to a record, the contents of which he could not read.   In Issaquena County, in 1874, every member of the board was alleged to be an illiterate negro.   Several were charged with official dishonesty, and two were forced to resign.[1] The members of the legislature, the sheriff, clerks, justices of the peace, and constables, were all colored.   In fact, there were only two white officers in the county.   In Madison County, every member of the board was colored, and the maximum of learning among them was the ability of one to sign his name mechanically.   There was not a justice of the peace in the county who could write his name.[2]   In the performance of their duties, they imposed but few fines, and shortly before the meeting of the grand jury, they usually got some friendly white neighbor to write up their dockets for presentation at the proper time.   They were, of course, almost wholly ignorant of the law, and often unable to read the processes which they issued against persons and property in the name of the law.   Their signatures were attached to these processes in the form of a mark, and the processes were in turn delivered to constables equally unable to explain their meaning, or attest their action under them.   The justices had jurisdiction of civil causes involving as much as $150, and of all petty criminal offences, such as larceny, trespass, assault and battery, etc.   It was a standing complaint of the whites that it was impossible to prevent the thefts of seed cotton and live stock, on account of the leniency of the colored magistrates. By the law, theft of property below $25 in value was classified as petty larceny, and was included within the jurisdiction of the justices of the peace.   For the theft of a cow, they imposed a fine of $5 or possibly $10, or imprisonment in the county jail five or six weeks.   Their ignorance of the law sometimes worked hardships on suitors, and caused the attorneys not a little embarrassment.[3]

Marshall County, in the northern part of the state, had in

---

[1] Testimony of J. W. Farrish, Boutwell Report, p. 616.
[2] Testimony of Robert Powell, *ibid*. p. 876.
[3] Mr. Andrews, a member of the Yazoo city bar, related with indignation to the Boutwell committee how the ignorance of one of these officials caused him to lose $100 in a case in which he was interested.   See his testimony, p. 1704.

1874 three colored representatives in the lower House of the legislature, and one in the Senate. Of the members of the board of supervisors, three were colored, and one was a white man from the North who not only believed in social equality between the races, but in practice daily lived up to his professions. The other member was a conservative. The colored officials "could barely read and write." [1]

Wilkinson County, in the southwestern part of the state, was politically in a bad way at the time of the inauguration of Governor Ames. The sheriff was a white radical, and three members of the county board and all the justices of the peace except two were negroes, none of them being able to write a summons. The senators and representatives in the legislature were colored. The county superintendent of education was a negro from Oberlin, Ohio, and most of the school teachers were " fancy colored mulattoes from abroad." [2] There were as usual charges of extravagance and corruption in the administration of the county affairs. Some idea of qualifications of the local officials is afforded by the following personal testimony of Alexander Branch, president of the board of supervisors. He was examined by the Boutwell congressional committee at Jackson in 1876.

Question. Were you a slave before the war ?
Answer. Oh, yes, sir ; one yet.
Q. Have you any education ?
A. Not a bit.
Q. Can you read and write ?
A. No, sir ; I do not know my a b c's. I never had any opportunities. I am a hard laboring man.
Q. Have you any property ?
A. Nothing but a mule, a horse, two cows, and a family.[3]

The adjoining county of Amite had a board composed of four negroes and one white man, " all ignorant and unfit for the place." [4] All were under indictment for making illegal appropriations. Yazoo County was, from the standpoint of the whites, in a melancholy condition. It is one of the large

[1] Testimony of Judge J. W. C. Watson, Boutwell Report, pp. 1003–1004.
[2] Testimony of Hon. J. H. Jones, *ibid.* p. 1639. This witness alleged that a Cincinnati firm supplied the county with school desks and chairs at $7.50 each when the cost was $3.50 ; that the county paid $126 per barrel for pork for the use of the poor house ; that the county was charged $1500 for three bridges containing four, eight, and twenty planks respectively ; and that the county debt had increased from $6000 in 1865 to $70,000 in 1876.
[3] Boutwell Report, p. 1591.
[4] Testimony of H. P. Hurst, *ibid.* p. 104.

wealthy counties in the Mississippi Valley, and had a population overwhelmingly colored. The sheriff was the well-known "carpet bagger," Colonel A. T. Morgan, an efficient officer but, for other reasons, very unpopular among the whites. The chancery clerk was a negro, formerly a member of the legislature. He had been a slave up to the close of the war, had no conception of his duties, and, in fact, seldom went about the office, which was farmed out to white deputies. He says he could write a little.[1] The circuit clerk was a negro of some intelligence, the assessor was a "carpet bagger" from Iowa, the circuit judge was from Pennsylvania, and the chancellor from New Hampshire. Of the three members of the legislature, two were negroes, one of them from Ohio. The other was a white "carpet bagger." The county treasurer was a negro, who, apart from bad spelling and punctuation, could write a very good letter.[2] Of the members of the board of supervisors, one was a white man from the North, another was a native, while the other three were illiterate negroes.[3] There was not a Democratic official in the county. It was alleged that the tax rate had increased four or five fold since the war, and that the county "was running deeper and deeper in debt."[4] The sheriff, however, denied these allegations, and declared that during his term the bridges burned during the war had all been repaired, that sixty schoolhouses had been built, and a $75,000 courthouse erected, and yet the increase of taxation had been slight.[5]

The situation in Warren County, so far as the conduct of county officials was concerned, will be dwelt upon in connection with the account of the Vicksburg riot. Of the members of the board of supervisors, the president and two others were alleged to have been illiterate. In Hinds County, the representatives and senators in the legislature and the sheriff were all negroes. Some of them were men of intelligence. Of the members of the board of supervisors, four were illiterate negroes, and the fifth was a Northern man, and at the time was one of the state printers.[6]

---

[1] See his testimony, Boutwell Report, p. 1682.
[2] See his letter in the Boutwell Report, Doc. Ev. p. 100.
[3] Testimony of J. M. Dickson (colored), Boutwell Report, p. 1684.
[4] Testimony of Garnett Andrews, *ibid.* p. 1704.
[5] Testimony of A. T. Morgan. ——
[6] Senator Furlong charges that this member received $6300 for doing the county printing during the first nine months of his term. This amount exceeded the average sum paid the state printer before the war. Only two members of the Hinds County board paid taxes on real estate. Speech in the Senate, Dec. 1874, p. 10.

Claiborne County was represented in the legislature by a negro boy whose occupation was that of a hotel waiter and boot-black.[1] The sheriff and circuit clerk were both colored, and the same was true of most of the local officials.

Washington County was the scene of many stirring political events during this period. It is one of the large " black " counties situated on the Mississippi River, and produces more cotton than any other county of equal area in the United States. During the period of Republican rule, the politics of the county were controlled chiefly by two negro preachers William Gray and J. Allen Ross. Gray was a state senator from 1870 to 1876, and was a strong personal friend of Governor Ames, who honored him with an appointment as brigadier general of state militia in 1875. In the Senate he was chairman of the committee on corporations, and seems to have taken a leading part in the proceedings of that body. The whites allege that he was insolent in his behavior, and was the terror of the community in which he lived.[2]

Ross was a more intelligent man, and was an eloquent speaker. He had held the office of chancery clerk, and had been elected to the office of sheriff, but was unable to give the requisite bond. The rivalry between him and Gray now and then created unusual excitement in the town of Greenville. Gray's alleged threat in 1875 that he intended to be sheriff at all hazards [3] led Ross to publish a letter advising his race to vote the Democratic ticket.

Nearly every officer in the county was colored. The sheriff's office, which yielded legitimately an income of $15,000 annually, was held by a negro. Another negro was superintendent of education. There was the usual complaint on account of the high rate of taxes. In addition to the regular state and county assessments, there was a levee tax of one cent per pound on cotton and fifteen cents per acre on land in cultivation. General Ferguson, the most prominent citizen of the county, told Senator Boutwell that the tax assessment on his land was $4.15 per acre, or about one-half its value, and that nearly the entire land of the county had been sold for taxes.[4]

The increase of the state levy from 1 mill on the dollar to 14 was accompanied by a similar increase in the county levy. The law allowed the county boards of supervisors to

---

[1] Testimony of J. D. Vertner, Boutwell Report, p. 191.
[2] Testimony of S. W. Ferguson, *ibid.* p. 1470.
[3] *Ibid.* p. 1468.   [4] *Ibid.* p. 1472.

levy a tax exclusively for county purposes, which, together with the state assessment, should not exceed 25 mills on the dollar. In every county, with half a dozen exceptions, the limit was reached, and it appears to have been exceeded in more than thirty instances. This violation of the law does not seem to have been confined to those counties under Republican rule, nor does the average county levy appear to have been much higher in the Republican centres than in the Democratic centres.

According to the report of the state auditor, thirty-four of the seventy-three counties of Mississippi had Republican administrations in 1874, and thirty-nine had Democratic administrations. From the table on the following page[1] it will be seen that the highest levy was that of Colfax (now Clay) County, the rate being 23.2 mills. This, with the state tax of 14 mills, made the amount nearly 4 per cent. Those who lived in the villages of that county had to pay, in addition, a municipal tax. In Warren, the county levy was only 14 mills, but the municipal levy of $21\frac{1}{2}$ mills in Vicksburg made the total contributed by the unhappy citizens of that town equivalent to about 5 per cent. The showing in the Democratic counties, according to the auditor's report, does not seem to have been much better than in the Republican counties. If the report of the auditor is a truthful statement of the situation, the Democratic charge of Republican extravagance does not seem to have been well founded.

It will not be seriously denied that a tax levy, ranging from $2\frac{1}{2}$ to 5 per cent on property which had decreased largely in valuation, was a grievous burden upon a people who had by no means recovered from the impoverishment of the war, and who had experienced a succession of droughts, floods, and bad crops almost unprecedented in the history of the state. The result was wholesale confiscation of property. The sheets that were fortunate enough to secure the public printing, contained whole pages of delinquent tax lists. In some communities, the tax payers decided that it was better to allow their property to be confiscated, and take the chances of being able to redeem it in after years.[2] *Over six million*

---

[1] This table is from a certified report of the state auditor, and is printed as a part of the documentary evidence in the Vicksburg Report, p. 533. I have no means of ascertaining its correctness. The total state and county levies, as given in the table, are smaller than the corresponding levies for the year previous. I find in the report of a special committee, House Journal, p. 1444, that the rate in Adams County was $43\frac{1}{2}$ mills, Claiborne County, $33\frac{1}{2}$, etc.

[2] See testimony of General S. W. Ferguson, Boutwell Report, p. 1470.

acres of land — one-fifth of the area of the state — were forfeited during this period, on account of the inability of owners to pay the taxes.[1]

Democratic Counties.	State Tax.	County Tax.	Total.	Republican Counties.	State Tax.	County Tax.	Total.
Alcorn	14	9	23	Adams	14	17.7	31.7
Attala	14	11	25	Amite	14	11	25
Benton	14	18½	32½	Bolivar	14	16	30
Calhoun	14	12	26	Carroll	14	11	25
Chickasaw	14	20.3	34.3	Claiborne	14	10.5	24.5
Choctaw	14	17	31	Coahoma	14	15	29
Clark	14	16	30	Copiah	14	11	25
Covington	14	11	25	Colfax	14	23.2	37.2
Franklin	14	14	28	De Soto	14	5.3	19.3
Greene	14	11	25	Grenada	14	18½	32½
Hancock	14	18½	32½	Hinds	14	11.4	25.4
Harrison	14	8.6	22.6	Holmes	14	11	25
Itawamba	14	11	25	Issaquena	14	16	30
Jackson	14	16½	30½	Jefferson	14	17½	31½
Jasper	14	7½	21½	Kemper	14	18	32
Jones	14	17½	31½	Lowndes	14	15	29
Lafayette	14	10	24	Le Flore	14	11	25
Lauderdale	14	11	25	Madison	14	11	25
Lawrence	14	10	24	Marshall	14	14	28
Leake	14	12½	26½	Monroe	14	11½	25½
Lee	14	15	29	Noxubee	14	14	28
Lincoln	14	10.7	24.7	Oktibbeha	14	13	27
Marion	14	11	25	Panola	14	10	24
Montgomery	14	10.8	24.8	Pike	14	11.8	25.8
Neshoba	14	18	32	Rankin	14	10	24
Newton	14	10	24	Sumner	14	11	25
Perry	14	10	24	Sunflower	14	11	25
Pontotoc	14	6.2	20.2	Tallahatchee	14	13½	27½
Prentiss	14	8½	22½	Tunica	14	10	24
Pearl	14	7½	21½	Tate	14	7	21
Scott	14	10	24	Warren	14	14	28
Simpson	14	11½	25½	Washington	14	13½	27½
Smith	14	9	23	Wilkinson	14	19	33
Tippah	14	17½	31½	Yazoo	14	10	24
Tishomingo	14	11	25				
Union	14	11	25	Average			13 7⁄17
Wayne	14	15½	29½				
Winston	14	16	30				
Yallobusha	14	8	22				
Average			12 7⁄13				

[1] Testimony of W. H. Gibbs, state auditor, in report of Vicksburg investigation committee, 2d Ses. 43d Cong. No. 265, p. 530. The following is the testimony of the auditor on this point : —

It was a special grievance of the whites that the great majority of those who enjoyed the honor and emoluments of office, as well as those who participated in the choice of the official class, had little share in the burdens of the tax payers. This was to a considerable extent true. In 1874, out of 140,000 voters, 75,000 were on the delinquent tax list. Warren County had 5000 colored voters, and 4686 delinquents. Hinds, with nearly 6000 voters, had 4972 delinquents. Washington had 4313; Yazoo, 2937, etc. The majority of the delinquents were, of course, colored voters. A comparatively small proportion of them owned real estate at this time. There were many counties in which the blacks did not pay $1000 in taxes, yet they held the majority of the offices and administered the government.

IV. STATE EXPENDITURES

During the period of Republican rule in Mississippi, there were no great railroad swindles as in Louisiana and Arkansas, and no such wholesale plundering of the treasury as in South Carolina. The reconstruction constitution wisely prohibited the loan of the credit of the state. It was true, however, as charged by the whites, that the number of offices and agencies with high salaries was needlessly multiplied, so that nearly the entire Republican party was in the pay of the state.[1] In communities where there were not enough competent Republicans to go around, one man sometimes held several offices, or the offices were distributed among the members of a family.[2] As an illustration of the

Q. Can you inform us what proportion of the lands of Mississippi have been forfeited to the state for taxes?
A. About one-fifth.
Q. You are correct in the statement that it is one-fifth?
A. Yes. The entire area is about 30,000,000 acres. There are owned by the state and the levy boards about 6,000,000 acres. This exceeded by 2000 square miles the states of Connecticut, Rhode Island, and Delaware. The lists of lands advertised for sale in Hinds County in 1875 covered two full pages of the *Jackson Pilot*.

[1] There were only twelve white Republicans in Noxubee County in 1875. The offices were distributed among them as follows : one sheriff, two deputies, one chancery clerk, one treasurer, one superintendent of education, one assessor, two magistrates, and one editor of a Republican paper. The others were members of the county board or of the legislature. Testimony J. W. Robbins, Boutwell Report, p. 1265.

[2] William Price, a Methodist preacher from the North, was state senator from Grenada County, was public printer of his district, and was postmaster until the President's order prohibiting postmasters from holding other offices, when he turned the office over to his wife. At the same time his nephew was super-

complaint that the increase in the number of public offices was unnecessary, the Democrats cited the organization of the judiciary. When the reconstructionists took charge, ten circuit judges performed all the duties which now required twenty chancellors and thirteen circuit judges. To this charge, the Republicans replied that the abolition of the office of county probate judge in 1870, and the transfer of most of the duties of that office to the chancery courts, made an increase in the number of chancellors necessary. Moreover, they said, the citizenship of the state had been doubled by the adoption of the Fourteenth Amendment, a fact which added vastly to the business of the courts. The Democrats met these assertions by saying that many of the duties hitherto performed by the probate judges had been transferred to the chancery clerks, of whom there was one in each county; that the recent constitutional amendment by which the jurisdiction of justices of the peace had been made to include all civil cases not exceeding in amount $150, and the general poverty of the people by which business transactions were very much limited in value, had taken away one-third of the civil business of the circuit and chancery courts.[1] There can be little doubt that the need for such an elaborate judicial machinery was more apparent than real. It is difficult to believe that there was sufficient chancery business in Mississippi in 1874 to require a term of the chancery court in each county at least four times a year.[2] Governor Ames in 1875 recommended a reduction in the number of chancellors from twenty to ten, but it was left to the Democrats to make the reduction in 1876.

There was one feature of the Ames administration which Charles Nordhoff characterized as "robbery pure and simple." It was the matter of the state printing, the cost of which was

intendent of education and deputy collector of internal revenue, his son-in-law was a chancery clerk, and he himself was an applicant for the office of sheriff and tax collector. Nordhoff, Cotton States, 1875: article, Mississippi. Also Price's testimony, Boutwell Report. The *Jackson Clarion* of Nov. 8, 1870, tells of a Smith family in Madison County who were thus favored. One was postmaster, one was public printer, one was a member of the county board, one was a member of the city council, one a city weigher, one a candidate for the legislature, and one a candidate for school director. The Senate Journal of 1873 contains a Democratic protest that Senators Morgan, Gibbs, Abbott, Campbell, and Bowles were at the same time holding other offices. C. W. Clarke, a member of the legislature in 1870, was also at the same time district attorney. There were other instances of this kind.

[1] Report Senate sub-committee, p. 398.

[2] This was the requirement of the constitution, Art. VI. Sec. 17. The provision was amended in 1875, so as to require the court to be held but twice a year in each county.

out of all proportion to the other expenses of the government. For the five years immediately preceding 1861, the average annual cost did not exceed $8000; for the five years commencing with 1870, it was $73,000, making an average annual excess of $65,000. In one year the amount reached nearly $128,000. The Democracy cut the amount down to $22,000 in 1876. The journals of the legislature contained a vast amount of matter utterly worthless to the public; they were bulky in size, and contained large appendices. Examples may be cited in illustration. In 1856, the journals of the two Houses contained 1163 pages; in 1873, 4363 pages, or nearly four times as many. The statutes were no less voluminous. For the five years preceding reconstruction, the total number of pages amounted to 2113, while for the five years of Republican rule it amounted to 3789 pages.

The official printer was accused of being notoriously corrupt, and was charged with having secured his appointment from the legislature by means of bribery,[1] and what was incomprehensible to many, he was one of the confidential advisers of the governor, and for a time a member of his household.[2] He turned his printing office over to another person and took a clerkship in the state treasurer's office at a salary of $1500 a year in state warrants worth seventy or eighty cents on the dollar. He was thus able to cash at par the warrants which he had received as state printer, amounting to $75,000 or $100,000 a year.

The subject of another complaint was the marked increase in the cost of administering the different departments of the state government. Frequent sessions of the legislature long

---

[1] G. E. Harris's letter to President Grant, Boutwell Report, p. 597.

[2] Nov. 24, 1875, the Attorney General wrote concerning him : "His office as state printer is about to expire, and he wants to be postmaster at Vicksburg. I regret to say that he is so degraded that the charge of corruption and bribery is no offence to him, and it comes from various sources." *Ibid.* p. 59. Another prominent Republican declared that the state printer was receiving $100,000 a year, that his "atrocities on the state treasury for the last two years would fill a volume," that he speculated in state warrants, that he collected four or five times as much on every printing bill as the law allowed him, and that Governor Ames knew this and yet used all his influence actively and persistently to keep him in the place. J. S. Morris to W. W. Huntingdon, *New York Herald*, Jan. 7, 1876. The following table compiled from the auditor's reports shows the cost of public printing before and after the war : —

1861	$8,028	1873	$74,702
1866–1867	6,228	1874	78,806
1867–1868	8,675	1875	50,803
1870	52,876	1876	22,295
1871	127,848	1890	13,500

drawn out, the large per diem of members, and the employment of a larger corps of clerks, doorkeepers, sergeants-at-
arms, porters, pages, etc., increased the expenditures on
account of the legislature far beyond those of ante-
bellum days. A Democratic proposition to reduce the per
diem of members was opposed almost unanimously by the
Republicans. Similarly, a resolution to limit the amount of
stationery allowed members met the same fate.[1] Before the
war, the cost of clerical service for the legislature rarely
exceeded $30 or $40 per day. In 1875, it was costing $150
per day. There were twenty-six attachés receiving from $3
to $6 per day. A number of these were committee clerks,
a luxury which the ante-bellum legislator never enjoyed.[2]

A proposition that no committee clerks be employed except
at the expense of the committees employing them was voted
down.[3]

The expenditures on account of the judiciary show the
same proportional increase. The disbursements under this
head were $144,565 in 1861. In 1870, they were $320,399, in
1871, $389,922, and in 1872, $434,973, which was the maximum
amount reached. The Democrats reduced the expenditures to
$95,185 in 1876.

The expenditures on account of the executive department
show the same results. This was due to the large emoluments of the state officers and the misapplication of the
executive contingent fund. Prior to the war, the compensation of the governor was $3500 per year and the use of the
executive mansion, while the salaries of other state officers ranged from $1500 to $2000 per year. In 1865, the

---

[1] A committee of investigation reported, Feb. 26, 1875, that the fifty-five
colored members who were entitled to $165 worth of stationery at state
expense had drawn $258.95 worth, whereupon the *Jackson Clarion* demanded
to know why the correspondence of the colored members was so large. The
stationery account for the first two months of the session of 1875 was $2281.

[2] The following comparative exhibit compiled from the auditors' reports
shows the increase in the cost of the several items under consideration :—

	PER DIEM OF MEMBERS.	MILEAGE.	CLERICAL SERVICE.
1865–1866	46,362	22,128	5,861
1870	166,632	29,664	28,201
1873	105,244	16,552	32,634
1878	79,100	9,230	5,816

[3] House Journal, 1873, p. 15.

salary of the governor was raised to $6000 by a Democratic legislature. At the same time, the per diem of members of the legislature was increased from $4 to $8, and the salaries of other state officers increased to $2500 or $3500 per year. This was one piece of Democratic legislation which the reconstructionists showed no disposition to repeal, although they were memorialized to do so. It matters little which party was responsible for this legislation, the complaint of the tax payers was well founded. New York and Louisiana were the only states in which the chief executive received as much compensation for his services as the governor of Mississippi did. With one-fifth of the population of Ohio and one-tenth of the taxable property, Mississippi paid her governor one-third more salary. With one-tenth of the taxable property of Massachusetts, she paid her governor nearly twice as much. With one-third as much property as Connecticut, and one-fourth as much as New Jersey, she paid six times as much.[1] In addition to the large salary of the governor, he was provided with a house, for the repair and furnishing of which liberal appropriations were made by the legislature.[2] Both Governors Powers and Ames used the executive contingent fund for household purposes, so that their personal expenses could not have been great.[3] The law did not specify in detail the purposes for which this fund was to be used, although it was intended to be devoted chiefly to the apprehension of fugitives from justice. It had never been used to defray the household expenses of the governor, or to provide furniture for the executive mansion. The compensation of the state superintendent of education and the

---

[1] The following were the salaries of the governors of several states at this time : Illinois, $4000 ; Iowa, $3000 ; Indiana, $3000 ; Maine, $2500 ; Massachusetts, $3500 ; Ohio, $4000 ; Wisconsin, $1250 ; Nebraska, Connecticut, Vermont, New Hampshire, Rhode Island, New Jersey, and Michigan, $1000 ; Mississippi, $6000 ; Virginia, $5000 ; Alabama, $4000 ; Louisiana, $6000 ; Georgia, $4000.

[2] Down to 1872, $44,000 had been appropriated for this purpose since the war.

[3] The following are some of the " contingencies " of Powers and Ames : —

POWERS (for 4 months, 1872).		AMES.	
Linen and tablecloths	$89.10	Two mouse traps	$.75
Kitchen utensils (repairs)	26.00	Two thermometers	1.00
Gas and coal	358.44	One wire line	1.75
Spoons and forks	46.75	One slop pail	2.50
Repairing linen	20.00	Tablecloths	71.00
Repairing silverware	72.36	Freight on peaches	1.50
Wood	95.00	Freight on fruit	.25
		One bed pan	1.75

attorney general were also unduly large. The salary of the former official was $3000 per year, and an allowance of $1500 for clerk hire. The pay of the attorney general was $3500 per year, and as reporter of the Supreme Court he received $7 per page for each volume of decisions reported. The *Jackson Clarion* charged that in 1872 he received $38,143 on this account alone. Prior to the war the reporter received $3 per page, and the legislature in 1872 reduced the compensation to that amount.

The office of lieutenant governor and commissioner of emigration were looked upon by the Democrats as sinecures created by the reconstructionists to reward their party adherents. Before the war, the president *pro tem.* of the Senate performed the duties of lieutenant governor at a salary double that of other members of the legislature. The lieutenant governor received $1500 per year. The department of immigration was established in obedience to a general feeling that something ought to be done to encourage capital and labor to flow into the state to aid in the work of restoration. This feeling was manifested in the organization of local immigration clubs, and the occasional despatch of a commissioner to the Northwest or to Europe. Had the department been placed under the supervision of an intelligent commissioner, identified with the state, familiar with its needs, and acquainted with its resources, it would no doubt have accomplished great good and met the approval of all parties. But instead of this, an unlettered colored member of the legislature was elected commissioner by the legislature in violation of the constitution, which prohibited members from holding offices of their own creation.[1] It was alleged that he employed five assistants in the office, three of whom were likewise members of the legislature. At the expiration of his term he was succeeded by a colored minister, formerly a member of the legislature, from Natchez. Twelve thousand five hundred dollars were appropriated annually for the use of the department. The whites charged that none but colored immigrants were encouraged to come into the state.[2] They refused to recognize the department, and at private expense sent Colonel Musgrove, a "carpet bagger," to the North to advertise the

[1] The Attorney General gave an opinion that the commissioner in question was ineligible, but in a mandamus proceeding a circuit judge decided in his favor. *Jackson Clarion*, June 12, 1873.

[2] I find in the files of the *Jackson Clarion* occasional mention of the arrival of a number of carloads of colored immigrants under the auspices of the Commissioner of Immigration. Furlong, a Republican senator, said in a speech

resources of the state and to encourage the immigration of white men of means and industry. The State Grange also maintained an immigration bureau at Meridian, and sent an agent to the North for the same purpose.

The following comparative table shows the state expenditures from 1860 to 1876, omitting the four years of the war, the expenses of those years being abnormally large: [1] —

YEAR.	DEMOCRATIC EXPENDITURES.	YEAR.	REPUBLICAN EXPENDITURES.
	Amount.		Amount.
1860	$ 663,536.55	1870	$1,061,249.90
1865	1,410,250.13	1871	1,729,046.34
1866	1,860,809.89	1872	1,596,828.64
1867	625,817.80	1873	1,450,632.80
1868	525,678.80	1874	1,319,281.60
1869	463,219.71	1875	1,430,102.00
1876	518,709.00		

It should, however, be said that if the testimony of Governor Ames may be followed relative to the expenses of the state government during the two years in which he was at its head, his was the most economical administration since 1856, with the exception of two years, 1861 and 1869.[2]

Among the sins charged to the " carpet baggers " in Mississippi was that after five years of extravagance and plunder they turned over the government to the democracy with a debt aggregating $20,000,000.[3] According to the report of the auditor for 1875, the total state indebtedness on Jan-

in the Senate, Dec. 18, 1874 : " Happily our first commissioner has not endangered us in any way, for it is not probable that he has induced or would induce, if he remained in office a century, one hundred immigrants, white or colored, to turn their faces in this direction."   " I submit that our present immigration department is a needless, unprofitable, and most mischievous expenditure of a vast amount of money, and if it cannot be promptly and completely regenerated, ought to be abolished."

[1] These figures are taken from the reports of the state auditor ; see also Boutwell Report, Doc. Ev. p. 118, and Vicksburg Report, p. 524.

[2] In his last message to the legislature in 1876, he says : " The expenses of the state government for 1874 were $908,330 ; for 1875, $618,259. It is possible, as Governor Ames suggests, that the auditor included in his estimates some expenditures that should not properly have been charged to the administration, and that the apparent discrepancy was the result of two different systems of book-keeping. I have preferred to follow the official report of the auditor."

[3] A table giving the debts of the Southern states at the close of the reconstruction period, in which the debt of Mississippi is placed at $20,000,000, appeared first in a speech delivered by the Hon. St. George Tucker in the 51st Congress (Record, 1st Ses. p. 6566) ; later, in Hon. H. Herbert's " Why

uary 1 of that year was $3,750,385.[1] It consisted of two
forms—a debt, the whole of which was to be discharged,
principal and interest, and a debt of which the interest
only was to be discharged.   The latter part of the debt
was commonly known as the Chickasaw school fund,
which, with the common school fund, constituted a trust held
by the state for the benefit of the schools.   The state paid
interest annually on that part known as the Chickasaw fund,
($814,743), the beneficiaries being those counties originally
constituting the Chickasaw cession.   The principal is never
to be paid.   The common school fund amounted to $718,946.22.
This was required to be invested in United States bonds, the
interest going to the several counties for the benefit of their
schools.   As the Chickasaw debt was incurred before the
war, it should not of course be charged to the "carpet baggers," and as the interest only was to be paid on the Chickasaw and common school funds, they should be deducted
from the total debt given above, in order to ascertain the real
indebtedness.   On January 1, 1876, two months before Ames
surrendered the government, he sent a message to the legislature, in which he gave a statement of the condition of the
finances of the state.   From this statement it appears that
the real state debt, that is, its outstanding obligations over
and above its ability to pay at once with its currency and
available funds, was but little more than $500,000.[2]   His
statement agrees substantially with the report of the state
treasurer for 1876,[3] and does not differ greatly from the findings of a special committee of Democrats, who reported that
the actual indebtedness of the state three months before
Ames resigned was but little more than a million dollars.[4]

the Solid South?" from which it was copied by Dr. J. L. M. Curry in the
Southern States of the American Union, p. 231, and has more recently been
used in President E. Benjamin Andrews' History of the United States during the last Quarter of a Century (Magazine edition, Scribners, May, 1895, p.
569).   Shortly after the publication of President Andrews' article, Ex-Governor Ames addressed a communication to him complaining that his authorities had led him into making a " $19,500,000 error in a $20,000,000 statement,"
so far as the debt of Mississippi was concerned.   President Andrews replied
that he had been seriously misled, and after procuring the official reports, was
pained to find that his statement as regarded Mississippi was without foundation.   The table alluded to was omitted from the book form of his history.
[1] Vicksburg Report, p. 534.   [2] Message, p. 3.   [3] Pp. 19–21.
[4] The Democratic legislature that impeached Governor Ames appointed a
joint committee of the two Houses "to investigate and ascertain the indebtedness of the state on Jan. 1, 1876."   On the 12th of April, they reported
that the total indebtedness was $2,631,704.24.   If from this be deducted the
school funds, there is left a remainder of about one million, which represents
the real indebtedness.   See Journal, House of Representatives, 1876, p. 623.

The state debt in 1870, when the Republicans took charge of the government was, according to one authority, \$221,522.75[1]; according to another, it was \$653,480, exclusive of the school fund.[2] It is difficult to see how any system of book-keeping could stretch a debt of half a million or even a million into one of twenty million.[3] It should also be said by way of explanation that the work of restoration which the government was obliged to undertake, made increased expenses necessary. During the period of the war, and for several years thereafter, public buildings and state institutions were permitted to fall into decay. The state house and grounds, the executive mansion, the penitentiary, the insane asylum, and the buildings for the blind, deaf, and dumb were in a dilapidated condition, and had to be extended and repaired. A new building for the blind was purchased and fitted up. The reconstructionists established a public school system and spent money to maintain and support it,[4] perhaps too freely, in view of the impoverishment of the people. When they took hold, warrants were worth but sixty or seventy cents on the dollar, a fact which made the price of building materials used in the work of construction correspondingly higher. So far as the conduct of state officials who were intrusted with the custody of public funds is concerned, it may be said that there were no great embezzlements or other cases of misappropriation during the period of Republican rule. It was charged and was the official opinion of the Attorney General that the bond of the state treasurer in 1875 was insufficient and not in due form of law. On August 28, the Attorney General informed the governor that the treasurer's bond had no oath or verification on it, nor did it appear that any of the sureties were worth anything in "freehold estate," as required by law. He advised the governor to close the office and take possession of the keys, safes, and vaults. The governor was charged by the legislature of 1876 with "unlawfully, knowingly, and

[1] Report of Democratic committee, Journal, House of Representatives, 1876. Really, the amount was much larger than this. The committee deducted from the real indebtedness, \$526,000, being the amount lost to the state by the bad management of stock which it held in two railroads.

[2] Report 10th Census, Vol. VII. pp. 554–595. In 1880 the debt was \$379,000. At present, 1900, it is \$1,030,946.07. Report state treasurer, Oct. 1, 1899.

[3] Of course the indebtedness here spoken of is the state indebtedness. Almost every county and every municipality of any size had debts of their own. Vicksburg, as we shall see, had a larger debt than that of the whole state.

[4] The Republican defence is well set forth by Hon. George E. Harris, Boutwell Report, p. 114, Doc. Ev.

corruptly" approving the treasurer's bond for "corrupt and partisan purposes," and for "unlawfully, knowingly, and corruptly" permitting him to remain in possession of the office.[1] The governor affirmed that he did not at the time know there was any defect in the form of the bond, that he signed the bond without noticing the absence of the word "freehold," and that, moreover, the treasurer upon going out of office had settled in full with the state without any defalcation or loss whatever.[2] The treasurer of the Natchez hospital seems to have been the only defaulting state official during the administration of Governor Ames. He was a "carpet bagger," and the amount of the shortage was $7251.81.[3] The colored state librarian during Alcorn's administration was charged with stealing books from the library.[4] The only large case of embezzlement among the state officers during the postbellum period was that of the Democratic state treasurer in 1866. The amount of the shortage was $61,962.

The increase in the expenditures of the government was, of course, accompanied by an increase in the rate of taxation. The increase began in 1869, and reached a maximum in 1874. The following is a statement of the levies for state purposes alone from 1869 to 1878:[5] —

YEAR.	AMOUNT ON $1 OF ASSESSED VALUATION.	YEAR.	AMOUNT ON $1 OF ASSESSED VALUATION.
1869	1 mill	1874	14 mills
1870	5 mills	1875	9¼ "
1871	4 "	1876	6½ "
1872	8½ "	1877	5 "
1873	12¼ "	1878	3½ "

[1] Impeachment Testimony, pp. 24–25.
[2] Correspondence of Governor Ames, 1875, p. 22.
[3] Impeachment Testimony, p. 33. The Testimony in the Impeachment of Adelbert Ames is the title of a volume of 323 pages printed by authority by the legislature to meet the assertion of the President of the United States that Governor Ames was a refugee from the state, and to "furnish to the world a complete vindication of the motives and actions of the legislature in preferring articles of impeachment, and to place the testimony beyond the possibility of loss by fire or otherwise." Besides the oral testimony, it contains one hundred pages of documentary evidence. Five hundred copies were printed. The Impeachment Trial of Adelbert Ames is a pamphlet of sixty-two pages, printed also by authority of the legislature in 1876. It is a record of the proceedings of the Senate sitting as a court of impeachment, and contains the answers of the governor to the charges preferred against him.
[4] *Jackson Clarion*, Oct. 18, 1870.
[5] This statement, except the amounts from 1875 to 1878, is from a communication of W. H. Gibbs, state auditor, to Hon. George S. Boutwell, June 10,

The one mill tax of 1869 represents the state levy at the time the democracy surrendered the government to the reconstructionists, while the six and one-half mills levy of 1876 is the amount fixed by the Democrats in the first year of their restoration. It will be seen that in the second year of Governor Ames's administration there was a reduction of several mills in the state levy. This was due chiefly to an act transferring much of the cost of maintaining the judiciary from the state treasury to the several county treasuries. Of course the shifting of the expense to the counties was not a reduction of the amount. However, Ames is entitled to the credit of reducing to some extent the state levy. There is good reason to believe that he was more disposed to economy than many of those by whom he was surrounded. If one may judge from his professions, his highest ambition was to give the state an economical administration.[1] But unfortunately his actions did not always accord with his professions.

V. UNPOPULAR LEGISLATION

One of the chief complaints of the whites during the period of Republican rule was the overabundance of legislation. Before the war, the legislature met biennially, and was seldom in session for a longer period than two months. As already pointed out, it was in session for a period of nearly six months in 1870, five months in 1871, nearly four months in 1872, and about four months in 1873. Besides, an extra session was held in the autumn of 1873, in consequence of the chaotic condition of the election laws. In 1874, the legislature was again in session for a period of three or four months during the winter and spring, and again an extra session was held in the autumn, a result of the

1876. Boutwell Report, p. 140, Doc. Ev. These figures are presumably correct. They are quoted as authority by both political parties, and I have never seen their correctness questioned. The auditor was a Republican and a Northern man. The rates for 1875–1878 are from the auditor's reports.

[1] For example, in his annual message to the legislature Jan. 5, 1875, he recommended the "most stringent economy in appropriations for the support of the government, and that every possible step be taken in the direction of retrenchment and reform." He recommended biennial sessions of the legislature, a reduction of the number of chancellors from twenty to ten, that the number of tax collectors in each county be reduced to one, that measures be adopted to secure the better safe keeping of public moneys, that a special tax be imposed on litigants, that the appropriations for the state universities be reduced from $120,000 to $50,000, that the expenses of public printing be reduced, that all exemption laws be repealed, etc. For the Republican view of Governor Ames's policy of economy see testimony of United States District Attorney Walton, Boutwell Report.

Warren County troubles. In 1875, it was in session from January 5 to the middle of April, and again an extra session was held in the autumn, this time in consequence of the Clinton riots. Thus, in five years, there had been nine sessions of the legislature. The constitution of 1868 left the question of annual or biennial sessions to the discretion of the legislature.[1] The platform of the Republican party in 1873 contained a pledge that thereafter the legislature should meet biennially, but instead of carrying out the promise, it almost reversed the process, and adopted the practice of meeting semi-annually. Doubtless, the per diem mode of compensation was one of the reasons for the protracted sessions, although it must be admitted that for several years after the war the necessities for legislation were much greater than before.[2] The taxpayers' convention urged a change to biennial sessions, and declared with truth that it would mean a saving of $100,000 a year to the people of the state. A resolution providing for biennial sessions passed the House, but was defeated in the Senate through the influence of the governor, who, it is alleged, advised his friends to vote against it.[3]

Complaint was not confined to the amount of legislation, but was also directed quite as much against its general character. One of its measures was the District Printing Bill, alleged to have been devised by Governor Ames to enable him to support a partisan press and control it in his interest. By the provisions of this act the several chancellors were authorized to designate certain newspapers in their respective districts to do the official and legal advertising, such as publication of delinquent tax lists, notices of sheriffs' sales, proceedings of boards of supervisors, etc.[4] There were

[1] Article IV. Sec. 6.

[2] The compensation of members was fixed in 1870 at $7 per day and 80 cents per mile going and returning. Every effort to have the compensation of members reduced was steadily resisted by the colored members. Finally the pressure became so great that the Republicans passed an act fixing the compensation of members at $500 per year. A motion to fix the amount at $400 was opposed by every colored member except one. At this time, the compensation of members of the legislature in New Hampshire, Connecticut, Delaware, New York, Michigan, Wisconsin, and Nebraska was $3 per day, and in some instances deductions were made for absences, and the sessions limited to forty days. In Illinois it was $5 per day, and in Maine, $150 per year.

[3] All the colored members, except ten, voted against biennial sessions. Of this course the *Plaindealer* (Republican) said: "It is a shame on the fair record of the colored members."

[4] Act approved April 3, 1874. The distribution of the public printing in the Holly Springs district may be taken as an illustration of the way in which

few Republican newspapers in the state at the time, but this
measure caused a number of small sheets, all of which were
short-lived, to spring into existence in order to get the public printing.   Property was frequently advertised for sale
under execution in a distant part of the judicial district, and
at a point removed from the county in which the sale was to
be made.   Publication under such circumstances could, of
course, be of no value, for not one property owner in a hundred ever saw the notice.[1]   With the repeal of the act which
called these sheets into existence, they disappeared.   Many
of them in 1876, changed names and became Democratic
papers.   Not one continued permanently as a Republican
paper.   The following notice from the *Jackson Clarion* contains the history of a majority of them : " Died at Jackson, Mississippi, on the morning of July 14, 1868, of too
much constitution, the state journal, aged about six months.
Its brief existence was sustained chiefly by convention warrants, which having lost their nutritious properties are no
longer healthy newspaper food.   The funeral ceremonies
were conducted at a late hour on Saturday evening last, its
editor being chief mourner, and a few negro women and
children putting in an occasional sob.   May it rest in peace."
    One of the most notorious swindles which the legislature
devised was the Pearl River Scheme, so called.   Several
members of the legislature organized the Pearl River Navigation Company, and induced the legislature to give them

the law worked. After the passage of the printing bill, a certain Republican
informed the governor of his desire to start a paper to sustain the administration, and asked him to *require* the judicial appointee for the district to designate him as official printer. The governor replied the following day and
assured the applicant of his hearty coöperation in the enterprise which he
had undertaken. The chancellor, upon receiving his appointment, wrote the
applicant saying : " It is understood, as a matter of course, that the printing
will go to you." He had no type, office, or subscribers. The paper was
printed on one of the old presses in Holly Springs. Lawyers who had important sales to advertise put them in some other paper at private expense.
Boutwell Report, p. 989.
    [1] The first Republican newspaper in Mississippi was established by General
James Dugan of the Federal army at Vicksburg in 1867. In the same year
Captain H. T. Fisher and General E. Stafford established the *Mississippi
Pilot* at Jackson. For several years it was the most influential Republican
journal in the state, and was the organ of the state administration. The
following is a partial list of the short-lived Republican newspapers established
during this period : the *Jackson Pilot, Jackson Times, Natchez New South,
Kosciusko Republican, Vicksburg Colored Citizen, Vicksburg Republican,
Meridian Chronicle, Corinth Republican, Friars Point Delta, Austin Cotton
Plant, Oxonian, State Register, Brookhaven Citizen, Fayette Vindicator,
Natchez Post, Seacoast Republican, Vicksburg Monitor, West Point Times,
Grenada Republican, Aberdeen Republican, Vicksburg Times, National
Republican, Okolona News, Holly Springs Tribune, Brandon Argus, Missis-*

certain lands granted by the United States for school purposes and for the improvement of the navigable streams of
the state, in consideration of which the company obligated
itself to remove all obstructions to navigation in Pearl River
and otherwise improve its navigable condition. The governor approved the bill without taking the proper bonds and
securities that the service would be faithfully performed.
They sold about 105,000 acres of the land, and used the
money without removing a snag from the river.[1]

Still another measure which became the subject of much
complaint was an act passed, at the instance of the governor
it was alleged, conferring upon him the power to appoint a
tax collector in each county. The collection of taxes had
always been one of the functions of the sheriff, who was an
elective officer, and the most influential one in the county.
This duty was now to be transferred to another set of officers, who would be equally as influential and independent
of popular control. The governor made a number of appointments under the act, but before it went into effect the
Supreme Court declared the law unconstitutional.[2]

Another measure authorized the governor to appoint a
special revenue agent for each county, whose duty it was to
investigate the accounts of sheriffs and treasurers, to enforce
the collection of revenue improperly withheld from the state
and county treasurers, and to hunt up frauds, defalcations, etc.
These agents were to receive 50 per cent of all shortages discovered, or delinquent taxes collected, and were supposed
to be electioneering agents for the governor, who was understood to be a candidate for the Senate. Some of the
appointees were members of the legislature. This was in
violation of the constitution, which prohibited members from
holding offices of their own creation.[3] Another proposed
measure was the Metropolitan Police Bill, by which a sort

sippi Leader, Holmes County Republican, Senatobia Signet, Meridian Gazette, Holly Springs Star, Canton Citizen, Summit Times, Prairie News,
Vicksburg Plaindealer, Jackson Leader, Columbus Press, Macon Free Opinion, Mississippi State Journal, Pontotoc Equal Rights, Copiah Republican,
American Citizen.

[1] Testimony of J. H. Estell, Boutwell Report, p. 325.

[2] French vs. Mississippi.   George E. Harris says this law was passed after
much caucusing, and after pistols were presented to force the members to
vote for it.   Testimony before Senate sub-committee, p. 592.

[3] Article IV. Sec. 38.   Ex-Attorney General Morris (Republican) said :
" These offices were in many instances unknown to the constitution, and unknown to the history of the state or to the history of any other state, and
wholly unnecessary to the public service.   Idle vagabonds belonging to the
legislature were appointed to fill them."   Letter in New York Herald, Jan.
7, 1876.   Boutwell Report, p. 1082.

of standing army was to be maintained in the state.   It was, however, defeated.[1]   One of the "notorious jobs" of the legislature in 1875 was the lease of the state convicts, several hundred in number, to one of its own members, for a period of five years, without compensation to the state, although the lessee immediately transferred them to another person by way of sub-lease, for a large sum.   The action of the governor in approving the contract was one of the grounds of impeachment.[2]

Such were the more notable instances in which the legislature was charged with abusing its power.

VI. THE VICKSBURG TROUBLES

The first trial of the strength of the Ames administration as to its power to preserve the peace and maintain order, came in September, 1874, at the time of the troubles in Warren County known as the Vicksburg Riots.   If we may believe the testimony of the whites, Warren County, and especially Vicksburg in 1874, had as corrupt and incompetent a government as ever afflicted an Anglo-Saxon community.   The senators and representatives in the legislature were colored, the sheriff could not write a simple return, and he was believed to be dishonest; the chancery clerk was corrupt beyond doubt, and not intelligent enough to enter a plain continuance on the records ; the circuit clerk and every member of the board of supervisors except one were colored, and scarcely one of them could read or write ; and four of the eight councilmen of Vicksburg were colored.   In fact, there were only three white officers in the county.[3]   The negroes, who were largely in the majority, had established the "color" line, and openly declared that the whites should not hold any of the offices.   The whites complained that they paid 99 per cent of the taxes of the county, all of which were assessed, collected, and disbursed by colored officials.   The town of Vicksburg, the chief seat of the troubles, had in 1874 a population of 11,000, the majority of which was black.

[1] The act provided for commissioners at salaries of $3000 each, sergeants at $1500, captains at $1800, and patrolmen at $100, per month.   The estimated cost was $200,000.   Only one white man in the House voted for the measure.   Every colored member voted for it.   Only one colored member in the Senate voted against it.   The Democrats presented him with a gold-headed cane for his stand against the measure.

[2] Impeachment Testimony, pp. 26, 29.

[3] The *New York Nation*, Vol. XIX. p. 412, gives some "shocking illustrations of incompetency and ignorance" among the officials of Warren County at this time.   Its authority is "an ex-Federal soldier who lived in Vicksburg for ten years."

The county and city debts, which in 1869 amounted to $13,000, had increased until the city debt alone aggregated $1,400,000.[1] Large sums of money had been squandered by the city government in grants to railroad companies and in public improvements.[2] Early in 1874, the whites organized a tax-payer's league, the chief purpose of which was to carry the municipal election in the fall. The Republicans nominated for mayor a white man then under indictment for twenty-three offences,[3] and for aldermen, seven negroes of poor character and little intelligence, and one white man who could neither read nor write, and who was the keeper of a low grog shop.[4] The ticket was so objectionable that but three white men in the city voted for it.[5] The tax payers nominated candidates under the name of the people's party. The ticket was supported by the better class of Republicans, among whom were Hon. George C. McKee, member of Congress, Judge Speed, General Furlong, and forty or fifty colored voters who had a substantial interest in the welfare of the city. For weeks before the election, white and colored militia companies paraded the streets, each trying to intimidate the other, and threatening bloodshed. Nothing illustrates better the imbecility of the state government than the fact that within three months after its inauguration it is found calling for United States troops to maintain the peace in a town of eleven thousand inhabitants. As early as April, acting governor Davis telegraphed Governor Ames, then in Massachusetts, that excitement was high in Vicksburg, and that they ought to have a company of United States troops, whereupon the governor applied to Major Allyn, commander of the post at Jackson, and being refused, telegraphed General Emery, at New Orleans, to send the troops.[6] Again, July 20, Davis wrote President Grant that serious disturbances were anticipated at Vicksburg, on account of the approaching election. "Immense armed bodies," said he, "are parading the street both day and night, and the city authorities are unable to protect life and property. I feel constrained to ask for two companies of United States troops.

---

[1] See on this point United States Census Report for 1870 ; testimony of Judge Speed (Republican) before the Vicksburg committee.

[2] Charles Nordhoff is authority for the statement that the Democrats received most of the money spent for public improvements in Vicksburg. He relates an instance in which a Democrat charged the city $500 for moving a safe from the wharf to the courthouse. Cotton States, p. 82.

[3] *Ibid.*   [5] Cotton States, p. 82.

[4] Testimony of Frederic Speed before Vicksburg Committee, p. 224.

[6] Correspondence of Governor Ames, 1874, p. 16.

I consider them absolutely necessary to prevent riot and bloodshed." He declared that the executive was powerless to execute the laws and preserve the peace.[1] Again, July 23, he wrote a long and doleful letter to the Secretary of War, imploring him to send troops.[2] On the 29th of July, Governor Ames returned to the state and at once wrote the President that a "serious and alarming condition of affairs exists in Vicksburg. Infantry and cavalry organizations exist, and a piece of artillery has been brought to the city." He declared that it was a political controversy between the Democrats on one side and the Republicans on the other, and that the former were masters of the situation, and were consequently opposed to the presence of troops. Again, he besought the President to send troops, adding almost pathetically that no harm could be done by sending them, as there were garrisons already in two cities of the state.[3] The governor was at once informed that the President declined to move the troops except under a call made strictly in accordance with the provisions of the Constitution. On August 1, his application was renewed, and the President was informed that "actual violence" existed. During all the time, there was no apparent effort on the part of the state government to bring about peace. During his administration as military governor, General Ames always had troops at his command to carry out his orders. To this method of government he was accustomed by habit and training. Upon the first breach of the peace, he turned almost instinctively to the military, a support without which his administration could hardly have stood. The election came off August 4, and the largest vote ever recorded in the city was polled. The reform ticket was elected, with the exception of two school trustees.[4]

---

[1] Correspondence of Governor Ames, 1874, p. 539.
[2] *Ibid.* p. 543.   [3] *Ibid.* p. 561.
[4] *Ibid.* p. 599.   Several other exciting municipal campaigns took place in Mississippi during 1874. One of these was in Columbus, in December. Like the Vicksburg election, it may be said to have constituted one of the initial skirmishes in the "Revolution" of 1875. That town was likewise afflicted with bad government, though not to the same extent as Vicksburg. General B. B. Eggleston, late president of the reconstruction convention, was candidate for mayor against Mr. Billups, the Democratic candidate. A few days before the election there was circulated through the town a handbill, with large headlines, "This Means Business," and under it, in large letters, "Bread or no Bread." Then followed the announcement that at a meeting of citizens it had been decided that the negro who voted for Eggleston would, as certain as fate, vote bread and meat out of the mouths of his wife and children, that the signers were pledged to employ no man who had been discharged by a member of the club, unless he produced a recommendation. They said, "You have driven the white man to the verge of ruin,

After the overthrow of the municipal ring in Vicksburg, the whites turned their attention to county affairs, which were in a melancholy condition. The chief grievance was the high rate of taxation and the existence of wholesale fraud in the county government. The state levy was 14 mills,[1] the county levy 14 mills,[2] and the levy for municipal purposes in Vicksburg was 21½ mills,[3] thus making the aggregate rate of taxation in the city of Vicksburg nearly 5 per cent. And what was worse, the tax payers had good reason to believe that the large sums of money thus collected were being stolen and otherwise misapplied. The sheriff, Peter Crosby, was, by virtue of his office, also tax collector. In December, he was to collect the state and county taxes aggregating $160,000. His bond was notoriously insufficient. It was not dated, no penalty was prescribed, and the sureties were all colored except one, a married woman whose signature did not bind her. Their signatures were made with marks and without witnesses, they lived in different parts of the state, and some were not worth one-tenth of the amount for which they were bound. The district attorney, a Republican, says there were men on Crosby's bond for $5000 who were not worth five cents.[4] The judge of the criminal court, an ex-Union soldier, and an appointee of Governor Ames, gave his opinion that $12,000 was the greatest amount that could be realized from the bond which by law should have been $81,000.[5] The district attorney advised the board of supervisors that the bond was insufficient. The whites petitioned and remonstrated with the board, urging it to require new bonds, but the board declined to act. Crosby published a card in one of the city papers, in which he declared that he would give no further bonds, nor would he vacate his office until ousted by a judgment of the Supreme Court. In the meantime, the state auditor, a Republican, had discovered that fraudulent jury and witness certificates had been issued by the circuit clerk

and he has determined to draw the color line, and if you can stand it, he can. Every negro who votes for Billups will be protected in every sense of the term, and every proper assistance will be afforded him in the power of the white men of Columbus." After the election, a private circular was sent around to the leading Democratic business men, headed: "(For Private Use.) Stand by Your Colors! Hew to the Line!" Then followed two lists of 69 names, one headed "Worthy," the other "Unworthy," and signed by "the Members of the Club." Billups was elected. Cotton States, p. 83.

[1] Report State Auditor, 1874. [2] *Ibid.*
[3] Testimony of Warren Cowan, Vicksburg Report, p. 332.
[4] Testimony of Luke Lea, Vicksburg Report, p. 313.
[5] Testimony of Frederic Speed, *ibid.* p. 216.

of the county, and that a large amount of county warrants
had been forged by the chancery clerk and were in circulation. Davenport, the colored chancery clerk, refused to allow the tax-payer's committee to examine his books.[1] At
the November term of the court, the grand jury, consisting of
ten freedmen and seven whites, found seven indictments
against Cordoza, ex-circuit clerk, and at the time state superintendent of education, for embezzlement of $2000, and for
forging witness certificates: five indictments against Davenport for forging county warrants; and two against Dorsey,
the circuit clerk, for forgery and embezzlement. The district
attorney testified that if the grand jury had thought necessary, it might have found one hundred indictments against
Cordoza and Dorsey, and fifty against Davenport.[2] After the
indictments were found, records essential to their conviction
were stolen from the sheriff's and chancery clerk's offices.
These papers were afterward discovered buried under Davenport's house.

In this situation, a "tax-payers' convention," was called, in
which Republicans as well as Democrats participated. It
resolved to take heroic action, and on December 2, demanded
the resignation of the sheriff, chancery clerk, and coroner.[3]
Crosby asked for time to consider the matter; later he refused
to resign. His refusal was reported to the convention,
whereupon that body, five hundred strong, proceeded to the
courthouse, repeated the request, and forcibly secured his
resignation. Davenport also tendered his resignation, and
left the state. Crosby notified the circuit judge that he had
yielded to force, and resigned his office. The judge then telegraphed Governor Ames that an armed mob was in possession
of the courthouse and jail, having forced most of the officers
to flee, and that he was powerless to execute the laws. The
convention detailed one of its number, an ex-Union soldier, to
take charge of the sheriff's office until another sheriff could
be elected. Crosby proceeded to Jackson to confer with the
governor, who advised him that his resignation was void, and
that he had the power to call the *posse comitatus* to his aid, to
hold his office, and to exercise its duties. The governor furthermore promised to coöperate with him in his efforts to
regain the office.[4] Crosby returned to Vicksburg accompanied by Colonel Lee and General Packer of the governor's

[1] Vicksburg Report, p. 215.
[2] Testimony of Luke Lea, *ibid.* p. 302.
[3] *Ibid.* p. 324.
[4] Testimony of Adelbert Ames, Vicksburg Report, p. 539.

staff, and shortly afterward had a hand-bill printed and distributed throughout the county by runners. He stated in this paper that he had been compelled by an armed mob to resign his office, and he appealed to all Republicans of the county, black and white, to "support him and fight the cause on its merits."[1] The card was read in all the colored churches throughout the county on Sunday, December 6, by ministers who impressed upon their congregations the duty of arming and marching to Crosby's aid. Meantime, Governor Ames had issued a proclamation reciting that riotous and disorderly persons had combined to deprive colored men in Vicksburg of their civil and political rights. All such persons were warned to disperse immediately. At the same time, he sent orders to the captain of a negro militia company to suppress the riot, and coöperate with Crosby in his attempt to regain possession of his office. This added fuel to the flame. There were two white militia companies in Vicksburg officered by white men, one of whom had been a brigadier general, and another a colonel in the Federal army. The governor did not communicate with either of these, and the negro captain was directed not to take orders from them. The reason assigned by the governor was his belief that neither of the white companies would treat his commands with the slightest respect, and that Captain Hall's color was an indication of his loyalty and patriotism.[2] On Sunday afternoon, it was reported in Vicksburg that the whole available strength of the negro population was massing, with the intent of marching upon the town next morning. The report was doubtless exaggerated into alarming proportions. The dread of negro insurrection, which has at one time or another darkened every hearthstone in the South, took possession of the people, and they saw visions of slaughter, rape, arson, and robbery. Adjutant General Packer went out to stop the negroes, but without success. At daybreak Monday morning, the alarm was sounded by the watchman from the top of the court-house. It proved false, however, but was again struck later in the morning by the same watchman, who announced that a large body of negroes was approaching the city. The streets were soon filled with excited men, and weeping women and children. At eight o'clock A.M. the mayor published and circulated a manifesto declaring that the governor's proclamation was false, warned all armed bodies to disperse at once, and commanded all good citizens to hold themselves in readi-

---

[1] Majority Report, Vicksburg Report, p. 24.
[2] Testimony of Adelbert Ames, *ibid.* p. 545.

ness to report at any call for the purpose of enforcing his orders. At twelve o'clock, he issued another proclamation closing the saloons, and advising the people to be "quiet and discreet, but firm." The city was then placed under martial law, and supreme command delegated to an ex-Confederate officer. With a force of one hundred men, he moved out to meet the approaching negro host. The two leaders had a conference, and the negroes agreed to withdraw. As they proceeded to do so, they were fired into, as they claim, with the result that seven were killed. While this was going on, another battle was taking place at the Pemberton monument. The testimony as to who began the firing is conflicting. The whites claim that the negroes fired upon them first. In the several conflicts which ensued, two whites and twenty-nine blacks were killed.[1] Thirty prisoners were taken, but were soon released. All the whites, Republicans as well as Democrats, were found together in the conflict. An ex-Federal army officer testified that one hundred ex-Union soldiers took part in the fight — a more conspicuous part than that taken by the ex-Confederates.[2] On December 21, two weeks after the riot, the President issued a proclamation commanding all "turbulent and disorderly persons" to retire peaceably to their respective homes within five days.[3] In a few days quiet was restored, although the governor continued to call upon the President for troops.

The legislature met in extraordinary session on December 17, at the call of the governor, who sent in a message in which he warmly denounced the whites as "insurgents," and declared that ample legal remedies existed for the wrongs complained of. He expressed sorrow that "a portion of the citizens could find it in their hearts to deprive by violence their neighbors and fellow-citizens of their political rights"; declared that the officials and prominent men holding views different from those held by the "insurgents" had been com-

[1] See Majority Report, Vicksburg Committee. Mr. Mayes, in his Life and Times of L. Q. C. Lamar, p. 237, says the number killed was one white man and fifteen negroes. Andrews, in his History of the United States During the Last Quarter of a Century, put the number at fifty-nine.

[2] See testimony of General C. E. Furlong, Vicksburg Report, p. 100. General Furlong served through the Civil War, and was on Sherman's staff at the time of the surrender of Vicksburg. He controlled a squad of cavalry in the Vicksburg Riot, and otherwise championed the cause of the whites.

[3] Richardson's Messages and Papers of the Presidents, Vol. VII. p. 322. The *New York Nation*, commenting on this action of the President, said: "It is difficult to make out what the grounds for the proclamation are now, and if the state government is not strong enough to keep the peace in a single town, it must be so feeble that it needs permanent assistance. XIX. p. 412.

pelled to flee; doubted whether there was any cause for complaint; declared that the acts of the insurgents bore a strong resemblance to Mexican and South American insurrections; and informed the legislature that he was without means to suppress the disorders.[1] He recommended that the legislature make provision for suppressing the "insurrection" in Warren County, and for suppressing similar outbreaks likely to occur elsewhere. The legislature responded by adopting a joint resolution calling upon the President for troops. Upon the passage of this resolution, forty-six members of the legislature published an appeal to the people of the United States, in which they charged the Republicans with attempting to introduce martial law in Mississippi, for political purposes. They protested against the action of the governor, and the majority of the legislature, which, they said, was based on no evidence whatever. The legislature also appointed a committee of investigation. January 4, 1875, the governor telegraphed the President that "the majority of the legislative committee sent to Vicksburg, report to me that a great feeling of insecurity prevails there, that certain officers cannot safely discharge their duties, that armed defiance of all law and authority holds full sway at the courthouse, and consequently I am compelled to ask you to send troops there to uphold and protect the lawful authorities."[2] Meantime, the board of supervisors had ordered a special election to fill the vacancy occasioned by the resignation of Crosby. The legislature, by special act, extended the period of notice to be given for special elections, thus invalidating the order of the board. The election, however, was held, the colored voters refusing to take any part in it. A Mr. Flannagan was elected, took possession of the sheriff's office, and entered upon the discharge of his duties. On January 5, 1875, General P. H. Sheridan telegraphed the governor from New Orleans that he had that day assumed control of the Department of the Gulf, and that a company of troops would be sent to Vicksburg the

---

[1] Of this message, the *Jackson Clarion* of Dec. 10, 1874, said: "If his purpose is to urge the passage of laws prescribing severe penalties for delinquent and thieving officials, and affording relief to the tax payers, all will be well. But if it is to organize a military force of cutthroats and vagabonds to overrun the state, and bully the people, we would earnestly advise him to desist. He must not misunderstand the temper of the people. He commenced the conflagration by the issue of his ill-timed proclamation. He can extinguish it as readily, by taking care that lawless officials are brought to punishment, and not sustained in their crimes."

[2] Correspondence of Governor Ames, 1874. The Majority Report of the legislative committee was signed by two white and three negro members.

following day.[1] The order was carried out, and on Monday, January 18, Major George E. Head, U. S. A., with a squad of soldiers, entered the sheriff's office, ejected Flannagan and reinstated Crosby.[2]

The whole course of Governor Ames in regard to the Warren County troubles was disapproved by the whites, both republicans and Democrats.[3] They said that he showed a lack of personal interest in their grievances, that he should have had some word of condemnation for the delinquent and criminal officials, and that he should have visited Vicksburg in person and urged Crosby to give a satisfactory bond, instead of advising him to call out the *posse comitatus* and resist the whites.[4] The charge that it was the design and purpose of Ames to bring on a conflict between the whites and the blacks does not seem to be well founded. The utmost that he can be accused of was bad judgment and possibly indifference in the matter. If any one more than another can be held responsible for the unfortunate affair, it is Crosby. His influence over the negroes of the county was absolute. The poor deluded creatures were fooled into marching upon the city in a mole-like way under the orders of Crosby, with a vague impression that it was Republican to do so. In fact there was a story afloat at the time that General Grant and Governor Ames were there in person, and desired them to attack the city. The negroes were fired into and dispersed as any mob would have been, Crosby, in the meantime, having deserted them.

The Vicksburg affair was the subject of investigation by a committee of Congress. The *Clarion* of December 17 declared that the investigation was courted, and asked that "the facts be allowed to go to the country." The members of the committee were Messrs. Hurlburt of Illinois, Conger of

---

[1] Correspondence, 1875, p. 238. On the same day, Sheridan sent his celebrated despatch to the Secretary of War, recommending Congress to declare the "ringleaders" in the Vicksburg affair banditti, and leave him to do the rest, remarking that no further action by Congress would be necessary. The legislature voted the general a resolution of thanks for this somewhat cruel threat. The Democrats, of course, protested against it.

[2] *New York Nation*, Jan. 21, 1875.

[3] Justice Tarbell of the Supreme Court said : "I advised against any attempt to reinstate Crosby, because I regarded him as unworthy." Impeachment Testimony, p. 120. Charles Nordhoff says he was told by honest Republicans in Mississippi that the riot could have been prevented had the governor done his duty. Cotton States in 1875.

[4] The *Jackson Clarion* of Dec. 10, 1874, in a long editorial, fixed the responsibility for the riot on Governor Ames, and declared that it was the beginning of the end.

Michigan, Williams of Wisconsin, Speer of Pennsylvania, and O'Brien of Maryland. They took testimony for two weeks at Vicksburg, examining in all 115 witnesses. As might have been expected, there was a majority and a minority report. The majority fixed the blame on the whites, but admitted that much misgovernment existed in the affairs of the county.

CHAPTER NINTH

THE KUKLUX DISTURBANCES IN MISSISSIPPI

THE so-called Kuklux Klan is said to have originated in Tennessee in 1866, during the administration of Governor Brownlow, and to have been at first an association of young men for mutual pleasure and amusement.[1] The nocturnal perambulations of the freedmen, their habit of running away from labor contracts, the large amount of petit larceny among them at this time, the abandonment of their crops to attend political meetings, their participation in the loyal leagues, and their alleged insolence to former masters created a necessity for some kind of restraint, as the whites believed. The Kuklux organization was designed to accomplish this purpose.[2] In its beginnings, it was similar to the old slave patrol, and was intended simply to scare the superstitious blacks into good behavior and obedience. The whites allege that it was to serve as a sort of offset to the Loyal Leagues.[3] These were secret political organizations among the colored people, and were generally organized and presided over by their white allies. Meetings were usually held at night in some out-of-the-way place, and were harangued by white Republican speakers. These organizations solidified the black vote, for there was a league in every community, and every colored man was a member.[4]

General N. B. Forest was reputed to have been at the head of the Kuklux organization in the South, and it was charged that he introduced it into Mississippi, while engaged

---

[1] D. L. Wilson, *Century Magazine*, Vol. VI. p. 398.

[2] For the alleged necessity for such an organization, see testimony of General John B. Gordon, before the Kuklux committee ; see also testimony of General Forest.

[3] The *Jackson Clarion* of March 21, 1871, said if the Kuklux Klan really existed, it would not recommend its disbandment during the existence of the Loyal Leagues, whose "conspiracies the Kuklux was intended to circumvent."

[4] The following is a part of the oath alleged to have been taken by members of the Lynch Council, No. 33, of the Jackson League : "I will do all in my power to elect true and reliable Union men and supporters of the government to all offices of profit or trust, from the lowest to the highest, in ward, town, county, and general government."

in railroad building in the eastern portion of the state.[1] At
first, the organization had among its members some of the
most influential citizens of the state — distinguished leaders
of the Confederate armies, but as soon as the original purpose
of the organization was perverted, the better class of men
abandoned it.[2] The original purposes of the organization as
set forth in the prescript were the protection of the weak,
innocent, and defenceless from the outrages of lawless
and brutal persons ; the relief of the injured and oppressed;
the aiding of widows and orphans of Confederate soldiers;
and assistance in the execution of all " constitutional " laws.[3]

The mysterious organization, gruesome rites, and the
strange language of the Klan were well calculated to strike
terror into the minds of a superstitious race emasculated by
centuries of slavery. Its sphere of operations was styled the
Invisible Empire ; the chief functionary was the Grand
Wizard ; each state was a Realm ruled over by a Grand
Dragon ; each congressional district was a Dominion, at the
head of which was the Grand Titan ; each county was a
Province under the rule of a Grand Giant ; and each county
was subdivided into Camps or Dens, each governed by a
Grand Cyclops. The members of a Den were called Ghouls.[4]
The mysterious constitution of the organization was not less
terrifying than the manner in which the members disguised
themselves when in active service. The prevailing costume
was a long white robe reaching to the knees, and slashed up
the sides for convenience in running. The covering for the
face was a white mask containing holes for the eyes. The
headgear was sometimes a high cardboard hat, but more frequently a sort of cap with long ears or horns attached. The
front part of the dress was often disfigured with skulls and
crossbones or other hideous designs. The horses ridden by
the Kuklux were disguised quite as effectively as the riders.[5]
Meetings were presided over by the captain, and admission
was by password only. Motions for " waiting upon " certain
individuals could be made by any member and were put by
the captain. It was alleged that sometimes the Klan in one
community would call upon the Klan in a neighboring com-

---

[1] Testimony of Governor R. C. Powers, Kuklux Report, p. 586.

[2] Testimony of S. J. Gohlson, pp. 854–860, and of J. F. Sessions, p. 216,
ibid.

[3] What purports to be the prescript is printed in the Kuklux Report, pp.
12–14.

[4] Lalor's Encyclop. of Pol. Sci. II. p. 680.

[5] For descriptions of disguises worn in Mississippi, see Kuklux Report,
pp. 274, 327, 343, 467.

munity to execute its decree.   This was said to have been a
common practice in the counties of Mississippi lying along
the Alabama line.[1]

The most exaggerated tales were circulated among the freedmen in regard to the character and strength of the Kuklux.
The mere rumor that they were "riding" in the neighborhood was sufficient to cause every black to retire to his cabin.
It was common among them to magnify a band of a dozen
into a hundred.   They were never visited by less than fifty,
and the number was usually reported to be two or three hundred.   The idea was widespread among the negroes during the
early days of reconstruction that the Kuklux were spirits of
dead Confederate soldiers, and were possessed of supernatural
powers, such as the ability to take themselves to pieces at
will, rattle their bones, and drink whole pailfuls of water.
The Kuklux practice of conversing in mysterious and unin-
telligible language, the negroes called "mummicking."   They
told of a horrible monster who lived in the Yazoo swamps,
and went about the land with a flesh bag in the shape of a
heart "hollering for fried nigger meat," a delicacy for which
it had an insatiable appetite.   The "decree" of the camp was
usually delivered to the person for whom it was intended by
the captain, in a pompous manner, and was pronounced as an
order of the Grand Cyclops registered in some corner of
Hades.   If the decree was simply a warning, the offender
was informed that it was the practice of the Klan never to
give its warnings but once.   The notice was usually posted
in some conspicuous place about the premises of the person
for whom it was intended.   The following notice found on
the door-post of a Freedmen's Bureau Agent in Rankin
County, in 1868, is typical of the manner in which the Kuklux
delivered its warnings.[2]

K. K. K.   *Dismal Swamp*

2 D, XIΛ͞.   *11th hour*

Mene, mene, tekel upharsin.   The bloody dagger is
drawn; the trying hour is at hand; beware!   Your steps are
marked; the eye of the dark chief is upon you.   First he
warns; then the avenging dagger flashes in the moonlight.

By Order of the Grand Cylops:

LIXTO

[1] Governor Alcorn in an interview in the *New York Democrat* of April 17,
1871, is reported as saying: "I have no doubt that there is such a thing as
Kukluxism in the Southern states, but there is none in Mississippi unless the
bands of desperadoes along the Alabama line can be called Kuklux."
[2] Put in evidence before the reconstruction committee.   H. Mis. Docs.
3d Ses. 40th Cong.

Here is another taken from the *Iuka Gazette:* —

$\bowtie \!\! \stackrel{=}{=} K : K : K :$

BLOODY MONTH

Skeleton Hollow, Dark Moon, Silent Hour

In hoc signum.   To the veiled brotherhood of subdivision No. 9.
The Grand Cyclops never sleeps.   His bony fingers have pointed
to the "Bleeding Band" and his messenger will greet you in the
24th revolution on the Spirit's Dial.   Mortals have threatened the
Band.   The Bloody hand is raised to warn.   Be cautious lest it
fall.   The Sword is unsheathed & red.   Let Tyrants tremble.

H. K. 3.   7.

O.

Sub. R. T. and Bearer of the Diadem.

Here is another : [1] —

(A picture of crossed swords, coffin, skull and crossbones, owl,
bloody moon.   Train of cars, each labelled K. K. K.)

Dam your Soul !   The horrible sepulcher and bloody moon has
at last arrived.   Some live today, tomorrow "Die."   We the undersigned understand through our Grand Cyclops that you have
recommended a big Black Nigger for Male Agent on our nu rode;
wel sir, Jest you understand in time if he gets on the rode you
can make up your mind to pull roape.   If you have anything to
say in regard to the matter, meet the Grand Cyclops and Conclave
at Den No. 4, 12 o'clock midnight Oct 1, 1871.

When you are in Calera we want you to hold your tongue and
not speak so much with your mouth or otherwise you will be taken
on supprize and led out by the Klan and learnt to stretch hemp.

Beware !   Beware !   Beware !   Beware !

PHILLIP ISENBAUM
Grand Cyclops

JOHN BANKSTON
ESON DAVES

You know who and all   WARREN THOMAS
others of the Klan.   BLOODY BONES

The Kuklux organization does not seem to have attracted
any attention in Mississippi until 1868.   It was charged by
the Republicans that in the campaign of that year against
the Constitution, the whites terrorized the negroes by the
Kuklux method, and either kept them away from the polls or
intimidated them into voting against the Constitution.   General Gillem, in his report for 1868–1869 said: "The great

[1] Put in evidence before the reconstruction committee.

defect in the administration of justice is not in the courts;
after offenders are once in custody their trial and punishment usually follow. The difficulty lies in identifying and
arresting criminals. In many instances crimes either of
murder or aggravated assault and battery are committed at
night by persons in disguise who cannot be recognized by
their victims or witnesses."[1] The election of 1869 for state
officers and members of the legislature was the occasion for
further alleged Kuklux manœuvres. It was not, however,
until after the readmission of the state to the Union that the
Kuklux disturbances became alarming, and for a while threatened to subvert the peace and order of the state. The
passing of the Freedmen's Bureau in 1869 with its officials
in every community, and the withdrawal of a majority of the
troops, removed a restraint, which had, to a great extent,
curbed the lawless spirit. Offences against freedmen and
Northern men now increased to such an extent as to embarrass the civil authorities in the execution of the laws.
Alcorn on November 10, 1869, while a candidate for governor, had published a card in which he declared that in the
event of his election, "Society should no longer be governed
by the pistol and the bowie knife."[2] He was elected, and
shortly after the meeting of the legislature, sent in a message recommending the enactment of drastic measures to
break up the Kuklux organizations. The legislature, in
accordance with his recommendation, passed, on July 21,
a stringent law for this purpose. It was made unlawful for
any person to appear in a mask or disguise, or to prowl about
the houses of other persons. The penalty for travelling
about in disguise to the disturbance of the peace was fixed
at not less than $100 and not more than $500, and imprisonment at the discretion of the court. The penalty for entering or attempting to enter any house in disguise was declared
to be a felony punishable by imprisonment in the penitentiary
for a period not less than one year and not more than five.
The penalty for committing assault in disguise was fixed at
imprisonment in the penitentiary for a period not less than
five years and not more than ten. It was made the duty
of peace officers to request all disguised persons whom they
might discover, to unmask, and upon their refusal, to arrest
them with or without warrant. They were empowered to
call upon bystanders for aid in making arrests, and the pen-

---

[1] Report Secretary of War, 1868–1869, p. 1054.
[2] Appendix to H. and S. Journal, 1871, p. 1214.

alty for refusal to render aid in such cases was fixed at not
more than $500, and imprisonment not exceeding six months.
Official neglect of duty was punishable by a fine not exceeding $1000, and imprisonment not exceeding one year.   The
governor was authorized to offer rewards not exceeding
$5000 for the arrest of any person guilty of attempting to
enter a house or attempting to commit assault in disguise,
and the reward was to be paid out of the treasury of the
county in which the offence was committed.   It was made
the duty of all judges of the criminal courts to give this act
in their charges to the grand jury at each term of the court.[1]
In spite of the law, the disturbances increased.   The governor offered large rewards without effect.   He then asked
the legislature to give him authority to offer rewards as
high as $25,000 which amount he thought would "draw the
cowardly assassins from their hiding-places."[2]   The chief
defence of persons charged with offences of this kind was the
alibi.   The governor attributed the failure to convict to the
sympathy of the juries for persons thus accused, and alleged
that witnesses were afraid to testify for fear of personal
violence.

On the 23d of March, 1871, President Grant sent a special
message to Congress, in which he declared that life and property were insecure in some of the Southern states, and that
carriers of the mail and collectors of the revenue were in
danger of personal violence.   That the power to correct the
evil was beyond the control of the state authorities, he felt
certain, and he recommended appropriate legislation to meet
the case.[3]   Accordingly, what is known as the Enforcement
Act was passed on April 20.   Its most important provision was the extension of the jurisdiction of the Federal
courts to Kuklux cases.   A heavy penalty was fixed for
"conspiring to levy war against the government of the
United States, delaying the execution of the Federal laws,
or attempting to deter any person from voting, holding
office, or acting as a witness or juror in the Federal courts.
It authorized the President to employ the land or naval
forces of the United States to suppress disorders in case the
state authorities were unable or unwilling to do so, and to
suspend the writ of *habeas corpus* during the continuance
of the Kuklux troubles.   The act also authorized Federal

---

[1] Laws of Miss. 1870, p. 89.
[2] Appendix to H. and S. Journal, 1871, p. 1213.
[3] Affairs in the insurrectionary states, Vol. I. p. 1.

judges to exclude from juries those who were deemed to be accomplices.[1]

The legislature of Mississippi memorialized the senators and representatives from the state to vote for the passage of the act, and they all complied with the request. The act seems to have accomplished the purpose for which it was designed, for by the end of the year 1872, the Kuklux troubles had practically ceased. An attempt to extend the provisions of the act passed the Senate, but failed in the House.[2]

Before the passage of the Kuklux Act, a joint committee of twenty-one senators and representatives had been appointed to inquire into the condition of affairs in the late insurrectionary states. Early in June, a sub-committee began taking testimony at Washington. On the 22d of September, a sub-committee of five was appointed to visit Mississippi and take further testimony. The committee went first to Macon, where it took testimony from November 6 to November 9, examining in all sixteen witnesses, of whom ten were white and six black. On the 9th, the committee went to Columbus, where it took testimony until the 17th, examining in all forty-six witnesses, of whom thirty-six were white and ten were black. The testimony relating to Mississippi embraces two large octavo volumes of twelve hundred closely printed pages, and contains a vast amount of material bearing upon the political and social condition of the state during this period.

One of the most prominent witnesses before the sub-committee at Macon was Governor R. C. Powers, a Northern man, and at that time an extensive planter in the county. He told the committee that with the exception of a half-dozen counties adjoining Alabama, there had been no difficulty in enforcing the law in Mississippi, and that the only lawlessness worth mentioning was that committed by disguised bands who went about the country at night.[3] Governor Powers expressed the opinion that much of the crime

---

[1] Lalor's Encyclop. of Pol. Sci. Vol. II. p. 681. The *Clarion* of April 14, 1871, said of this act : " It is predicated on no other foundation than the malice and cowardly hatred of its authors for the white inhabitants of the Southern states, and their desire to retain power at the cost of honor and principle will intensify the opposition to Republican rule and hasten its overthrow."

[2] The only speech of note made by Adelbert Ames while representing Mississippi in the United States Senate was in favor of this measure. He gave a gloomy picture of affairs in the state. His colleague, Senator Alcorn, vigorously opposed the measure, and denied the allegations of Ames in regard to affairs in Mississippi. Globe, 42d Cong. 2d Ses. App. p. 393.

[3] Kuklux Testimony, p. 584.

in Noxubee County was committed by men from an adjacent county in Alabama. It was his further opinion that the man who took a bold and open stand against the Kuklux would be in danger of personal violence. With a few honorable exceptions, the most influential men did not take the lead in calling indignation meetings for the purpose of denouncing Kuklux outrages. That such a policy would have done much to discourage the lawless spirit there can be little doubt. Until the evidence became indisputable, the Democratic press denied the existence of such an organization as the Kuklux.[1] Some of the papers assumed a sort of apologetic tone, and sought to excuse and palliate their acts. There were, however, some papers that denounced them as assassins and midnight banditti. Such a paper was published in the town of Macon.[2]

Some of the most sensational testimony before the general committee at Washington was that of one John R. Taliaferro of Noxubee County. Taliaferro was a Southern man, and claimed to be an ex-Confederate soldier and a Democrat in his politics. He alleged that, although not a member of the Kuklux organization, he had, upon invitation, gone along with them in several of their raids. The pass-words " Hail " and " Mount Nebo," he said, admitted to the camps of Winston, Lauderdale, Kemper, Lowndes, and Oktibbeha counties in Mississippi and in Pickens County, Alabama. The signal for distress, he said, was generally " Kosciusko." In some communities the words " Avalanche " or " Bleecher " were the signals. In public places, the sign of recognition was the drawing of the hand across the chin, and the response was given by placing the hand on the lapel of the coat. Meetings were held regularly every two weeks at such time and place as was appointed by the captain. No written communication was permitted. Minor punishments, such as

---

[1] The *Clarion* of Dec. 13, 1870, said it did not believe that such an organization existed in the state. In the issue of March 21, 1871, it admitted the existence of the Kuklux Klan, and said its origin was due to the "instinct of self-preservation."

[2] This was the *Macon Beacon*, a Democratic journal, published by Ward and Ferris. In the issue of May 14, 1870, it was said : "These midnight banditti are doing more to thwart the peace and prosperity of our country than a wise legislation of years can counteract. Our people should personally endeavor to remove these foul ulcers that now and then break out where bad blood exists, and apply remedies that will finally restore these diseased parts to healthy action. It can be done calmly and soothingly, but it must be done firmly. It should be made disreputable to aid or countenance such outrages, and the very perpetrators will then pause and look back with horror on the deeds of darkness which they have blindly committed."

whippings or warnings to leave, were usually attended to
by the local Klan, but if life was to be taken, a Klan from
another county or from Alabama was called upon to execute
the decree.[1]

Mr. Baskerville, a merchant and planter of Noxubee County,
and an ex-Confederate lieutenant colonel, testified that there
was no such organization as the Kuklux Klan in the state of
Mississippi, although he admitted that occasionally disguised
men committed deeds of violence here and there.   He positively denied Taliaferro's allegations in regard to the Kuklux
organizations in Noxubee County.[2]

Winston, Lowndes, Monroe, Chickasaw, and Kemper
counties were all the theatres of more or less disturbances,
and each was the subject of special investigation by the Committee of Congress.   Kemper County for ten years after the
war was the scene of animosities and feuds which finally
culminated in the assassination of the most prominent figure
in the troubles.   This was the sheriff, W. W. Chisholm, an
ex-Confederate soldier, but a radical of the most pronounced
type.   His friends allege that he was the subject of persecution from the time of his conversion to radicalism until the
time of his death in 1877.   The Democrats, on the other
hand, claim that he was a violent person, and an enemy to law
and order.   He testified at Washington on the condition of
affairs in the county, and asserted that great lawlessness existed there.[3]

One of the most notable cases of kukluxing in Lowndes
County was that of the Rev. Mr. Galloway, a Congregational
minister, and the teacher of a negro school near Caledonia.

---

[1] Taliaferro's testimony is printed in Vol. I. of the Kuklux Report on Mississippi, pp. 223–246.

[2] Kuklux Report, pp. 373–483.

[3] The Kemper County troubles have been made the subject of two volumes
written from very different standpoints.   One of these volumes, entitled the
Chisholm Massacre ; or a Picture of Home Rule in Mississippi, was written
by J. M. Wells, an ex-Union soldier and a United States deputy revenue
collector.   The book gives a terrible and no doubt overdrawn picture of
affairs in the county.   The chief theme is the alleged massacre of Chisholm
and his daughter and son in 1877.   The author gives a somewhat pathetic turn
to the story, and it aroused considerable feeling in the North.   It should be
said that the killing of the children was purely accidental.   Kemper County
Vindicated — A Peep at Radical Rule in Mississippi, is the title of the other
history of the Kemper County disturbances.   The author is James Lynch of
West Point, Mississippi, and the book is written as an answer to the charges
made by Wells.   He fixes the responsibility for the troubles on Chisholm,
and gives an interesting, but no doubt exaggerated, account of the abuses of
radical government.   Wells's book was published by the Chicago Monumen-
tal Association, 1880 ; Lynch's, by E. J. Hale & Co., New York, 1879.

He was called on by a band of "one hundred disguised men," who ordered him to stop teaching. They informed Mr. Galloway that they were the spirits of dead Confederate soldiers, and had come all the way from Manassas to see that poor widows were not imposed upon. He says they delivered their order to him in a "lordly manner," and endeavored to make him promise that he would stop teaching. In a few days, he closed his school. Shortly thereafter, he received another visit from the Kuklux, who ordered him to stop preaching to the negroes. They accused him of preaching doctrines calculated to inflame the minds of his colored parishioners against the whites, and even with drilling the negroes at night for the purpose of making war upon the Kuklux. This Galloway positively denied. They plainly told him that there were preachers enough in Monroe County without him. He refused to make any promises, and they finally went away without doing him harm, but warned him of the consequences of his disobedience. He admits that he advised the negroes to shoot into the Kuklux, in order to frighten them, but steadily discountenanced every suggestion of armed resistance, in fact, used his personal influence to prevent them from attacking the Kuklux. He continued his preaching and was not again molested.[1]

Perhaps no case of kukluxing in the South was the subject of more comment throughout the country than the whipping of Colonel A. P. Huggins in Monroe County. Huggins was an ex-Union soldier, born in Ohio, and reared in Michigan. At the close of the war, he became an agent of the Freedmen's Bureau in Mississippi, which office he held for about eighteen months. He then became assistant assessor of internal revenue, and superintendent of public schools, both of which offices he held at the time of his whipping in March, 1870. He had made himself obnoxious to the whites of the county by his extravagant administration of the public school system. While making an official tour through the county, he stopped, upon invitation, to spend the night with a respectable white Democratic citizen, by the name of Ross. He had been warned during the day that the Kuklux were "riding" for him the night before, and would in all likelihood pay him a visit the following night. About ten o'clock, he was awakened by a loud call at the gate, and upon looking out of the window, he saw the premises covered with men dressed in white. They demanded that he come out;

[1] His testimony is found in the Kuklux Report, pp. 662–675.

informed him that at a regular meeting of their camp, his case had been under consideration, and that they had certain warnings which it was necessary for them to deliver to him privately, as it was against their rules to deliver warnings in the presence of women and children. He at first refused to appear. Mr. Ross was then ordered to bring him out, or to place a light in his room. Upon his refusal to do so, they threatened to set fire to the house. Upon the solicitation of Mr. Ross, Colonel Huggins agreed to leave the house. Upon reaching the gate, he asked the chief to deliver his little bit of warning and allow him to go. The captain then pronounced the decree in a pompous manner, saying that it had been given in a certain den and registered in some corner of hell, the exact location of the registrar's office having escaped his memory. The substance of the decree was that he should leave the county within ten days, and relieve the people from all taxes. The captain further informed him that the rule of the camp was, first to give the warning, second, to enforce obedience to their laws by whipping; third, to kill by the Klan altogether; and fourth, if the offender still refused to obey, they were sworn to kill him "privately by assassination or otherwise." They told him that his chief offence was in collecting taxes to keep radicals in office. Not deterred by their threat, Huggins says he told them that he would leave Monroe County at his pleasure, whereupon a number of men sprang over the fence, seized him, and disarmed him. They then carried him a quarter of a mile down the road, when they stopped and asked him if he had changed his mind. He replied that he had not. Both he and Mr. Ross, who had followed, attempted to reason with them, but they could not be moved, and insisted that he must leave the state. Presently, one of the crowd appeared with a stirrup strap of stout leather and proceeded to whip him. They gave him seventy-five lashes, and then went away, leaving him with Mr. Ross.[1]

In Chickasaw County several persons were whipped by the Kuklux, the best known cases being the whipping of E. C. Echols and Cornelius McBride. Echols was a Southern man, but a Republican in politics.

The only noteworthy Kuklux demonstration in Pontotoc County was a raid into the town of Pontotoc on the night of

---

[1] Colonel Huggins's testimony, as given at Washington, July 19, embraces thirty-three pages in the Kuklux Report, beginning with p. 265. He testified again before the sub-committee at Columbus, Mississippi, November 13. See pp. 820, 828.

May 12, 1871. The purpose of the raid was to capture Mr. Flournoy, who enjoyed the distinction of being the most extreme and obnoxious radical in the state.[1] He was the editor of a sheet called *Equal Rights*, and held the office of county superintendent of education. Judge Austin Pollard, chancellor of the seventh judicial district, was holding court in the town, and upon being informed of the presence of the band, he and Colonel Flournoy went out to meet them. Judge Pollard held a parley with them, and demanded their surrender. He had no sooner repeated the demand than one of the Klan fired, presumably at the judge. The firing then became general on both sides, with the result that a young man was killed. The young man testified in his dying moments that there were about thirty men in the crowd, and that their purpose was to get hold of Colonel Flournoy.[2]

One of the subjects of investigation by the Kuklux committee was the riot at Meridian on March 6, 1871. The affair grew out of the relations between the whites and blacks of the town, the immediate cause being the act of a Northern school-teacher with several negroes in assaulting a deputy sheriff who had come over from Alabama to make some arrests. The white man was arrested and bound over for his appearance at court, but upon the advice of his white friends he forfeited his recognizance and left for parts unknown. The officers of the town were all Northern white men or freedmen, and were all appointees of General Ames as military governor. They complained of the manifestation of public sentiment which made it advisable for one of their leaders to leave, and sent a committee of colored men to Jackson to represent to the governor the "true condition of affairs" in the town.

On the 3d of March the colored committee returned from Jackson, accompanied by Mr. Moore, a colored minister and the representative of the county in the legislature. They called a mass meeting of Republicans for the following day at the courthouse, in order to make a report of their mission to Jackson. The meeting was largely attended by colored people, and addresses were made by Warren Tyler, a colored school-teacher, William Dennis, a notorious negro, and the Rev. Mr. Moore. The whites charged that the speakers advised the colored people to "take things into their own

[1] See his own testimony on this point, Kuklux Report, p. 95.
[2] Flournoy's testimony is in Vol. I. of the Kuklux Testimony, pp. 82–95; Judge Pollard's testimony is in Vol. II. of the Kuklux Testimony, pp. 1100–1110.

hands." About an hour after the adjournment of the meeting, the store of the mayor was discovered to be on fire. The fire spread until a number of buildings had been consumed, the negroes refusing to help extinguish it, on the ground that it was a " white man's fire." During the following day great excitement prevailed in the town, and groups of excited men could be seen here and there holding street corner meetings and discussing the situation. A mass meeting was held Monday morning, at which resolutions were adopted condemning the speeches of the colored men. A committee was appointed to wait on the governor and request him to remove the mayor.

Shortly after the adjournment of the mass meeting, the trial of the three negro orators for " creating disorder " began before a Republican magistrate. The trial had proceeded for some moments when a tremendous firing began in the courtroom. The magistrate fell at the first shot. Twenty or thirty shots rang out almost simultaneously. When the smoke cleared away several dead bodies were found. Dennis, badly wounded, was carried to the sheriff's office and left on the floor. During the night he was killed. Tyler was found concealed in a barber shop and was quickly despatched. During the firing Moore feigned death by falling to the floor. He afterward escaped and made his way to Jackson, pursued by a body of armed citizens. He never returned to Meridian. After the expiration of his term as a member of the legislature he became a night watchman at the capitol. He is at present a blacksmith in Jackson.

In the meantime three other negroes had been arrested, carried to the courthouse, and put in charge of a deputy sheriff for safe keeping. During the night, they were taken out and killed. The riot ended by the burning of Moore's dwelling house and the colored Baptist church near his residence. In the meantime the mayor was informed that it was the desire of the white citizens that he should leave the town. He was accordingly escorted to the train by three or four hundred men, and left for the North.[1] The affair caused considerable excitement throughout the state, and the legislature called on the President for troops. Governor Alcorn

---

[1] My chief source of information for the facts relating to the Meridian troubles is the report of a special committee of investigation appointed by the legislature, and the report of the congressional committee on affairs in the insurrectionary states. Both committees took a large amount of testimony. The report of the state committee is printed as a part of the testimony of the congressional committee. See Vol. I. Affairs in the Insurrectionary States.

telegraphed to Washington, March 17, that the "riot had been suppressed," that the affair was undergoing investigation, and that there was no need for troops. Except some "minor outrages" in east Mississippi, he said the state presented an unbroken evidence of civil obedience and order.[1]

In this, as in most of the so-called riots which occurred in the state during this period, each race accused the other of responsibility for the affair. It happened in this, as in the others, that political conditions were the remote cause, and when once the explosion came, the negroes suffered most.

In the meantime an effort was being made to enforce the act of Congress for the prevention of Kuklux outrages. Mr. Wells, the United States attorney for the northern district of Mississippi, told the congressional committee in November that he had under indictment between two and three hundred persons charged with violation of the Federal enforcement law. He stated that he commenced the prosecutions in the United States court about the 15th of May, 1871 — less than a month after the passage of the act, and that he had been engaged constantly in travelling or otherwise prosecuting his duties.[2]

On Tuesday, the 28th of June, 1871, the first important trial in the United States under the Kuklux Act began at Oxford before Hon. R. A. Hill, United States district judge.[3] The case was entitled *Ex parte* Walton *et al.*, and was a proceeding by writ of *habeas corpus* upon application of twenty-eight persons charged with the killing of a negro in Monroe County on the night of March 29. Forty odd witnesses were examined, their testimony covering sixty-one pages of the printed record. Able counsel were employed on both sides, and rarely has a criminal trial in Mississippi been conducted with more ability.[4] The trial lasted eight days, and was attended with great interest and excitement. A com-

[1] *Jackson Clarion*, March 28, 1871.
[2] Testimony, p. 1148.
[3] My chief authority for the account of the trial is a pamphlet entitled : A Full Report of the Great Kuklux Trial in the United States District Court at Oxford, published privately. It contains the argument of the counsel, copies of the indictment and other processes, the testimony of all the witnesses, and the decision of the court, making a volume of one hundred pages. The pamphlet, except the argument of the counsel, was incorporated in the report of the Kuklux committee, and embraces sixty-one closely printed pages. See pp. 936–997.
[4] The counsel for the United States were G. Wiley Wells, United States Attorney for the northern district ; E. P. Jacobson, United States Attorney for the southern district ; H. C. Blackman, H. W. Walter, Van H. Manning, and G. P. M. Turner. For the petitioners were W. F. Dowd, S. J. Gholson, Reuben O. Reynolds, Robert E. Houston, J. D. McCluskey, and E. O. Sykes.

pany of United States infantry and one of cavalry were on hand to maintain order.

The petitioners denied the allegation in the bill of indictment, and declared that the witnesses who swore to the facts therein, perjured themselves; and that the district court of the United States had no jurisdiction, since the deceased and his alleged murderers were all citizens of the state of Mississippi, whose courts alone could try offences between its citizens. The question thus involved the constitutionality of the Enforcement Act. The court decided that the act was a constitutional measure; that Congress had the power, by virtue of the Fourteenth Amendment, to enact legislation for the protection of colored citizens and those who had supported the cause of the Union, even to the extent of depriving the state courts of jurisdiction over crimes committed against such persons; that, consequently, the court had jurisdiction of the cases in question. The judge refused to discharge the petitioners from prosecution, but released sixteen of them upon their own recognizance in the sum of $500 each, conditioned upon their appearance at the next term of court. Eight others were released upon a recognizance of $5000.

There was a general rejoicing among the whites at the release of the prisoners, for the belief seems to have been widespread among them that the prisoners had been wrongfully arrested and kept away from their families and crops.[1] Upon their arrival at Aberdeen, they were met by a large crowd of citizens, who offered their congratulations. There was cheering and firing of cannon, and other demonstrations of rejoicing.[2]

The first trial in the southern district began at Jackson, in February, 1872. It was the case of L. D. Belk, and grew out of the Meridian riot.

On April 10, 1872, district attorney Wells reported to the Attorney General of the United States the names of 490 persons who had been indicted in the northern district of Mississippi in pursuance of the Kuklux law; 172 who had been arrested and bound over; 28 who had pleaded guilty; and 14 who had confessed and turned state's evidence.[3] It appears from his report that the twenty-eight persons charged with the murder of the negro in Monroe County, and who were released upon writ of *habeas corpus* by Judge Hill,

---

[1] See on this point the testimony of General Gholson, pp. 878–879, and of Colonel Reynolds, p. 910.

[2] For account of this demonstration, see testimony of A. P. Huggins, p. 820 ; of S. J. Gholson, p. 878, and of R. O. Reynolds, p. 910.

[3] Ex. Docs. 2d Sess. 42d Cong. No. 268, pp. 30–44.

in June, 1871, pleaded guilty at the December term of the court, and it also appears that the sentence was not carried into execution.   The district attorney reported that no parties had been convicted except those who pleaded guilty, as the time of the court, up to the date of his reappointment, had been occupied in hearing petitions for writs of *habeas corpus* and motions to quash indictments, generally upon the ground of the unconstitutionality of the Kuklux law.   In a subsequent report he gave the names of 678 persons who were indicted in the northern district.   Three hundred and twenty-five of these cases were disposed of during the year 1872, there being 262 convictions.[1]   During the year ending June 20, 1873, 268 cases were disposed of, 184 of which were convictions.   On July 1, 1874, 171 cases were pending.

Mr. Jacobson, the United States attorney for the southern district, reported February 17, 1872, the names of 152 persons who had been indicted for violation of the Kuklux Act, the majority of the cases being "conspiracies to injure citizens because of the exercise of the right of free speech."   He gave the names of twelve persons who had confessed their guilt. It appears that there had been no convictions, up to the time of his report.[2]

It remains to be said in conclusion that much of the responsibility for these so-called Kuklux disorders must rest ultimately upon the authors of the congressional policy of reconstruction.   The policy by which political power in the South was suddenly transferred from the hitherto dominant class to a race emerging from slavery was one of the most dangerous experiments ever undertaken by the law-makers of any country.   That such a policy could have been carried through, unattended by social and political disorders, especially in view of all the attendant circumstances, no intelligent man will for a moment expect.   History abounds with illustrations of the truth that the secret conclave, the league, and the conspiracy are the sequences of political proscription and disfranchisement.   The Illuminés in France, the Tugendbund in Germany, the Carbonari in Italy, and Nihilism in Russia, are notable examples.   In the Southern states, opposition to the congressional policy of reconstruction did not take the form of armed and organized resistance, but of secret retaliation upon its agents, and especially favored beneficiaries, regardless of race, color, or nativity.

---

[1] Ex. Docs. 42d Cong. 3d Ses. No. 32, p. 11.
[2] Ex. Docs. 42d Cong. 2d Ses. No. 268, pp. 30–44.

CHAPTER TENTH

Educational Reconstruction

One of the schemes of the reconstructionists in Mississippi was the establishment of an elaborate system of public schools for the benefit of both races. Prior to the war, almost the only free schools in the state were those maintained out of the proceeds arising from the sale or lease of the so-called sixteenth section lands, granted to the state by Congress in the early part of the century. But as most of these lands had been lost by mismanagement, the number of such schools was not very large.[1] They were open, of course, only to white children.

The traditional preference for the private school, due largely to historical conditions in the South, had militated against the establishment of a uniform system of public education. However, a tendency in this direction had been in process of development at the outbreak of hostilities.

With the occupation of the state by the Federal armies, the work of teaching the negroes began. The first schools established for this purpose were at Corinth shortly after the occupation of that town by the Union troops in 1862. The American Missionary Association, the Freedmen's Aid Society, and the Society of Friends had established schools about Vicksburg before the close of the war. Upon the organization of the Freedmen's Bureau, a more systematic and comprehensive plan of negro education was undertaken. Joseph Warren, chaplain of a negro regiment, was appointed superintendent of freedmen's schools for the state at large. These schools were under military supervision, and benevolent associations supplied them with books and, in many cases, furnished clothing to the students. The following exhibit from the report of Superintendent Warren shows the number of schools and the enrollment on March 31, 1865 : —

[1] Joseph Bardwell, state superintendent of education in 1876, says there were 1116 public schools in Mississippi in 1860, attended by 30,970 pupils. See his report for 1876.

	SCHOOLS.	TEACHERS.	ENROLLMENT.
Vicksburg	11	22	1854
Camps near Vicksburg . . .	4	9	720
Davis Bend Colony	4	9	739
Natchez	11	20	1080

The teachers were, for the most part, supported by the Northwest Freedmen's Commission, the Friend's Society, the United Brethren, the American Baptist Home Missionary Society, the National Freedmen's Relief Association, the American Missionary Association, and the Reformed Presbyterian Board.

The bureau officials reported, in 1867, that Vicksburg had a negro normal school attended by 450 pupils, while the common schools of the city had an enrollment of 1700. In 1869, they reported that 81 negro schools, attended by 4344 pupils, were in operation in the state with 105 teachers, 40 of whom were colored.

The reconstruction convention, many of whose members were freedmen or Northern white men, was thoroughly imbued with the idea of education for the negro race. The constitution which they adopted made it the duty of the legislature to encourage by all suitable means the promotion of intellectual, scientific, moral, and agricultural improvement by establishing a uniform system of public schools for all children between the ages of five and twenty-one years. Constitutional provision was made for a permanent school fund, and the legislature was empowered to levy a poll tax not exceeding $2 per capita.[1]

Governor Alcorn in his inaugural announced emphatically that the government during his term would devote a large part of its energies and resources to the establishment of a system of common schools for the " poor white and colored children of the state who had been permitted in the past to grow up like wild flowers." [2] Some weeks later, he sent in a special message reminding the legislature of the constitutional obligation resting upon them in this matter, and urged immediate action upon the subject.[3] On the Fourth of July, the legislature passed an elaborate act " to regulate the sup-

[1] Constitution of 1868, Art. VIII. Secs. 5, 6, 7, 8.
[2] Senate Journal, 1870, p. 51.
[3] Appendix to Senate Journal, 1870, pp. 12–20.

port, organization, and maintenance of a uniform system of public education for the state." The act guaranteed to each child the advantages of a public school for at least four months of each year. A state board of education was created and vested with the power of general supervision of all public school interests. A state superintendent elected by the people was to be *ex officio* president of the board, and was charged with prescribing rules and regulations for the management of public schools. His salary was fixed by statute at $3000 per year, and he was allowed $1200 for clerk hire. County superintendents were to be appointed by the state board, and were charged with examining applicants, granting certificates, and performing such other duties as the state superintendent might designate. There was to be a board of six directors in each school district of the county. They were charged with establishing schools, hiring teachers, selecting text-books, and estimating the cost of constructing or renting buildings. Their compensation was fixed at $3 per day and mileage. Each board was also to have a secretary at a salary of $3 per day. Boards of supervisors were authorized to levy a tax sufficient to defray the expenses as estimated by the directors, except that they were limited to a tax rate of fifteen mills on the dollar. It was made the duty of the directors to establish a school wherever the parents or guardians of twenty-five children of school age should make written application for it.[1] Serious objections were at once urged against the law by Democrats and Republicans as well. In the first place, it provided for a system of education entirely too expensive, in view of the impoverished condition of the people. The desolation of a long war, a succession of crop failures, a Federal tax on cotton equivalent to one-fourth of its value, the loss of the slaves, and the increased taxes necessary for rebuilding and repairing public institutions, bore heavily upon a people who had never been accustomed to heavy taxes, even in the days of their prosperity. Moreover, the additional expense of educating their former slaves was naturally not very popular. It does not appear, however, that there was any opposition by the more intelligent whites to an economical scheme of negro education, for they clearly foresaw that the higher interests of society required that freedmen, who were now their political and civil equals, should receive at least the rudiments of

---

[1] Laws of 1870, pp. 1–20. All the members of the House Committee on Education were Northern men except two who were native freedmen.

an education. The chief source of objection was the needlessly expensive machinery provided for the administration
of the system.[1] The provision for boards of salaried school
directors and secretaries was entirely unnecessary.[2] The
county superintendents could easily have performed the
duties assigned to these boards. The authors of the system soon discovered and admitted this fact.

Another objection to the law was the requirement that
county superintendents, who were to be paid from the local
treasuries, should be appointed by the state board of education, thus depriving the people of the several counties of
the privilege of choosing competent residents to manage
their educational affairs, and compelling them in some instances to accept non-residents — " carpet baggers " selected
by the central authorities at Jackson.

Moreover, the tax payers were not only denied the right
of electing the county superintendents, but they were not
permitted to choose the still more important officials, the
directors who estimated the school taxes. These officials
were appointed by the boards of supervisors, who were themselves appointees of General Ames as military governor, for
it must be remembered that there was not until November,
1871, a general election for county and local officers. Thus
it happened that the entire management of the schools, from
the assessment of the taxes to the employment of the teachers, was in the control of the non-tax-paying class. These
officials, some of whom were familiar with the excellent systems of public education in the old states from which they
came, sought to create a similar system in the South, without,

---

[1] Ex-Senator A. G. Brown, in an address to an audience of colored people
in Copiah County, declared emphatically in favor of educating the freedmen.
The *Columbus Index* of Dec. 19, 1866, contains a long letter from the Bishop
of Mississippi urging planters to establish schools for the instruction of colored children on their farms. A state teachers' convention held at Jackson,
July 31, 1867, advised the establishment of a system of public schools for
the freedmen. It is probable that this would have been done by the native
whites had not the "carpet baggers" forestalled their action. The *Jackson
Clarion* of Feb. 11, 1866, urged that provision be made for the education of
the negro. It said : " The negro educated by the Yankee will be more dangerous than the Yankee himself. The negro educated by ourselves will double
our strength. Let us encourage Southern men to educate the negro." The
Hinds County Gazette of July 13, 1866, stated that " organized plans for the
intellectual improvement of the negro are being generally adopted throughout
the state." It announced that a school for the benefit of colored children
was in operation at Holly Springs, and was under the superintendence of
Judge Watson, and that Hon. Kinloch Falkner, formerly secretary of state,
was one of the teachers. There was also a school at Oxford, conducted by
Chancellor Waddell and several professors of the state university.

[2] The amount expended as compensation for directors in 1874 was $70,000.

apparently, taking into consideration the general impoverishment of the people and the traditional opposition to schools
maintained by the state.   Contributing little themselves to
the public burdens, they were often unable to appreciate the
real situation of those who did.   They proceeded on a scale
which would not have been considered burdensome in one
of the Northern states, but it was unduly expensive for a
Southern state in 1870.[1] It was alleged that the ordinary
log schoolhouses used before the war were not good enough
for the reconstructionists, but that they had to have substantial frame buildings, costing from $500 to $1000 each, and
supplied with furniture purchased by special agents in Northern cities.   Wherever twenty-five pickaninnies could be
assembled, a schoolhouse had to be built and a high-salaried
teacher employed.   The Southern whites refused to teach
negro children.   Negro teachers were not to be had.[2] Northern men and women were willing to teach freedmen's schools,
but a four months' term at ordinary wages did not afford
a sufficient inducement to attract them to the South.   It was
necessary, therefore, to pay salaries out of all due proportion
to the value of the service performed and the ability of the
people to pay, or else have the schools go without teachers.
During 1870 and 1871, teachers' salaries in Mississippi
ranged from $40 to $150 per month, according to the grade
of certificate, the average for the former year being $60.[3]

Examinations for teachers' licenses were not such as to
ascertain the real fitness of applicants or conduce to a

---

[1] State Superintendent Pease said of the law : " It would operate successfully in Ohio or Massachusetts, but not in Mississippi.   The experience
of the last twelve months shows that notwithstanding we have succeeded
in establishing a large number of schools, the work has been accomplished
at the expense of an enormous and unnecessary outlay of labor and money."
Report for 1871, p. 16.

[2] In Leflore County, in 1874, there were twenty-four schools and only nine
teachers available.   This was the case in most of the river counties.   Report
of state superintendent for 1875.

[3] The following exhibit, compiled from the annual reports of the state
superintendents, shows the average monthly salary of public school teachers
in Mississippi from 1870 to 1877 : —

1870	$60.
1871	58.90
1872	51.32
1873	50.
1874	55.47
1875	55.47
1876	39.87
1877	29.19½

The highest average in any one county was $75.26 in Chickasaw in 1873.

high standard of scholarship. They were asked a few oral questions by the superintendent in his private office, and the certificate was granted as a matter of course. The teachers from the North, it was alleged, became political emissaries among the negroes, organized them into "loyal leagues," and impressed upon them the duty of voting the Republican ticket. This was particularly true of negro teachers who went from Oberlin and other abolitionist centres.

Teachers of negro schools could not secure board in the homes of respectable white citizens, and consequently had to lodge with their colored patrons. Living upon terms of social equality with the negro was a grave offence in the mind of the Southern white, and was sure to cost the offender whatever respect the community might otherwise have entertained for him. It was too often taken as *prima facie* evidence of loose moral character, whereas, there can be little doubt that the great majority of the Northern white men and women who taught negro schools in the South were persons of high moral and intellectual character. However this may be, as time wore on, this prejudice disappeared to some extent, and a feeling of genuine admiration was cherished for the Northern teacher. It came to be a common remark that the "Yankee schoolmarm" with her twang, abominable pronunciation, and other faults, was *par excellence* the successful teacher and disciplinarian.

In October, 1870, the new system of free schools went into operation. In several counties where the blacks largely outnumbered the whites, the attempt to collect a heavy school tax met with more or less opposition. In Monroe County, where the black population exceeded the white population in the proportion of three to one, there was great dissatisfaction at the manner in which the authorities were alleged to have appropriated money for the maintenance of the schools. The county superintendent of education was Colonel Huggins, a Union soldier, and a former agent of the Freedmen's Bureau, who held at the same time the office of United States assessor of Internal Revenue. It was alleged that his estimates for the support of the public schools were unnecessarily large, and that he refused to make use of schoolhouses offered him without charge, but instead, erected new frame buildings throughout the county, and paid teachers unreasonably large salaries.[1] The superintendent charged that the

---

[1] The salaries of teachers in Monroe County ranged from $50 to $150 per month, according to the grade of certificate, the average being $70 in 1873.

Kuklux attempted to break up the schools, and that they notified two of the school directors, who had been particularly prominent in fixing the estimates, to resign their positions within a certain time or they would be "dealt with" according to the well-known customs of the Klan. The directors promptly complied with the request.[1] Nearly all of the teachers in that part of the county east of the Tombigbee River, twenty-six in number, were notified to close their schools. One of these was a lady from Geneseo, Illinois. She had been sent to Mississippi by the American Missionary Society, and was engaged in teaching a small school at Cotton Gin Port at a salary of $75 per month. She had endeavored to secure board with a white family, but being unsuccessful, had taken up her abode with a family of negroes. She was visited by the Kuklux in March, 1871, and was ordered to leave. She promptly obeyed the order.[2] Dr. Ebart, one of the school directors, a Southern man and the teacher of a white school in Aberdeen, received a similar notification. On account of opposition to the extravagances of the school authorities, the board of supervisors declined to levy the special tax of 10½ mills.[3]

In Lowndes County, there was also more or less opposition to the course of the school authorities.[4] Lowndes, like Monroe, had a large negro population, there being four times as many colored children of school age as white children. Sixty public schools were opened and teachers employed at salaries ranging from $50 to $150 per month, the average being $78. A number of school buildings were erected, and the superintendent was authorized to proceed to St. Louis and purchase furniture and apparatus, his expenses being paid out of the county funds. The board of supervisors levied a special tax of $95,000 in addition to the poll tax. The whites protested, called a meeting at Columbus, and appointed a committee to urge a reduction of the levy, and another to

In addition to the poll tax, the school directors in that county levied a property tax of 10½ mills on the dollar. The law allowed 15 mills. Colonel Huggins testified before the Kuklux committee at Washington that the whole amount expended for school furniture in Monroe County was $2100, and that the purchases were made in St. Louis. The average cost of the buildings erected was about $400 each. One was built in Aberdeen, at a cost of $6120. Seventy-five schools were established and twenty-four buildings erected at an aggregate cost of $10,000.

[1] Testimony of A. P. Huggins, Kuklux Report, p. 281.

[2] Kuklux Report, p. 777.

[3] Testimony of F. H. Little, Kuklux Report, p. 367.

[4] The superintendent was Dr. J. N. Bishop, a Northern man, at present a physician of note in New York City.

investigate and report upon the financial condition of the county.[1] The opposition became so strong that the board decided to reduce the assessment one-half. Several teachers were whipped, and a number of schools broken up by the Kuklux. One of the teachers who was thus dealt with was a Northern man, who boarded in a negro family and taught a negro school about seven miles from Columbus. He was visited by a band of disguised men, and told that he had no business teaching "nigger" schools, and that the whole system was a humbug and an imposition on the people.[2]

The Rev. Mr. Galloway, a Congregational minister from the North, and teacher of a negro free school at Caladonia, received a call of a similar character.[3] Two other teachers who received orders to close their schools were old citizens of the county, and one of them was a one-armed Confederate soldier.[4] It will thus be seen that the victims of these proceedings were limited to no particular class of teachers, but included Southern as well as Northern teachers and ex-Confederate as well as ex-Union soldiers. They all appear to have been honorable and well qualified. It is reasonable to conclude, therefore, that the opposition was not in any sense political, nor does it seem to have been directed against the public school system *per se*, but rather against its abuses.

In Noxubee County, the only interference with the public school system was the burning of three or four schoolhouses.[5] The county superintendent was notified by the "Grand Cyclops" to resign his position.[6]

In the adjoining county of Winston, the opposition was more marked, and likewise took the form of schoolhouse burning. Governor R. C. Powers told the congressional committee in March, 1871, that no one had been permitted to teach a negro school or a white public school in the county for seven or eight months, and that every house in the county where a school was being taught, except one, had been burned.[7] On the 6th of April, a mass meeting of citizens was held at the county seat, and resolutions were adopted

---

[1] The report of the committee is printed in full in the *Columbus Index* of June 1, 1871.

[2] Testimony of Lewis Perkins, Kuklux Report, p. 899 ; also Testimony of H. B. Whitfield, p. 420.

[3] Testimony of J. F. Galloway, *ibid.* p. 663.

[4] Testimony of H. B. Whitfield, *ibid.* p. 420.

[5] Testimony of A. K. Davis, *ibid.* p. 477.

[6] Testimony of J. B. Allgood, *ibid.* p. 499.

[7] Testimony of R. C. Powers, *ibid.* p. 588.

condemning these acts, after which it appears that no more houses were burned.

The most notable case of interference with the schools in Chickasaw County was the whipping of Cornelius McBride, a young Irishman from Cincinnati, who had previously taught a negro school in Oktibbeha County. With the consent of the whites he opened a school in Chickasaw County, and was kindly treated by his neighbors. On account of his popularity and intelligence he was asked by the whites to take charge of their Sunday school. For a while, after the beginning of the Kuklux raids, he was not molested, but in the latter part of March, 1871, they went to his house, took him out, and severely whipped him. Refusing to be deterred by the threats of the Kuklux, he returned to his school the following morning, and taught it out without further molestation. According to McBride's testimony, two hundred free schools had been opened in the county, all being supplied with teachers at salaries ranging from $40 to $100 per month.[1]

Mr. Schneider, the teacher of a negro school in Warren County, received the following notice from the Kuklux : —

HEADQUARTERS K.K.K. March 3, 1871.

MR. S : — As it is customary for our order never to attack any one without just telling him the cause and giving him fair warning, we wish to say, that having had your case before the order at its last meeting, you were found guilty of certain misdemeanors by a unanimous vote.

Charge 1. Associating with negroes in preference to the white race as God ordained. Guilty.

Charge 2. For being instrumental in the removal of one of our fellow citizens from the office of justice of the peace in the county and beat where you reside and placing a carpet bagger, negro, and scallawag in his stead. Guilty.

There was one other charge, but there being a few dissenting votes on this — not guilty.

It is an established rule of the order never to give a man more than three days to leave the county, but taking it into careful consideration your situation and the size of your carpet bag, we have concluded to extend the time to five days ; at the expiration of said time, we will wait upon you if you are in the county. Hoping that you will view the subject in a sensible light and

---

[1] See Kuklux Report, pp. 325–342. He was doubtless in error as to the number of schools in the county. None of the counties, except Hinds and Warren, had as many as one hundred and fifty public schools at that time.

leave, as we always dislike to use harsh means, our object being to purify our state, and we commence our work on scallawags and carpet baggers first.

Yours, etc.

A wronged and outraged Mississippian
and chief of the Kuklux Klan.[1]

In Pontotoc County, a number of the teachers were notified by the Kuklux that unless they closed their schools, they would be "dealt with." In every instance they were teachers of negro schools, and oddly enough all except one were Democrats. Sixty-four free schools had been established, and all of the teachers except eleven were Democrats. An attempt to "Kuklux" Mr. Flournoy, the superintendent, resulted disastrously for one of the members of the band. He proved to be a young man of respectability in the neighborhood.[2]

At first the belief was general that it was the purpose of the reconstructionists to force mixed schools upon the whites, and, to be sure, there was no express provision in the constitution for separate schools, a proposition to incorporate such a provision having been voted down, every colored member opposing the motion. On this subject, the *Jackson Clarion*[3] said: "No intelligent and true friend of the negro, much less of the white race, can look upon the measure (the provision in the constitution of 1868 relative to public schools) with any other feeling than that of disgust and loathing. Its authors have sown the seeds of discord between the two races. They cannot and will not intermingle on terms of social equality as contemplated by this odious scheme." Again the *Clarion* declared that it would require a standing army to enforce such a provision.[4] When it became evident, however, that there was no intention of establishing mixed schools, much of the opposition wore away, so that Superintendent Pease was able to report in 1871 that "a most marvellous revolution of sentiment" in regard to negro education had already taken place. As the sentiment in favor of negro schools increased, State Superintendent Gathright, a native Southerner, advised the white teachers in a public address in 1876, to lay aside their prejudices and teach negro schools. He argued that such a policy would keep in the state the large sums that went to pay Northern teachers. It would also

---

[1] Report state superintendent of education, 1871, p. 69.
[2] Testimony of R. W. Flournoy, Kuklux Report, pp. 82–95.
[3] Issue of Feb. 21, 1868.
[4] Issue of March 11, 1868.

remove what was regarded as an objectionable element, namely, the class of teachers that organized and controlled the negroes politically. The address was widely commented on at the time. The *Vicksburg Herald*, under the caption " Wheat *vs.* Chaff," said: " The recent pronunciamento of Professor Gathright, the head centre of the educational interests of the state, contains some sound wheat and more or less chaff. His advice to the teachers of the state now working under him was good to a certain extent; but when he endeavors to persuade the daughters of our state to enter the field as teachers of negro schools, it would be strange if the proposition created much enthusiasm. A lady who is capable of teaching at all must be sore in need if she has to resort to a colored school to eke out a precarious existence, and we hope the time will never come when any true daughter of the South will ever be put to that necessity. . . . Professor Gathright no doubt means well, but that does not help his proposition." [1]

The results of the first year of free education in Mississippi were encouraging to the reconstructionists, notwithstanding the undoubted difficulties which they had to confront. State Superintendent Pease reported that more than 3000 free schools had been opened, with an attendance of 66,257 pupils. Of the 3600 teachers employed, all except 399 were white. Five hundred school sites had been donated and 200 buildings erected by private subscription. The total expenditures, on account of public education for the year, were $869,766.76, an amount which exceeded the government expenditures for all other purposes.[2] This burden

[1] Issue of May 12, 1876. The *Hinds County Gazette*, as early as July 13, 1866, lamented that "Cape Cod schoolmarms" were swarming into Mississippi, and to counteract the evil of which, the white citizens in every neighborhood where there was a colored school, were advised to select some " well-known, competent, and unobjectionable" woman to teach the school, as a "full and free indorsement of the community" would prevent ostracism of her. The editor noticed a great desire among the negroes for " Yankee " teachers.

[2] The *Jackson Clarion* did not think the educational outlook afforded much cause for congratulation. It said: "The present system of common schools is a humbug. One million dollars was spent last year, with very little advancement in learning. The *modus operandi* is a very few hours of instruction each day — school closed eight months in the year : a greedy swarm of useless drones in the shape of school officers doing nothing and living high on extravagant salaries, squandering the vast school funds in thieving combinations and contracts for fine furniture and useless books, and for building fine schoolhouses. The whole thing is an abortion, a swindle, a carpet-bag fraud, on the people." The same paper announced that the Democratic party proposed to reform all abuses, maintain good schools for ten months in the year, cut off all lazy and useless officers, get good teachers, reduce the number, and pay them well, build plain, cheap houses, and give all the children, black and white, a good education for half the money that was being spent.

might have been much lighter, had it not been for the mismanagement of the school funds prior to the war.[1] More
than a million dollars of sixteenth section funds, to say nothing of the Seminary and Chickasaw funds, were lost through
poor management. Few things in the history of the state
afford more cause for regret than the manner in which
these munificent endowments were administered. Had they
been judiciously managed, they would have yielded revenue
enough in 1870 to defray the entire cost of the public school
system.

Governor Alcorn, in his annual message to the legislature
in 1871, recommended that county superintendents be made
elective by the local magistrates of the school districts, as,
under the appointive system, men "absolutely unacquainted
with the people of the counties to which they were sent"
had been selected in many instances. In a special message
of April 1, he charged that the school directors "presented
an administration which threatened, by the wantonness of its
extravagance, to impress the more restive of the population
with a sense that they are being oppressed by taxation."
"While the average pay of the teachers in the Northern
schools," he said, "is less than $300 a year, salaries in Mis-
sissippi range from $720 to $1920 a year." Relative to the
extravagances of the school authorities in certain counties,
he said: "With the purchase or erection of brick schoolhouses in some districts, and the furnishing of schoolhouses
in others with elegant desks and office chairs, and the supplying in others of apparatus better suited to the demands of
the academy than of the common school, we may accept the
conclusions that there is some foundation for the general
outcry against the alleged plunder of the school funds. In a
few short months of actual work in the county of Lafayette,
the school board is charged, on very grave authority, with
having expended $3500 in cash and $4000 in credit, with
little or nothing to show for the money. In the interests,
not only of the school funds, but of the peace and order of
the state, I recommend to you earnestly to set some limit on
the option of school boards as to their outlays."[2]

By an act of April 17, 1873, the public school system was
reorganized and simplified. The boards of school directors
were abolished, and trustees were made elective by the
patrons. A general property tax of four mills on the dollar

---

[1] Nineteen of the sixty-four county superintendents in 1870 reported a
loss of $418,765 of the sixteenth section school funds.
[2] Appendix to H. and S. Journal, 1871, p. 1198.

was levied for school purposes, and teachers' salaries were fixed at from $35 to $75 per month. It was still thought, however, that the popular election of county superintendents would be " a disastrous blow " to public education in the state.[1]

After the restoration of the democracy in 1876, the system was still further changed, and expenditures largely reduced.[2]

The first reconstruction state superintendent of education was Henry R. Pease, a Northern man, an ex-Union soldier, and an agent of the Freedmen's Bureau. In 1865, he became superintendent of education in Louisiana by military order. Later, he became superintendent of the educational department of the Freedmen's Bureau in Mississippi, and upon the readmission of the state to the Union, was elected superintendent under the new constitution. It devolved upon him to organize the system of free schools. His competency was never questioned, but the demand of the colored race for office, in 1873, caused him to be set aside for a negro named Cordoza. Cordoza, at the time of his. election, was under indictment for malfeasance as circuit clerk of Warren County. Upon his impeachment and removal from office in 1876 for misappropriation of school funds, Mr. Gathright, a Southern man, became superintendent.

It remains to notice briefly the condition of higher education in Mississippi, so far as it was directly or remotely affected by the Civil War and Reconstruction. Soon after the adoption of the ordinance of secession, most of the students of the university organized themselves into a military company and applied to the governor to muster them into the service. In spite of the appeal of President F. A. P. Barnard and Professor Lamar, the governor sent up a mustering officer, and the boys were enlisted. The president then addressed a circular letter to the parents of the young men, asking for authority to demand their discharge. Most of the replies assured the president that the enlistments were approved by the parents and guardians concerned. The company was shortly afterwards ordered to Richmond, and took part in the first great battle of the war. Soon after the outbreak of hostilities the university closed its doors, the members of the Faculty resigned, and most of them entered

[1] Report of state superintendent, 1874, p. 6.

[2] Thus the expenditures on account of the state superintendent's office in 1874 were $17,816 ; in 1877 they were $3768. The cost of clerk hire was reduced from $2000 to nothing; the cost of printing was reduced from $13,000 in 1874 to $1000 in 1876. The aggregate salaries of county superintendents were reduced from $48,350 in 1875 to $9760 in 1876.

the service of the Confederacy. President Barnard, although a slaveholder, and although his sympathies were in some degree with the people of the South, among whom he had lived for twenty years, was a Union man, and declined to join the secession movement. He went North, and in 1864 became president of Columbia University, where he had a long and brilliant career.[1]

During the war, the buildings and university grounds were occupied first by the Confederate and then by the Union troops. No permanent injury seems to have been done the institution by either army, so that the work of reorganization was comparatively easy.[2] Governor Sharkey, in the proclamation announcing his appointment as provisional governor, directed the trustees to meet at Oxford, July 31, for the purpose of reopening the university. The meeting was duly held, a Faculty appointed, and in September, the university opened its doors. The work of the university was not materially affected by the reconstruction policy. The district commanders did not interfere with its administration, but regularly issued the warrants for its support, and showed no disposition to impair its usefulness.[3] The trustees ap-

---

[1] Professor Barnard was one of the many Northern men who were living in the South at the beginning of the war. He became president of the University of Mississippi in 1856, and his administration was in the highest degree satisfactory to the board of trustees. An incident of his administration was the investigation of a charge that he was "unsound" on the slavery question and guilty of advocating the acceptance of negro testimony in a case of discipline in which one of the students was accused of assaulting a negro servant. Barnard, with two other Northern-born members of the Faculty, voted in favor of a motion to convict the student upon the testimony of the servant, while the Southern members voted against it. The matter seems to have excited a good deal of comment, and immediately after the publication of the charge concerning his "unsoundness," the president demanded an investigation. The board of trustees made a full investigation, and reported that the charge was "wholly unsustained by the evidence." Professor Barnard testified before the board as follows: "I am a slaveholder, and if I know myself, I am sound on the slavery question." Jefferson Davis strenuously urged him to accept government service under the Confederacy, but he declined. His departure from the state was the cause of great regret among the University trustees, Judge Sharkey declaring it to be nothing less than a "public calamity."

The testimony and proceedings in the "trial" of Dr. Barnard are published in the appendix to the House and Senate Journals of 1859. See also Fulton's Memoirs of F. A. P. Barnard, ch. x.

[2] On the 7th of December, 1863, the legislature passed a resolution reciting that the university buildings had been occupied by state and Confederate troops who had done "great damage to the buildings, grounds, furniture, and books, and had destroyed the beautiful groves, much of it in apparent wantonness, reflecting no credit upon the officers, and calculated to add very little to the character of the army." Laws, p. 232.

[3] Mayes's Hist. of Education in Mississippi, p. 162.

pointed by the district commanders were old and highly respected citizens of the state, and the appointments were approved by all parties. The reconstruction legislature, however, was not disposed to pursue a non-interference policy, and in May, 1870, it passed an act to "reconstruct" the university. A new board of trustees, among whom were several "carpet baggers" and a number of native Republicans, was appointed in pursuance of the act. The "radicalization" of the university was the subject of loud complaint, and some of the newspapers called upon Democratic members of the Faculty to resign, and Democratic citizens were advised not to patronize an institution where their sons were likely to have their political principles corrupted.[1] This view was not favorably received, and it appears that but one or two members of the Faculty left the university in consequence of the reorganization of the board. The attendance, however, fell off in a marked degree.[2]

It appears that no attempt was made to "radicalize" the faculty, and there is no evidence that more than one appointment was influenced by purely political considerations.[3] During this period a good deal of nervousness existed among the whites, for fear that some colored student would demand admission to the university, for there appeared to be no legal ground on which he could be excluded. The constitution and laws had distinctly provided that all distinctions and discriminations founded on race or color should be prohibited, and the Supreme Court had upheld the Civil Rights Act in the case of a negro who refused to occupy a particular seat in a Jackson theatre.[4] The Republican party, in its platform of 1873, declared that it recognized no distinctions in the rights of all children to equal privileges, and access to all public schools, colleges, and universities, and declared, moreover, that should any of the said institutions deny admission to any child on account of color, the party was pledged to enforce this declaration by appropriate legislation.

[1] Mayes's Hist. of Education in Mississippi, p. 164.
[2] The university opened in September, 1870, with only sixty students, and as late as January, there were only one hundred present. The *Jackson Clarion* of Oct. 11, 1870, said : "The people have revolted at the thought of placing their sons under radical patronage, when the country abounds with schools uncorrupted by radical influences."
[3] Some of the Republicans arraigned the Faculty for permitting certain students in their commencement addresses to make use of "partisan language," and on one occasion, when a young man was discoursing on "Our Dead Heroes," a radical member of the board "insulted" him by leaving the hall. The affair was the subject of a good deal of newspaper comment at the time. *Jackson Clarion*, July 24, 1873.
[4] Donnell *vs.* Mississippi, 48 Miss. 661.

The uncertainty as to what action the university authorities would take in the event the radicals should insist upon the admission of negro students led Judge Hudson of Yazoo City to address an open letter to the Faculty propounding this question : " Will the Faculty, as now composed, receive or reject an applicant for admission as a student on account of color ? " The chancellor and seven professors, in a signed statement, replied that they would be " governed by considerations of race and color," and that should the applicant belong to the negro race, they would, without hesitation, reject him, and as the university was established exclusively for the white race, they would " instantly resign if the trustees should require them to receive negro students." " This," said the *Jackson Clarion*, " is a declaration of war against the fundamental principle of the Republican party, and we warmly endorse their stand."[1] Governor Alcorn denounced the letter of the professors as the " stuff of political tricksters," told them if they wished to resign they were perfectly welcome to do so at any time, and taunted them with being an " obsequious faculty, acting under the fear of such men as Judge Hudson."[2] Shortly after the publication of the correspondence referred to, Mr. Flournoy, the radical editor of *Equal Rights*, published at Pontotoc, announced in his paper that he purposed bringing the matter before the United States courts under the Civil Rights Act. " We shall," he said, " endeavor to find a colored boy competent to enter the university in a year or two at least, present him for admission, and test the question whether the professor or the Constitution is supreme."[3] The board of trustees knew that to dismiss the Faculty or open the doors to colored students would mean the breaking up of the university, consequently their insistence on these points was abandoned. No colored students ever applied for admission to the white university. This was probably on account of the liberal provision made for their race elsewhere; namely, the establishment of several normal schools and a state university. The university was located at Rodney, and its first president was ex-United States Senator Revels. The same appropriations were made for its support as for the white university, and for several years it was in a flourishing condition. Governor Ames, however, in 1874, removed Revels, his policy being to retain

---

[1] The correspondence between Judge Hudson and the Faculty is printed in the *Jackson Clarion* of Oct. 11, 1870.
[2] *Jackson Clarion*, July 31, 1871.
[3] Quoted in *Jackson Clarion*, Nov. 25, 1870.

as few of Alcorn's appointees as possible.[1] Revels's successor, unfortunately, did not command the respect of the students, and there were charges affecting his personal integrity and private character.   The students revolted at the removal of Revels, and about sixty of them withdrew.   The president was unable to maintain discipline, the university was declared to be in " rebellion," and a joint committee of the legislature was appointed to investigate its condition.   They reported that there was a president whose sole duty was to hold evening prayers and exercises on Sunday at a salary of $2500 a year; that the charges of drunkenness, profanity, and lewdness against several officials of the university were found to be true; that the president should be required to teach at least one class; that the offices of superintendent and treasurer should be abolished; and the annual appropriations for its support reduced from $50,000 a year to $15,000.[2]

One of the features of the educational system of the reconstructionists was the establishment of a series of fellowships in the two universities, with stipends of $100 each in addition to free tuition.   Each county was entitled to as many annual fellowships in each institution as it had representatives in the legislature.   As the course embraced six years' work, it might easily have happened that some counties would have had as many as thirty fellows in each university. It does not appear, however, that more than $1200 was appropriated by any county in one year on this account.

Two state normal schools for the colored race were established at Holly Spring and Tougaloo, and were liberally supported by the legislature.

When the reconstructionists surrendered the government to the democracy, in 1876, the public school system which they had fathered had become firmly established, its efficiency increased, and its administration made somewhat less expensive than at first.   There does not seem to have been any dis-

---

[1] Governor Ames wrote letters to the presidents of a number of Northern colleges and universities, asking them to recommend a suitable person for the head of the university.   One of these was directed to a gentleman in Washington who was requested to ascertain if Frederick Douglas would accept the position, and if he was a supporter of Alcorn.   Correspondence of Governor Ames, May 25, 1874.

[2] The report of the committee is signed by three colored and two white members.   Senate Journal, 1875, p. 321.

The *Jackson Clarion* of June 30, 1875, said: " During the last four years Alcorn University has cost the state $240,000.   It would have been more economical for the state to have boarded the students at the Fifth Avenue Hotel, New York, and sent them to Columbia University."

position upon the part of the Democrats to abolish it or impair its efficiency. On the other hand, they kept their promise to the negroes, made provisions for continuing the system, and guaranteed an annual five months' term instead of four, as formerly. Moreover, the cost of maintaining the schools was very largely reduced, and the administration decentralized and democratized, thereby removing what had been a strong obstacle to peace and good order. And thus the system of public education, unpopular at first, on account of the circumstances surrounding its establishment, has grown in favor with the people, until to-day it is the chief pride of the commonwealth, and is destined to be the chief means of solving the great problem which the Civil War left as a legacy to the white race.

CHAPTER ELEVENTH

The Revolution

I. THE ELECTION CAMPAIGN OF 1875

THE election campaign of 1875 was the most exciting in the history of the state, and in some respects it will compare favorably with any political struggle that ever occurred on American soil. The officers to be elected that year were the state treasurer, members of Congress, members of the legislature, and all county and local officers. The Democrats resolved to make a supreme effort to carry the election. For the first time since 1868, they were strongly united, and with some hope of success, although a Republican majority of 30,000 was to be overcome. Since 1868, they had made no effort to carry the election, with the exception of the feeble attempt to elect Judge Dent in 1869. In 1873, they virtually disbanded and declined to even nominate a ticket, gave up their party name, and supported Alcorn for governor, and Greeley for President. They were now encouraged by the schism in the Republican party, having reason to believe that they would secure the support of many of the white Republicans and negroes who were identified with the state. The result of the recent election in the North, by which the House of Representatives had become Democratic, also gave them hope. The initial movement in the campaign of 1875 began as early as the 3d of March, when a caucus of Democratic members of the legislature was held in the capitol. It appointed a committee of 42, under the chairmanship of John M. Stone, to effect the reorganization of the party. The committee met on the 17th of May, and set August 3 as the date for the state convention, and recommended the nomination of the ablest and best men for Congress, for the legislature, and for the state offices.[1] The convention which met August 3 was a large and representative one. It was addressed by the Hon. L. Q. C. Lamar, fresh from his eulogy on Sumner, and at the time the idol of his party. He advised strongly against

[1] Mayes's Lamar, pp. 249–250.

the "color line," and urged the whites to do nothing to abridge the rights of the colored race.[1] The platform adopted recognized the civil and political equality of all men, favored public education, the selection of honest officials, economy in the administration of the government, biennial sessions of the legislature, an able and competent judiciary and the restriction of its duties to judicial functions only, the discontinuance of excessive local and special legislation, and the elevation of the standard of official character. The chief arraignment of the Ames government is found in plank number twelve. It reads as follows: "The building up of partisan newspapers by legislation, the arming of the militia in time of peace, the unconstitutional attempt to take from the people the election of tax collectors, the attempted passage of the Metropolitan Police Bill, the attempted corruption of the judiciary by the use of executive patronage, we denounce as great outrages upon constitutional liberty; while, as evidence of the utter incapacity of our present rulers to administer the affairs of the state, we point to the mass of confusion in which the revenue and registration laws of the state has been placed, the necessity of extraordinary sessions of the legislature to cure the blunders and follies of the regular sessions, and to the repeated executive and legislative acts which have been by the Supreme Court declared unconstitutional and void."

Another important duty of the convention was the selection of an executive committee to conduct the campaign. J. Z. George, a late brigadier general in the Confederate army, and at that time one of the leading attorneys of the state, was appointed chief manager of the campaign.

The campaign was one of unprecedented vigor and enthusiasm. The whites left their fields, shops, and stores to take part in the canvass, and for three months little else seems to have been done. Every man was pressed into service. "Mississippi demands," said the *Macon Beacon*, "that every man shall do his duty in the campaign." The Republicans were almost equally active and determined. They devoted themselves to organizing and drilling the negroes, who were enrolled in clubs, usually one in each community; weekly meetings were held, generally in out-of-the-way places and at night, at which the negroes were harangued by white leaders, who carefully instructed them how to register, how to approach the polls, and how to vote. Judge Watson says he

---

[1] The *Clarion* of August 4 said that his speech was "the ablest made in the capitol since the war; massive in argument, irresistible in logic, statesmanlike in the policy it advocated, and eloquent."

heard them on the stump advise the negroes never to follow their old masters in politics, but to watch them and be sure to take a different course, and they would certainly be right.[1] They were told that the Southern white man was their enemy, and that Democratic success meant the reinslavement of the colored race. This was the most effective argument of the Republicans — it was a scarecrow that had not entirely disappeared as late as the presidential election of 1884. The negroes were also made to believe that the defeat of the Republican party would insure the disestablishment of the public school system, or the denial of its benefits to the colored race. They were told that General Grant wanted them to vote the Republican ticket. These, and many other representations of a similar character, were made by those interested in securing the negro vote. Upon the advice of the state committee, the whites organized themselves into clubs, generally of a semi-military character, had parades, barbecues, mammoth torchlight processions with banners and transparencies, fired anvils and even used cannons in their demonstrations.[2] Many of their organizations were furnished with military equipments, for which purpose extensive importations of arms were made, almost every town receiving a consignment. A Vicksburg hardware merchant testified that his business was larger in 1875 than at any time in its history, except the first year after the war. A well-known Mississippian who occupied a judicial position in Washington told the *New York Times* correspondent, October 22, that both parties in Mississippi were arming, each determined to carry the election, that 500 Spencer rifles had been brought to the small town in which he had formerly resided, and upward of 10,000 had been brought into the state at large. Another judge testified that $4000 had been spent for arms in his county.[3] These preparations were the subject of much edi-

---

[1] Boutwell Report, p. 42.

[2] In Monroe, Lowndes, Hinds, Kemper, and other counties, cannon were purchased, furnished by the national committee, or borrowed from municipalities in other states. Constant calls were made upon Chairman George for cannon to be used in firing salutes on barbecue days and similar occasions. The cannon were dragged from point to point, and discharged along the public roads and in the neighborhood of Republican meetings. The commander of the United States post at Jackson loaned the Democrats a cannon, and on the occasion of a parade, they fired it so near the governor's house as to break the window panes. The commander of the post was court-martialled for allowing the United States ordnance to be used for this purpose. The Republicans alleged that this kind of demonstration terrified the negroes and kept them at home. The allegation was not without foundation.

[3] Boutwell Report, p. 1143.

torial comment in the Republican press.   The *Clarion* replied that it was not unusual for gentlemen of means to purchase improved firearms.

Monster open-air meetings were held in almost every neighborhood of the state.   The chairman of the executive committee was overwhelmed with requests for speakers.[1] Orators of national repute were brought from other states to aid in arousing the people to a sense of the importance of the contest.   The *New York Tribune* said the only campaign in the country that had any life in it was the one in Mississippi; that the Democrats were holding immense mass meetings throughout the state, and a notable feature of these gatherings was the attendance of large numbers of negroes.

II. RIOTS AND DISTURBANCES IN 1875

The peace and quiet of the state were disturbed several times during the progress of the campaign by conflicts between the whites and blacks.   The first of these occurred at Vicksburg on the occasion of a Fourth of July celebration. It resulted in the breaking up of the meeting and the death of several negroes.

Another " riot " occurred at Yazoo City, September 1.   On the occasion of a political meeting at which Colonel Morgan, the leading Republican politician of the county, was speaking, a disturbance was raised which resulted in the death of one white man and three negroes.   The news soon spread that the negroes were " rising " and coming to sack the town. Great excitement prevailed, the city was put under martial law, and an ex-Union soldier deputed to assume control of affairs.   He organized patrols, and picketed the roads leading into the town.   Two military companies were hastily organized for defence, and were joined by " Northern men and Southern men, Democrats and Republicans." [2]   The expected

---

[1] Hon. L. Q. C. Lamar was the most popular speaker in the campaign of 1875.   Every community wanted him.   Editor Barksdale of the *Clarion* and Judge Wiley P. Harris came next in demand.   During the two months preceding the election, General George sent and received more than five hundred telegrams, relating to the management of the campaign.   They are printed in the Boutwell Report as a part of the documentary evidence.

[2] See testimony of W. H. Foote, a colored member of the legislature. Boutwell Report, p. 1666 ; also the testimony of Garnett Andrews, the ex-Union soldier referred to, p. 1699.   It is utterly impossible for a Northern man, unacquainted with conditions in the South, to understand correctly the terror which an apprehended negro insurrection creates in the minds of the whites.   Colonel Andrews testified as follows, on this point : " From the

invasion never took place. Colonel Morgan fled from the city, and went to Jackson to lay his case before the governor, who finally offered to send him back and reinstate him in his office by means of an escort of three hundred colored militia. The citizens of the county were "alarmed" at the proposed invasion of their county by negro troops, and accordingly organized to resist it. The borders of the county and the roads leading thereto were watched night and day, and the whites were kept informed by telegraph of every movement of the state authorities. The *Jackson Clarion* of October 13 declared that "the invasion of Yazoo with an armed negro militia, fired with bloody intents," would justify whatever measures the citizens might "see fit to adopt for the protection of their lives and sacred honor." The excitement became so intense that Colonel Morgan wisely declined to return under such circumstances. There is reason to believe that had the "invasion" been attempted, few colored militiamen would have escaped to tell the tale. The purpose of the whites in this respect was open and avowed.[1]

On October 9 occurred the Friars Point conflict in Coahoma County. Coahoma, like most of the river counties, had colored officials. The sheriff was from Oberlin, Ohio. The

time of this riot up to the time of the election, and a short time after, I have never suffered such an amount of anguish and alarm in all my life. I had served through the whole war as a soldier in the army of northern Virginia, and saw all of it ; but I never did experience such fear and alarm. And this was the universal feeling among the white people. It showed itself upon the countenances of the people. Men looked haggard and pale after undergoing this sort of thing for six weeks or a month, and I have felt, when I lay down to sleep, that neither myself nor my wife and children were in safety." Boutwell Testimony, II. pp. 1201–1255.

[1] Colonel Morgan made a lengthy report to the governor, on affairs in Yazoo County. It fills ten columns in the *Jackson Pilot*. Subsequently, he published a volume of 512 pages, giving an account of his varied experiences in Mississippi. The work is entitled Yazoo, or the Picket Line of Freedom (Rufus H. Darby, Washington, 1884). The career of the "carpet bagger" is well illustrated in the life of this man. He was a Union soldier from Wisconsin, settled in Mississippi at the close of the war, and engaged in cotton-planting and lumbering. Like many Northern men who went South after the war, he failed in the business of cotton-planting, and entered politics. He says he was received by the Southern people with the greatest kindness, when he first went among them, but lost his popularity on account of his championship of the Freedmen's Bureau and his association with the negroes. After the revolution, he went to Washington, where, like many other carpet baggers in a similar position, he secured employment in one of the executive departments. Here he remained until ousted by Secretary Lamar in 1884. He then went West, where he now lives. Morgan's correspondence shows that he is a man of education, and his political opponents testify that as an officer he was able and faithful.

state senator was colored, and was also from Ohio. While holding the office of senator he was appointed receiver of public moneys, and within a year he defaulted with a large sum and ran away. Another Ohio negro was sent over to the county from Jackson to fill the senatorial vacancy, and was easily elected. While holding this office, he was appointed county superintendent of education, and special agent to collect taxes. The sheriff wanted him to be elected clerk of the county. A convention was held, the sheriff getting his ticket through, whereupon the dissatisfied Republicans, among whom were United States Senator Alcorn, General Chalmers, Judge Reed, and other large property holders, issued a call for a mass meeting, at which Alcorn denounced the colored ring in severe terms. The sheriff announced his intention of replying to the speech on the following Monday, and sent runners throughout the county to bring in negroes to protect him in his right of speech. On Monday, a messenger came in and reported that an armed body of negroes was approaching the town with the intention of sacking and burning it. Alcorn and Chalmers hastily organized a force of whites and went to meet the invading host. The negroes were ordered to disperse; a battle ensued in which eight men were killed, two being whites.[1]

The riot at Rolling Fork in December was, like the others, a race conflict. Issaquena County, of which Rolling Fork is the county seat, is situated in the Mississippi " bottoms," and was made up of large plantations upon which, in some instances, as many as five hundred negroes lived, with perhaps but one or two white families. The owners of the land usually lived in the hilly portion of the state. The management of the county affairs was almost entirely in the hands of the negroes, there being at this time but two white officers in the county. The " massacre " grew out of a drunken brawl between a young white man and a negro, in which the white man was stabbed and left for dead. The news spread throughout the county, the report being no doubt greatly exaggerated. Then again came the report that the negroes were arming and threatening to destroy the town and kill the whites from the cradle up. The whites formed a semi-military organization, and chose for their leader the Rev. Mr. Ball, a Baptist preacher, a Northern man and an ex-Union soldier, and

---

[1] Letter of James L. Alcorn in *New York Tribune*, Oct. 11, 1875. Alcorn says the affair had its origin in the party schism between his adherents and those of Ames. Ames charges Alcorn with being solely responsible for it.

marched out to meet the negroes. In the fight that ensued, six of them were killed.[1]

The most noteworthy of the riots of 1875, and really the last race conflict in the state of Mississippi, was that which took place at the little seminary town of Clinton in Hinds County, September 4, the occasion being a Republican barbecue. It appears that twelve or fifteen hundred negroes and about one hundred white men were present. The Republicans consented to have a joint discussion with the Democrats, the Democratic speaker to have the first speech. After he had spoken, and the Republican speaker had ascended the stand, a tremendous firing commenced, and the negroes began to run. How the disturbance started is a question upon which the testimony is conflicting. The Republicans charge that it was brought about by four or five drunken young white men. The Democrats, on the other hand, claim that it was begun by the negroes. In the fight that ensued several negroes and three white men were killed, two of the latter being young men, who, it was alleged, were pursued across the field, overtaken, and horribly murdered and mutilated. The news spread rapidly, and the county was wild with excitement. Soon special trains with companies of armed men came from Jackson, Vicksburg, Bolton, and other places, to aid the whites, for it was believed that there was to be a general massacre. During the days following the riot, a sort of reign of terror existed in the community. Negroes suspected of being implicated in the killing of the white men at Clinton were killed, the number being variously estimated at from twenty to thirty.[2] Many negroes in fear abandoned

---

[1] A few days after this, the whites of Rolling Fork entered into a treaty with the negroes, delegates from a dozen plantations being present and signing the treaty. Several of the more desperate negroes were excluded from the benefits of the amnesty, and the colored signatories pledged themselves to be peaceable, and to deliver up certain of these offenders. The whites, in turn, pledged to protect the negroes in every way. The treaty is printed in Boutwell Report, p. 699, and is signed by seventeen whites and blacks.

[2] Judge Alderson thought the number was fifty. Boutwell Report, p. 295. Soon after the riot, Chairman George, of the Democratic state executive committee, appointed a committee of three persons to investigate the causes of the affair, and report the results to him. They took the sworn statements of three negroes and twenty white men, five being classified as Republicans. The committee reported that only fifteen took part in the "premeditated massacre" of the whites; that the beginning of the quarrel was involved in obscurity; that as soon as the firing began, the colored men made a rush with the cry: "Kill the white men"; that the whites retreated; that two negroes were killed on the spot, and four or five wounded; that young Sively and Thompson were murdered, and their bodies mutilated; that Mr. Chilton, an innocent white man, was killed in his own yard; and that Captain White was

their homes and crops and fled to the swamps, or lay out in the woods, sleeping on the ground or in out-houses. Others fled to Jackson to seek the protection of the governor, and took up their abode about the United States courthouse, where they were left to the charity of the people for support. There they remained in large numbers for many days, while their cotton was spoiling in the fields. They besieged the governor for the state arms, demanding that they be given an opportunity to defend themselves. The whites, fearing that the governor would yield to their entreaties, detailed thirty or forty of their number to guard the state house where the arms were stored.

Three days after the riot, the governor issued a proclamation reciting that persons in various parts of the state had formed themselves into military companies without authority of law; that they moved from point to point in support of each other without the appearance and consent of the peace officers, and without the knowledge or authority of the state government; that these organizations had overthrown civil government in Yazoo County, set it at defiance in Hinds, and created distrust and fear in Warren, causing loss of many lives, ard compelling many persons to flee from their homes. The governor commanded all members of such organizations to disband forthwith, and required all citizens to render obedience to and assist the peace officers in the preservation of order and the enforcement of the law. The whites denied the existence of such a state of things as was set forth in this proclamation, denied that the law was being defied or peace disturbed, and, furthermore, offered to place at the disposal of the governor a number of military companies made up of white men, without respect to party affiliations, to maintain order should the occasion require it.[1] But the governor had no faith in the white militia, and accordingly fell back upon his old resource, namely, an appeal to the President for Federal troops. He telegraphed the President, September 8,

stabbed and left for dead. The report was published and circulated as Campaign Document, No. 2. It is printed in the Boutwell Report. The grand jury of Hinds County made a thorough investigation, examining more than one hundred witnesses, and reported March 25, 1876, that while it was evident that many persons, both white and colored, were killed, they were unable to find any single witness who saw any man kill another ; that no witness was able to tell just how the affair began ; and that the riot was entirely unpremeditated.

[1] The citizens of Aberdeen telegraphed, offering one hundred good men ; Natchez offered to furnish one hundred and twenty-five ; Holly Springs, one hundred or more.

that "domestic violence in its most aggravated form prevails in various parts of the state beyond the power of the authorities to suppress."[1] The following day, Chairman George telegraphed Attorney General Edwards Pierrepont that there were no disturbances in the state and no obstruction to the execution of the laws, and that "peace prevails throughout the state, and the employment of United States troops would but increase the distrust of the people in the good faith of the present state government." Two days later, he again telegraphed Pierrepont that offers of help were freely made to the governor of assistance to preserve the peace, and reassured him that there was no danger of disturbance unless initiated by the state authorities. Governor Ames first tried to get the troops under Grant's Vicksburg proclamation of December, 1874, but failing in this, he asked for them "because the legislature could not be convened in time to meet the emergency." Pierrepont, on September 10, asked the governor by wire some questions about the nature of the emergency, but could get no satisfaction, and finally, on the 14th, wrote him a letter which was widely published and commented upon at the time. He quoted from a despatch of the President, who was absent from Washington, saying that the whole public was tired out with the annual autumnal outbreaks in the South, and that the majority were ready to condemn any interference on the part of the government, and that Governor Ames should exhaust his own resources before receiving aid from the United States government. The Attorney General furthermore assured the governor that he had given no proof, had made no allegation, in fact, that the legislature could not be called together, and that if called together, it would not support any measure that he might propose in order to preserve the public order. He was, however, given the promise of troops when the requirements of the constitution should have been complied with, either by summoning the legislature or by doing his best to suppress his "domestic violence" with the state forces. The

---

[1] The despatch called attention to disturbances in Yazoo, Hinds, Warren, and other counties, and concluded as follows: "After careful examination of all reports, I find myself compelled to appeal to the general government for the means of giving that protection to which every American citizen is entitled. I do not now make formal application under the provisions of the Constitution, but telegraph you to know first if you can and will regard the proclamation issued by you in December last upon the application of the legislature of this state as still in force. A necessity of immediate action cannot be overstated. If your proclamation of December is not in force, I will at once make a formal application under the Constitution of the United States." A copy of this despatch is among the unpublished papers of Governor Ames.

President said to the Attorney General in regard to the application of Governor Ames; "I heartily wish that peace and good order may be restored without issuing the proclamation; but if it is not, the proclamation must be issued, and I shall instruct the commander of the force to have *no child's play*. If there is a necessity for military interference, there is justice in such interference as to deter evil-doers. I would suggest the sending of a despatch (or better, a private messenger) to Governor Ames, urging him to strengthen his own position by exhausting his own resources before he receives government aid. He might accept the assistance offered by the citizens of Jackson and elsewhere. Governor Ames and his advisers can be made perfectly secure. As many of the troops now in Mississippi as he deems necessary may be sent to Jackson. If he is betrayed by those who offer assistance, he will be in a position to defeat their ends and punish them."

In transmitting this despatch to Governor Ames, Pierrepont said: "You see by this the mind of the President, with which I and every member of the Cabinet who has been consulted are in full accord. You see the difficulties; you see the responsibilities which you assume. We cannot understand why you do not strengthen yourself in the way the President suggests. Nor do we see why you do not call the legislature together and obtain from them whatever powers and money you may need. I suggest that you take all lawful means and all needed measures to preserve the peace by the forces in your own state, and let the country see that the citizens of Mississippi, who are largely favorable to good order, and are largely Republican, have the courage and the manhood to *fight* for their rights and to destroy the bloody ruffians who murder the innocent and unoffending freedmen. Everything is in readiness; be careful to bring yourself strictly within the Constitution and the laws, and if there is such resistance to your state authorities as you cannot by all the means at your command suppress, the President will swiftly aid you in crushing these lawless traitors to human rights."

The governor continued to insist upon troops, and declared his willingness to have the "odium in all its magnitude descend upon him," if only they might be sent. It should be said that the sentiment in favor of Federal interference was by no means unanimous among the Republicans of the state, and to this fact, as much as to anything else, may be attributed Governor Ames's failure to get troops.[1]

[1] Nearly all the native white Republicans of the state indorsed President Grant's non-interference policy. Among those especially active in defeating

III. PREPARATIONS FOR WAR

The governor, having failed to get Federal troops, proceeded to organize the state militia and put the state on a
" war-footing," as the whites expressed it. The legislature
in the spring had passed what was commonly known as the
"Gatling Gun" Bill. This act authorized the governor to
organize two regiments of ten companies each, and to purchase four or more Gatling guns, and to organize a corps of
select officers and men from the infantry to send with the
guns. Sixty thousand dollars were appropriated to carry the
act into execution, $5000 to be used in the purchase of arms.
No action was taken toward organizing the militia under this
act until the Clinton and Yazoo riots made it the governor's
duty, as he believed.[1] Warlike preparations now began in
earnest. D. Appleton & Co. were telegraphed for one hundred copies of Upton's " Infantry Tactics"; the chief of ordnance was asked for fifteen hundred haversacks, and the
state's quota of arms (one thousand Springfield breech-loaders)
were ordered to be purchased in Hinds County; and the
United States commissary department at New Orleans was
asked if it could furnish five thousand rations of pork and
bacon.[2] On the 22d of September, the governor wrote
General Emery, commanding the Department of the Gulf,
introducing Colonel Morgan, " who," he says, " will represent the true condition of things in Mississippi," and added
that he would have to reorganize the militia and possibly
to fight. He asked that " a company of troops be sent
to Yazoo, and some to Jackson, as the latter would be the
chief seat of war, if war we have." [3] These preparations

the governor's plan were United States Senator Pease and Representative
George C. McKee, both " carpet baggers." They were severely censured by
the governor, and were charged with having sold out to the Democrats.   His
course was also condemned by some of the leading colored politicians of the
state, among whom were ex-United States Senator Revels and Ham Carter,
the latter a member of the legislature from Vicksburg.   In a letter to General
Grant, Carter says, " The large majority of the Republicans indorse your
policy of non-intervention."   *New York Herald* of Jan. 10, 1876.

[1] Testimony of A. G. Packer, Adjutant General, Impeachment Testimony,
p. 131.

[2] See Boutwell Report, I. p. 470.

[3] Correspondence, 1875, p. 158.   On the 11th of September, Governor
Ames telegraphed Pierrepont that the necessity which called forth his despatch of the 8th to the President still existed.   " This violence," he said,
" is incident to the political contest now pending.   The race feeling is so
intense that protection for the colored people by white organizations is

"alarmed" the whites, who asserted that the purpose of the governor was to provoke a conflict between the races such as would induce the sending of United States troops which, together with the negro militia, would enable the governor to control the approaching election in the interests of the Republican party. The *Clarion* of October 13 said: " Ames is organizing a war of races with all its attendant horrors, in our otherwise peaceful state. The time has arrived when the companies that have been organized for protective and defensive purposes should come to the front. There are three of them in the city of Jackson. There are others in Hinds — let still others be formed all over the state as speedily as possible, and armed and equipped with the best means that can be extemporized for the occasion. We hope to see a large and imposing display of these defensive organizations as soon as practicable. Let every citizen hold himself in readiness to join one or other of these companies for the emergency that the bold, reckless, and desperate adventurer, who is in the executive office, seems determined to force upon us." There seems to have been an honest impression in the minds of the whites that the governor desired to provoke a conflict between the races, but when we consider what must have been the appalling consequences of such a conflict, we are forced to believe that the impression was not well founded. As the organization proceeded, the indignation of the whites increased. The chief places of honor were given to men thoroughly hated and distrusted by the whites.[1] For this, Ames was hardly to blame, since none other would accept places in the militia. In view of the opposition of the whites to negro militia, it was suggested that the whites should enlist, and be able thereby to counteract the evil of the negro militia. They were so advised by General George on October 2.

despaired of. The Republican party of this state has been opposed to organizing a militia of colored men. It has been believed by them that it would develop a war of races which would extend beyond the borders of this state. The organization of the whites alone, where the issue is one of race, would be equally ineffectual. I am aware of the reluctance of the people of the country to national interference. Permit me to express the hope that the odium of such interference shall not attach to President Grant or the Republican party. As the governor of a state, I made a demand which cannot well be refused. I cannot escape the conscientious discharge of my duty toward a class of American citizens whose only crime consists in their color."

[1] The appointee for Adjutant General was a " carpet bagger " whose character was impeached by men of his own party. One of his two aides-de-camp was a negro, and the other a defaulter and criminal who afterwards fled the state. All of the five brigadier generals were Republicans and three were negroes. There were a number of negro colonels.

There was nothing in the law to prevent them from enlisting. But they charged that the governor did not want white companies in his organization, and that every difficulty was put in their way to prevent them from enlisting.[1] There was doubtless a preference for negro militia, since the governor believed that he could not rely on the white troops to execute his orders.

In Hinds County, seven companies were organized, of which only two were white, the colored companies being composed largely of refugees from Clinton, and some of whom were charged by the whites with complicity in the "massacre" of the three white men. One or two companies under the command of white officers were enlisted in Amite County, and the organization was proceeding elsewhere when, late in September, a bombshell was thrown into the ranks of those who were supervising the organization. It came in the form of an injunction sued out by the Democrats, restraining the auditor from issuing warrants for any part of the amount appropriated by the legislature for military purposes. The injunction was granted by Chief Justice Peyton on the ground that no state may keep troops in time of peace and when there is no obstruction to the execution of the laws and no riot or insurrection to suppress.[2] Shortly before the set-back to the governor's military preparations, an incident occurred which came near causing a conflict between the negro militia and the whites. The governor had detailed one of the colored companies, made up of Clinton refugees, and commanded by Senator Caldwell, a courageous and dangerous negro, and an alleged participant in the Clinton riot, to escort several wagon loads of arms through the country to Edwards Station for the purpose of arming colored companies in that town. The arms were not shipped by rail for the reason, as the governor alleged, that they would

[1] See testimony of H. Barksdale, Impeachment Testimony, pp. 144–145, for an account of the obstacles alleged to have been placed in the way of a white company which desired to enlist.

[2] *Aberdeen Examiner*, September 30. Alexander Warner, the chairman of the Republican state executive committee, telegraphed Attorney General Pierrepont that the organization of the militia had been enjoined by the Democratic state executive committee, in order to carry the election by fraud. October 24, there was a full meeting of the committee at Jackson, and they telegraphed the Attorney General that the injunction was granted by a Republican judge upon the petition of a private citizen and a tax payer of Jackson. The Attorney General was also reminded that only the payment of the money was enjoined, not the organization of the militia. The committee said, "We take pleasure in assuring you that the most profound peace and good order prevail throughout the state." Boutwell Report, p. 290.

be seized by the whites.[1] The escort proceeded along the
highway to Edwards with drums beating, banners flying, and
bayonets fixed, until the town of Clinton was reached. Here
they paraded the streets and encamped for the night. The
rage of the whites knew no bounds. They telegraphed General George, asking if they should attack the company or
submit, declaring that they could do either. He advised
them not to interfere with the escort, although it required
strenuous efforts on his part to prevent them from attacking
it.[2] The escort proceeded to Edwards, delivered the arms,
and returned to Jackson with two other companies, without interruption, whereupon the *Jackson Pilot* declared that
the Senator could exclaim, " *Veni, vidi, vici!* " About the
same time, the governor was making preparations to send a
consignment of arms to a colored company in De Soto County,
but the excitement it occasioned, and the belief that they
would be seized by the whites, induced the abandonment of the
project. It was also at this time that the excitement at Yazoo
was at its highest, on account of the governor's proposal to
send Colonel Morgan back with an escort of colored militia.

Nothing illustrates better Governor Ames's want of tact in
dealing with the whites, for he should have known that few
things were more offensive to them than a body of negro
soldiers equipped with all the paraphernalia of war, marching
and countermarching through the country with the purpose,
as was commonly asserted, of striking terror into the minds
of the whites. They declared that the governor's course in
arming the negro militia was one of hostility to them, and
that he desired a conflict. The governor by way of reply
insisted that he was only trying to do his duty, which he was
bound by oath to do, that the state government was powerless to execute the laws, that he could not secure the assistance of the Federal government, and that he was compelled,
as a last resort, to call in the aid of the state militia, and that
as the state government commanded the respect of the
colored race only, it must depend for military support on
colored troops. The governor declared that he had no faith
in the promises of the white troops. He believed, sincerely,
that in the first conflict between the whites and blacks, which

[1] A consignment of arms shipped by boat from Greenville to Vicksburg to
be used for a similar purpose had been seized by the whites. Boutwell
Report, p. 230. The arms intended for the white company at Edwards were
shipped by express and were not interfered with.

[2] Leading citizens of Jackson remained at the telegraph office until one
o'clock in the morning, sending telegraphic appeals to Clinton urging the
whites not to interfere with the company. Impeachment Testimony, p. 146.

the militia was called upon to suppress, the white troops would go over in a body to the side of the white rioters. In this situation, he argued, was it not wise to give the preference to colored troops upon whom he could depend? But it was his distrust of the whites, his want of confidence in their integrity, that hurt them most. He should have encouraged the enlistment of the white troops and discouraged the enlistment of negroes, in view of the universal prejudice against the colored troops, and then waited for the faithlessness of the white soldiers to show itself. It was the constant complaint of the whites that Governor Ames regarded them as unworthy of his official preferment as long as colored men could be forthcoming. There is no doubt that much might have been done to remove this impression, and consequently to secure the moral support of the race which constituted the wealth and intelligence of the state. It should also be said that in pursuing this course of arming the colored militia, Governor Ames opposed the judgment of many white Republicans of the state.[1]   L. Q. C. Lamar expressed the general feeling of the whites at this time when he said: " I think the future of Mississippi is very dark.   Ames has it dead.   There can be no escape from his rule.   His negro regiments are nothing.   He will get them killed up, and then Grant will take possession for him.   May God help us ! " [2]

About the 5th of October, Mr. C. K. Chase of New York arrived in Mississippi as an accredited agent of the department of justice, having been commissioned by Attorney General Edwards Pierrepont to investigate the condition of affairs, and report to the President if, in his opinion, the necessity for United States troops existed, and if possible to quiet the political excitement which was now at fever heat. He took up his abode with Governor Ames, and was the recipient of his hospitality while in Mississippi. Mr. Chase says he found the city of Jackson in great excitement, and un-uniformed militia, both white and colored, were parading the streets. It was at this time that the organization of the

---

[1] Judge Alderson says that Governor Ames did wrong in arming the colored militia, and that he refused to accept proffers of aid from some of the best citizens that he had ever seen.   Boutwell Report, p. 294.   Hon. George T. Swann says he advised the governor not to organize the militia because it would be composed mostly of colored men who would be gobbled up as fast as they could be enlisted.   Boutwell Report, p. 300.   J. H. Estelle, another prominent white Republican, said, "The feeling was universal among us that the negroes ought not to be armed and suffered to march about as soldiers."
[2] Mayes's Lamar, p. 211.

militia was proceeding under the direction of Governor Ames, and plans were in preparation for sending Colonel Morgan back to Yazoo City, both of which Mr. Chase advised against. Shortly after his arrival, he sought an interview with General George and Editor Barksdale, and it was through his offices, as he claims, that the conference between the governor and the citizens was held, at which he was a spectator. Mr. Chase remained in Jackson until after the election, using his influence to bring about a fair election. He took with him to Mississippi a number of detectives from New York and Washington, who were sent to operate in different parts of the state and keep him informed of the condition of affairs. As complaints of disturbances came to Governor Ames, they were turned over to Mr. Chase, who in turn laid them before the Democratic chairman for explanation. General George would then telegraph to the seat of the trouble, asking for a statement of the cause of the disturbances. Upon receiving a reply, he submitted it by way of explanation to Mr. Chase. In a number of instances, each party sent out a special agent to investigate jointly the causes of alleged disturbances.[1]

What would doubtless have resulted in a bloody conflict between the whites and blacks, and perhaps a violent overthrow of the state government, was prevented by a treaty between the Democrats and the governor, commonly known as the Peace Agreement. Some days previous to the conclusion of the treaty, an unsigned call had been published in the *Jackson Clarion,* and in the Vicksburg papers, calling upon all good citizens to meet in Jackson, for the purpose, it was understood, of taking action in regard to the governor's course in arming the militia.[2] It was believed by the Republicans that the action to be taken was to demand the disbandment of the militia, and if this was not done, to declare war upon the governor.[3] The meeting was held at Angelo Hall,

[1] Chase says the explanations General George furnished were not satisfactory to him, and he finally reported to the Attorney General that there was no chance for a fair election without the aid of United States troops. Testimony Boutwell Report, p. 1804. His report to the Attorney General was made October 27, and is printed in the Boutwell Report, p. 92, documentary evidence. He said the Democrats were determined to carry the election, and declared that they had intimidated the negroes by hanging several of their leaders, that the Republicans dared not put out a ticket in some counties, and were forced to make compromise tickets in others, that the governor was powerless, that refugees were coming in daily, complaints hourly, and an invasion from Alabama was expected.

[2] Testimony of C. K. Chase, Boutwell Report, Vol. II. p. 1802.

[3] Testimony of H. B. Ware, Republican chancellor, Boutwell Report, p. 1217. Judge Ware says that on the day of the meeting train-loads of men

and was largely attended. In the course of the deliberations, it was suggested that a committee of the citizens should wait on the governor and have a conference with him in regard to the militia. Judge Ware was requested to ascertain if the governor would consent to receive the committee. He called upon Governor Ames and earnestly advised him to disband the militia. The governor said that he desired peace, and it would be the happiest moment of his life if he could effect that purpose by disbanding the militia.[1] He readily consented to receive the committee, whereupon General George, with a dozen of the prominent gentlemen present, called at the mansion, and a full and frank interview took place, in the course of which the governor announced that in consequence of Colonel Morgan's refusal to go back to Yazoo City he had abandoned the attempt to reinstate him, and that he had also countermanded the shipment of arms to De Soto County. He then expressed fears that peace and good order would not be preserved, and that colored men would not be allowed to vote as they desired; that his whole object in calling out the militia was to preserve order and suppress disturbances; that he was originally opposed to arming the militia, but was under the circumstances forced to do so; but in view of the assurances from the citizens that they desired peace and good order and a fair election, and that they would by example and precept do all in their power to maintain peace and secure a fair election, he was willing to meet their views as far as he could, and with this end in view he would promise to disband the militia; that no more companies should be organized; and that their arms should be deposited in certain depots and there guarded by United States troops to be detailed for that purpose, or by men selected by himself and General George.[2] The result of the interview was then reported to the meeting, the agreement was ratified, and a committee of twenty citizens was appointed to return to the mansion and express the thanks of the meeting for what the governor had done. There can be little doubt that this arrangement prevented bloodshed. Much credit for the treaty was due to Mr. Chase, the special agent of the department of justice. No one was more pleased with the arrange-

came in from different parts of the state, most of whom had on their side arms. To carry out their purpose they went so far as to organize a battalion and elect Mr. Joshua T. Green major.

[1] Boutwell Report, p. 1218.

[2] The text of this agreement is printed in Impeachment Testimony, pp. 230–233.

ment than Governor Ames. On the following day, he wrote the Attorney General of the United States: " Through the timely intervention of Mr. C. K. Chase, a bloody revolution has been averted. The condition of affairs which preceded the Clinton riot grew worse from day to day, and assumed gigantic proportions under the feeling of hostility to the militia I was organizing. The danger became apparent to all, and in the interest of peace and a fair election, an understanding was had to the effect that the opposition was to do all in their power to preserve peace, and I to suspend further operations with my militia. I have full faith in their honor, and implicit confidence that they can accomplish all that they undertake. Consequently, I believe that we shall have peace, order, and a fair election. I write this letter to you chiefly to thank you for sending here a gentleman who has succeeded in inspiring us all with confidence, and who, by his wisdom and tact, has saved the history of this state from a bloody chapter."

On October 23, the Attorney General replied as follows: " Yours of the 16th came duly, and yesterday I presented it to the President, who read it to Senator Bruce; and I also presented it to the Cabinet. I delayed answering it until the meeting of the Cabinet, and I have to say that the course you have taken meets the approval of the President and of the Cabinet, and that they are each and all much gratified that your judicious course in making this settlement and producing peace without bloodshed proves that you have acted wisely. I sincerely hope that those with whom you have negotiated will keep their agreement, and that you will have a peaceful election. You may be assured that to produce this result without the necessity of calling out the Federal troops will redound greatly to your credit throughout the entire North. You will be advised of the preparations made to aid you in case the opposition violate their honor and break their faith. You may feel assured that this department will always be ready to aid you in any lawful way to preserve order and to give the right to every citizen to vote as he pleases." [1]

IV. THE TRIUMPH OF THE DEMOCRACY

As the campaign progressed, it became evident to the Republicans that their prospects of success were diminishing. As early as August 18, Governor Ames wrote Merimon

[1] These letters are among the unpublished papers of Governor Ames.

Howard, a colored member of the legislature: " The political sky is somewhat overcast. I fear through violence and fraud that Louisiana and all the Southern states except South Carolina, where elections are held, will go bodily Democratic." Again, September 5, he wrote to Hon. S. W. Dorsey of Little Rock, Arkansas, heartily indorsing his suggestion for a convention of Southern Republicans, and observing that "the times are full of danger for our cause."[1] The *Vicksburg Plaindealer* (Republican) said "there is no use disguising the fact — the Republican party has reached a crisis." The *Greenville Republican* predicted that it would require the utmost caution in management to save them from overwhelming defeat. Before the end of the month, it was apparent that their only hope was to get United States troops "to prevent the intimidation of Republican voters by the Democrats." On September 25, Governor Ames sent General Dedrick to St. Louis to meet President Grant and to ask that United States detectives be sent to Mississippi " to penetrate the designs and schemes of the ' white liners ' who are preparing to deprive colored men of their civil and political liberties by violence."[2] Two days later he wrote General Grant asking if United States marshals might call on Federal troops to make arrests.[3] Mr. Warner, the chairman of the Republican state executive committee, says he felt satisfied soon after the meeting of the state committee in August that the will of the people could not be expressed in the coming election without some kind of "protection"; that riots and disturbances were occurring almost daily; that the Republican meetings were broken up here and there, so that it was difficult to get speakers to canvass the state.[4] Accordingly, the Republican chairman with a committee of " Ames " Republicans went to Washington to see what protection " our people " could get.[5] They styled themselves the "genuine representatives of the Republican party in Mississippi." They subsequently had a conference with the President in New York City, and advised him that he

---

[1] Correspondence, 1875, p. 98.

[2] *Ibid.* p. 159.

[3] *Ibid.* September 2, the governor suggested to Chairman Warner of the Republican state executive committee that "great advantage would result to the party if the executive committee should go to the expense of telegraphing North to such papers as the *Chicago Inter-Ocean* and *Washington Republican* the lawlessness and murders committed by the democracy of this state." *Ibid.* p. 151.

[4] Testimony of A. Warner, Boutwell Report, p. 962.

[5] The committee were Chairman Warner, B. K. Bruce, A. R. Howe, James Hill, John R. Lynch. They were all candidates. Correspondence of Governor Ames, 1875, p. 152.

could not err in recognizing them as the true representatives of the party in Mississippi. United States Senator Pease of the anti-Ames wing of the party denounced the course of the committee, and telegraphed the President that a posse of citizens could be got in any county to keep order, and that Federal interference would be a positive injury to the state.[1] This faction now sent a committee [2] to wait on the President and induce him to recognize them as the "genuine" Republicans, and to assure him that there was no need for Federal interference in the approaching election. Governor Ames characterized the Pease committee as "sore-heads," charged them with being "venomous and vindictive" toward him, and declared that they had been repudiated by the Republican party.[3] They assured President Grant that the Ames Republicans were opposed to his policy, and had purposely refused to indorse the national administration in the state convention, against the protest of the Pease Republicans.[4] In the end, the Pease Republicans won, the Federal patronage was withheld from Governor Ames and his party adherents, and they were left to fight their battle at the polls without the presence of United States troops.[5] Governor Ames attributed their failure to get troops mainly to the activity of Senator Pease, whom he denounced bitterly.

As the election day drew near, proclamations and addresses fell thick and fast from the hands of the two campaign managers, and the press contained columns of advice to the voters. The Republican chairman's final address reminded the colored voters that the government had expended millions of dollars to secure their right to vote, and millions more would be expended if necessary; that President Grant had declared that there would be no child's play in Mississippi if the troops were called out, and if the Democrats could afford to risk their lives for the sake of a few offices, the Republicans could

---

[1] His despatch is printed in the *Clarion* of Sept. 14, 1875.

[2] The members of this committee were Senator Pease, George C. McKee, and G. Wiley Wells, the two latter being members of Congress — all were "carpet baggers."

[3] Correspondence of Governor Ames, 1875, p. 152.

[4] In reply to this charge Governor Ames wrote General Grant that the failure of the state convention to indorse his administration was simply an oversight, and assured him that he had nowhere truer friends than in Mississippi. Whether the failure of the convention in this respect was inadvertent or not, the state executive committee, fearing to lose the support of the national administration, made haste to adopt a resolution indorsing it, and had it incorporated as a plank in their platform. *Ibid.* p. 152.

[5] The only troops in the state at the time of the election were 100 at Vicksburg, and 120 at Jackson, and 200 at Holly Springs.

well afford to do the same.   The Democratic press denounced
this language as "incendiary, and calculated to inflame the
passions of the blacks."[1]

The *Clarion* of October 13 contained the following rallying
cry: "*Democrats, Conservatives, old men and young men, black
and white, push onward the organized columns!   Advance our
glorious standard into the broken ranks of the plunderers and
follow them up with the proud symbol of redemption!   Onward!
Onward!*" It announced that the funeral obsequies of the radical party would be conducted on the 3d of November, that the
Times and *Pilot* would be the chief mourners, and that General
George would deliver an appropriate address.   In the issue
of October 20, it declared that the victory was already won,
and advised that if an attempt was made to throw out the
Democratic boxes, to hang the man that did it.   The whites
were urged to keep the peace agreement, but to remember
their inalienable rights, and not forget that the price of
liberty is eternal vigilance.   "Work night and day.   Gather
at the polls by daylight, and stay until dark.   Do not be
crowded away.   For eight years you have had to stand back
and allow the radicals to vote first.   Do not submit to stand
in the rear of a long line.   If that game is tried, *break the line.*
See that your votes are counted and properly returned.   Be pru-
dent and calm, but determined.   Hang the registrar who pro-
poses to throw out a vote." The *Times* and the *Pilot* applied the
"incendiary" argument with some effectiveness to this advice.

The election took place November 3, and with a few exceptions passed off with unusual quietness; in fact, it was about
the most peaceful election since the war.   In many instances,
the negroes did not go to the polls.   In others, they voted
with the Democrats.   The Republicans charged that the
absence of the negroes from the polls was due to intimidation
and threats which they had received during the weeks prior
to the election, that they had been coerced by their employers, driven away from the polls, their meetings broken up,
and that in some counties they were forced to abandon the
struggle early in the campaign.   There was more or less
interference with the Republican canvass in several of the
"black" counties, particularly in Warren, Hinds, Yazoo,
Holmes, Lowndes, Monroe, and Copiah.   In a number of
instances, Republican meetings in these counties were broken
up by the whites, so that public discussion had to be abandoned to some extent several weeks before the election.   It

[1] *Jackson Clarion*, Oct. 13, 1875.

is also true that a number of local politicians, leaders of the
party, and club organizers, both black and white, were killed
during the weeks prior thereto.[1] Others were overawed,
threatened, and compelled to make Democratic speeches.[2]
The whites claimed that they were morally justified in withholding employment from those who voted to inflict a corrupt and ignorant government upon them, and did in many
cases use the power which they had as owners of the land
which the negroes cultivated, and of the cabins which they
tenanted, to control their votes. On Monday, before the
election, there appeared in the *Aberdeen Examiner* a pledge
signed by 190 prominent farmers and business men of Monroe
County to discriminate in making labor contracts against
those who should vote the Republican ticket ; that they
would discharge at least one-third of the more active politicians, club leaders, and drummers ; that they would not
knowingly employ any one who had been discharged by any
signer of the pledge, or permit to live in their houses or on
their lands those who had been introduced into the county in
the interests of the radical party ; and that they would furnish
the county executive committee a list of those persons who
might have been refused labor on political grounds, to be enrolled in a book kept for the purpose, and which list was to be
printed in the *Weekly Examiner* as a standing advertisement for
the protection of the citizens. There were similar agreements
among the whites in Lowndes, Chickasaw, Colfax, Noxubee,
and other counties.[3] They claimed to be simply pursuing
General Grant's policy as President in making appointments
to office, namely, to extend no favors to those who were not

---

[1] One Republican witness puts the whole number of Republicans killed
during the canvass at three hundred. The number is, of course, exaggerated.
Report of Senate sub-committee, p. 979.

[2] Caradine, a colored member of the legislature from Clay County, was
subjected to treatment of this kind. He says : "They told me that I would
have to go around and make some speeches for them ; they came by my
house and 'fotched' a buggy for me. I got in and went along with them,
and made three speeches, but they did not appreciate them at length." Senator Price, the much hated "carpet bagger" of Grenada, had an experience
somewhat similar to Caradine's. See his testimony in the Boutwell Report.

[3] The text of the above pledge is printed in Boutwell Report, II. p. 141.
Colonel Reynolds, at Buena Vista, September 4, declared that "whoever eats
the white man's bread must vote with the white man or refrain from voting
at all," and the immense applause with which the sentiment was greeted
showed that he had reached the heart of every auditor. The *Aberdeen Examiner* said that this utterance was the keynote of the campaign. Judge Houston the following night spoke at the courthouse in Monroe County and declared
that the whites were justified in demanding the coöperation of the colored
voters in their effort to free themselves from a rule that was oppressive and
odious to every man who had an interest in the welfare of the state, and that

their friends.[1] It must be said to the credit of General George that he used his best efforts to secure a fair election. The following telegram to Mr. Vertner of Claiborne County was typical of many that he sent out: " Tell our people to use every effort to secure a peaceful election and prevent disorder. This must be done if possible, so far as we are concerned. Faith must be kept in the peace agreement." Again he telegraphed a prominent Democrat that full protection must be allowed all negroes who wished to vote. " Be sure of this," he said. Upon receipt of information that a movement was on foot to assassinate Mr. Warner, the chairman of the Republican state executive committee, while at the polls, he telegraphed Campbell and Calhoun, prominent attorneys of Canton: " If Warner goes to Madison Station, see by all means that he is not hurt. We are nearly through now, and are sure to win. Don't let us have any trouble of that sort on our hands." [2]

The exceptions to the general quiet of election day were the disturbances in Claiborne, Kemper, Amite, Copiah, and Clay counties. In Aberdeen, a cannon in charge of a half-dozen men was alleged to have been trained on the voting-place during the day, while a cavalry company, made up largely of men from Alabama, paraded the streets. The sheriff abandoned the polling-place and concealed himself in the county jail. The fordways across the Tombigbee River, the crossing-place of the negroes from the great black belt on the east side, were guarded by squads the night before. The whites claimed that their purpose was not to intimidate the negroes, but to prevent them from seizing the state arms in the jail and from massing at the polls.[3] In Amite County, the occurrences were highly discreditable to the whites. The election inspectors were compelled to resign, a body of

if the negro would not assist them in redeeming the state from this terrible incubus, he took the position of a covert, if not an avowed enemy, and was entitled to no consideration at their hands. *Aberdeen Examiner*, Sept. 9, 1875.

[1] Testimony of H. A. Rice, Boutwell Report, p. 1193.

[2] The following day General George received this answer, " Your telegram last night saved A. Warner.   G. A. JOHNSON."

[3] The whites allege that it had been customary in all the elections since the war for the negroes to mass themselves in an unbroken phalanx at the polls for the purpose of preventing the Democrats from voting. The law permitted any voter in the county to cast his vote at the county seat, although the spirit of the law intended that they should vote in their respective precincts. Upon the advice of the Republican leaders, the negroes generally went to the county seat where they might vote in a body with less likelihood of being interfered with.

men from Louisiana invaded the county and drove the
negroes from the polls ; the sheriff, the county superintendent of education, both "carpet baggers," together with the
United States deputy collector of internal revenue were
driven from the county, and the latter official was even pursued beyond the limits of the county and was not able to
return to perform his duties until furnished with an escort of
United States troops.[1] In Columbus, on the night before the
election, fires broke out about the same time in half a dozen
different places. The town was put under martial law, and
an ex-Confederate brigadier general assumed control by appointment from the mayor. He at once issued a proclamation detailing a number of military companies to preserve
order. Four negroes were killed and three wounded. Each
side charged the other with having started the fire for political purposes.

The election resulted in an overwhelming victory for the
Democrats. They carried the state by a majority of over
30,000, elected all the members of Congress except two, the
state treasurer, a majority of both Houses of the legislature,
and a majority of the local officers.[2] Sixty-two of the 74
counties elected Democratic officials.[3] In Kemper County
the Republicans polled only four votes; in Yazoo, one of the
large black counties, with a negro majority of 2000, only
seven Republican votes were cast ; Hinds, with a Republican
majority equally as large, went Democratic by a majority of
1515, which was increased to 3026 in the presidential election
of 1876; Tishomingo polled only twelve Republican votes,
and the Republican vote in other counties was equally small.
In the presidential election of the following year, all the counties, except four, along the Mississippi River, went Democratic,
Lowndes and Yazoo, both Republican counties, casting only
two votes for Hayes and Wheeler. The announcement of the
result was the occasion of great rejoicing among the whites,
and they celebrated their "political emancipation" in various
ways. This election ended the rule of the "carpet bagger" in

[1] Testimony of W. B. Redmond, Boutwell Report.

[2] For state treasurer, Hemmingway was elected over Buchanan ; for Congress, Lamar of the first district had no opposition ; in the second district
Wells, Republican, was supported by the Democrats, and was elected over
Howe, the Ames candidate ; in the third district Money was elected over Ex-
Governor Powers ; in the fourth district Singleton defeated Niles ; in the fifth
district Hooker defeated Hill ; in the sixth the Democratic candidate, Seal,
was defeated by John R. Lynch, his majority being 231.

[3] Among the counties that continued Republican were Oktibbeha, Noxubee, Monroe, Jefferson, Issaquena, Tunica, Bolivar, and Adams.

Mississippi, and marks the beginning of a new era in the history of the state. It possessed many of the elements of a real revolution. In regard to the Republican charge of intimidation, it is undoubtedly true, as alleged, that intimidation was successfully practised by the whites, but, in most cases, it was resorted to before election day. There was a variety of demonstrations during the days preceding the election, which gave the negroes to understand that the whites were determined to carry the election at all hazards. This, no doubt, kept many of them from the polls. Those, however, who attempted to vote, with a few exceptions, were not disturbed. It should also be said that there was intimidation on the other side. Charles Nordhoff declared that it was a serious mistake to suppose that intimidation was exclusively a Democratic proceeding. "It has," he said, "been practised quite as much, or even more, vigorously by Republicans, and the negroes were the most savage intimidators of all." He said he had visited communities where it would have cost a negro his life to vote the Democratic ticket.[1] Those of the negroes who dared vote the Democratic ticket, lost standing in the community, and were summarily dismissed from membership in their social and religious organizations. Republicanism was the sure test of orthodoxy, and the colored minister, the most influential of his race in politics, warned his parishioners of the consequences of party infidelity. In Madison County, a colored minister was dismissed by his church for voting the Democratic ticket.[2] In spite of the party lash, however, they voted with the whites, in many instances voluntarily, as it appears, and colored men like Senator Revels, Ham Carter, and other prominent leaders of the race came out openly on the side of the whites.[3] The Democrats made a strong appeal

[1] Cotton States, p. 11.

[2] In regard to the dismissal of the colored preacher alluded to above, Mr. Britton (colored) testified as follows before the Boutwell committee : Q. You got rid of him after that? A. Yes, sir. We were ready to jump him there quicker than we did them Democrats, because he went back on us. Q. You turned him right off? A. Yes, sir. We would not let him come into the church any more, would not let him go into the pulpit, and would not hear him preach. Q. Because he voted that ticket? A. Yes, sir. Boutwell Report, p. 903. The Clarion printed a letter signed by four negroes, informing their representative in the legislature that if he acted with the Democratic party they would hang him when he returned home, adding that they were sworn to hang any man who betrayed them.

[3] Testimony of H. R. Revels, Boutwell Report, p. 1015 ; letter of Ham Carter to President Grant, supra. The Jackson Clarion of Sept. 22, 1875, contains a long letter from the Rev. J. G. Johnson (colored), of Holly Springs, advising his race to "join hands with the white people in redeeming from the spoiler our common country." "Since you were free," he said, "the whites have been friends to you ; they have aided you when you were

to the colored voters, solemnly pledging their honor that if they carried the election, the colored people should be secured in the full enjoyment of their rights and privileges, that they should not be discriminated against in the legislation adopted by the party, that the public school system should be continued as before, and the education of the colored children amply provided for. Editor Barksdale stated it as his solemn conviction and firm belief that the colored people wished a change of administration. He says he saw five hundred negroes in a Democratic procession in Raymond, and a similar spectacle in Jackson. Judge Watson says he noticed a great change in the negroes, and that they went out by the hundreds to hear Democratic speeches. There is little doubt that some negroes, who had accumulated property, and who were naturally opposed to the heavy taxes levied by the state government, preferred to see a change of administration.

A more important reason for the overthrow of the Republicans was the schism in their own ranks. The overwhelming election of Ames in 1873, the favorable auspices under which he was inaugurated, and his promises of an economical administration had done much to unite the party, but it was alleged that within six months after the inauguration, the governor had thrown off the better element of the party, and allied himself with the worst class of colored Republicans and "carpet baggers." [1] The governor's course alienated many of his own party leaders. He was charged with making an undignified attack upon United States District Attorney Wells, a Republican, and at the time a candidate for Congress. [2] He declared that United States Senator Pease, another Republican leader, and like himself a "carpet bagger," was a traitor to the party. [3] Judge Stearns, another, was in his opinion cor-

in trouble, and when death entered your households they have sympathized with you." The same paper of October 13, published a letter from J. Allen Ross, a negro ex-senator from Washington County, expressing similar views.

[1] Letter of J. S. Morris to W. W. Huntington, *supra*.

[2] Correspondence of Governor Ames, 1875, pp. 22, 43. He wrote the Attorney General to appoint Stone, Bliss, Whitfield, Niles, anybody except Wells, who was a man without principle or honor, and whose assertions were not worth the paper on which they were written. Letters of May 15 and 22. Wells had assailed the administration for its alleged extravagance and corruption, and the failure of the governor to redeem his pledges made in the inaugural address, and his course in the Vicksburg affair. Boutwell Report, p. 1017. See Wells's letter in the *Clarion* of August 13, 1875.

[3] Correspondence of 1874, p. 66. May 15 he writes Pease: "I quite agree with you that 'carpet baggers' should not fight each other — a correct principle as a general one, but to go on the principle that no 'carpet bagger' should be opposed, cannot hold."

rupt beyond doubt.[1] Lieutenant Governor Davis had gone
over to the sore-heads.[2] He broke with the Attorney General,
and never sought his advice on any point of law, nor accepted
it when offered voluntarily. He charged Alcorn with being
exceedingly corrupt.[3] Not only was he opposed by many of
the Republican leaders of the state, but he failed to command
the support of the national administration. He could not get
troops, and his recommendations for Federal office were disregarded, and candidates appointed against whom he had urged
the most strenuous objections. In a letter of February 2, 1875,
he informed a correspondent that he had no influence at
Washington.[4] The Attorney General, he said, doubted his
integrity, and held him responsible for the appointment of
corrupt, inefficient, and dishonest United States district
attorneys and marshals.[5] "With one or two exceptions,"
said he, "the entire Mississippi delegation in Congress are
hostile to me, and my word goes for nothing, and I hesitate
to speak to them on any subject."[6] The naked truth is, less
than a baker's dozen of the prominent Republican leaders who
had a substantial interest in the welfare of the state were supporters of Governor Ames in the election of 1875.[7] It should
be said, however, that the schism was confined more largely
to the ranks of the leaders of the party than to the common
voters, although in a number of counties the Republicans had
two tickets in the field, each as bitter against the other as they
were against the Democrats. Fights were almost as common
occurrences between the different wings of the Republican
party as between the Democrats and Republicans. A notable
instance of this kind was a political row in Holmes County
between a faction of the party led by Mr. Warren, a "carpet
bagger" and ex-Speaker of the House, and one led by Mr.
Holmes, with the result that two negro politicians were shot

[1] Correspondence of 1875, letter of May 15.
[2] Correspondence of 1874, p. 66.
[3] Letter to Senator Conkling, Correspondence of 1875, May 22. He wrote
Conkling: "Be careful how you follow his [Alcorn's] leadership in levee
matters. We, especially the whites, believe him exceedingly corrupt."
[4] Correspondence of 1875, p. 183.
[5] *Ibid.* pp. 40, 60.
[6] *Ibid.* pp. 109, 183. Sept. 30, 1875, he wrote to President Grant begging
for the removal of Lake, United States marshal, and Wells, United States
district attorney. He said: "Such men with Pease embarrass us and give
heart to white liners. We pray you for some quick blow at such men." *Ibid.*
p. 164. The prayer was not granted.
[7] A prominent white Republican told the Boutwell committee that
the governor's policy and his association with corrupt men had disrupted the
party. "I do not know," he said, "any people more antagonistic than the
two wings of the party." Boutwell Report, p. 325.

and killed by a member of the governor's staff. He fled from the state, and was never caught.[1] Such occurrences made the Democratic victory easy in many counties.

Four days after the election, ex-United States Senator Revels wrote a long letter to the President, in which he gave his views on the course of Governor Ames, and the reasons for the defeat of the Republican party. The letter was widely published at the time, and was the subject of not a little comment throughout the Union.[2]

HOLLY SPRINGS, MISS., November 6, 1875.

To HIS EXCELLENCY, U. S. GRANT, *President of the United States:*

. . . Since reconstruction, the masses of my people have been, as it were, enslaved in mind by unprincipled adventurers, who, caring nothing for country, were willing to stoop to anything no matter how infamous, to secure power to themselves, and perpetuate it. My people are naturally Republicans, and always will be, but as they grow older in freedom so do they in wisdom. A great portion of them have learned that they were being used as mere tools, and, as in the late election, not being able to correct existing evils among themselves, they determined by casting their ballots against these unprincipled adventurers, to overthrow them. . . . My people have been told by these schemers, when men have been placed on the ticket who were notoriously corrupt and dishonest, that they must vote for them; that the salvation of the party depended upon it; that the man who scratched a ticket was not a Republican. This is only one of the many means these unprincipled demagogues have devised to perpetuate the intellectual bondage of my people. To defeat this policy, at the late election men, irrespective of race, color, or party affiliation, united, and voted together against men known to be incompetent and dishonest. I cannot recognize, nor do the mass of my people who read, recognize the majority of the officials who have been in power for the past two years as Republicans. . . .

The great mass of the white people have abandoned their hostility to the general government and Republican principles,

---

[1] Testimony of Judge W. B. Cunningham, Boutwell Report, p. 844.

[2] The letter was first published in the *Jackson Daily Times* in November, 1875. In June, 1876, Mr. Revels testified before the Boutwell committee, and declared that he still stood by that letter. He said: " I believed then, as I do now, that certain imprudent men who called themselves Republicans had broken our party down, and after the defeat they rushed to Washington and were trying to mislead the President and throw the blame on the pure Republican party and the innocent old white Republicans, both of whom I felt it my duty as a Christian man to defend." In this connection it is but fair to state that Mr. Revels was likely prompted in some degree by personal prejudice, the governor having removed him from the presidency of Alcorn University.

and to-day accept as a fact that all men are born free and equal, and I believe are ready to guarantee to my people every right and privilege guaranteed to an American citizen. The bitterness and hate created by the late civil strife has, in my opinion, been obliterated in this state, except perhaps in some localities, and would have long since been entirely obliterated, were it not for some unprincipled men who would keep alive the bitterness of the past, and inculcate a hatred between the races, in order that they may aggrandize themselves by office, and its emoluments, to control my people, the effect of which is to degrade them. As an evidence that party lines in this state have been obliterated, men were supported without regard to their party affiliations, their birth, or their color, by those who heretofore have acted with the Democratic party, by this course giving an evidence of their sincerity that they have abandoned the political issues of the past, and were only desirous of inaugurating an honest state government, and restoring a mutual confidence between the races. I give you my opinion, that had our state adhered to Republican principles, and stood by the platform upon which it was elected, the state to-day would have been upon the highway of prosperity. Peace would have prevailed within her borders, and the Republican party would have embraced within her folds thousands of the best and purest citizens of which Mississippi can boast, and the election just passed would have been a Republican victory of not less than eighty to a hundred thousand majority; but the dishonest course which has been pursued has forced into silence and retirement nearly all of the leading Republicans who organized, and have heretofore led the party to victory. A few who have been bold enough to stand by Republican principle, and condemn dishonesty, corruption, and incompetency have been supported and elected by overwhelming majorities. If the state administration had adhered to Republican principles, advanced patriotic measures, appointed only honest and competent men to office, and sought to restore confidence between the races, bloodshed would have been unknown, peace would have prevailed, Federal interference been unthought of; harmony, friendship, and mutual confidence would have taken the place of the bayonet. . . .

H. R. REVELS.

Other notable letters written to the President by prominent Republicans shortly after the election, and which, like that of Senator Revels's, received much attention at the time, were those of Attorney General Harris and Ham Carter. In each of these letters, the responsibility for the Republican defeat was placed upon Governor Ames. No Democrat ever arraigned his administration with such severity as did these three Republicans, two of whom were colored men. Ex-Attorney

General Morris, about the same time, published a long letter in the *New York Herald*, in which he criticised in unmeasured terms the course of Governor Ames, and like the others, endeavored to make it appear that Ames alone was responsible for their overthrow.[1] For some weeks after the election, it was the fashion for Republicans of the anti-Ames persuasion to write letters North, for the purpose of informing prominent Republicans that Governor Ames had killed the party in Mississippi.

V. THE IMPEACHMENT OF STATE OFFICIALS

It was generally understood by the Republicans that in the event of their success, Governor Ames was to be transferred to the United States Senate; the understanding among the Democrats was that if they secured the legislature, he was to be impeached and removed from office, along with certain other state officials, notably the lieutenant governor and the superintendent of education. Soon after the result of the election was known, the *Clarion* took strong ground in favor of impeachment.[2] The governor was fully expecting this, and had expressed a desire to resign the day before the election, and again the day after the results were known, but General George, Editor Barksdale, and a few other white leaders, horrified at the prospect of a negro governor, are said to have implored him to withhold his resignation, assuring him that there was no objection to him personally, but only to some of his advisers and counsellors.[3] On December 17, he wrote to a friend that he did not expect to make any more appointments until the question of impeachment was settled. Again he wrote to H. W. Lewis of Columbus, December 27: "Should I appoint the tax collectors,[4] Mr. George or some one else would issue a proclamation forbidding payment of taxes. I am rather expecting impeachment. A party that will secure one branch of the

[1] Harris's letter is printed in Report Senate sub-committee, p. 590, and is dated November 24 ; Carter's, in the Boutwell Report, p. 1083, and is dated November 15, and Morris's, in the Boutwell Report, p. 1081, dated November 23. Revels's letter is printed in the Boutwell Report, p. 1019, and in the Report of the Senate sub-committee, p. 595.

[2] In the issue of November 24, it demanded that Ames be removed from the governorship, and forever disqualified from holding office in the future.

[3] Testimony of C. K. Chase, Boutwell Report, *supra.*

[4] This was in pursuance of the law creating a new set of officials to collect taxes.

2 D

government by fraud, intimidation, and murder will not hesitate to vote themselves into possession of all the other branches."[1] On the same day, he wrote to another friend, " You are doubtless aware that the revolution is to be completed by the Democrats voting themselves into all the other offices."[2] February 15, he wrote Colonel Bolton of Greenville: "Impeachment is progressing, and my Winchester-rifle friends will vote me out."[3] On the same day, he wrote to James G. Blaine: " I think they will go on with my impeachment. A Republican and an ex-Union soldier cannot live in the South. His position is similar to what would have been that of an abolitionist here in the days of slavery, or a Union soldier at Andersonville during the war. Our late election was a revolution. By it the legislature was gained. This is not a republican form of government."[4] March 7, he wrote Charles Carlton of New York:[5] " Of course a Republican and an ex-Union soldier has no more consideration or justice here under Democratic Winchester-rifle rule than the Union prisoner had at Andersonville. Nothing is charged beyond political sins; of course, with them that is a sin which to Republicans is of the highest virtue. Their object is to restore the Confederacy and reduce the colored people to a state of serfdom. I am in their way, consequently they impeach me, which done, Jeff Davis will be restored to his former supremacy in this part of his former kingdom."[6]

The legislature chosen in the November election assembled at Jackson January 4, 1876. The legislature was composed of thirty-seven senators and one hundred and sixteen representatives. Of the senators, twenty-six were conservatives and eleven Republicans, five of whom were colored. Of the representatives, ninety-seven were conservatives, all but two calling themselves Democrats. There were nineteen Republicans, of whom sixteen were colored. There was one colored Democrat and three colored independent Republicans. All the colored Republicans in this legislature, however, usually acted with their white colleagues when they had such, as was the case in Noxubee, Oktibbeha, and Washington. There was one Democratic " carpet bagger " and one Republican " carpet bagger " in the Senate, and three or four in the House. The Boutwell committee reported to Congress that if there had been a free election, there would have been sixty-six Republicans to fifty Democrats in the House, and

[1] Correspondence of 1875, p. 183.
[2] Ibid. p. 186.
[3] Ibid. p. 253.
[4] Ibid. p. 240.
[5] Ibid. p. 270.
[6] Ibid. p. 270.

twenty-six Republicans to eleven Democrats in the Senate, consequently the legislature was not a legal body, and its acts not entitled to recognition by the political department of the United States, although the President might, in his discretion, recognize it as a government *de facto* for the preservation of the public peace.[1] In point of ability, this legislature will compare favorably with any in the history of the state. The executive committee had urged the people in the late contest to nominate for office the best men who would consent to serve. This advice was followed, and as a result, a number of the most prominent men in the state were elected.

In his last annual message, that of January 4, Governor Ames declared that the legislature was an illegal body, and that the late election had been carried by fraud and violence. The legislature resented the charge, declared that the governor was not giving them information of the state of the government as required by the constitution, and that his message " was calculated, if not intended, to impair that good feeling which had been established between the people of the North and those of the South." That body accordingly passed a long resolution "repelling his insinuations, and respectfully returning his communication with the statement that they would be pleased to receive from him information of the state of the government, together with recommendations of such measures as he might deem necessary and expedient, as provided by the constitution." [2]

A day or two after this incident General Featherston, a representative from Holly Springs, offered a resolution that a committee of five be appointed by the speaker to inquire into the official conduct of "acting Governor" Ames, and report to the House whether there were good reasons for his impeachment. After striking out the word "acting" the resolution was adopted.[3] The committee made a thorough

---

[1] Boutwell Report, p. 28. Many of the Republican members seem to have regarded the legislature as an illegal body, although they continued to sit in it and draw their per diem. They refused to vote on questions relating to the impeachment of Governor Ames, and at a caucus held January 17, they declared Mr. Warner as their choice for United States Senator, but deemed it unwise to cast their votes for him because they believed the legislature an illegal and revolutionary body. Correspondence of 1876, p. 216.

[2] *Jackson Pilot*, Jan. 5 and 6, 1876.

[3] The members of the committee were W. S. Featherston, H. L. Muldrow, W. A. Percy, W. F. Tucker, Fred Parsons (Rep.). Although the Republicans had but one representative on the committee, he testified that no evidence of unfairness was manifested by the majority, and expressed his thanks for the uniform courtesy which he received. Impeachment Testimony, p. 7.

investigation, extending through a period of thirty-eight days, from three to five hours per day. Forty-five witnesses were examined, twenty-six being classified as Republicans and nineteen as Democrats. Five volumes of testimony were taken. On February 22, the committee reported a resolution in favor of the impeachment and removal of the governor for official misconduct on eleven separate and distinct charges. March 2, twenty-one articles of impeachment were exhibited by the managers. The pardon of Alexander Smith on March 11, already alluded to, led to the addition of two more articles, making twenty-three in all. The first twenty-one articles were adopted by a vote of seventy-one to eight, thirty-seven members, all Republicans, being absent and not voting. The last two articles were adopted by a vote of fifty-eight to nine, forty-nine members being absent.[1]

In the meantime the lieutenant governor and the superintendent of education were being disposed of. On the 14th of February, a resolution directing that articles of impeachment be prepared against Davis was adopted, and managers appointed to conduct the case before the Senate as a court of impeachment. Ten colored members voted in favor of the impeachment charges. The principal charge against him was accepting a bribe while acting-governor in June, 1875, for granting a pardon to Thomas Barrentine, convicted of the murder of Ann Thomas in Lowndes County. He attempted to resign, but the Senate proceeded with the trial. His trial ended on the 13th of March, resulting in his conviction by a vote of thirty-two to four, six Republicans, one of whom was a negro, voting for his conviction. The *Jackson Times* (Republican) said: "It must be admitted by fair-minded and unprejudiced Republicans that the verdict rendered was, under the circumstances, just and proper."

On the 16th of February, a resolution directing the impeachment of Cordoza was adopted. The resolution was supported by eleven Republicans, eight being colored. It charged him with official malfeasance in twelve instances. They were as follows: for retaining money belonging to the state, received by him when clerk of the circuit court of Warren County for lands forfeited for non-payment of taxes; for converting to his own use funds of Tougaloo University while treasurer of that institution; for obtaining money from the state for unnecessary books for the public schools, a portion of which was for his own benefit; and with proposing to another to

---

[1] Impeachment Testimony, pp. 48, 50.

divide and convert to their own use a portion of the school-teacher's fund of Warren County. While the impeachment was still pending, he asked permission to resign and have the proceedings dismissed. This request was granted, and on the 22d of February, his resignation was accepted by the House by an almost unanimous vote.

On March 16, the chief justice entered the bar of the Senate, assumed the presidency of the court, and administered the oath to senators. The managers of the impeachment reported the articles, and the trial of Governor Ames proceeded.[1] He had employed able legal counsel, among whom were Roger A. Pryor of New York City, and Michael Clancy and Thomas Durant of Washington, the latter formerly a member of the New Orleans bar.[2] On the second day, the governor appeared through his counsel and asked for a reasonable length of time for the preparation of his answer to the articles of impeachment. He was given five days, in accordance with his wishes, and the trial set for March 28. On Wednesday, March 22, the court of impeachment met for the third time, when the answer and pleas of the governor were filed.

A week later the governor's counsel addressed him the following communication: —

Jackson, Miss., March 28, 1876.

To His Excellency, Adelbert Ames, *Governor of Mississippi* :

The fact disclosed to us to-day, that before proceedings of impeachment were begun against you, you had resolved to resign your office, has led us to consider whether your purpose might not be resumed and carried out without any sacrifice of your honor

---

[1] After articles of impeachment had been preferred, Chief Justice Peyton being required to preside, the legislature passed a resolution asking him to resign his position as chief justice until the "emergency" had passed, when he could be reëlected by his brethren. He accordingly did so, and Justice Simrall was elected in his place, and presided over the impeachment trial. The reason assigned by the Democrats for this somewhat novel proceeding was the extreme ill-health of the venerable chief justice, and the little personal difficulty he had had with the governor. The Republicans made capital out of this, alleging that it was on account of Simrall's politics that his participation in the trial was desired. This was tampering with the judiciary, they insisted, one of the things for which the Democrats were impeaching the governor. As Simrall was an appointee of Alcorn, and supposed to be a Republican, and as the chief justice was really incapacitated (he died a few months afterward), it does not appear that the Republican charge was well founded. See Laws of 1876, p. 126 ; Testimony of George E. Harris, Report Senate sub-committee, pp. 817, 819.

[2] He had expected Judge Jeremiah Black of Pennsylvania, but failed to secure him.

and dignity. Appreciating the sensibility which restrains you from resigning while charges are pending against you, we are nevertheless, clearly of the opinion that in the event the charges are withdrawn, you may retire without the least compromise of your reputation.

An examination of all the evidence adduced against you satisfies us that your acquittal would be the result of a thorough and impartial trial; but when we contemplate the expense you must incur in procuring the attendance of the hundreds of witnesses whom it will be necessary to summon from various parts of the state, we do not see why you should suffer so great a sacrifice, when your vindication may be accomplished by a withdrawal of the charges. Awaiting your reply to the suggestion hereby conveyed, we have the honor to be

Your Excellency's obedient servants,

THOS. J. DURANT.
ROGER A. PRYOR.

The governor at once replied to the suggestion of his counsel as follows: —

EXECUTIVE MANSION, JACKSON, MISS., March 28, 1876.

GENTLEMEN : In regard to your suggestion, I beg leave to say that, in consequence of the election of last November, I found myself confronted with a hostile legislature, and embarrassed and baffled in my endeavors to carry out my plans for the welfare of the state and of my party. I had resolved, therefore, to resign my office as governor of the state of Mississippi. But, meanwhile, proceedings of impeachment were instituted against me, and, of course, I could not and would not retire from my position under the imputation of any charge affecting my honor or integrity. For the reasons indicated, I still desire to escape burdens which are compensated by no possibility of public usefulness; and if the articles of impeachment presented against me were not pending, and the proceedings were dismissed, I should feel at liberty to carry out my desire and purpose of resignation. I am very truly yours,

(Signed)   ADELBERT AMES.

To Messrs. DURANT AND PRYOR, Jackson, Miss.

The House at once adopted a resolution by a vote of seventy-eight to ten, directing the managers to dismiss the articles of impeachment against the governor.[1] Thereupon the Senate adopted a resolution by a vote of twenty-six to three, dismissing the charges.[2] On the same day the governor sent the following brief message to the legislature: —

---

[1] Impeachment Testimony, p. 51.
[2] Impeachment Trial, p. 60.

EXECUTIVE OFFICE, JACKSON, MISS., Mar. 29, 1876.

TO THE PEOPLE OF THE STATE OF MISSISSIPPI:

   I hereby respectfully resign my office of governor of Mississippi.

    (Signed)   ADELBERT AMES.[1]

This closed his eventful career in Mississippi. He might have avoided this humiliation had he been a prophet, abandoned the office to the lieutenant governor, and, like Alcorn, accepted a seat in the Senate. "It was," he says, "my hope that after an indorsement of the people by election as governor, I could exchange the office for a seat in the Senate. But unfortunately for my aspirations the lieutenant governor was a colored man. Of those who came to me and begged me to remain in the governor's chair, none were more earnest than my political opponents, who said, 'a negro governor will humiliate and disgrace the state, and destroy its prosperity.' I made the sacrifice; whether it was meritorious depends on one's point of view."

Shortly after tendering his resignation, Governor Ames left the state, and has resided in the North ever since. While in Washington, he testified before the Boutwell committee relative to affairs in Mississippi. In regard to the charge that he constantly appealed to the prejudices of the negro against the white man, and through ambitious motives sought to prevent harmony between the races, he is quoted as saying: "When I first went to Mississippi, nine years ago, my duties brought me into constant intercourse with the whites, and I adopted their version of the condition of affairs without investigation, and sympathized with them. It was only when the trials over which I presided [military trials] revealed the fact that their conduct toward the negro was almost universally characterized by an utter disregard of their rights as citizens, that I was forced to become, if you may call me so, their champion. Since then I have always taken a very prominent part in Mississippi politics. I have made hundreds of speeches, and yet no man can point out a single line

---

[1] Hon. Roger A. Pryor in a letter to General Benjamin F. Butler, father-in-law of Governor Ames, thus describes how an agreement was reached: "Accordingly, I opened negotiations with the leading men against us, with many of whom I had had old and intimate associations, and after a strenuous struggle it was arranged that they should dismiss the charges, and that the governor should resign. This plan was carried out without any reflection on the governor's character. Indeed, he stands better to-day in the estimation of his enemies than ever before. Throughout the trying crisis he bore himself as a brave and honorable gentleman."

I have written or sentence I have spoken calculated to arouse a hostility of race. On the contrary, I have used all my influence, both personal and official, to produce a sentiment of harmony, on the basis of exact and equal justice."

The cause of Governor Ames's downfall in Mississippi is not difficult to discover. His political opponents testify to his personal integrity, courteous demeanor, and his education and refinement. No well-informed Democratic politician ever accused him of peculation or plunder. The unanimous testimony is that his failure was due to the circumstances surrounding his advent into Mississippi. His education, his connection with the war, and his surroundings were such as to give him, if not a prejudice against, at least a strong suspicion of the Southern whites, and an over-confidence in the mental and moral ability of the black race, so far as their ability to govern themselves was concerned. He did not know then that a superior race will not submit to the government of an inferior one.[1] He went to Mississippi wearing the uniform of a Union soldier, at a time when the people were impoverished and the land desolate from the ravages of war. The people were filled with strong passions and prejudices, and so was General Ames. The times were ill fitted for the establishment of cordial relations between the conquerors and the conquered. In the discharge of his official duties, he enforced the Congressional policy with perhaps more severity than the spirit of the law required, though this is doubtful. The circumstances under which he abandoned the army to accept a high civil office cost him much of his popularity. His preference for colored men and Northern Republicans in the formation of his official relations cost him the confidence of the substantial citizenship of the state, namely, the property-owning class. His failure properly to appreciate real conditions, in the direction of his policy, intensified race feeling, led to violent outbreaks, and ultimately to revolution. His mistakes were for the most part errors of judgment.

Shortly after the occurrence of the events related above, a congressional committee visited Mississippi to investigate political affairs in general and the late election in particular. On December 15, Senator Morton had offered a resolution for the appointment of such a committee, and he supported his resolution in a series of speeches in which he bitterly denounced the methods which the Democrats had employed

---

[1] This is an acknowledgment which he has recently made in a letter to the author.

in the late election, and declared that it had been carried by fraud and intimidation. The resolution slept until the 29th of March, when it was taken up, again debated, and passed March 31. The political complexion of the House at this time was such that the Senate did not desire an investigation by a joint committee, but wished it to be exclusively a senatorial affair. The committee was appointed, and the investigation began April 27.[1] The appointment of Senator Boutwell, a man of somewhat rabid views on Southern questions, and the quality of whose mind entirely unfitted him for the work of reconciliation, as chairman of the committee, virtually determined the character of the investigation and the report.[2] The report of the committee was the principal event in Congress during the first week of August, 1876. It embraces with the testimony two mammoth volumes of over two thousand printed pages. As was to be expected, two reports were made. The report of the majority declared that the testimony indicated that fraud and intimidation were generally and successfully practised in the canvass; that the allegation of unfitness against Governor Ames was unfounded; that he was not amenable to any just charges affecting his personal integrity, his character as a public officer, or his ability; that many of the officials in Mississippi were incapable and dishonest, but they were not approved by the governor or the great mass of the Republican party; and that a small number of newcomers had misused the confidence of the negro, secured office, and betrayed the trust confided to them. The report endeavored to explain the reason for the increased taxation and expenditures of the state government by saying that they were far less than in some of the Northern states; declared the legislature recently chosen was an illegal body; and that Ames, whose resignation had in the meantime been extorted by the said body calling themselves the legislature, was of right the governor of the state. They made three recommendations to Congress: first, that the state might be denied representation in Congress; second, the

---

[1] The members were George S. Boutwell, Massachusetts, chairman; Angus Cameron, Wisconsin; S. J. R. Miller, Minnesota; Thomas F. Bayard, Delaware; James E. McDonald, Indiana. Senator Oglesby of Illinois was first appointed a member, but was excused. McMillan took his place. Messrs. Bayard and McDonald were the Democratic representatives of the committee.

[2] The committee first held a twenty days' session in Washington, taking testimony. It then visited Mississippi, and took testimony for fourteen days at Jackson, beginning June 9; and two days at Aberdeen. The whole number of witnesses examined was one hundred and sixty-two.

enactment of laws for the protection of the rights of citizens; third, if the disorder increased and mild means proved ineffectual, the state should be remanded to a territorial form of government, and through a system of education and kindred means of improvement change the ideas of the inhabitants and reconstruct the government upon a republican basis.[1] " A wicked and imbecile report," said the *New York Nation*.[2] "The Massachusetts legislature must see that Boutwell has done his full duty to the American republic, and that it can spare him for a period of seclusion and meditation."[3] The almost pathetic appeals of Governor Ames for troops have already been described. The President refused to interfere. The state went Democratic. The President on July 26, more than a week before the appearance of the Boutwell report, wrote to Governor Chamberlain of South Carolina confiding to him that "Mississippi is governed to-day by officials chosen through fraud and violence such as would scarcely be credited to savages, much less to a civilized and Christian people."[4] On July 31, six days later, in his annual message to Congress, he says the report on Mississippi had not been made public, "but perhaps it will sustain my allegations."[5] His anticipation of the report can hardly be construed in any other light than evidence of prejudice against the Southern people. Most of the allegations in the majority report were denied by the minority. Both the reports are strongly tinged with partisanship for the evident purpose of influencing the presidential election.

VI. COMPLETION OF THE REVOLUTION

The work of turning out Republicans did not end with the removal of the governor, lieutenant governor, and superintendent of education. Although there were no more impeachments, many offices and agencies — sinecures, as the Democrats called them — were abolished either directly or indirectly. One of the first of these officials to feel the effects of the revolution was the colored commissioner of

---

[1] Boutwell Report, p. 29.   [2] Aug. 10, 1876.   [3] Aug. 17, 1876.
[4] Boutwell Report (minority). The *Nation*, speaking of this somewhat extravagant statement of President Grant, said rather sarcastically : "If he knows this now, he must have apprehended it then, and his refusal to interfere must be characterized as an act which would scarcely be accredited to savages, much less to the President of a civilized and Christian people." Aug. 10, 1876.
[5] Richardson, Messages and Papers of the Presidents, Vol. VII. p. 376.

immigration. His salary was reduced from $2000 a year to $100, and he was requested to provide himself with an office at his own expense, unless he could find a vacant room in the state house. The special agents to look up shortages among county treasurers and tax collectors were next legislated out of office. This was followed by the abolition of the state board of equalization; the office of cotton weigher; the office of postmaster of the two Houses; and the office of liquidating levee commissioner. The number of chancellors and circuit judges was largely reduced. An amendment to the constitution for the abolition of the office of lieutenant governor was proposed, and boards of supervisors were forbidden to employ counsel at stated salaries.

The Gatling Gun Bill was repealed, and the militia was paralyzed by the reduction of the pay of its officers, when in actual service, to five cents per day. The compensation of all state officers, members of the legislature, and judges and chancellors was reduced in amount, and the purposes for which the executive contingent fund could be drawn upon were specified with the minutest detail. None of it could be spent on the governor's house, except where the building would be damaged by neglect. The state treasurer was made custodian of the funds belonging to all state educational and charitable institutions. The fees of the public printer were reduced so that the cost of the state printing fell from $50,803, in 1875, to $22,295, in 1876. The district printing law was repealed, and with it passed away the subsidized Republican press. Payment for printing the proceedings of the legislature in daily newspapers was forbidden. The number of employees about the legislature, such as messengers, pages, porters, clerks, night watchmen, etc., was reduced. Their pay was proportionately decreased. The per diem of trustees of state institutions was abolished, and provision made for the payment of only their actual expenses while travelling to and from the places of meeting. All county officers were required to furnish their own stationery, and provisions were enacted to secure a more sufficient guarantee for the safe keeping of public funds. The penitentiary was made self-supporting by a lease for a goodly sum. It was alleged that this measure meant a saving of $75,000 annually. An economical registration law was enacted, and its meaning was made sufficiently clear to obviate any more extraordinary sessions of the legislature. An amendment to the constitution was proposed, the purpose of which was to secure biennial sessions of the legislature. A new school law was enacted, and its administration simplified, and the expense reduced. In 1874, the amount appropriated for the state superintendent's office was $17,816; in 1876, the amount was $4195. The average salary of teachers was reduced to $39.87 per month. Fellowships in the state university were abolished. The special school tax of four mills on the dollar was abolished, and a fund derived from the sale of public lands, licenses, etc., was established. The Democrats kept their promises to the negroes, and guaranteed an annual school term of four months in every county.

The state tax was reduced from $9\frac{1}{4}$ to $6\frac{1}{2}$ mills on the dollar. It was still further reduced the following year.

Other measures provided: for the reorganization of the judicial districts; for the reorganization of the congressional districts;[1] for the revision of the criminal code; for funding the floating debt; for the cancellation of $185,000 of state warrants; for securing the prompt payment of fines collected by justices of the peace; for securing the agricultural land scrip fund; for requiring boards of supervisors to ascertain the outstanding indebtedness in their respective counties; for the appointment of an agent to investigate funds and collect revenues due to the state, counties, and levee boards; an act for granting relief to the tax payers by extending the time for payment of taxes; and for a sweeping reform of the whole financial and administrative system.

One cannot fail to see in this legislation the signs of a revolution. The legislature of 1876, the first of its kind after the inauguration of the reconstruction policy, evidently proceeded on the belief that the work of the " carpet baggers " was unworthy to stand. The majority of the Democratic members honestly believed that much official corruption existed in the administration of the state government when they took hold. The most searching investigation was instituted in every department, with the confident expectation of unearthing numerous frauds.[2] The legislature continued in session until April 15, a period of three and a half months, endeavoring to wipe out every trace of the old régime, and to

---

[1] A feature of this law was the celebrated gerrymander known as the " shoe-string " district. It included all the counties on the Mississippi River, from Tennessee to Louisiana, being nearly three hundred miles in length, and not more than twenty wide in some places. The purpose of the law is well known.

[2] The *Jackson Pilot* is authority for the statement that at one time thirty-one investigations were being conducted by the legislature. The sum of $500 was appropriated for the purpose of facilitating these investigations. Laws of 1876, p. 43.

restore the government to a "systematic and economical" basis. Judged from the standpoint of its legislation alone, it deserves to be ranked as one of the most important in the history of the state. There is little doubt that most of its legislation was wholesome and wise — certainly it was economical — and it had the result of restoring the confidence of the people in the government. This is shown in the almost immediate appreciation of the state securities. State warrants, which in January, 1875, were sold at seventy-three cents on the dollar, rose during the session of the legislature to seventy-five cents, and before the end of the year they were only one cent below par.[1]

The retirement of Chief Justice Peyton and Justice Tarbell from the Supreme Court, with the appointment of Democratic successors, and the return of a solid Democratic delegation to Congress in November, 1876, completed the revolution. In July of the following year, the Republican executive committee adopted a resolution formally dissolving the party in the state. That a political party claiming a majority of 30,000 should thus quietly disband, would be considered an astounding occurrence, were it not for the fact that it no longer had a reason for prolonging its existence.

While the legislature was removing the "carpet baggers" from office and repealing the laws which they had enacted, many of them were preparing to emigrate. There was no longer any likelihood that they would ever again get possession of the offices, and as some of them were in bad standing among the native whites, there seemed to be little encouragement for them to remain. During the year 1876, a large majority of those who had at one time or other held office moved away. A comparatively small proportion of them had acquired real estate in Mississippi, and hence they were not beset by any serious difficulties in transferring their domicile to other states. Of those who were prominent in the politics of the state, less than half a dozen remained. They were good citizens, and were highly respected by the native whites among whom they lived.[2]

[1] Appleton's Annual Cyclopædia, 1876, p. 563.

[2] Of the Northern men who became prominent in Mississippi politics during the reconstruction period, the following are survivors at the present writing, May, 1901 : —

Ex-Governor Ames, Lowell, Massachusetts ; Ex-Governor Powers, Phœnix, Arizona ; Ex-United States Senator Pease, Watertown, North Dakota ; Ex-United States District Attorney G. W. Wells, Los Angeles, California ; Hon. Legrand W. Perce, ex-member of Congress, Chicago ; Judge W. B. Cunningham, Chicago ; Hon. Alexander Warner, Salisbury, Maryland ;

A number of those who emigrated succeeded in getting government positions at Washington. Several local colored politicians, who were alleged to have been outlawed, were taken under the care of the administration and were appointed watchmen about the Capital.[1]

It is difficult to form a correct estimate of the character of the Mississippi "carpet baggers" as a class. It can perhaps be said that as a class they were superior in character to the "carpet baggers" in South Carolina and Louisiana. It can also probably be said that many of them were men of personal honesty and integrity. But these had to bear the odium of those who came to the state for the purpose of peculation and plunder. The charge sometimes made that they were all thieves and plunderers has no foundation in fact. At the same time, it is undoubtedly true that as a class they were not animated by that spirit of economy which every consideration of propriety and justice plainly dictated as a policy of expediency. They unnecessarily multiplied the burdens of the people, did not exhibit an over-delicacy in their desire for the emoluments of office, and by their alliance with the colored race against the native whites finally brought on revolution. This was the final fruition of the congressional policy of reconstruction.

Hon. H. T. Fisher and Hon. C. W. Loomis, Cleveland, Ohio ; Colonel A. T. Morgan, Silverton, Colorado ; Hon. O. C. French, Hayden, Colorado ; General Charles E. Furlong, New York City. The number of genuine "carpet baggers " in Mississippi was never very large. In some counties there were none. In few did the number exceed a dozen. But as they generally held office, or were prominent in the politics of their respective communities as organizers of the freedmen, the impression conveyed was that they almost outnumbered the native whites. In 1870, there were 1610 persons living in Mississippi who had emigrated there from the Northern states since 1860. Of these, more than 1000 were from Illinois and Ohio. As this includes the women and children, and those who did not go South to get office, it is reasonable to suppose that the number of real carpet baggers in the state in 1870 did not much exceed 1000.

[1] Relative to the movement of the "carpet baggers" upon Washington, the *Jackson Times* (Republican), said : " The recent political earthquake in Mississippi left many Republicans who had labored faithfully and with self-sacrificing zeal for the party, without position, and with means exhausted. These have naturally flocked to Washington to ask of the administration assistance in the hour of our undeserved defeat and disaster."

INDEX